Business Communication
Canadian Edition

Business Communication
Canadian Edition

Marty Brounstein
Arthur H. Bell, PhD
Dayle M. Smith, PhD
with Connie Isbell
and Alan T. Orr, MEd

John Wiley & Sons Canada, Ltd.

Library and Archives Canada Cataloguing in Publication

Brounstein, Marty
  Business communication : communicate effectively in any business environment / Marty Brounstein, Arthur H. Bell, Dayle M. Smith ; with Connie Isbell and Alan T. Orr. — 1st Canadian ed.

ISBN 978-0-470-67816-9

  1. Business communication.   I. Bell, Arthur H. (Arthur Henry), 1946-   II. Smith, Dayle M III. Isbell, Connie   IV. Orr, Alan T.   V. Title.

HF5718.B744 2010   651.7   C2010-901273-9

Production Credits
Acquisitions Editor: Zoë Craig
Vice President & Publisher: Veronica Visentin
Vice President, Publishing Services: Karen Bryan
Creative Director, Publishing Services: Ian Koo
Marketing Manager: Aida Krneta
Editorial Manager: Karen Staudinger
Developmental Editor: Andrea Grzybowski
Typesetting: Thomson Digital
Cover Design: Mike Chan
Cover Image: Alex Slobodkin
Printing and Binding: Edwards Brothers
Printed and bound in the United States of America
1 2 3 4 5 EB 14 13 12 11 10

John Wiley & Sons Canada, Ltd.
6045 Freemont Blvd.
Mississauga, Ontario L5R 4J3
Visit our website at: www.wiley.ca

PREFACE

College classrooms bring together learners from many backgrounds with a variety of aspirations. Although the students are in the same course, they are not necessarily on the same path. This diversity, coupled with the reality that these learners often have jobs, families, and other commitments, requires a flexibility that our nation's higher education system is addressing. Distance learning, shorter course terms, new disciplines, evening courses, and certification programs are some of the approaches that schools employ to reach as many students as possible and help them clarify and achieve their goals.

Business Communication, Canadian Edition, is designed to help address this diversity and the need for flexibility. It focuses on the fundamentals, identifies core competencies and skills, and promotes independent learning. The focus on the fundamentals helps students grasp the subject, bringing them all to the same basic understanding. The text uses clear, everyday language, presented in an uncluttered format, making the reading experience more pleasurable. The core competencies and skills help students succeed in the classroom and beyond, whether in another course or in a professional setting. A variety of built-in learning resources promote independent learning and help instructors and students gauge students' understanding of the content. These resources enable students to think critically about their new knowledge, and apply their skills in any situation.

Our goal with *Business Communication, Canadian Edition,*—with its brief, inviting format, clear language, and core competencies and skills focus—is to celebrate the many students in your courses, respect their needs, and help you guide them on their way.

CASE Learning System

To meet the needs of working students, *Business Communication, Canadian Edition* uses a four-step process: The CASE Learning System. Based on Bloom's Taxonomy of Learning, CASE presents key business communication topics in easy-to-follow chapters. The text then prompts analysis, synthesis, and evaluation with a variety of learning aids and assessment tools. Students move efficiently from reviewing what they have learned, to acquiring new information and skills, to applying their new knowledge and skills to real-life scenarios:

- **C**ontent
- **A**nalysis
- **S**ynthesis
- **E**valuation.

Using the CASE Learning System, students not only achieve academic mastery of business communication *topics*, but they master real-world business communication *skills*. The CASE Learning System also helps students become independent learners, giving them a distinct advantage whether they are starting out or seeking to advance in their careers.

Organization, Depth and Breadth of the Text

Business Communication, Canadian Edition offers the following features:

- **Modular format.** Research shows that students access information from textbooks in a non-linear way. Instructors also often wish to reorder textbook content to suit the needs of a particular class. Therefore, although *Business Communication, Canadian Edition* proceeds logically from the basics to increasingly more challenging material, chapters are further organized into sections that are self-contained for maximum teaching and learning flexibility.
- **Numeric system of headings.** *Business Communication, Canadian Edition* uses a numeric system for headings (for example, 2.3.4 identifies the fourth sub-section of section 3 of chapter 2). With this system, students and teachers can quickly and easily pinpoint topics in the table of contents and the text, keeping class time and study sessions focused.
- **Core content.** Topics in the text are organized into six parts and fifteen chapters.

Part I: Foundations of Business Communication

Chapter 1, Understanding Business Communication, familiarizes students with the basics of business communication; the role of assumptions in effective communication; the steps of the communication process; and common patterns of communication. Guidelines for communicating in teams are also offered.

Chapter 2, Mastering Communication Skills, presents the four types of speaking approaches, giving special attention to assertive speaking. Nonverbal methods of communication, including their impact and pitfalls; the three stages of the listening process; and the four approaches to listening, as well as the role of listening in effective communication, are also discussed.

Chapter 3, Effective Conflict Resolution, is unique to business communication texts, yet its inclusion is vital. This chapter suggests four common approaches to resolving conflict, and offers useful strategies on how to apply the idea of respect, use assertive communication tools, and keep conflicts under control. The resolving-concerns conflict resolution model and the needs-based model are described, as are ways of handling challenging reactions in conflicts.

Part II: The Writing Process

Chapter 4, Writing for Business Audiences, outlines the benefits of learning good writing skills, the importance of audience, and the need to explore ideas, as well as critical factors that affect the writing process. The most commonly used organization techniques, along with the most common writing mistakes, are also presented, as is a discussion of how details and examples can strengthen written work.

Chapter 5, Writing and Revising Business Communications, emphasizes the importance of word choice and voice in writing, and provides guidelines for writing effective sentences and paragraphs. Revision tools and proofreading techniques, as well as their benefits, are also included.

Part III: Letters, Memos, Email, and Other Brief Messages

Chapter 6, Managing Memos and Email, underscores the importance of memos in business communications, highlights the four most common types of memos, and outlines how to make memos persuasive and skillful. The timely topic of email is also presented, along with a discussion of both when an email is a useful means of communication, and when another form of communication would be better. Guidelines for writing effective emails conclude the chapter.

Chapter 7, Writing Positive Business Letters, describes how letters communicate information in the business world. Students learn the standards and optional parts of a business letter and examine common letter formats. They also learn about positive business letters: their purpose, how they serve a customer's needs, and how they can resolve difficult business situations and maintain goodwill.

Chapter 8, Writing Negative Messages, shows how to use the indirect pattern when delivering negative messages and the benefits of using a direct approach to deliver negative news, with suggestions for when to use each. Common types of negative letters are also presented.

Chapter 9, Writing Persuasively, discusses how persuasive letters address a reader's needs and identifies three common types of persuasive letters. In the context of underscoring the power of salesmanship as a business tool, the chapter presents a step-by-step plan for writing a sales letter. The role of persuasion in claim letters is also explored, as are the four most common claim letters. The relative merits of various writing tools and techniques are also explored.

Part IV: Developing Speaking Skills

Chapter 10, Spoken Communication, describes the benefits of speaking assertively and outlines ways of delivering a positive, direct, honest message. Techniques for using telephones, cell phones, and voicemail effectively to planning, participating in, and leading business meetings are presented.

Chapter 11, Giving Speeches and Oral Presentations, shows students what makes and breaks a presentation, highlighting the importance of planning, organization, visual aids, and non-verbal communication. Ideas for channelling anxiety and staying composed in front of an audience are also presented.

Part V: Reports and Proposals

Chapter 12, Writing Business Reports, discusses the importance of reports, how they communicate information to an audience, and the key elements they contain. The formats of short and long reports are presented, along with guidelines for choosing the right kind of report for a business situation. Rounding out the chapter are 10 steps for efficient report writing.

Chapter 13, Writing Business Proposals, outlines how to determine a proposal's audience and how to organize a proposal to be maximally effective. The five steps of the proposal-writing process are outlined, and the pros and cons of using visual aids is discussed.

Part VI: Employment Messages

Chapter 14, Writing Resumés and Cover Letters, offers ways of conducting an employment search, describes the three types of resumé formats, and offers guidelines for choosing the one that is best suited to a given job-search need. Guidelines for writing effective resumés and cover letters tailored to a job description are included, along with examples.

Chapter 15, Interviewing for Employment, concludes the text, offering ways of preparing for an interview, tips for presenting yourself assertively and successfully in an interview, and guidelines for following up after an interview, including the importance of thank-you letters.

Pre-Reading Learning Aids

Each chapter of *Business Communication, Canadian Edition* features the following learning and study aids to activate students' prior knowledge of the topics and orient them to the material:

- **Pre-test.** This pre-reading assessment tool in multiple-choice format not only introduces chapter material, but it also helps students anticipate the chapter's learning outcomes. By focusing students' attention on what they do not know, the self-test provides students with a benchmark against which they can measure their own progress. The pre-test is available online at www.wiley.com/canada/brounstein.
- **What you'll learn in this chapter and after studying this chapter.** These bulleted lists tell students what they will be learning in this chapter and why it is significant for their careers. They also help students understand why the chapter is important and how it relates to other chapters in the text. The "What You'll Learn . . ." lists focus on the *subject matter* that will be taught (e.g., the parts of a standard business letter). Each bullet in the list corresponds to a chapter section. The "After Studying This Chapter . . ." list emphasizes *capabilities and skills* students will learn (e.g., provide examples of the three different letter formats).

Within-Text Learning Aids

The following learning aids are designed to encourage analysis and synthesis of the material, and to support the learning process and ensure success during the evaluation phase:

- **Introduction.** This section orients the student by introducing the chapter and explaining its practical value and relevance to the book as a whole. Short summaries of chapter sections preview the topics to follow.
- **"For Example" boxes.** Found within each section, these boxes tie section content to real-world organizations, scenarios, and applications.
- **Figures and tables.** Line art and illustrations have been carefully chosen to be truly instructional rather than filler. Tables distill and present information in a way that is easy to identify, access, and understand, enhancing the focus of the text on essential ideas.
- **Self-Check.** Related to the "What You'll Learn" bullets and found at the end of each section, this battery of short answer questions emphasizes student understanding of concepts and mastery of section content. Though the questions may

either be discussed in class or studied by students outside of class, students should not go on before they can answer all questions correctly.

- **Key terms and glossary.** To help students develop a professional vocabulary, key terms are bolded in the introduction, the summary, and when they first appear in the chapter. A complete list of key terms with brief definitions appears at the end of each chapter and again in a glossary at the end of the book. Knowledge of key terms is assessed by all assessment tools (see next section).
- **Summary.** Each chapter concludes with a summary paragraph that reviews the major concepts in the chapter and links back to the "What you'll learn" list.

Evaluation and Assessment Tools

The evaluation phase of the CASE Learning System consists of a variety of within-chapter and end-of-chapter assessment tools that test how well students have learned the material. These tools also encourage students to extend their learning into different scenarios and higher levels of understanding and thinking. The following assessment tools appear in every chapter of *Business Communication, Canadian Edition*:

- **Quick Questions** help students summarize the chapter's main points by asking a series of multiple choice and true/false questions that emphasize student understanding of concepts and mastery of chapter content. Students should be able to answer all of the Summary Questions correctly before moving on.
- **Give It Some Thought questions** in short answer format review the major points in each chapter, prompting analysis while reinforcing and confirming student understanding of concepts, and encouraging mastery of chapter content. They are somewhat more difficult than the *Self-Check* and *Summary Questions,* and students should be able to answer most of them correctly before moving on.
- **Applying This Chapter questions** drive home key ideas by asking students to synthesize and apply chapter concepts to new, real-life situations and scenarios.
- **The Next Step questions** are designed to extend students' thinking, and so are ideal for discussion or writing assignments. Using an open-ended format and sometimes based on Web sources, they encourage students to draw conclusions using chapter material applied to real-world situations, which fosters both mastery and independent learning.

Instructor and Student Package

Business Communication, Canadian Edition is available with the following teaching and learning supplements. All supplements are available online at the text's book companion website, located at www.wiley.com/canada/brounstein.

Instructor Companion Site. This password-protected site provides the following aids and supplements for teaching an Introduction to Business Communication course:

- *Instructor's Resource Manual.* This manual gives teaching suggestions for each chapter of the text. These include a chapter summary, learning objectives, definitions of key terms, lecture notes, answers to select text question sets, and at least three suggestions for classroom activities, such as ideas for speakers to invite, videos to show, and other projects.
- *Diagnostic Evaluation of Grammar, Mechanics, and Spelling.* A useful tool that instructors may administer to the class at the beginning of the course to determine each student's basic writing skills. The evaluation is accompanied by an answer key and a marking key. Instructors are encouraged to use the marking key when grading students' evaluations, and to duplicate and distribute it to students with their graded evaluations.
- *PowerPoint Presentations.* Key information is summarized in 10 to 15 PowerPoint slides per chapter. Instructors may use these in class or choose to share them with students for class presentations or to provide additional study support.
- *Test Bank.* One test per chapter, as well as a mid-term and a final. Each includes true/false, multiple-choice, and open-ended questions. Answers and page references are provided for the true/false and multiple-choice questions, and page references for the open-ended questions.

Student Companion Site. These tools are provided to students to help enhance their understanding of the material presented in this text:

- *Pre-tests.* These multiple-choice tests introduce the chapter material to students and help them to anticipate what they will learn from reading each chapter.
- *Post-tests.* These online tests are designed to be taken after students have read the chapter and give students an opportunity to test their own understanding. Each test includes all of the questions from the chapter's pre-test so that students can see how their learning has progressed and improved.
- *Sample Long Report.* A properly formatted long report demonstrating the techniques and structure discussed in Chapter 12 of the text will be available in PDF form for students to examine online or print out.
- *Additional samples.* A collection of letters, memos, and other communication materials discussed throughout the text will give students further opportunity to enhance their understanding by seeing effective business communication in use.

BRIEF CONTENTS

CONTENTS

Part VI: Employment Messages

1

UNDERSTANDING BUSINESS COMMUNICATION

Building a Foundation for Communicating at Work

STARTING POINT

Go to www.wiley.com/canada/brounstein to assess your knowledge of the basics of business communication. After reviewing the website, you'll be able to determine where you need to concentrate your effort.

What You'll Learn in This Chapter:

- the steps of the communication process
- common patterns of business communication
- barriers to effective communication
- guidelines for communicating in teams.

After Studying This Chapter, You'll be Able to:

- examine the importance of each step of the communication process
- use diagrams to compare communication patterns
- identify the positive and negative effects of assumptions, including your own
- describe the guidelines for productive team communication.

INTRODUCTION

Who needs to communicate effectively with others to be successful at work? Most people must interact in the workplace with bosses and low-level employees, superiors and subordinates, managers and the managed—all types of co-workers—to be successful at their jobs. In this chapter, the tools for communicating success- fully are discussed. The role of assumptions is examined. Also reviewed are the five steps of the communication process, as well as patterns of communication and their obstacles. The chapter concludes with guidelines for improving team communication.

1.1 Becoming an Effective Business Communicator

It's difficult to find any job function or field of employment where communicating effectively with people isn't vital. Regardless of your job title or the type of organization or industry you work for, if you're like most people, the greatest challenges you face lean less toward the technical side of your job (your area of expertise) than they do toward interacting with other people.

Fewer and fewer jobs today require employees to do tasks by themselves. Instead, many organizations—in the public as well as private sectors—stress that they have customers that they must communicate with and serve. The two basic types of customers are:

- **External customers:** People outside the workplace with whom you need to build good working relationships for success on the job. These can range from suppliers to investors, and include people outside your organization who need the products and services that your business provides.
- **Internal customers:** Your fellow employees, inside and outside the department where you work, to whom you provide services or assistance.

In addition, the workplace is often structured so that many employees do their jobs in cooperative, team-like situations for part or most of their workdays. And if you work in management, most of the demands placed on your job require being able to effectively interact with others—staff, peers, and bosses. Interactions between people at work often are like games of tug-of-war. The rope serves as a metaphor for the bond or connection between two people as they interact. The more it gets tugged between the two parties, the higher the tension, and the less productive the conversations. Alternatively, when neither party makes an effort to hold onto the rope, the bond is broken. In either case, you have varying degrees of a tug-of-war—the stresses and strains that block effective communications.

The goal of successful communications is sharing the rope so that it is strongly held but no one gets dirty—this is a challenge, but key to the success of communicating on the job.

1.1.1 Training for the "Game"

Despite years of schooling, for the most part, we have not been properly trained to effectively communicate with others. Your task is to identify where your weaknesses lie, and then take steps to strengthen them.

As a human being, your communication skills fall into four categories:

- listening
- speaking

- reading
- writing.

Although the advent of the computer and the Internet has increased the use of reading and writing skills, human beings generally spend more time in face-to-face forms of communication: listening and speaking (speaking includes both the verbal and non-verbal ways people express their messages to one another).

Although you're taught to read and write in school, you probably didn't receive any formal instruction about how to listen effectively and express yourself constructively while interacting with others. These interpersonal channels of communication are seldom a part of the curriculum in basic education. Yet listening and speaking are more critical for people to understand each other, work together, and solve problems with one another.

Once you add elements like stress, tension, and challenge to your workplace—from dealing with differences of opinion to facing demanding customers—you can see how easy it is to get caught up in that tug-of-war feeling. Because the skills needed to effectively handle stressful situations simply aren't taught, you may have trouble sharing the rope. Instead, communication becomes more adversarial, ranging from waging verbal war against the other person to appeasing that person just to get past a difficult situation. Adversarial ways of communicating essentially block people from working out their differences and interacting respectfully.

SELF-CHECK

- Identify and define external customer, internal customer, sender, and receiver.
- List and describe the four categories of communication skills.

1.2 Examining the Communication Process

Many of the problems that occur in an organization are the direct result of people failing to communicate. Faulty communication leads to confusion, errors, and can ultimately lead to the failure of a team or of a plan. Understanding how the communication process works can give you useful insight into how you can make it work for you.

1.2.1 Finding Your Place in the Process

Our communication skills are constantly being tested in the business world. Technological advances such as email, voice mail, and video conferencing have brought on a revolutionary change in that a huge amount of information is now available to us. At times, it may seem as if we're drowning in a constant flood of letters, reports, faxes, emails, junk mail, and data of every kind and every form. This onslaught of information means that you must be able to:

- handle more business documents and other business messages
- sift through more information to choose the information you need
- understand more information
- communicate more effectively to customers, co-workers, suppliers, and others.

To do all these things, you must be a highly skilled communicator. So how do you become one? Before answering this question, consider the definition of **communication**: a process by which information is exchanged between individuals through a common system of symbols, signs, or behaviour. "Communication" springs from the Latin verb *communicare,* which means "to make common." Notice that the primary meaning of communication is not to recite, deliver, speak, or write. All of these activities fall short of "making common" the flow of ideas and feeling. Mere speaking is a one-way activity, but communication involves common interests shared by all parties involved in the communication.

Effective communicators share in the give-and-take of ideas and feelings. Even when they give speeches, they notice responses from their audiences. For example, a man smiles in the front row. An older person leans forward to hear from the back row. Two teenagers yawn. All of these responses show that others actively participate in the speaker's communication process. The speaker alone can only make speech noises. The audience alone can only wait to hear or see something. Together, they can communicate in the mutual activity of making thoughts and feelings common to the group.

1.2.2 Breaking Down the Process

As an effective communicator, you are able to send your information to an intended receiver so that he or she understands it. To do this, you use each of the five aspects of the communication process:

1. An *information source* (a "message"—an idea, thought, or fact).
2. A *signal* (a stream of words, images, or gestures that expresses the message).
3. A *transmittal* (an act of sending, delivering, or transferring the message).
4. A *channel* (a "medium," such as a report, TV image, or speech).
5. A *receiver* (an "audience"; may be listeners, viewers, or readers).

The way in which this process works is that an information source is translated into → a signal that is → transmitted through → a channel to → a receiver.

This description of communication is deceptively simple; within it you'll find plenty of opportunity for things to go wrong. Problems with communication are often at the core of many of the errors, misunderstandings, and conflicts that occur in the workplace.

SELF-CHECK

- Define communication.
- List the five aspects of the communication process.

1.3 Seeing Communication Patterns at Work

Communication patterns are either structured or unstructured. Examples of structured communication include the company newsletter, the weekly meeting of teaching assistants, and the annual shareholders' meeting. Unstructured communication includes the office grapevine, the after-class chat, and water-cooler conversations. Structured communication is usually:

- **recorded or documented in some form.** This may include printed copies of a newsletter, the written minutes of a meeting, and the printed agenda for a conference.
- **less subject to change than unstructured communication.** The messages in a newsletter, for example, are usually fixed in a way that a chat over coffee is not.
- **more widely known and more easily accessed.** Structured communications such as quarterly financial reports are visible to a broad public and open to scrutiny. Private conversations, on the other hand, cannot be accessed without eavesdropping.

Unstructured communication is just as important as structured communication to the effective functioning of a business. Notice these three characteristics about unstructured communication:

- **It is dependent upon personal emotional factors.** For example, two employees both receive a company memo whether they like one another or not, but their conversation over a cup of coffee depends almost entirely on their attitudes toward one another.
- **It is more flexible and open-ended than structured communication.** Conversations tend to raise questions and express feelings more than they pose arguments and answers.

- **It is more personalized than structured communication.** Because they are for a general audience, most memos, reports, and speeches are couched in general terms. However, unstructured communication can change the message to suit an individual. The rumour of an impending layoff based on seniority, for example, can be told in very different ways to a long-term vice-president and to an employee hired just last month.

1.3.1 The Grapevine

Because of the way it branches and grows, the flow of gossip and rumour in an organization is called the grapevine. Of all the forms of unstructured communication within an organization, one of the most useful—and potentially most destructive—is the company grapevine. Somehow, good news never gets better, but bad news always gets worse when it travels along the grapevine. Inevitably, each participant adds a layer of personal prejudice or anxiety to the rumour as it moves along.

Learn to involve yourself in the grapevine for positive ends. The grapevine exists, after all, because people without knowledge in an organization are people without power. You can use this need to know to build team spirit and mutual trust rather than crippling suspicion and jealousy. Here are three suggestions for nurturing a fruitful grapevine:

- **Make contact in the grapevine in several different places.** Don't restrict your casual knowledge of what others say to the bits and pieces you hear from others at your level. Find interesting associates at other levels in the company.
- **Make time to tune in to the grapevine.** Make regular contact with key people in the grapevine. These should not be scheduled as formal meetings, of course.
- **Participate in the grapevine in a natural way.** Don't lecture or spy. The grapevine grows on trust, and it won't include you if you openly stand on a soapbox or take notes on who's saying what.

1.3.2 Types of Communication Patterns

The following simple diagrams lay out some common patterns of business communication. Although they apply primarily to structured communication patterns detailed above, several also can be found in unstructured settings.

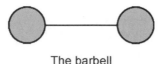

The barbell

In this barbell pattern, both partners depend on the other's confidence. Typically, neither wants to be isolated, so each relies heavily on the partner. This barbell pattern is all about discretion, confidence, and trust.

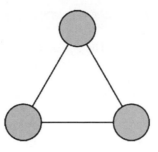

The triangle

Three people joined in a triangle pattern face the challenge of dealing with different points of view without making any one party in the triangle feel left out. Communication triangles work well in an atmosphere of mutual trust. You can recognize the breakdown of the triangle when it begins to take the shape of a broken triangle:

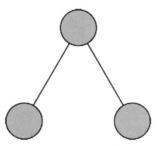

The broken triangle

In the broken triangle, two of the parties have severed communication. With time, they may also sever communication with the one party they have in common. Usually, it's difficult to remain the one trusted associate of two enemies.

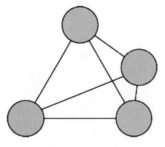

The pyramid

In a pyramid, one party usually assumes the leadership role. In some cases, this party generates or gathers much of the information received by the group. In other cases, the leader acts as a clearinghouse for information to be shared among members.

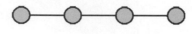

The series

The series presents the same challenge as the party game called "Gossip," "Telephone," or "Rumour." In the game, one person whispers a sentence or two to the next person, who then passes it down the chain. By the time it gets to the last person, the message has usually changed—usually with hilarious results.

In business, the results may not be so funny. If linked chains are necessary, keep the chains as short as possible; for example, have contact with parties farther down the line.

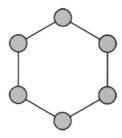

The circle

The circle pattern helps to avoid the problems associated with communication chains. The message is sent around the circle, but eventually finds its way back to who started it. He or she can then alter the message, if necessary, or start a new one on its way.

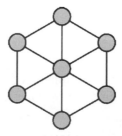

Hub and spokes

The hub and spokes pattern combines aspects of the pyramid—the hub is like the peak of the pyramid—and the circle. The leader initiates a message that is then sent throughout the group. At any point, however, individuals can respond to the leader or to each other.

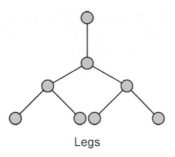

Legs

In the legs pattern, messages are communicated through levels of responsibility to more and more workers. The legs pattern frees the time of the central decision maker; he or she need only to explain the message once, instead of many times to many parties. When misused, however, this pattern can isolate company leaders from important feedback from within the company.

The cross-fire

Freedom is the key word for the cross-fire pattern. Members can speak freely to anyone in the group; the pattern works well for brainstorming sessions. This pattern has the danger, of course, of leading to communication chaos.

1.3.3 Directional Differences

Each of the communication patterns, when translated into actual business contexts, could be described in terms of direction. Were lower-level employees talking to upper-level employees? Were employees on the same level talking to each other? The direction becomes important as you see the possibilities and pitfalls emerge.

- **Upward Communication:** Allows the upper level to keep informed and gives the lower level the chance to participate in the decision-making process. However, can cut into an executive's time, as well as involve upper-level managers in petty decisions that could be handled at a lower level.
- **Downward Communication:** Builds a sense of team spirit and mutual dependence through shared knowledge. However, may lead lower-level employees to expect to be informed of all company matters.
- **Lateral Communication:** Helps to create social bonds and build credibility for an organization's message. However, may be used to isolate certain individuals or groups who are purposely excluded by their peers.

You don't have to wait for your first day in your new career to observe the fascinating working of upward, downward, and lateral communication. Watch for them in your everyday experiences. Do people act differently when they speak in the different directions? Does their use of language change? Do they choose different media? The answers you discover will help you use upward, downward, and lateral communication to your business advantage.

FOR EXAMPLE

Management Style

Michael was the kind of boss who was well liked by his staff. Much of this had to do with his open-door policy of management. As much as he could, he made himself available to his staff to discuss decisions, personnel issues, and so forth—even when they could have been handled at a lower level. When Michael was asked to take on additional duties, however, his time became much more limited. To avoid any disruption in management, Michael assigned the office manager with the job of screening out and resolving a portion of the simpler issues that came across his desk. By doing so, Michael could still maintain much of the feeling of his open-door style, without having to deal with every decision that needed to be made.

1.4 Giving Feedback

A message cannot truly be communicated unless it has been understood by the receiver. So how do you know when you've really communicated? You pay attention to feedback. A receiver interprets a message and, by word or expression, sends feedback to the sender. If the communication continues, the sender uses the feedback received to adapt any new messages.

Feedback may present itself either immediately or at a point later in time. Regardless of when you receive it, consider it a critical part of your ability to communicate effectively.

- **Immediate feedback:** Feedback does not wait for an obvious pause. An audience flashes a sign of approval, disapproval, frustration, curiosity, and so forth on a second-by-second basis. An effective communicator responds to it almost unconsciously by watching the eyes, faces, and physical gestures of the audience. Such clues guide them to adjust their content and delivery to better suit their audience's needs.
- **Delayed feedback:** In many situations, feedback arrives too late to make on-the-spot adjustments. In the case of a business letter, for example, you may not know for days or weeks how it was received. In other cases, a speaker may chat informally with members of the audience after a presentation, or a writer may attach

a questionnaire to a proposal or report. Regardless of when it comes, delayed feedback gives you an opportunity to learn and improve as a communicator.

> **FOR EXAMPLE**
>
> **Feedback or No Paycheque**
> The financial manager of an engineering firm was frustrated by the lack of attention being paid to him by employees at his monthly "State of the Business" addresses. So he tried a bold experiment. In the middle of his next address, without changing his tone of voice, he repeated the same sentence over and over again: "Permit fees are going up once again." It wasn't until the third and fourth repetitions that some employees looked up; many continued to doodle and daydream until the fifth. "Okay," he said, "I'm up here working hard to communicate with you. I'd like you to do the same for me. Sit up, ask questions, shake your head." The experiment worked. With the feedback that followed, he made some minor but successful changes, making everyone happy.

1.5 Barriers to Communication

Anything that prevents your audience from understanding your message is a barrier to effective communication. Consider the following barriers, both physical and psychological:

- **Physical Barriers.** You've put a lot of work into your speech or report, and you expect your audience's polite attention. Not so. A number of physical forces can wreak havoc on your ability to communicate your message:
  - **Time restraints.** Is a 20-page report or a 20-minute speech too long?
  - **Environmental conditions.** Heat, cold, noise, and drafts can distract an audience.
  - **Presentation.** Fuzzy type, narrow margins, and an otherwise unattractive document look unprofessional and won't capture the attention of your audience.
- **Cultural Barriers.** Your culture, background, and bias can interfere with the communication process when you attempt to interact with people from a different social group. To communicate with other cultural groups, you must be willing to adapt—but not discard—your own patterns of thought and behaviour to meet the needs of your audience. To prepare for this, you need to know your audience and know yourself.
- **Motivational Barriers.** Your audience may simply not want to be motivated by what you have to say. And, even after they do begin to move with your thoughts, they might need help to keep going. This mental inertia is increasingly common among hassled business people. The communication tools covered in this book will help motivate an uninterested audience.

- **Emotional Barriers.** Business situations are rarely able to entirely avoid the personal element. People's feelings get hurt; they can also develop strong emotional attachments. When you send a message with strong negative or positive emotions, you shouldn't expect the messages to sail undisturbed through the heavy emotional weather.
- **Language Barriers.** This is not a compliment: "I didn't understand much of what he said, but it was an excellent speech." Don't use technical or specialized vocabulary beyond the limits of your audience. Language shouldn't be a mirror in which to admire your own intelligence.
- **Non-verbal Barriers.** Non-verbal cues such as body language and gestures can create a serious barrier for your message. A sagging posture can undo the effect of the most enthusiastic words, telling the audience "I don't really believe what I'm saying." Lack of eye contact in most Western cultures communicates insecurity over your words. (See Chapter Two for more details.)

1.5.1 Working with Assumptions

A critical part of being able to communicate effectively is becoming aware of how your assumptions affect your interactions with others.

- **Assumption:** A belief that something is true without proof or demonstration, or that a person is going to behave a certain way before they've had a chance to act.

   You've probably been making them (and have had them made about you, too) all your life. But not all assumptions are negative.

- **Processing stimuli:** Assumptions help you gather the information and stimuli to make sense of the world around you. When you're driving, for example, assumptions help keep you alert and aware of what other drivers may do so that you stay safe.
- **Anticipating problem situations:** Assumptions can help you prepare for problems and plan how to respond appropriately if difficult challenges arise.
- **Trying new things:** Assumptions can help you make educated guesses about new people or situations. They can aid you in drawing upon past experiences and determining how to apply them in future situations—in essence, allowing you to take risks and do something new and different.

1.5.2 Avoiding the Downside of Assumptions

When you assume, you can make a fool out of yourself, but you can also affect others and make them look or feel pretty silly, too. Worst of all, by acting on your assumption, you've probably hurt someone else. Using assumptions a lot—especially when dealing with other people—is a mistake.

The problem with assumptions is that they can lead to mistakes, misunderstandings, and strained relationships when they're acted upon as absolute facts. The following is a list of common assumptions that people make:

- **Jumping to conclusions:** In this scenario, you *think* you know what someone is going to say or whether something can work before you get the whole story. This assumption usually manifests itself in several (often annoying) ways, including:
  - ○ finishing people's sentences for them
  - ○ interrupting before a message has been fully stated
  - ○ tuning out as soon as a person you find unfavourable starts talking.
- **Focusing on intentions:** People have intentions and they have actions, and you can only see the actions. Yet people often make assumptions on what they perceive are someone else's intentions—and quite often assume the worst. When you focus on someone's intentions, you often approach people with undue suspicion and interpret inconsequential actions (the little things) as destructive or of ill will.
- **Thinking you know best:** When you think you know best, you're already taking actions or making decisions for someone else without first checking with the person who is affected directly by what you do. These actions range from making commitments to initiating changes. Quite often, the person most affected doesn't find out about these changes until after they're made.
- **Stereotyping:** Assuming that everyone who is from a different group than you behaves the same. Stereotypes can be based on groupings like ethnicity, gender, religion, sexual orientation, or occupation. Stereotyping involves ideas like engineers all do one thing, men are all like that, all women do that, and so on. Stereotypical remarks often offend others and do nothing more than show your ignorance and biases.

FOR EXAMPLE

Assuming the Best, Getting the Worst

A project manager assigned a teammate the task of writing an article for the company newsletter. She gave him a deadline and guidelines on content, but assumed he knew enough to have the item proofread before submitting it to the newsletter. Unfortunately, he didn't—and the item contained a major error. With her assumption, the manager opened the way for an embarrassing situation for herself and her team.

1.5.3 Becoming Aware of Your Own Assumptions

Although assumptions are a normal part of the human thought process, you need to become aware of your own assumptions in order to have effective interactions. Here are a few tips to help:

- **Deal with each person as an individual.** Get to know each person you work with or each customer you serve as an individual. The more you understand others, the better you can communicate with them.
- **Listen first.** Once you've heard someone's message, ask questions and check your understanding so that you know what someone really means. When something sounds contrary to your thoughts, avoid reacting quickly with a negative comment or disagreement. Instead, ask the person the rationale of the idea or proposal at hand.
- **Avoid generalizations.** Generalizations about people often come off as stereotypical remarks. Rather than talking in generalizations, tie the comments you make to your own experiences and do so only when it is relevant.
- **Communicate first; act second.** Because being in the workplace requires cooperating and coordinating with others, make sure that everyone is consulted before you take action. No matter how well intentioned you are or how brilliant an idea you have, when you don't consult important people first, they're often upset, and as a result, may even reject a legitimate action or idea.
- **Make the safest assumption of them all.** The safest assumption to make when working with others is to assume that the other person means well. This assumption allows you to see and deal with the actions and ideas of others at face value.

SELF-CHECK

- Define assumption and describe a positive use of making an assumption.
- Discuss four ways that assumptions can lead to mistakes and misunderstandings.
- List five tips for avoiding the negative side of assumptions.

1.6 Culture and Communication

Intercultural communication involves making connections between people with different views of the world. In today's global marketplace, every business communicator needs to know how to interact successfully with members of different cultures, whether in business relations with a foreign company or while employed in multicultural workforces.

When you and your own cultural background come into contact with persons of another culture, a middle ground, or **transaction culture**, should emerge. For example, consider the cultural rules that would guide a business conversation between you and a manager from Japan. You would not speak and act entirely as you would when conversing with Canadian co-workers, nor would the Japanese manager hold fast to Japanese conversational rules and behaviours. Both of you would consciously and subconsciously bend your own cultural habits and assumptions to accommodate the communication needs of the other.

Many forces can interfere with the desire to meet other cultures in a productive, mutually satisfying way. The following misconceptions frequently get in the way of successful intercultural communication:

- **Everyone is essentially like me.** We too easily assume that others think as we think, feel as we feel, and therefore should act as we act.
- **Others lack my advantages.** Many people believe the reason that some people aren't like them is that there's something wrong with the people who are different. They explain away cultural differences as deficiencies.
- **Our differences won't matter once we get together.** Putting different cultures into contact will not automatically lead to mutual understanding and respect.
- **Don't worry, I speak the language.** Unfortunately, formal language training does not guarantee successful intercultural communication. Knowing the language does not guarantee that you know the culture.
- **They have to respect my knowledge.** Not so. Many cultures place more importance on mutual trust than on technical know-how.
- **We're all interested in the "bottom line."** Some North Americans are used to doing away with formalities and procedures when they threaten profits or efficiency. In some other cultures, however, you may never violate the established process—including working through a hierarchy, observing customary waiting periods, and completing elaborate paperwork.

Prepare yourself to interact in a new culture by becoming aware of your own assumptions and blind spots. Doing so will help you avoid the devastating effects of crossed signals based on a misunderstanding of gestures, expressions, and innocent actions. Think about the following areas of sensitivity as you work to overcome your own assumptions and stereotypes:

- **How do men relate to women, and women to men?**
- **How does the culture indicate respect?** Consider the roles of silence, seating arrangements, eye contact, gifts, and compliments.
- **How does the culture view human time and space?** Does a 7 p.m. appointment mean "7 sharp" or "sevenish," or "closer to 8"? What about personal space? Should you stand a bit closer to a person from France or Japan than you are used to standing to a Canadian?
- **What are strict taboos in the culture?** For example, is alcohol accepted, winked at, or absolutely unthinkable?

- **How are business commitments made in the culture?** By handshake? By signing of documents? Is a verbal agreement enough for a business commitment?

- **What non-verbal cues are used in the culture to pass information to you or to pass private understandings between members of a culture?** For example, an apology delivered with a big smile in Japan is considered to be utterly sincere.

- **How should you handle the matter of language and translation?** What words should you learn to indicate your interest in another culture? Should you supply your own translator? Will he or she be trusted?

- **How should you dress for business and social occasions in the host country?** Will dressing in native clothes cause you to lose your identity? Or will North American street clothes be viewed with irritation and impatience?

- **What aspects of the host country's religious or political life must be understood for effective business relations?** Are certain times of the day set aside for worship? Must certain work groups be separated because of political differences?

FOR EXAMPLE

Getting Personal

When travelling to Venezuela, Calgary oil broker Lisa Farnswell could not help but compliment the Venezuelan manager on her flowing, black hair. Obviously pleased, she received the compliment with a smile. The two had a few minutes to wait before starting their meetings, so Lisa continued with what she thought were more pleasantries, asking the manager if her hair was difficult to care for. The smile quickly faded. The Canadian had trampled on an important Latin American custom: avoid personal questions about the private lives of acquaintances.

SELF-CHECK

- Using examples, define structured communication and unstructured communication, and discuss the differences.

- List nine common patterns of business communication.

- Explain the differences between immediate and delayed feedback. Give at least one example of each.

- Discuss six barriers that prevent an audience from understanding a message.

- List six misconceptions that get in the way of successful intercultural communication.

1.7 Approaches to Team Communication

In today's competitive world, organizations increasingly rely on employee teams to handle projects. Therefore, team communication is crucial to an organization's success. Whether you are a member of a team, the leader of a team, or the manager of a number of teams, the foundation for your success will lie in your team's communication skills.

Many types of communication coexist within an organization or business. When possible, a face-to-face meeting is the most effective, but when another mode of communication is needed at certain times, your team will have a number of choices to choose from. Here are a few of the ways a team can communicate, whether formally or informally, internally or externally:

- **Traditional:** Bulletin boards, letters, paper memos, reports, telephone calls, and faxes still have their place in the business of communication.
- **Electronic:** Email, Internet, and video telephones can reach others instantly, even crossing international borders in the blink of an eye.
- **Conversational:** Everyday chats and informal conversations keep co-workers connected. Be careful to avoid the pitfalls of the office grapevine.

Keep in mind that these communication methods should only be a part of your approach. They cannot substitute for old-fashioned, face-to-face meetings.

FOR EXAMPLE

Getting the Message
As the manager of a shipping company, you insist on one-hour lunch breaks for your employees. You've posted a general memo, in fact, demanding "compliance with company procedures regarding punctuality." Some workers understood the message, but many have not. An area supervisor suggested a different approach, one that emphasized the workers as part of a team. Over the next week, each of the supervisors brought it up during meetings, making a point of talking about how all the workers depend on one another—hence the importance of getting back from lunch on time. As a result, punctuality rates rose, and the memo was removed.

1.7.1 Keep Information Flowing

In team situations, the need for members to keep each other informed is extremely important. Think of the flow of information as a **loop.** By opening and closing the loop, you keep the flow moving.

Closing the loop means following through and getting back to others, informing them of what happened or what you found out about an issue.

Opening the loop means taking the initiative to let others know something in advance, or passing on helpful information—without being asked.

Closing and opening the loop involves thinking of others and keeping communication going at all times so that each person associated with the team feels well informed (in the loop).

1.7.2 Teach So That Others Can Learn

Part of what often is needed in teams involves cross-training or showing new team members how to do certain tasks, and most teaching involves communicating with others. To teach effectively, first remember that the person you're instructing doesn't know the task or job as well as you do. Explain the process step by step and translate any unfamiliar terms into common language.

In addition, allow for—and be receptive to—questions. Answer them clearly and directly. When people feel comfortable asking questions, they're engaged and learn well. You can also check the understanding of your trainees by asking questions of your own. In particular, use open-ended questions so that trainees must provide feedback on what they're learning. Doing so lets you know what's sinking in and what's still confusing.

1.7.3 Offer Assistance

When your vocabulary includes comments like "What can I do to help you?" or "Let me give you a hand with that," or "I can help you get that assignment done, if you'd like," you speak the language of a valuable team player. People want to know that they can count on you to help when they need it, and that you're willing to do so. When you're asked for assistance, always answer with a yes. If not now, then say when you can help and follow through. Someone who speaks and acts in the language of helpfulness and cooperation is a positive member that everybody wants as part of their team.

1.7.4 Ask for Help

Part of the benefit of working on a team is that you don't have to figure everything out yourself. You have other resource people who can share their expertise and help you when you need it. Asking questions is a sign of interest and assertiveness, not of stupidity. The only stupid thing you can do is not to ask when you don't know or you're uncertain about something. Don't apologize for asking—just speak up with confidence, stating your need simply and clearly. Then listen for the answer and ask if you need more information or explanation. You may also want to paraphrase the answers you receive to make sure you understand.

1.7.5 Speak Up in Meetings

The more you get involved in team situations, the more you're asked to attend team meetings. Teams need meetings to coordinate their activities and to collectively communicate to get everyone going in the same direction. For effective teamwork, teams need their members to do more than just show up to the meetings.

Speak up assertively in every meeting. Offer your ideas and express opinions that help the team move forward in getting results. Even if you're the soft-spoken type, pump up your volume a bit and say what you have to offer to help the team—your thoughts and contributions are truly needed.

Actively listen, too, and show your interest in the meetings. Help turn your meetings into constructive two-way conversations. (More on assertive speaking and active listening can be found in Chapter Two.)

1.7.6 Talk in Terms of Outcomes

A common pitfall for many teams is argument among the team members about how to get a job done. The outcomes needed are often lost in the debate over "your way versus my way."

Make outcomes the focus of these discussions, especially when you're problem solving and planning with your team members. Ask:

- "What goals are to be met?"
- "What results do we need to accomplish?"
- "What customer needs must be met?"

Ask questions like these during your discussions and you'll generate a focus on achieving outcomes, not on methods.

1.7.7 Give Supportive Feedback

You can offer feedback to your team members about their performances. Doing so enhances teamwork, because it opens up honest communication. Just make sure that you *describe* your observations based on actions, instead of providing subjective commentary about other people's performances. (Read more on describing in Chapter Three.)

Give feedback to recognize good performance. When others help you or take other actions that help the team achieve results, express appreciation for it. Just be sure to give specific positive feedback, not general praise.

If something doesn't go well, providing observations about such issues in a straightforward and supportive manner helps team members reflect on their efforts and learn from their experiences. You're not giving feedback to judge others; you're doing so to reinforce performance and behaviours that make for effective teamwork.

1.7.8 Take Problems to the Right Source

One way to determine whether a team will be effective is to look at how its members deal with problems and concerns that arise: Do they snipe at each other? Do they gossip behind each others' backs? Form factions? That doesn't encourage teamwork.

Team members need to work through their problems to grow and become effective as a team. When issues affect the team as a whole, put them on an agenda for a team meeting so that team members can deal with them collectively. When issues deal with an individual, go to that person to address the problem. In both cases, help facilitate the process by using the communication tools and problem-solving models of conflict resolution (outlined in Chapter Three).

1.7.9 Make Newcomers Feel Welcome

One of the challenges teams sometimes face is integrating new members. New members need to go through the learning curve and need to pay attention to the dynamic among all the members of the team. When little is done to help the new members fit in and feel like a part of the team, the team tends to pull apart.

When you're an established part of a team, always try to help the new person fit in as fast as possible. Use your active-listening skills to find out about the individual's work background. Ask what the person needs and help meet those needs. Ask others to help in showing the new person the ropes, and include the new person in social gatherings.

1.7.10 Maintain a Sense of Humour

A sure sign that you have an effective team is people laughing with each other as a normal occurrence. Their humour keeps a light touch that eases the stresses that come with the job.

Remember, teams are made up of a collection of personalities. Trying to get them to work together effectively is no small task. If you can see the humorous side of this challenge and act upon it with your team members, you can transition from focusing on yourself in your own job to focusing on the group as a team.

SELF-CHECK

- Discuss examples of traditional, electronic, and conversational types of communication within an organization.
- Explain what closing the loop means.
- Explain ten ways of enhancing the communication in a team.

SUMMARY

In order to achieve success in business, most people need to communicate effectively with others, whether they are superiors, customers, or co-workers. Assumptions, which typically have a negative implication, play an important role. The communication process itself, from source to receiver, involves active participation to be a success. In those instances when team communication is involved, techniques can be applied to enhance effectiveness.

KEY TERMS

Assumption	A belief that something is true without proof or demonstration, or that a person is going to behave a certain way before they've had a chance to act.
Communication	A process by which information is exchanged between individuals through a common system of symbols, signs, or behaviour.
External customers	People outside the workplace with whom you need to build good working relationships for success on the job. These customers include suppliers and investors.
Intercultural communication	Making connections between different views of the world.
Internal customers	Your fellow employees, inside and outside the department where you work, to whom you provide services or assistance.
Receiver	A person who listens to one or more speakers.

Sender	The speaker expressing his or her message to other parties.
Stereotyping	Assuming that anyone who is from a different group than you—whether in race, ethnicity, gender, religion, sexual orientation, occupation, or other grouping—behaves and thinks in the same way as the group.
Transaction culture	The middle ground that emerges when speakers and their own cultural background come into contact with persons of another culture.

ASSESS YOUR UNDERSTANDING

Go to www.wiley.com/canada/brounstein to evaluate your knowledge of the basics of business communication. Measure your learning by comparing pre-test and post-test results.

Quick Questions

1. External customers are customers who need the products and services that your business provides. True or false?

2. An assumption is having proof that a person is going to behave in a certain way before they've had a chance to act. True or false?

3. Ways to prevent yourself from making negative assumptions include:
   (a) treating each person as an individual
   (b) avoiding making generalizations
   (c) using active listening to check someone's meaning
   (d) all of the above

4. Communication is a one-way activity in which ideas or feelings are delivered, spoken, or written. True or false?

5. Which of the following could serve as a form of feedback for a presentation?
   (a) applause
   (b) question-and-answer session
   (c) opinion
   (d) all of the above

6. Which of the following is *not* a form of structured communication?
   (a) company newsletter
   (b) conversation over coffee

(c) weekly staff meeting

(d) office-wide email

7. The office grapevine is a useful, though sometimes destructive, part of an organization's communication system. Which of the following can help you make the most of it?

   (a) ignoring it

   (b) taking part in it only when you have something to contribute

   (c) participating in it on different levels

   (d) reporting its misuse to others

8. Which communication pattern avoids the problems associated with the series pattern?

   (a) hub and spokes

   (b) circle

   (c) legs

   (d) pyramid

9. In thinking about the flow of information as a loop, opening the loop means cutting off individuals from the information. True or false?

10. Feedback is critical to successful team communication. Feedback should *not*

    (a) recognize good performance

    (b) provide subjective comments

    (c) describe observations based on actions

    (d) be sincere

Give It Some Thought

1. The communication process is like a game of tug-of-war. What happens in the game when two participants can't communicate with each other (when both speak at the same time, for example, or one tunes out the other)?

2. What kind of assumptions would you be safe in making if you were the store manager of a small hardware store in an area where weather forecasters are forecasting a major snowstorm?

3. In many cases, making an assumption about another person can often lead to communication problems. To avoid problems, what *should* you assume about the people you are dealing with?

4. Describe the five aspects of the communication process in the correct order.

5. What role does feedback play in the communication process?

6. How does unstructured communication generate more emotional responses from receivers than structured communication?

7. Which communication patterns could be described as both efficient and inefficient?

    (a) cross-fire

    (b) hub and spokes

    (c) broken triangle

    (d) pyramid

8. Which physical and psychological barriers are involved in the following scenarios?

    (a) An audience loses focus when poor presentation materials are used.

    (b) An audience interprets poor eye contact as insecurity over the message.

    (c) An audience can be distracted by noise, drafts, and other discomforts.

    (d) An audience can be put off by stereotypes or cultural differences.

9. What are different ways that business commitments are made in different cultures, and how can these lead to misunderstandings?

10. Team communication is a critical part of an organization's success. How does teaching play a part in enhancing the effectiveness of a team?

11. Even a team member who is not an assertive speaker can contribute to a team's success. What are two things such a person can do to overcome insecurity or fear?

Applying This Chapter

1. You direct credit card services for a large furniture company. You've argued for months that the company's collection letters are sadly out of step with what's going on in the business world; the "Pay up!" approach is simply not working during these difficult economic times. Discuss how you could avoid the negative use of assumptions and at the same time address the needs of your "audience."

2. Draw a graphic that represents the grapevine among a group of friends, colleagues or fellow students. Describe the speed, accuracy, and motives of the grapevine.

3. You supervise ten other employees in an insurance company. On what occasion would you use the cross-fire pattern of communication with your workers? On what occasions would that approach be inappropriate?

4. Assume you're a member of a hospital's development team put together to come up with ideas for recruiting new volunteers. A fellow teammate who is new to the hospital staff is showing a lot of enthusiasm during your brainstorming meetings, but nearly all of her ideas have been way off base. Others on the team are showing their frustration. Which of the team communication guidelines could you use to help with the situation?

5. Cecile, a friend from high school, has just landed a great new job in a firm that creates websites for small businesses. She's a bit nervous, though, because

everyone in the new firm seems to work closely in teams and she's used to working solo. Cecile was relieved when you told her you would write up some practical suggestions for her based on what you were learning about teamwork in your new business communications course. Write up a friendly, supportive email to Cecile; she's especially interested in giving feedback during strategy planning sessions.

THE NEXT STEP

Wrong Assumptions
Jot down three instances in which making an assumption about someone (or, alternatively, when someone has made an assumption about you) has backfired. Think about why it happened. Did you jump to a conclusion or resort to a stereotype? What were the consequences? How could you have avoided the situation in the first place?

Communication Barriers
Sometimes, the way an organization is arranged can itself become a barrier to communication. Describe any organizational barriers to communication that you see at your workplace, school, or organization. Go on to suggest ways in which you could reduce or eliminate these barriers.

Succeeding in a New Country
Pick a country that you would like to visit on business some day. Do some Internet and library research on issues like personal space, levels of formality, or the relationship between men and women in that country. How might issues like these affect your communication with your host? Additionally, identify any strict taboos that you'll want to be aware of. Which taboos might you have violated if you had not taken time to investigate the cultural differences between your country and the foreign country?

Choosing a Candidate
Your company is opening an office in a foreign country. Consider what you've learned from Question #3 and get together with two or three other classmates to devise an insightful list of interview questions that will identify potential biases or other problems so that you are able to determine which candidates are most likely to succeed in a different culture.

Feedback
List the various forms of feedback you receive during a typical day. Which influence your actions the most? Why?

2

MASTERING COMMUNICATION SKILLS

Tools for Sending and Receiving Messages

STARTING POINT

Go to www.wiley.com/canada/brounstein to assess your knowledge of the basics of communication skills. After reviewing the website, you'll be able to determine where you need to concentrate your effort.

What You'll Learn in This Chapter:

- the four types of speaking approaches
- non-verbal methods of communication
- the three stages of the listening process
- the four approaches to listening.

After Studying This Chapter, You'll be Able to:

- discuss the relationship between assertive speaking and other approaches
- identify the impact of non-verbal communication skills
- review ways of avoiding non-verbal pitfalls
- discuss the role of listening skills in effective communication.

INTRODUCTION

Success in your work comes from more than just having expertise in your field. It also comes from being able to express yourself, listen to others, and build relationships with the people you work with.

The four types of speaking approaches—aggressive, non-assertive, passive-aggressive, and assertive—are reviewed. The chapter examines non-verbal types of communication, including eye contact and body language. The importance of listening and the stages of listening are discussed. The chapter concludes with a look at the four approaches to listening: passive, selective, attentive, and active.

2.1 Recognizing the Four Approaches to Speaking

People express themselves in four ways: aggressively, non-assertively, passive-aggressively, and assertively. This section discusses each pattern of communication in detail so that you can recognize each one, understand what makes assertiveness the most effective approach, and then move your own way of speaking toward assertiveness.

If you're like most people, you've used all four speaking approaches at various times. But you may find that when you deal with certain people or encounter certain situations—especially challenging and stressful ones—you often fall into one of the less-productive patterns of expressing yourself (aggressive, non-assertive, or passive-aggressive). If you do, join the club known as the human race. You become a successful communicator by dealing with these situations assertively, the most positive and respectful way of resolving issues with others.

2.1.1 The Aggressive Approach

Aggressive speaking is a hard-charging approach that's often hostile and comes across as controlling or dominating. Here are some common messages you may hear when someone speaks aggressively:

- "You must . . ."
- "You always/never . . ."
- "Whose fault is this?"

There's nothing subtle about the aggressive approach. The following are common behaviours that an aggressive speaker displays:

- **Blaming, accusing:** In problem situations, an aggressive speaker is quick to find fault and focus on the wrongs that the other person supposedly committed.
- **Intimidating body language:** An aggressive speaker sometimes uses threatening or intimidating body language, such as demonstrative finger pointing, moving closer to you, getting in your face to argue a point, or pounding on a table with his or her fist.
- **Demanding, ordering:** The aggressive approach to getting something from another person is to demand it or give orders. Aggressive speakers tell you what you must do.
- **Raised voice:** When someone is making a point aggressively, his or her voice gets louder and the tone becomes sharper.

- **Harsh, personal language:** An aggressive speaker focuses more on the person than on the issue. The language is often filled with a lot of *you* insults and, at times, with profanity. Tact or diplomacy is tossed aside.

2.1.2 The Non-Assertive Approach

Non-assertive speaking comes off as the softest of the four approaches. A non-assertive speaker is passive and allows others to dominate the conversation.

Here are some common messages you hear when someone speaks in a non-assertive manner:

- "Uh . . . if that's the way you want to do it . . . um, that's fine with me."
- "I'll talk to him soon about that problem; I've just been really busy."
- "I hate to bother you."

There's nothing strong or certain about the non-assertive approach. Instead, non-assertive speakers often display the following behaviours:

- **Overly agreeable, no point of view expressed:** A non-assertive speaker agrees with you in order to keep everything nice. A non-assertive speaker also seldom expresses his or her point of view and certainly doesn't express an opinion that's contrary to yours.
- **Avoidance:** The non-assertive way to deal with a concern is to avoid dealing with it: Avoid talking to the person, let the problem linger, and try to put off dealing with the situation for as long as possible, especially if it has to do with an uncomfortable matter.
- **Withdrawn body language:** A non-assertive speaker doesn't make direct eye contact with other people, stays at a distance, and may slump or cower. Nothing confident comes across in the speaker's physical effort to communicate the message.
- **Sounding unsure:** When someone speaks non-assertively, he or she hesitates and sounds unsure. A non-assertive speaker may use language such as *maybe* or *hopefully,* or may start sentences with comments like, "I don't know if this idea will help."
- **Beating around the bush:** Non-assertive speakers express critical or sensitive points by talking around the issue and rambling, leaving the point—at best—implied. The speaker never states the point clearly and directly.
- **Sounding hopeless or helpless:** A common non-assertive speaking characteristic is language of despair or inaction. A typically resigned or hopeless message, such as, "I tried that once, but it didn't work, so what can you do?" is common. You may hear a lot of *I can'ts* and *I don't knows* such that no plan or possible solution is introduced.

> **FOR EXAMPLE**
>
> **Non-Assertive and Ineffective**
> Ethan finally got up the nerve to talk with Noah, a co-worker whose performance
> was negatively impacting the team. During the meeting, Ethan talked about how
> a good team needs members who are supportive and follow through on their
> assignments. Noah agreed that those are good qualities for a team member. This
> 15-minute meeting ended with Ethan feeling that Noah understood the problem
> and with Noah feeling that this was a strange conversation—and nothing he
> needed to be concerned about.

2.1.3 The Passive-Aggressive Approach

Passive-aggressive speaking is an approach in which a person comes off as subtle and
indirect, but the underlying tone of voice may hurt or manipulate others.

Take a look at some messages you hear when someone speaks in a passive-aggressive
manner:

- *"I knew that wouldn't work."*
- *"If that's the way you want it . . ."*
- *"How could you even think that?"*

The subtleties of the passive-aggressive approach are not pleasant. Someone speaking passive-aggressively often displays the following behaviours:

- **Appears to agree but really does not agree:** One of the common behaviours of
  passive-aggressiveness is that the speaker sounds as though he or she is going
  along with something, but his or her actions that follow don't show support or
  commitment. Instead, the passive-aggressive speaker claims that any agreement
  was actually a misunderstanding or carries out actions that are contrary to the
  supposed commitment.
- **Talks to others but not to the source of the concern:** A passive-aggressive
  person does not deal directly with concerns about others. Complaining about that
  person to other people—behind that person's back—is a common way to handle
  concerns. Generally, such behaviour stirs up gossip and divisiveness.
- **Makes subtle digs and sarcastic remarks:** In this behaviour of passive-
  aggressive speakers, put-downs are concealed with sarcasm. Sometimes a passive-aggressive speaker expresses displeasure not through words but through
  non-verbal means, such as rolling the eyes, shaking the head, or making sighs of
  disgust.

- **Non-verbal message contradicts the verbal message:** In passive-aggressive behaviour, stated words sound positive, but body language or tone of voice gives the words the opposite meaning. "Everything is fine" means that something *is* wrong. "That's a good idea" means that it *isn't,* and so on.
- **Holds back expressing concerns or providing assistance:** A passive-aggressive speaker may withhold information or other forms of support when others can use it to get a job done. In addition, he or she holds emotions in, although you may get a sense of them in the speaker's body language. But nothing is said directly, and when asked about a concern, the speaker often responds by saying, "Never mind" or "No big deal."
- **Criticizes after the fact:** A passive-aggressive speaker is quick to pass judgement. After an event or action has taken place, a passive-aggressive communicator responds with what you should've done or what you did wrong—sometimes even when you requested input beforehand and he or she gave none.

2.1.4 The Assertive Approach

Assertive speaking involves expressing yourself in a positive and confident way and allowing and encouraging others to do the same.

This pattern of speaking requires the most skill and effort, for unlike the other three approaches, it requires you to think before you speak. Here are some common messages you hear from assertive speakers:

- *"Yes, that was my mistake."*
- *"As I understand your point, . . . "*
- *"Please hear me out and then work with me to resolve my concern."*

The following are some of the behaviours that someone who speaks in an assertive fashion displays:

- **Takes responsibility:** The assertive approach says that each individual is responsible for his or her own actions—no excuses, no blaming others for problems. The speaker accepts what has happened and focuses on what needs to be done next.
- **Takes initiative:** An assertive speaker doesn't play games. If something needs to happen, he or she takes the initiative to get the process rolling—no waiting for others to say what to do and when to act. The assertive approach is action oriented.
- **Listens actively:** Assertiveness allows for two-way conversation. Assertive speakers are willing to hear the other person out and understand his or her point of view.
- **Speaks up, and is direct and constructive:** If a point needs to be made or a thought needs to be expressed, an assertive communicator speaks up. He or she

states the point directly without beating around the bush. Assertive speakers use language *constructively;* that is, they communicate the message in the best way possible and make the point clearly. The language focuses on the issue at hand.

- **Shows sincerity:** When you express yourself sincerely, you say what you mean and mean what you say—and do so with respect for others.
- **Is focused on solutions:** In problem situations, an assertive speaker takes a problem-solving approach. He or she examines the problem, not to blame or find fault with anyone, but to understand the issue and move toward developing a solution.
- **Assumes a confident voice and body language:** The voice of an assertive speaker sounds strong, certain, and firm when needed. The speaker's posture, gestures, and facial expressions support his or her message. He or she sounds and looks alive when speaking, coming across non-verbally as positive and enthusiastic.
- **Addresses concerns directly to the source:** An assertive speaker addresses issues directly to the source as opposed to telling others about the problems. At the same time, the speaker states the problem constructively and places the emphasis on collaborating with the other person to work out a resolution. No browbeating or blaming occurs.
- **Requests needs:** Whereas an aggressive speaker demands or orders to get what's needed, an assertive speaker *asks for* or *requests* what's needed. The message makes the sense of importance clear so that the request and any rationale for it are understood.

Don't Confuse Aggressive with Assertive

People sometimes confuse the words **aggressive** and **assertive.** What they share in common is that the speaker is willing to share his or her viewpoint and is willing to take action to deal with issues. But after that, the two approaches are quite different.

Aggressive	Assertive
Blunt	Direct
In conflict situations, harsh in tone	In conflict situations, firm in tone
In conflict situations, blame and browbeat the other person	In conflict situations, collaborate on solutions
Push your own way	Speak up, yet hear what the other person has to say
One-way conversation flow	Two-way conversation flow

2.1.5 Contrasting the Four Approaches to Speaking

To see the true impact of choosing one approach to speaking over another, try taking a situation and demonstrating each of the four common speaking approaches for that situation. Here's one such scenario.

Say you just received an important assignment with a tight deadline. You know that you need assistance from Jill, a co-worker, to get it done. Using each approach, how would you communicate this need? Take your thoughts and compare them to the following samples:

- **Aggressive approach:** "Jill, look, I'm in a jam right now. You need to help me get this critical project done right away! I don't have time to hear that you're busy with something else. That excuse just won't fly. So let me show you what I need you to do."
- **Non-assertive approach:** "Hi, Jill. I hate to bother you, I know you're probably busy right now. I have a tough assignment. If you have a chance, maybe you could lend me a hand for a little bit. But, uh, it's okay if you don't want to."
- **Passive-aggressive approach:** "Jill, I know you're the type who doesn't want to put yourself out too much. Hey, I'm just kidding. But look, when you were in a pinch last week, who helped you out? ? That's right—me. So look, I'm in the same boat now. Don't worry, I won't have you do most of the work anyway."
- **Assertive approach:** "Jill, I was just assigned a critical project that needs to be done in a week. I would appreciate it if you could lend some assistance. The project involves an area in which your experience will really come in handy. I'd like to take a few minutes with you now or this afternoon to determine what time and support you can lend. Does that work for you, and if so, what time can we meet?"

As you see in this example, the same message can be communicated in four different ways. Only an assertive speaker is able to directly and positively request Jill's help and communicate the importance of the situation. The aggressive message comes on as a strong demand, the non-assertive approach leaves you wondering whether anything is being asked at all, and the passive-aggressive message tinges with sarcasm and you-owe-me conditions—all of which are turnoffs to most fellow team members.

2.1.6 Becoming an Assertive Speaker

As discussed in the preceding section on the four ways people express themselves, the assertive approach is the most effective for achieving success on the job. If you're like many people, you can see yourself in the other approaches—and probably see people you've met in both your professional and personal lives in each approach, too.

You may have noticed that you have to listen effectively to speak assertively. The better you understand where the other person is coming from—you do so through active listening—the better you can tailor your message so that the other person understands it well. You can find more on active listening later in this chapter.

To change your pattern of behaviour so that you become an assertive speaker, apply the following principles:

- **Collaboration:** Conversations work best when they're two-way—that is, where both parties contribute and work to understand each other.
- **Flexibility:** Not everyone you interact with is the same; however, being direct, positive, confident, and willing to listen is a good place to start with everyone. From there, you can adjust to the individual after you get to know the person. For example, with some people, the less you say the better. With others, you have to be firm to be taken seriously.
- **Self-control:** The toughest person to manage in any interaction is yourself. Assertive speakers are in control of their emotions. Aggressive, non-assertive, and passive-aggressive speakers allow their emotions to control them.
- **Consistent respect:** Assertive speakers take a long-term view to working relationships. People you deal with today will remember you tomorrow. You may not like everyone you meet at work, but if you treat everyone with unconditional respect, you build more partners and allies for the future. You can take actions to deal with situations you don't like (see Section 3.3), but you always do so with respect.
- **Fix problems, not blame:** Problems are inevitable in any work situation, and many involve other people. When speaking assertively, your focus is on problem solving versus problem dwelling—on creating solutions together versus blaming one another.

The stressful and challenging situations you encounter, how often they occur, and with whom they occur vary greatly from individual to individual. For some people, the workday is filled with constant stress, whereas for others, the day is peaceful and friendly. Your approach to interacting with others greatly influences how stressful and challenging your work situations have been and will become.

SELF-CHECK

- Define aggressive speaking, non-assertive speaking, passive-aggressive speaking, and assertive speaking.
- Describe how assertive speaking is the most effective for achieving success in communicating on the job.
- Describe the characteristics of aggressive speakers.
- Discuss the difference between assertive speaking and aggressive speaking.
- Describe the principles for becoming an assertive speaker.

2.2 Mastering Non-Verbal Communication Skills

Assertive speaking is about delivering your message in a positive, direct, and confident manner while maintaining respect for the person or persons to whom you're expressing that message. However, your words alone aren't the only component of speaking. Much of the impact of your message has nothing to do with *what* you say but rather *how* you say it. The non-verbal tools covered in this section can greatly impact how your message is expressed and received by others. In fact, the following is true:

- **What you say is important, but how you say it often carries more weight.** Much of the emotion in a speaker's message is presented through non-verbal means of communication—body language and tone of voice. Emotion is what engages people's attention as they listen to you—or causes them to disengage and not listen.
- **Most people haven't been taught how to truly listen;** therefore, you can't count on them to listen fully and effectively when you speak to them. Non-verbal tools help you engage your listeners and keep their attention focused on your message.

2.2.1 Communicating with Eye Contact

Your eyes give your spoken message much of its meaning and affect whether the listener believes and trusts it. More often than not, however, the listener provides more direct eye contact to the other person than the speaker. What is the speaker doing with his eyes? At times, the speaker looks at the person with whom he's conversing, but quite often, his eyes are wandering around, gathering thoughts about what to say next.

The eye-contact assertive-speaking tool works differently; you provide steady and sincere eye contact with the other person while expressing your message. Here's how you use this tool:

- **Make steady eye contact.** The idea is to look at people when you're talking to them. Steady eye contact is the key to this subtle tool. Steady does not, however, mean constant. Blinking and occasional glances away are expected and normal. Add a touch of sincerity to your looks and you'll attract people's attention to you and your message.
- **Maintain eye contact.** The more familiar and comfortable a relationship you have with someone, the longer the eye contact can be maintained without discomfort for either party. In general, eye contact can range comfortably from 6 to 20 seconds in one-on-one interactions, while in group situations, the time is less per individual—3 to 6 seconds—because you want to address everybody in the group.

- **Look in the right places.** Look directly at your listener's face, near the eyes. Looking above and below the face captures less of the listener's attention and can make the listener uncomfortable.

2.2.2 Avoiding Eye-Contact Pitfalls

When speaking to others, avoid eye-contact behaviours that make your message less than assertive:

- **Staring and glaring:** Such looks often are interpreted as aggressive, which is far too strong for any message. Staring and looking below face level at the same time causes discomfort and may even offend your listener.
- **Looking away and all around:** This is the most common eye-contact pitfall for speakers. Whether they're searching for their thoughts or deeply absorbed in their messages, speakers who maintain little or no eye contact cause listeners to drift away.
- **Focusing in on one person, not everyone:** This behaviour happens in group situations. It's fine to address someone who has asked you a question. However, when your eye contact stays with only one person, the other listeners feel isolated and left out.
- **Glazing over:** Sometimes this happens when you're overly absorbed in your own thoughts or when you lose your train of thought. Once is no big deal, but have it happen more than that in a conversation and you appear to have tuned out your own message.

2.2.3 Supporting Your Message with Body Language

Body language refers to everything you do with your body to express your message, including facial expressions, posture, and gestures.

The idea behind assertive speaking is getting these myriad expressions and cues involved in your message; that is, coming alive when you speak.

You have to decide what to do with your face and body when you speak: You can use them or keep them dormant. In assertive speaking, you can use them in ways that positively engage others in your message and that enable you to come across as confident, animated, and relaxed. Here's how you use the body-language tool:

- **Posture:** Posture is how you carry and position yourself. Sit up and face your receiver as a means of expressing your message assertively. It is sometimes helpful to lean forward a bit as well. Sitting up also helps put strength in your voice.
- **Gestures:** Gestures are what you do with your hands when you're talking. Use gestures to come across assertively, to help your message flow properly, and in essence, to punctuate or emphasize key points when you're talking.

Figure 2-1 Comparing a negative facial expression to a positive one (dyonisos/iStockphoto)

- **Facial expressions:** Your face communicates emotions to others. The idea in expressing yourself assertively is to show enthusiasm through your facial expressions. Have your facial expressions match what you're saying in your message. Figure 2-1 illustrates two different facial expressions. Consider how different a message might sound coming from someone who looks unhappy (left) and someone who looks positive and friendly (right).

FOR EXAMPLE

Everyone Look Into the Mirror
Kavita managed a large group of customer service representatives who answered customers' technical questions over the telephone. As competent as they were, many of the staff spoke in monotone, becoming almost robotic in their explanations. Merely telling employees to sound livelier was not enough, so Kavita decided to place mirrors next to each rep's telephone. That meant when they picked up their phones, they saw themselves talking in the mirrors. With some instruction for the reps to put a smile in their voices, they became more animated in their facial expressions. The material they talked about started to sound more interesting. Most of all, the customers heard a difference.

2.2.4 Avoiding Body-Language Pitfalls

You want your posture, facial expressions, and gestures to come across as confident, animated, and relaxed. Certain behaviours, however, make you less than assertive and create emotions that range from disinterest to disgust:

- **Slouching:** When you lean back and relax in a chair, you come across as too relaxed. It's not good if you want to assertively communicate and be taken seriously by others. Less energy gets behind your voice as well.

- **Invading space:** This pitfall occurs when people are standing and attempting to engage in lively conversation. It's where you're getting too close for comfort to the other person. Generally, Canadians like to keep a "safe zone" of at least 35 centimetres (14 inches) around themselves. The space should be larger between men and women and between strangers. Certainly; if the person you are speaking to is leaning away from you, that's a sure sign you've crossed the comfort zone of physical space.

- **Looking stern:** This facial expression usually is displayed with furrowed eyebrows and a near frown or scowl. It has an uninviting—if not intimidating—feel to it and more often than not causes your listener to want to disengage.

- **Displaying threatening gestures:** The most common examples here are demonstrative finger pointing or pounding a fist on the table. These gestures often are part of strong messages and have you coming across aggressively instead of assertively.

- **Showing no gestures:** Sometimes people tuck their hands in their pockets when speaking. Others keep them under the table or folded tightly together. Without using gestures, you can appear stiff or timid—behaviours that have you moving on the non-assertive track. Have a look at Figure 2-2 below. The presenter on the left looks timid and stiff because he is speaking with his hands in his pockets. The presenter on the right is using his hands to engage with the presentation material on the chart beside him; this helps to draw in the audience's attention.

- **Folding your arms:** Folding your arms when speaking is different from folding them as you listen. When you're listening, as long as you don't look closed off, folding your arms helps you appear relaxed and receptive to hearing someone else's message. When you're speaking, however, folding your arms makes you come across as stiffer and less interested in your own message.

- **Exhibiting distracting habits:** Scratching, twirling hair, and pulling on jewellery are a few examples of habits that people exhibit when they're talking to someone else. These habits bring attention to you rather than what you have to say.

Figure 2-2 Using ineffective versus effective body language when presenting (Andy Cook/iStockphoto)

2.2.5 Using Your Voice

Your voice is a powerful tool for delivering your message in an assertive manner. When not used wisely, it can easily cause you to come across as non-assertive, passive-aggressive, or aggressive. When used wisely, however, it makes others pay attention to what you have to say.

The emphasis on the vocal tool for assertive speaking is not about the physical quality of your voice. You have what you have. The emphasis is on using the richness of your voice in terms of volume, inflection, and tone, so that your delivery commands positive attention. Here are some tips for using this tool:

- **Project your voice.** Are you audible enough when you speak? The idea is to be heard loud and clear. This effort becomes even more important when you're interacting in group situations such as meetings. Therefore, vary your volume for the situation. Go a little louder in group situations, and then turn it down slightly for one-on-one interactions. Always keep it at a volume that makes your voice easy to be heard.
- **Vary the volume of your voice to help to add emphasis to your message.** Increasing your volume at an important point commands attention, and some-times softening your volume at a particular point of emphasis can draw people's attention closer to you.
- **Show inflection in your voice.** Inflection deals with your pitch. If you're at a high pitch, your voice comes across as shrill, which nobody wants to hear. More commonly, if you stay at one pitch, you sound dull. The key to being assertive is to have variety—known as **modulation**—in your pitch.
- **Display sincerity in your tone.** Tone wraps up the volume and inflection in your voice. It conveys the feeling of your message and, therefore, plays a huge part in what your message means and how others receive it. You want your tone to communicate sincerity. When you're sincere, your message is better received.

2.2.6 Avoiding Vocal Pitfalls

Your voice can often be your greatest tool for communicating your message positively and effectively to others. However, when it isn't used assertively, your voice can be your greatest hindrance to being understood in the best possible way. Here is a list of pitfalls that make you sound less than assertive:

- **Sounding uncertain:** Your voice serves as a barometer of the amount of confidence you show in your message. If you sound hesitant or uncertain of your own message, no one will have confidence in you or what you say.
- **Being too soft-spoken:** When you're not audible enough to be heard well, the likelihood that no one is listening to you increases. If you can't speak up to be heard, you come across as lacking confidence in your own message.

- **Mumbling:** Sometimes you mumble as you're talking out loud to yourself or as you're changing directions in your message. Because people can't make out what you say when you mumble, some make the assumption that you're saying something negative under your breath. Others just get the impression that you're unsure about what you're talking about. Overall, mumbling detracts from a confident message.
- **Being too loud:** When the volume in your voice is too strong, especially when dealing with problem situations, you'll come across as aggressive and sometimes intimidating. If you sound too loud for what the situation calls for, you seem out of control. If you have to shout to be heard, generally no one wants to listen.
- **Dropping your voice at the end of a sentence:** This is a common pitfall for many people. You're hearing them fine but as they get to the end of a sentence or key point, the volume of their voice becomes almost silent. The sentence then sounds incomplete. When you sound like you lack the energy to complete your sentences, your receivers often lose your message and lose interest in hearing your message.
- **Sounding monotonous:** Monotone is the dreaded low-pitch sound in your voice, which, when it is heard continually, creates considerable disinterest in the message. No inflection in your voice usually translates to no attention gained from others.
- **Putting people down with your tone:** Tones that sound like you're arrogant, patronizing, or condescending hit people quickly with a feeling of disrespect— regardless of your intentions.

2.2.7 Getting Your Message Across by Managing Your Pace

Pace is the rate at which you speak. It determines how fast or slow the words come out of your mouth and how clearly those words are heard and understood.

People from different geographical regions speak at different rates. For example, English-speaking Canadians tend to speak more quickly than people from the southeastern US. In today's workplace, people often have grown up in places far different from where they're working now, including many other countries around the world. In other words, a wide variety of people come into our workplaces with a wide variety of communication styles.

This tool is about finding the happy medium with your rate of speaking. A steady pace can help you speak effectively with a wide variety of people. At the same time, this tool tells you to sometimes vary the rate a bit, especially based on the type of audience you're addressing. Here are some tips for applying the pace tool:

- **Enunciate your words clearly.** Enunciation is about saying words as they are meant to sound. "Are you goin' to the meetin'?", or "Are you going to the meeting?" These subtle kind of differences are often noticed by your receivers, and at times create a sense that you're not certain or knowledgeable about your own message.

- **Insert pauses occasionally in your message.** Thinking before you speak and allowing yourself the chance to breathe comfortably enhances your message. Pauses help you smooth out your pace, gather your thoughts, and enunciate your words clearly. Simply give yourself permission to think and breathe as part of your speaking habits.
- **Show a variation in your pace.** Changing your pace adds flavour and significance to key words. It also helps those words to stand out more clearly to your listeners. Sometimes this means speeding up from your steady pace as you say a key phrase or sentence. Sometimes this means slowing down from your steady pace at these critical points.
- **Match your pace of speaking with your listener's pace of speaking.** If you are speaking to someone whose pace is quicker than yours, speed up. If your listener speaks slower, slow down. This subtle change helps you to establish rapport. This last aspect of pacing is similar to a technique called **mirroring**. With mirroring, you aim to match all aspects of your communication to what the other person in the conversation is doing in order to establish rapport—from body language to use of words and rate of speech. The hazard of mirroring is that sometimes that effort can go too far. You either try to mirror so much that you lose track of the message you're listening to, or you come across as mimicking someone else.

2.2.8 Avoiding Pace Pitfalls

Four main pitfalls of speaking pace are highlighted here. You may see yourself in one of them, and if you do, welcome to the human race. Now go after correcting them and managing your pace to come across assertively:

- **Speaking too quickly:** When your pace of speaking is at a rate that's so much faster than your listener's speaking style, emotions are heard at an exaggerated level—you're too excited, you're overly anxious. As a result, your sincerity and confidence levels don't come across, so your listener isn't connecting with your message.
- **Slurring words:** Words sometimes are slurred because someone's speaking pace is too fast, but at the heart of the problem is the repeated unclear enunciation of your words that sometimes sounds like they're being combined together.
- **Speaking too slowly:** Saying one sentence in the time it takes someone else to say three may cause your listener to lose patience in following what you're trying to say. The point is to tune into your speech pattern and be aware of how you come across. Then look at your rate of speaking like driving a car. Sometimes you need to hit the brake and slow down, and sometimes you need pick up your speed.

- **Using excessive non-words: Non-words** are filler sounds or words that people say that aren't really words that attach to their messages. Common forms include "uh," "um," "like," "okay," and "you know." When used occasionally in a message, non-words aren't that noticeable, but when they're used frequently, they distract, clutter your message, and make it difficult to listen. The key to minimizing the non-words is to make better use of pauses. As mentioned before, pausing allows you to think first and provides a smooth delivery to your pace—much more appealing to listen to.

SELF-CHECK

- Define body language and pace.
- List four examples of non-verbal communication.
- Discuss the impact that non-verbal types of communication can have on a speaker's message.
- Describe how an audience might react to a speaker who fidgets, paces, and mumbles.
- Explain ways of avoiding body language pitfalls.

2.3 Mastering Listening Skills

If you're like most people, you interact with people every day in your job, so you do some talking and some listening. But are you *really* listening? Many people don't know the difference between hearing and listening and don't know what effective listening really means:

- **Listening** is defined as the process of receiving a message from a speaker, processing that message to make sense of it, and then responding to it in ways that show understanding of what the speaker means.
- **Hearing** is simply the physical effort of taking in the speaker's message, but doesn't necessarily mean that the message was received, processed, or responded to.

This chapter walks you through this process, shows you the ways that people commonly engage in listening, and helps you understand the most effective way to listen (called **active listening** and sometimes referred to as **reflective listening** or **responsive listening**).

> **FOR EXAMPLE**
>
> **Hearing without Listening**
> Nav was on his way to Saint John, New Brunswick to deliver a sales presentation to a potential big customer. He was running late and didn't want to miss his flight, so he asked an assistant to ship his presentation materials overnight to his hotel in Saint John, where he'd be able to get them in time for the meeting. The package never arrived, and Nav lost the customer's business as a result. A few days later, the package was discovered to have been sent to St. John's, Newfoundland and Labrador.

2.3.1 Recognizing the Impact of Listening

You can gain a lot when you listen effectively; you can lose a lot when you don't. You've probably experienced both the benefits of good listening and the costs of poor listening. The key is to recognize both the benefits and the costs so that you can maximize the benefits of your own listening.

Think about how it feels when someone really listens to you. Whether you feel respected, cared for, rewarded, or satisfied, or some other good feeling, when someone listens well to you, the experience is definitely positive.

Now, what would be the impact on your job if the people you interact with—from co-workers to customers—walked away from interactions with you with these kinds of positive feelings? You're likely to have results such as increased productivity, stronger work relationships, better customer satisfaction, greater cooperation, and less stress.

Listening is a powerful means of communication that can increase your effectiveness on the job. When you become aware of the power that active listening gives you, you're ready to develop and use listening tools and begin to have a positive impact on others.

2.3.2 Minimizing the Negatives

Stories of woe, from big to small, usually roll out when people are asked to tell about situations in which they were listened to poorly. Consider the following ways that poor listening can affect work situations:

- strained working relationships
- messed-up customer orders
- loss of current or potential business
- increased errors and the need for rework
- greater inefficiency.

In simple terms, poor listening can be quite costly. The key is to recognize the impact of effective listening and work hard to gain the benefits that come from it. Remember, too, that this stuff about listening makes your job easier, not harder.

2.3.3 Following the Three Stages of Listening

The listening process occurs in three stages:

Stage 1—Receiving: In this first stage, you take in the speaker's message through your senses, most notably through hearing and seeing (except when you're talking to someone over the telephone). Your eyes help you read the non-verbal cues that play a part in how the speaker expresses his or her message.

- ○ This is why, if you have an issue to work out with someone, you should get together face-to-face if possible. Seeing the person live helps you gain a better understanding of what that person is thinking and feeling.

Stage 2—Processing: After you take in the speaker's message with your senses, the internal processing begins. This activity takes place in your mind and involves analyzing, evaluating, and synthesizing. It's done to help you figure out the answer to the question, "What does the speaker mean?" This stage requires a great deal of concentration so that you get what the speaker is truly saying without being distracted.

Stage 3—Responding: This third stage in the listening process is the one in which the speaker sees and hears what the listener does. In this stage, the listener verbally and non-verbally acknowledges that he or she has received and understood the message.

2.3.4 Avoiding Ineffective Patterns for Listening

One of the common ineffective patterns that occurs in conversations is that a speaker speaks to a speaker instead of a listener. Little true listening takes place.

The example in Table 2-1 illustrates the pattern people often have in conversations: two people talking at each other and no one really listening. Although the conversation

Table 2-1: Calm conversation with no listening

Tom	Raymond
Begins as speaker: "Raymond, we need to increase efficiency in our operation by creating some process improvements."	**Reacts as speaker:** "Tom, I think the answer lies in putting in some organized training for the staff."
Reacts as speaker: "I disagree. The inefficiencies that occur in our operation are all process related. If we find ways to streamline our processes, we can serve our customers better."	**Reacts as speaker:** "No, Tom. If you look at the kinds of errors that staff members make, most are because of not knowing how the processes work. We tend to throw people into their jobs as opposed to training them how to do the job right."

between Tom and Raymond is not heated, and they're both talking about related subjects—they are still busy expressing opinions back and forth to each other. Neither is making the effort to understand the other's thinking.

SELF-CHECK

- Discuss the difference between listening and hearing.
- Discuss ways ineffective listening can damage a work relationship.
- List the three stages of listening.
- Explain ways of avoiding ineffective listening.

2.4 Recognizing the Four Approaches to Listening

As discussed earlier in the chapter, people express their messages to each other by using four common approaches. The same applies to how people listen. Because most people don't receive formal instruction in how to listen effectively and don't usually have standout role models for it, either, they engage in listening in the following ways:

- passive listening
- selective listening
- attentive listening
- active listening.

Of the four common patterns in how people listen to others, passive listening and selective listening occur the most often. You may see yourself, plus others in your life, in the patterns described in the following sections.

2.4.1 The Passive Approach

Passive listening is a common way that people listen to others. In this approach, the listener is present non-verbally but verbally provides little feedback to the speaker.

Here are some common behaviours exhibited by someone who is listening passively:

- eye contact with the speaker
- fairly expressionless look on the face
- occasional nods of the head
- occasional verbal acknowledgements, such as, "Uh huh," especially on the telephone.

As you can see in these behaviours, the listener is with the speaker but adds little to stimulate the flow of conversation. As the speaker, you're on your own. Talking to a passive listener is quite frustrating because you generally want more participation from the other person and you wonder whether that listener really cares or understands your message. The result is a one-way conversation like the one you can see illustrated in Table 2-2:

Table 2-2: Conversation with a passive listener

Tom	Raymond
Begins as speaker: "Raymond, I'd like to discuss our department's need to increase operating efficiency by creating some process improvements."	**Reacts as passive listener:** "Uh huh."
Continues as speaker: "In my opinion, the inefficiencies that occur in our operation are all process related. I think that if we find ways to streamline our processes, we can serve our customers better."	**Nods his head in agreement:** "Hmm."

2.4.2 The Selective Approach

Selective listening is nearly as common as passive listening. Selective listening is most commonly defined as "hearing what you want to hear."

When you hear the message you want to hear, you may function as a more engaged and understanding listener. But when you don't want to hear about the particular message being delivered, you tend to tune out or become reactive to the speaker. In other words, you're consistently inconsistent in your listening efforts when you function as a selective listener.

Someone who is listening in a selective manner to a message that he or she doesn't want to hear displays these behaviours:

- disinterested facial expression
- looks away at other things—a watch, papers, and so on

- reacts in a highly emotional manner, such as being defensive
- jumps in before the speaker has finished and takes over the conversation
- changes the subject
- asks a question about a point of self-interest, sometimes in an interrogating manner, that doesn't fit in the speaker's current message.

Falling into the trap of being a selective listener is easy to do. Humans have emotions and biases, and sometimes, something a speaker says triggers those emotions and biases. Table 2-3 illustrates an example of selective listening:

Table 2-3: Unsuccessful conversation with a selective listener

Tom	Raymond
Begins as speaker: "Raymond, we need to increase efficiency in our operation by creating some process improvements."	**Responds as selective listener:** "I can't believe you're telling me this after we've had three good years following the same processes! You people in the head office have no idea what it's like to work with customers!"
Continues as speaker: "No, listen Raymond, we've not unhappy with what you've been doing. From my thinking, our current order-fulfillment processes can be quite cumbersome. They create a lot of work and…"	**Shuffling papers while Tom is speaking. Interrupts Tom's message:** "But if you're not unhappy, why do we have to change things? We all like working this way."
Tries to get back on track: "But Raymond, we're trying to reduce the amount of work and confusion. If we can find ways to streamline them, I think we can better serve our customers."	**Fails to focus on Tom's message:** "The customers are happy with us! Acme Sprockets say we're their favourite supplier!"
Sees Tom's emotions blocking the conversation: "Raymond, you're not listening. Why don't you take some time to calm down and we'll talk again this afternoon."	**Continues to take it personally and ignores the point of the conversation:** "Well, I'm pretty unhappy about this, Tom. I've always liked working here and now this comes out of the blue."

2.4.3 The Attentive Approach

Functioning as an **attentive listener** is more productive than functioning as either a passive or a selective listener. An attentive listener is more engaged and less judgemental, both non-verbally and verbally.

Attentive listeners display these behaviours:

- steady eye contact with the speaker
- interested looks and sincere facial expressions

- nods to indicate understanding
- simple verbal acknowledgements ("I see," "Okay," "Yes," and so on) to encourage the speaker to express his or her message
- raises questions to begin to draw out the message
- asks questions that seek greater detail out of the message.

A speaker's message contains two parts: the facts or content and the feelings or emotions. Together, they comprise the meaning of the speaker's message. This concept is fundamental to results-oriented communication.

As an attentive listener, you focus on the facts that the speaker wants to relay to you in your conversation. When the message is mostly factual, you do well. When the message involves much emotion, you tend not to deal with it or neglect to acknowledge it directly. In essence, you say, "I can tell you what you're talking about; I hear your words, but I may not be able to tell fully what you mean." This is where attentive listeners fall short. Table 2-4 shows what happens when Tom uses attentive listening when discussing with Raymond possible changes to procedure. Raymond is sensitive about the subject and though his words indicate that he agrees with Tom, his actions and tone of voice show his hostility. Because Tom is using attentive listening, he hears Raymond's responses (what he is saying) but does not acknowledge the accompanying emotional clues that are part of Raymond's message (how he is saying it).

Table 2-4: Emotional conversation with an attentive listener

Tom	Raymond
Begins as speaker: "I'd like to speak with you about making some changes to the way we do things around here so we can improve our operation efficiency."	**Rolls his eyes, picks up the newspaper and begins reading it:** "Sure Tom, I'm all ears."
Responds as attentive listener, responding to Raymond's verbal message, but not acknowledging Raymond's physical messages: "Great, I'm glad you are open to the discussion. From my thinking, our current order-fulfillment processes can be quite cumbersome. They create a lot of work and much confusion. If we can find ways to streamline them, I think we can better serve our customers."	**Responds in a sarcastic tone:** "If you say so, Tom. I've been here three years but I am sure you know the department better than I do since you are the boss."
Continues as attentive listener, acknowledging only the verbal message: "Good, I'm glad you are in agreement."	

2.4.4 The Active Approach

Active listening, sometimes referred to as **responsive listening** or **reflective listening,** is the most powerful way in which people engage in the effort of listening.

An active listener receives a speaker's message with care and respect and then works to verify his or her understanding of that message—as the speaker meant it to be.

When you function as an active listener, you capture the speaker's whole message—the facts *and* the feelings. The speaker is able to get his or her message out and then walk away knowing that the listener has understood it.

Among the behaviours displayed by active listeners are the positive ones listed for the attentive approach (see Section 2.4.3), plus the following:

- showing patience
- giving verbal feedback to summarize understanding of the message
- acknowledging the emotions being expressed with the message to fully understand where the speaker is coming from
- exploring the reasons for the emotions being expressed when they are significant to the overall message
- speaking up when something is unclear or confusing.

Active listeners do talk. But what they talk about and where their attention goes is to the speaker's message—not their own message or their commentary on the speaker's message. Table 2-5 illustrates what Tom and Raymond's conversation would look like if they both used active listening:

Table 2-5: Respectful conversation between two active listeners

Tom	Raymond
Begins as speaker: "Raymond, we need to increase efficiency in our operation by creating some process improvements."	**Responds as listener:** "Help me understand more of your thinking behind this suggestion."
Continues as speaker: "From my thinking, our current order-fulfillment processes can be quite cumbersome. They create a lot of work and much confusion. If we can find ways to streamline them, I think we can better serve our customers."	**Responds as listener again:** "So you're seeing the root of our operational problems as being centred around processes?"
Confirms as speaker and then becomes listener: "That's right. What do you see as the main factors for our operational problems, Raymond?"	**Becomes speaker:** "In my view, the area we need to tackle most is training. That's the quickest and best way to start to make the improvements we need."
Responds as listener: "Training, hmm? What's your reasoning?" (And the conversation continues from there.)	

Unlike in their previous conversations (refer to Tables 2-1 to 2-4), you can see that the active listening is the most effective approach. Tom and Raymond are now talking *with* each other as opposed to speaking *at* each other. They are expressing opinions, but this time the opinions are explored and heard out. The conversation flows as a two-way interaction instead of two one-way interactions.

2.4.5 Making Active Listening Work

The best aspect of active listening, which makes it more effective than attentive listening, is that it removes doubt from your conversations. When you function as an attentive listener, you walk away from interactions thinking that you understood the other person. Often, the speaker also thinks that you have understood him or her. With active listening, the parties no longer think that understanding has been achieved; they *know* that it has.

To prepare you to get the best out of the powerful tools of active listening, here are a few tips:

- **Hold off on the assumptions.** Avoid jumping to the conclusion that you know what someone is saying before he or she states the entire message. (Sections 1.5.2 and 1.5.3 cover the problems with making assumptions.) Hold back and hear the whole message.
- **Avoid being quick to offer advice.** Unwanted advice may make the recipient feel dictated to or imposed upon—major turnoffs for most people.
- **Exercise patience.** Patience as used in active listening means exercising control over your own emotions. For active listening to work, you need to take control of your emotions so that you can deal with the variety of people who come your way.
- **Eliminate distractions and physical barriers.** When someone is talking to you, create the best possible conditions to allow for a comfortable conversation: turn your cell phone off, close the door, and arrange your chairs so you can sit across from each other.
- **Be consistently respectful.** Passing judgement on what people say or who they are turns you into a selective listener. When you come across as respectful, you build confidence and trust. Without consistent respect, active listening won't work.
- **Shift attention.** Everyone has a lot on his or her mind. Thoughts pass in and out all the time. If, as you attempt to listen, your mind's attention is focused more on what's going on around you or on what your next word back to the speaker is going to be, you're not really listening. Active listening puts attention on the speaker, not on you.

The key to success is to give verbal feedback during the conversation. Because most people aren't taught how to listen when they go through school, they tend not to give feedback to show understanding.

> ## FOR EXAMPLE
>
> **The Meaning Behind the Words**
>
> Rich hadn't worked with Josh for very long, but because they had travelled to a number of sales meetings together, they were beginning to get to know each other. As they prepared for the next day's sales presentation, Rich couldn't focus. He lost his place several times and fumbled with the equipment. When Josh asked him what was wrong, Rich assured him that everything was fine, but he didn't quite look Josh in the eyes when he said it, and he quickly changed the subject. When Josh brought it up again, Rich assured him that he "might be a little tired," but he could handle the presentation. Sensing from Rich's words and behaviour that it was more than being a "little tired," Josh switched responsibilities with Rich, giving him the more supportive role of handling the audience.

SELF-CHECK

- Define passive listening, selective listening, attentive listening, and active listening.
- Discuss how active listening is more effective than attentive listening.
- Discuss types of body language that can tell the speaker you are engaged in the conversation and actively listening.
- List six ways of making active listening work.

SUMMARY

People express themselves and listen to others in a variety of ways, some more effective than others; therefore, you need an arsenal of communication tools to increase your effectiveness on the job. The assertive approach to speaking is the most effective of four types of speaking. Much of the impact of what you say has to do with your non-verbal communications skills. To successfully communicate with others, a speaker must truly listen. Of the four approaches to listening, the active approach is the most effective.

KEY TERMS

Active listener	A person who receives a speaker's message with care and respect and then works to verify his or her understanding of that message.
Active listening	Listening that captures both the facts and the feelings of a message; involves verification of the understanding of a message; sometimes referred to as responsive listening or reflective listening.
Aggressive speaking	A hard-charging speaking approach that's often hostile and comes across as controlling or dominating.
Assertive speaking	An approach to speaking that involves people expressing themselves in a positive and confident way and allowing and encouraging others to do the same.
Attentive listener	Person who is engaged both non-verbally and verbally.
Body language	What a person does with their body to express their message, including facial expressions, posture, and gestures.
Hearing	The physical effort of taking in the speaker's message; hearing doesn't necessarily mean that the message was received, processed, or responded to.
Listening	The process of receiving a message from a speaker, processing that message to make sense of it, and then responding to it in ways that show understanding of what the speaker means.
Mirroring	A person's communications match what the other person in the conversation is doing—from body language to use of words and rate of speech.
Modulation	Having variety in pitch; a key element of assertive speaking.
Non-assertive speaking	A passive approach to speaking; a non-assertive speaker allows others to dominate the conversation.
Non-words	Filler sounds or words that people say that do not contribute to the meaning of a message. Common forms include "uh," "um," "like," "okay," and "you know."

Pace	The rate at which a person speaks. It determines how fast or slow the words come out and how clearly those words are heard and understood.
Passive-aggressive speaking	An approach in which a person comes off as subtle and indirect, but whose underlying tone may hurt or manipulate others.
Passive listening	A common way that people listen to others. In this approach, the listener is present non-verbally but verbally provides little feedback to the speaker.
Reflective listening	Listening that captures both the facts and the feelings of a message; involves verification of the understanding of a message; also known as active listening.
Responsive listening	Listening that captures both the facts and the feelings of a message; involves verification of the understanding of a message; also known as active listening.
Selective listening	An approach nearly as common as passive listening; most commonly defined as "hearing what you want to hear."

ASSESS YOUR UNDERSTANDING

Go to www.wiley.com/canada/brounstein to evaluate your knowledge of the basics of communication skills. Measure your learning by comparing pre-test and post-test results.

Quick Questions

1. The passive-aggressive approach to speaking gives the appearance of being subtle and indirect, but is actually manipulative or hurtful. True or false?

2. Which of the following is the most effective type of speaking?

   (a) non-assertive

   (b) selective

   (c) passive aggressive

   (d) assertive

3. Speaking out of turn if you need to make your point is one way of speaking assertively. True or false?

4. The way in which a speaker says his or her message has little effect on the message itself. True or false?

5. Which of the following is *not* a form of non-verbal communication?

    (a) eye contact

    (b) facial expression

    (c) patience

    (d) all of the above

6. Pace is an important communication tool. Pauses serve to distract an audience from the speaker's message. True or false?

7. The most effective approach to listening can be described as

    (a) reflective

    (b) responsive

    (c) active

    (d) all of the above

8. *Listening* is the same as *hearing*. True or false?

9. The final stage of the listening process is

    (a) processing

    (b) mirroring

    (c) responding

    (d) evaluating

10. Passive listening and selective listening are the most common approaches to listening. True or false?

11. Which of the following is the most effective type of listening?

    (a) passive

    (b) active

    (c) assertive

    (d) attentive

12. An active listener

    (a) asks questions to seek greater detail

    (b) nods to indicate understanding

    (c) gives steady eye contact to the speaker

    (d) all of the above

Give It Some Thought

1. Which of the following is an example of an assertive statement?

    (a) You always forget . . .

    (b) I'd like to point out . . .

    (c) I don't mean to be a bother, but . . .

    (d) I could have told you that before you tried it . . .

2. Discuss at least two ways that assertive speaking is different than aggressive speaking.

3. What are three things you can do to maintain an assertive approach to speaking?

4. Describe three common pitfalls of eye-contact behaviours.

5. Discuss the importance of one of the three types of body language.

6. What steps can you take to moderate your pace or find the most appropriate pace for each situation?

7. Discuss one way in which poor listening can negatively affect a professional situation.

8. Describe what takes place in the processing stage of an effective conversation.

9. What is a shortcoming of the attentive approach to listening?

10. Which of the four approaches to listening must you use to capture both a speaker's message and feelings?

Applying This Chapter

1. You are the direct supervisor for a group of sales trainees. Each trainee has a very different approach to speaking: aggressive, non-assertive, passive-aggressive, and assertive. The most effective approach for sales at your company is the assertive approach. As a result, your aggressive, non-assertive, and passive-aggressive speakers are struggling in their training. What advice should you give to each to direct them toward a more assertive approach?

2. As a customer service representative at a major electronics company, you deal with many customer complaints over the phone. Because you can't see the person's body language cues over the phone, you sometimes miss out on what a person is really saying. In a small group, brainstorm some tactics you could take to overcome this problem.

3. You are the administrative assistant for the director of sales at an international shipping company. Your boss has put you in charge of coordinating the planning team for this year's company barbecue. The planning team is made up of assistants from all areas of the company. Using the assertive voice, write an email to your team members requesting that everyone sign up for the following committees: decorations, activities, food, and publicity. Specify a deadline date by which everyone must respond.

4. You are the manager of a special project that you thought was going well. One of your staff members asked to speak to you about a situation at work and had

this to say: "I was excited when this project started a couple of months ago but that changed recently. We've lost a few resources that were helping us, and we've had the direction of the project changed twice. Almost every day now I get the feeling that something is going to happen to make this project harder for us to do well and on time." Using active or responsive listening, what should your response be?

5. Break into three groups to develop scenarios about a customer attempting to return an item to a retail store. The scenarios should involve either attentive, passive, or selective listening. Present your scenarios to the class as dialogues using full body language and gestures as discussed in this chapter. Challenge the rest of the class to determine what kind of listening you are illustrating and ask them to suggest improvements to make the transaction go more smoothly.

THE NEXT STEP

Passive-Aggressive Situation
Think of three statements you made or heard today that were ineffective because they were delivered with aggressive, non-assertive, or passive-aggressive approaches. Recast each in an assertive way. For more of a challenge, stop yourself before making such an ineffective statement in a real situation and instead present your message in an assertive manner.

Eye Contact
Ask someone to listen to a short message of two to three sentences and start out by saying, "Something important to me is . . ." First say your message while giving steady eye contact; and then repeat the exact same message while looking away most of the time. Ask your test subject to let you know which message evokes a more favourable response.

Listening Mode
The next time you find yourself in a conversation with someone, make an effort to shift into active listening mode. Receive the speaker's message, showing interest and maintaining steady eye contact. Give simple acknowledgements such as "I see" and "Yes." Give verbal feedback, keeping in mind that you should be capturing both the speaker's facts and feelings. Does your approach have any effect on the speaker?

Investigating Personal Space
Ask six to ten people to participate in a short experiment about personal space. About half of the participants should be close friends or family members; the rest should be

acquaintances or strangers. Be sure to explain the details of your experiment and get the person's permission before you begin. While both of you are standing, begin about 2 metres away from the participant and slowly step towards them. Ask them to tell you the instant they become uncomfortable with you being in their personal space. Keep a record of how well you knew the person and how close you were when they became uncomfortable. Present your findings to the class and discuss your theories for reasons for the differences.

3
EFFECTIVE CONFLICT RESOLUTION
Keeping Peace on the Job

STARTING POINT

Go to www.wiley.com/canada/brounstein to assess your knowledge of the basics of effective conflict resolution. After reviewing the website, you'll be able to determine where you need to concentrate your effort.

What You'll Learn in This Chapter:

- four common approaches to resolving conflict situations
- how to apply the idea of respect in conflicts
- how to use assertive communication tools in conflict situations
- steps of the resolving-concerns conflict-resolution model
- steps of the needs-based model
- ways of handling challenging reactions in conflicts.

After Studying This Chapter, You'll be Able to:

- discuss the relationship between constructive behaviours and conflict
- identify the factors that distinguish the four approaches to conflict
- describe communication tools that keep conflicts under control
- discuss the merits of the describing, stating-thoughts, and stating-feelings tools
- understand the purpose of entering into a conflict resolution with the appropriate plan.

INTRODUCTION

Conflicts are a part of life. Because much of your life takes place at work—as do many of your interactions—the workplace is an environment rife with conflict. Behaviours associated with a constructive approach to conflict are covered in this chapter. Four types of resolution approaches are detailed. Also explained is the value of using respect in all your interactions. Assertive communication tools that play a key role in conflict resolution are outlined. This chapter focuses on the importance of having a conflict-resolution plan, typically based on one of two resolution models. The chapter concludes with ways of handling particularly challenging reactions in conflicts.

3.1 Approaching Conflicts Constructively

A **conflict** is a problem in which two or more people have a difference of opinions, methods, goals, styles, values, and so on. These differences are a normal part of most workplaces.

Conflicts within the workplace generally involve two issues—those about business concerns and those about working relationships—but they all involve people. Because people are the source of problems and the key to the solutions, interpersonal communications, from listening to speaking, play a major role in the course that conflicts take.

Before you can apply communication tools that help you deal effectively with conflicts, you must first be aware of the behaviours and communication efforts that make or break potential conflict situations.

In other words, whether the outcome you get out of a conflict situation is positive or negative is greatly determined by the approach you take. When your approach sends you down a destructive path, the likelihood of arriving at a good resolution is slim to none. When your approach sends you on a constructive path, you increase the likelihood of achieving positive results. You're in control; you decide which path you take.

3.1.1 Knowing What Not to Do in Conflict Situations

Being aware of what not to do is an integral part of figuring out how best to resolve conflicts. The list of behaviours in this section put you on the destructive track; they make conflicts much more difficult to deal with and resolve. If you're like most people, you've probably had some experience with these behaviours: both exhibiting and receiving them:

- yelling
- blaming
- reacting defensively
- making negative assumptions
- not dealing with the situation

- making subtle digs and sarcastic remarks
- making personal insults
- complaining constantly about the situation
- issuing ultimatums
- arguing or pushing harder and harder for your way
- sending negative email messages
- going to others rather than the source.

These behaviours do nothing to work out resolutions in conflict situations. Instead, they escalate tensions, strain working relationships, prevent important improvements from happening, and destroy communication and information sharing.

FOR EXAMPLE

The Blame Game
Don was working with Sanjay on a critical assignment for a class project and presentation. As the deadline approached, Don realized that an important element had not been completed; when he confronted Sanjay, he said that Don was responsible for it. Somehow, each thought the other was responsible for the task. Instead of accepting it as a miscommunication and figuring out a way they could meet the deadline together, Don fired off an email blaming Sanjay—making matters even worse by copying the email to their professor.

3.1.2 Taking the Path to Success

It is important to learn how to approach conflict situations constructively rather than destructively. Certain skills are necessary when implementing these behaviours (see the following sections of this chapter), but you first must know and incorporate the essential constructive behaviours into your approach so those tools can work:

- **Go to the source.** No invention can ever take the place of face-to-face interactions for resolving disputes and conflicts. People need to meet directly, the old-fashioned way, and use conversation to settle their differences.
- **Stay in control.** The toughest person you have to manage in interactions is yourself. When you're in control of your own emotions, you're better able to influence the direction of a conversation toward achieving a positive outcome.
- **Stay focused on issues.** This action is related to staying in control. Your opponent may exhibit destructive behaviours that can distract your attention from the issues. The key is to focus on the issues, not on your or the listener's personal opinions.

- **Actively listen.** Sections 2.4.4. and 2.4.5 explain how to listen actively in your interactions. In conflict situations, your ability to listen to and understand where the other person is coming from is critical in achieving positive outcomes.
- **Be straight and sincere.** People sometimes worry so much about being nice to others that they can't be clear and honest when they attempt to address their concerns. Conflict situations are simply about working out issues and differences to make positive results. Save being nice for social situations.
- **Go for solutions.** When you're dealing with problems or conflicts, you want to be **solutions focused** so that your end result creates an improvement, corrects an error, or makes things better than they were in their previous state.
- **Assume the other person means well.** Section 1.5.2 touches on the many problems that assumptions can cause. They often lead you to think and act negatively in your interactions. Rather than worry about what you *think* is the meaning of someone causing you concern, you can deal with the actions and issues and focus on solutions.

SELF-CHECK

- Define conflict.
- Describe what to do and what *not* to do in conflict situations.
- Discuss the role of active listening in a conflict resolution.
- Explain how being solutions focused affects a conflict situation.

3.2 Handling Conflicts: The Four Approaches

People use four common approaches to express their messages to others—aggressive, non-assertive, passive-aggressive, and assertive (see Section 2.1). Because most people aren't ever taught to constructively express messages or to constructively listen, many find it difficult to handle stressful and challenging situations such as conflicts in positive ways.

This section contrasts the four common approaches to resolving conflict situations and shows you how the assertive approach offers you the best choice for dealing with the potentially challenging workplace conflicts you'll face: those that involve business issues and those that involve working relationships.

3.2.1 The Aggressive Approach

The **aggressive approach** is hard charging, is often interpreted as hostile in manner, and is one in which you come across as seeking to control or dominate. In conflict situations, you don't back down; in fact, you go on the attack. The conflict is a competition to be won.

If you take the aggressive approach to a conflict situation, you're likely to do several of the following:

- **You blame.** Finger-pointing and finding fault with others for the concern or problem dominate the interaction. When you're on the receiving end of this behaviour, you may want to say, "I got my head bitten off" by so-and-so.
- **You interrupt and talk over.** Using the aggressive approach often leads to an argument or debate as you become a combatant, getting louder, preventing the other person from getting a word in—all behaviours that tend to escalate tensions.
- **You push to get your way.** Compromising and listening to the other person's point of view? No way! The aggressive way to resolve the conflict is by pushing harder for your own view, being unyielding, and verbally browbeating the other person to get your way.
- **You demand and order.** With this behaviour, your solution is telling the other person what to do. Directives that sound like orders usually are stated loudly and harshly—characterized by comments like, "What you need to do is . . ."

Quite often, in the aggressive approach, all four of these behaviours come together at once. The aggressive approach doesn't focus on solutions; nor does it seek to build agreements that both parties can feel good about. Instead, it invites defensiveness and resistance—not ingredients for resolving conflicts.

3.2.2 The Non-Assertive Approach

With the **non-assertive approach,** you maintain a passive manner and do not express your rights or views. You let others dominate or control the situation, even if it doesn't result in a positive outcome for you.

When you fall into the non-assertive approach, conflicts are situations that breed great discomfort, and your comfort zone, not the issue at hand, becomes the focus of the situation. Here are actions common to the non-assertive approach to conflict situations:

- **You avoid conflict.** Because such situations often create a great feeling of discomfort, they are commonly avoided even when the problem gets worse. A lot of reasons, which usually sound like excuses, are given for not dealing with the concern.
- **You appease the other person.** In this action, you give in to the other person's demands just to go along and keep the peace—even if those demands aren't in your best interests. Those who take an aggressive approach in conflict love dealing with individuals who take a non-assertive approach.

- **You become hesitant and apologetic.** You sound uncertain and say a few "I'm sorry" comments along the way, because you don't want to hurt the other person's feelings. All this hesitancy, however, communicates a lack of confidence and importance in your messages and, not surprisingly, you're not taken seriously.
- **You ramble and beat around the bush.** The problem with rambling is that the message has no focus; the problem with beating around the bush is that points of discussion are indirect and implied at best. As a result, nothing gets resolved and the other person walks away thinking there's been much ado about nothing.

More often than not, in the non-assertive approach to conflicts, an avoidance behaviour emerges. The other common behaviours are reactions to challenging situations and usually appear when the conflicts are thrust upon you. Taking the initiative to get an issue of concern addressed seldom shows itself in the non-assertive approach.

3.2.3 The Passive-Aggressive Approach

With the **passive-aggressive approach,** negative and manipulative communications and actions are conveyed in a subtle and implied way. With the passive-aggressive approach, a person's actions appear quiet or nonthreatening on the outside, but on the inside, the actions are meant to be hurtful or deceitful.

Here are common actions that the passive-aggressive approach displays in conflict situations:

- **You tell others, not the source.** This is the classic passive-aggressive behaviour in conflicts. You engage in behind-the-scenes complaints about the source of the concern, telling everyone except that source. Such actions often stir much gossip, create negative energy around an office, and can become quite disruptive.
- **You withhold.** In this passive-aggressive behaviour, you refuse to cooperate. You don't pass on information that the other party can use or give assistance that is helpful. You give the source of your concern the silent treatment and refuse to talk to him or her.
- **You make subtle to not-so-subtle critical remarks.** Sometimes you display this behaviour through little put-downs or sarcasm. Sometimes you make openly critical remarks in group situations about something someone else has done; you may also hide behind email messages. In all cases, the subject of your remarks feels the criticism and experiences a lack of direct and constructive communication.

- **You hold in for awhile, and then unload.** This behaviour is the aggressive side of passive-aggressive. If you're the recipient of this behaviour, nothing visible is displayed for awhile about concerns with what you've been doing. Then one day the person verbally explodes with pent-up woes and lashes out with personal attacks. You may get an apology later, but you're sure they still think everything was your fault.

In the passive-aggressive approach, people shy away from addressing issues directly and constructively but are not shy about showing their negative emotions.

3.2.4 The Assertive Approach

When using the **assertive approach,** you express your rights and views in a positive and confident manner, and enable others to do the same with the intent and effort to work out resolutions. If you need to address an issue of concern, you tackle it, but do so respectfully so that you promote two-way communication.

When using the assertive approach, here are the common actions you can take in conflict situations:

- **Go to the source.** In the assertive approach, you go to the other person with whom you have your difference to open up dialogue—not through email, not through voice mail, not through a messenger. This action takes place one-on-one and privately.
- **Be direct and constructive in language and tone.** Assertive people don't shy away from expressing problems and describing them as they see them. But language and tone are to the point and tactful (the opposite of being blunt) and focused on the issue—the *actions* of the other person, not directed at the *person*.
- **Collaboratively problem solve.** The problem is stated but the emphasis from that point forward is to dwell on solutions (not on problems) and to work through the issues together as partners (not adversaries).
- **Stay firm yet willing to compromise.** Being firm means being strong in your convictions and confident in your manner, but not harsh in your tone or language. Your views and the other person's views are looked at together, along with what's good for the job at hand.

When you're using the assertive approach, you're willing to deal with conflict situations regardless of the comfort level you feel. Emphasis is placed on working through the issue with the other person and, more importantly, to work out solutions. Treating others with respect and problem solving with them are expected—and that's the assertive approach, the most effective in tackling conflict situations.

3.2.5 Using the Best Approach—Be Assertive

Being assertive takes the most constructive stance in dealing with conflict situations. A big part of handling conflicts assertively is exercising judgement and choosing the best course of action for dealing with an issue.

Here are three descriptions of when assertiveness works best in conflict situations:

- **Dealing with the matter now:** Sometimes, as the expression goes, no time is better than the present. Addressing the concern right away with the other party is better for turning the problem around and preventing it from building up and becoming a bigger problem. You feel in control of yourself and your emphasis is on resolving the conflict. You're also in a setting, or can create one right away, in which you and the other party can talk privately in a one-to-one interaction.
- **Dealing with the matter at a time in the near future:** You know you have a problem you need to address, but now isn't the best time to do so. If you can't address a conflict right away, set a time to meet with the other party while the issue is still fresh. Delaying for a brief time can be helpful because you have time to prepare.

FOR EXAMPLE

When Later Is Better

Stacy had just seen the final copy of the brochure that her company had printed for the city's winter festival weekend. In it, the brochure outlined the times and locations for nearly 30 different events and activities. Because Al, her assistant, had proved himself on his last five assignments, Stacy had given him the job of proofing the brochure before shipping it out. The brochure looked great, until the last page, which listed an event from the previous year. Al had probably let his guard down or become distracted by the end of his task and missed the mistake. Stacy, who had already dealt with two other contentious work issues that morning, decided to wait until after lunch to deal with this one. Because the issue with Al was not immediate, she decided that it would be best to give herself some time to clear her mind after such an intense morning. She simply sent Al an email asking him to bring his materials with him to meet with her at 2:00.

- **Leaving the matter alone:** This third option works only when the matter at hand isn't really that important. Assertiveness isn't about addressing everything that bothers you; it is about picking and choosing your issues.

Should You Talk About This Now?

When using the assertive approach to handle conflicts, you evaluate the best course of action to take before you act. That is, you think before you speak. Use the following checklist when deciding if you're ready to handle a conflict:

- **Are you in control?** When you're in control of your own emotions, you're in position to constructively deal with, and not be deterred by, someone's strong emotions.
- **Are you prepared?** The bigger the issue, the more prepared you should be. Get your thoughts in order, set your objective, and outline how you'll manage the meeting.
- **Is the other person ready?** People address problems better when they're calm, not stressed or emotional. For those people that never appear calm, choose the moment closest to when this can occur.
- **What impact is the problem having (or will have)?** The greater the negative impact of a problem or conflict, the greater the need to address it sooner rather than later.
- **Can you get over this?** If the issue you've attempted to put aside keeps gnawing at you, it probably needs to be addressed. Not doing so is a non-assertive approach.
- **Is this a good time?** Avoid situations with tight deadlines or heated arguments. Catch people at quieter times of day or set an appointment for a time that will work.

SELF-CHECK

- Define the following approaches to conflict: aggressive, non-assertive, passive-aggressive, and assertive.
- Describe typical reactions to the four conflict-resolution approaches.
- Discuss the negative effects of the passive-aggressive approach.
- Explain why the assertive approach is the most effective.

3.3 Respect: The Key to Becoming Assertive

You can build foundations that make assertive approaches to future conflict situations possible and effective. Such foundations serve as a basis for the way you approach working relationships that you create with staff members, peers, managers, customers, and vendors—everybody that you frequently to occasionally work with.

This approach is called being **consistently respectful.** When you have it working, you're in position to handle any conflict that confronts you and thus keep the molehills from turning into volcanoes.

Being consistently respectful relies on the following two points about how you interact and work with others:

- I should do those actions that are good for me, considerate of you, and good for the relationship overall and the job we have to do—regardless of whether you reciprocate.
- My approach is to be constructive in all interactions and focus on getting the job done well—regardless of whether I like you personally.

The *regardless* parts of this definition are aspects that give many people the most trouble. Who can argue with a constant desire to have consistently respectful working relationships? But others sometimes act or behave in ways that make it hard to maintain a constructive relationship with them. That's the challenge of being consistently respectful, but that's what makes it so powerful.

Being consistently respectful is not about putting conditions on working relationships, such as "I'm going to help you only if you help me." It isn't about deciding to treat with respect only those whom you like or with whom you get along. It also isn't about avoiding issues of concern because you're afraid of how the other person may react.

Being consistently respectful means working out issues as best as possible for the parties involved, while maintaining the dignity of the relationship. This means dealing with issues, but doing so in a respectful manner with a focus on the job to be done.

3.3.1 Applying the Keys to Being Consistently Respectful

Being consistently respectful paves the way to a strong foundation for tackling issues and especially conflicts with others. The following key principles make this approach to relationships work in your day-to-day interactions on the job:

- **Operating collaboratively:** This means people you interact with are viewed as partners, not adversaries. They don't have to become your friends, but they aren't your enemies whenever you have a disagreement. It also means that you work with, rather than against, others in a cooperative manner to get the job done.
- **Working to understand others:** This means making as much of an effort to understand where someone else is coming from as you do when you're letting the other

person know your own point of view. It means actively listening so that you can show a true understanding what others have to say, especially in conflict situations.

- **Building relationships for the long term:** Remember the advice not to burn your bridges? In brief, don't do things that hurt or disrespect others, because you're likely to run into those people again. Treating them with respect makes your job easier and builds allies for you today and in the future.
- **Fixing problems rather than blaming:** Recognize that people are a part of every problem. Blaming them for problems solves nothing but creates animosity and distrust. Working with others to solve problems is the best way to get solutions that work.

FOR EXAMPLE

Treating All Customers Alike
Will is a salesperson at a local car dealership. Every couple of months, his boss offers free incentives (coolers, umbrellas, radios, etc.) to customers who come in to test drive new models. The majority of these customers won't ever buy a car, but Will knows that he must treat them all the same, as if they will earn him a commission some day.

3.3.2 The Benefits of Being Consistently Respectful

We're all human, and humans make mistakes. But when you deal with others in a consistently respectful fashion, you build trust with them and they're more forgiving of your occasional mistakes. And when problems come up, they're more willing to resolve these problems with you in an emotionally controlled manner.

In fact, conflicts can then be dealt with in manageable sizes and kept on the constructive track. Best of all, conflicts don't have to be terrible and tense; they can even have positive benefits, including the following:

- **Sparking creativity:** Good conflict resolution explores ideas and options for making something better, challenges the status quo, and enables you to listen to others' perspectives to reach outcomes—great endeavours for stimulating creative thinking.
- **Opening lines of communication:** When people deal with conflicts constructively, they're talking face-to-face about the issues and maintaining respect while doing so. Such behaviour does wonders for enhancing communication.
- **Building teamwork:** In the consistently respectful approach, people are pulled together to work through conflicts. They must collaborate to reach resolutions.
- **Making things work better:** When you constructively deal with conflicts, the ultimate focus is on reaching solutions. When you collaboratively fix problems, as opposed to fixing the blame, you make a situation work better than it did before.

You can thrive on conflict. Conflicts can have a positive connotation, especially when you use an assertive approach and build working relationships to be consistently respectful as you resolve them.

SELF-CHECK

- Define consistently respectful.
- Describe ways of being consistently respectful.
- Discuss key benefits of treating others with respect.

3.4 Communicating to Keep Conflicts Under Control

Successfully resolving conflicts at work starts with taking a constructive approach to them. In particular, you want to take actions that are assertive. Go to the source, listen, focus on the issue, state your views directly and sincerely, and collaboratively come up with solutions. Quite often, however, this is easier said than done. Assertive action doesn't just happen because you want it to happen. It requires skill.

In order to take an assertive approach you must apply assertive communication tools. This section reinforces the assertive speaking and active listening tools discussed in 2.1.4 and 2.4.4 and explains how to apply them in conflict situations. It also gives you a few more tools to help you keep conflicts on the constructive track.

3.4.1 Getting Started on the Right Foot

You need to start your discussions on a positive track when you address conflicts or concerns with others. Introductions are important for managing discussions involving conflicts, especially when emotions run high. Regretfully, people quite often skip this critical step.

People have intentions and they have actions. But you can see only someone's actions. Of course, people make assumptions—usually negative ones—about someone's intentions, but the truth is that intentions are invisible. When you address concerns with others, you want to express a *positive intention* as part of a strong opening statement before you get into the specifics of your issue. A **positive intention** is a statement that says you mean well. It tells the other person in your conversation that the discussion and actions that follow are meant to be good. A positive intention is one of the most important tools to have in resolving conflicts.

Here's an example of a statement of positive intention, one that won't be easy to argue with or get defensive about:

George, as we address this issue today, I want you to know my whole focus here is on helping us clear the air and getting back on track toward having a working relationship in which we support one another.

A good statement of positive intention meets the following criteria:

- It's usually said in one sentence. Rambling messages tend to lose their impact.
- It's said in a sincere tone. Without sincerity, your statement has negative intentions.
- It's stated in positive language, and it avoids words such as *but* or *not*.
- It defines the positive outcome you're seeking.

You can use one of two types of positive intentions, or you may even want to use both. One type of positive intention is your own; the other type is the one you state for the other person.

As you can see in the *my* emphasis of the following type of positive intention, you *own* the statement. Words like "I," "me," "my," or "mine" show you have possession of the message. It is coming from your perspective:

Sue, my emphasis with you today is on working out solutions that help us do our jobs well.

Here is an example of a positive intention you give to the other party:

Sue, one thing I want you to know is that I greatly appreciate the passion you bring to your work and regardless of what we come up with, I want to see that continue for you.

In this second type of positive intention, the emphasis is on the other person. Its intent is to communicate your respect for the other person and acknowledge your understanding of his or her good intentions. The conflict to be worked out can, therefore, be more about the issue on which you differ than on the people who are involved.

3.4.2 Setting an Agenda

In addition to setting a positive tone, you want to establish a structure for the meeting so that it doesn't wander aimlessly. Conflict discussions without organization are less likely to reach a resolution. To set a good structure when you initiate a conflict resolution meeting, do the following:

- **State that you have an issue.** Let the other person know you have an important matter to address. Do this right at the start and do it in one sentence. It is a general statement that either names the overall subject you want to discuss ("Sue, I want to discuss some challenges I see happening with our ABC project") or simply states that you have an issue of concern that you want to address with the other person.

- **State your positive intention.** Make sure your listener is aware that you mean well by stating your own positive intention, by stating the positive intention of the other person, or by stating both if necessary. (See Section 3.4.1.)
- **Outline your agenda.** Another good thing to do when setting the structure for your meeting is to briefly highlight your agenda. The agenda outlines the flow of your meeting. When you do it right, it describes the problem-solving process you're going to use to guide the discussion. For example:

Sue, in our meeting today, I want to first share with you my concerns about what's been happening recently and then hear your point of view. From there, I want us to brainstorm ideas of how we can make things work better, evaluate which of those ideas will be mutually beneficial, and then close by finalizing our plan and even setting a follow-up time to review our progress.

No matter what problem-solving process you choose to follow in the meeting (two models will be covered later in this chapter), this is the kind of introduction you want to have for initiating conflict-resolution discussions. It gives you an organized flow with a constructive tone—a winning combination for getting started on the right foot.

3.4.3 Showing Understanding: A Tool for Success

When a conflict situation generates an especially high degree of emotion, both parties spend a lot of energy trying to outtalk each other. As the great debate ensues, you end up with two or more people sometimes vehemently talking and no one really listening. The more the tension rises, the further you get from reaching any kind of solution.

Being an active listener isn't always easy because conflict situations can spark a high degree of emotion. The tool that helps you listen actively is referred to as **shifting and showing understanding**. The following sections explain what the tool means and how to use it in conflict situations.

Shifting and showing understanding includes two main efforts:

- shifting your attention away from your own message and toward capturing the other person's message
- responding by showing understanding of the other person's message before continuing any efforts to express your own views.

This shifting of your attention from your own message to that of the other person brings your emotions under control when you see the tensions rising in a discussion—whether in a conflict or everyday situation. When you're in control of your own emotions, you increase the likelihood of influencing the other person to control his or hers.

> **FOR EXAMPLE**
>
> **Shifting the Approach**
>
> To prepare for a campaign celebrating the fiftieth anniversary of one of their products, Tony, a marketing project manager, was able to get help from Rashida, a member of another team. At first she'd been a big help. But in the last week or so, he'd seen her productivity and morale dip. When he tried to address this concern, she snapped, "I was asked to help you out nearly a month ago, but you keep asking me to do more. You know, I've got other work to do." The project manager's reply showed that she understood what Rashida was feeling: "You're feeling upset because you see this arrangement turning out quite differently from what you understood it would be. Is that right?"

3.4.4 Shifting into Gear: Making Shift and Show Understanding Work

To make shifting and showing understanding work, follow these key steps:

- **Mentally focus your attention on the speaker.** Stop speaking and put your attention into capturing what the other person is saying. (Try mentally saying the word "shift" just as a reminder to listen.) Then focus on the meaning of the message.
- **Give verbal feedback to show understanding.** After you get a sense of what the message means, paraphrase or reflective paraphrase what the speaker has said to you.
- *Paraphrasing* and *reflective paraphrasing* are two important tools of active listening.
  - **Paraphrasing:** *Restating the main idea of a speaker's message to verify or clarify your understanding of the facts or content of that message.*
  - **Reflective paraphrasing:** *Identifying the emotion and the meaning of a message and summarizing it in your own words.*
- Through your own words and observations, generally in one sentence, they help you show understanding of the message you've heard.

- **Gain confirmation or clarification of your verbal feedback.** Invite a direct response from the other person to find out if you're hearing the message correctly. To let your speaker know you need a response, you can raise your sentence-ending tone to make your feedback message sound like a question or simply ask, "Is that correct?"
- **Ask questions when you need more information to understand the message.** Before you can provide verbal feedback to check your understanding, you

sometimes need to get more out of the message. You may also need to get more information to further understand why the person thinks or feels the way he or she does.

- **Stay non-judgemental.** When you're looking to show understanding of the other person's message, your role is not to interpret it but to understand it as that person meant it. Likewise, avoid judging the speaker's view as right or wrong; it is merely *different* than yours, which is why you're having a conflict. You don't have to agree with it—just understand it.

- **State your view as needed or just move forward.** When you've shown that you understand the other person's message, you then have the opportunity to get your point across next in the conversation. Sometimes you can simply move forward into the solution stage of the discussion.

In conflict situations, you don't have to agree with the other person's viewpoint and feelings, but you do need to understand them. Doing so will lead you in the right direction toward a solution.

3.4.5 Telling It Like It Is: The Describing Tool

A big part of a police officer's job is writing reports about the incidents he or she deals with while on duty. The best officers write reports that cover just the facts. You can read such a report of an incident and see the scene in your mind as if you were watching it on videotape. That's the idea of the *describing tool*. **Describing** is reporting behaviours that someone displays in observable and objective terms. It's telling what you see, not giving your opinions about what you see. It's telling what someone has done, not stating your assumptions about the person's motives.

To clearly understand what describing means, keep the following points in mind:

- **Behaviour, not attitude:** Describing focuses on behaviours but not on attitudes. Behaviour involves someone's actions—you can see them and hear them. Attitude, on the other hand, is how someone thinks or feels about something. You can't see them; they're locked away in the individual's mind. Certainly, attitudes influence behaviour, yet they aren't the same. In fact, a person can have a lousy attitude about an issue but still manage to keep it in check by displaying respectful behaviours in any interaction.

- **Substance, not generalities:** Describing, sometimes referred to as constructive feedback, is providing substance to your message so the stated observations are clear and concrete. Sometimes, people comment on your behaviour in general terms. For example, "You were not constructive at the team meeting today." In this case, the receiver of this message didn't get a clear picture of what was done badly.

When describing, the receiver gets a clear picture of what you saw in that person's behaviour. Here is an example of describing:

As I facilitated today's team meeting, I was concerned about the behaviours you displayed that were different from your usual positive participation. On three occasions, I noticed you interrupted other team members before they were done expressing their points. On one of those occasions, I heard your voice get loud and you told Joe that his idea to solve the shipping delays was "a waste of time." What I saw happen for the rest of the meeting was that you sat quietly, had your arms folded, kept your chin down, and gave no response when asked for your thoughts to help on other ideas.

As you can see, describing gives you a clear, specific, and concrete picture of the events that took place as if you were watching them again on videotape. In conflict situations, describing is an important skill for expressing the concerns you have about what someone else is doing. Describing is much better than general criticism.

Here are guidelines to follow when describing:

- **Focus on the issue and use I-messages to help. I-messages** have you owning your observations. They help you focus on what the person did, the actions that have been seen, the issues, and not the person. I-messages are phrases such as the following:

  I've noticed . . .
  I've observed . . .
  I've seen . . .

- **Give specifics.** Without specifics, you end up with a description of general praise or criticism. Examples and quotes give your descriptions substance.
- **Report observations, not interpretations.** Knowing the difference between observations and interpretations is key to effectively using describing when dealing with behaviours. An observation is what you have seen. An interpretation is what you think or feel about what has been seen. Take a look at these examples:
  - **Interpretation:** "I noticed you were in a bad mood at today's meeting."
  - **Observation:** "I noticed you sat quietly and said nothing at today's meeting and even when asked a question, you replied with a one-word answer."
- **Be direct.** Don't beat around the bush, ramble, or talk around a point. Such forms of communication cause confusion and apprehension. In describing, being straightforward—without being blunt or aggressive—is the most effective way to make a message clear to someone else.

- **Show sincerity in your tone and language.** In addressing conflicts or concerns, a level of seriousness, respect, and care exhibits the importance of the message so that you prevent your tone from moving from sincere to harsh.
- **Avoid mixed messages.** Mixed messages lessen sincerity. Mixed messages attempt to say something nice in the first part of your message, but are followed by a "but" or "however" that introduces criticism, which the recipient understands to be the real point. For example, "Jim, I know you were trying hard on this project, but the report you did missed the mark and was poorly written."

3.4.6 Sharing Thoughts and Feelings

Conflict resolution is a matter of problem solving. Two communication tools—the **stating-thoughts** tool and the **stating-feelings** tool—help define and solve problems by getting your points across so the other party can understand where you're coming from.

Sometimes in the course of a conflict-resolution discussion, you need to offer an opinion. This primarily happens in the course of examining the problem situation but also can occur during dialogue about the solution. So as not to come across as opinionated, use the stating-thoughts tool. When stating thoughts, you indicate how the situation is impacting you, and you respond to the person through comments with constructive feedback.

When stating thoughts, you can usually use up to a few sentences. Don't be long-winded or you'll sound opinionated, but be sure to place your emphasis on being constructive and providing views supported by factual reasons. Here are some guidelines:

- **Own the thought.** Use the words "I," "me," or "my" to indicate the view is yours.
- **Tell your thought in positive terms.** Use language constructively, presenting the message in the best way possible and avoid words such as "not" and "but."
- **When defining impact, clarify the effect the problem is having on you.** Give facts to support your views or conclusions. Usually this is done right after you've used the describing tool to state observations about your concern. For example:

  Based on the concern I just described to you, not getting the information I was expecting at the agreed-upon dates has caused delays for me on this project and is affecting my ability to meet the final target date for the project.

- **When responding with feedback, focus on issues and behaviours.** Focus your feedback on observations and facts, avoiding interpretations or analysis of other people's perceived intentions.

  For example, say,
  "I'm having difficulty understanding your explanation of the circumstances. Your dates and events aren't coming across in a clear fashion to me." Don't say, *"You're not making much sense here. You don't explain things very well."*

Conflict situations evoke emotions. Your ability to control your own feelings has great influence on what happens with the other person's emotions. On the other hand, to act as though no emotions exist isn't realistic. The key is to express your emotions rather than show them, and this is where the stating-feelings tool comes in to play. With the stating-feelings tool, you talk about the emotion that you feel rather than put it on display. This tool often is used right after you use the tool of describing.

With the stating-feelings tool, you describe your concern or problem, after which you can state feelings in a few sentences that let the other person know how the situation has made you feel. Here are some guidelines for constructively using the stating-feelings tool:

- **Show ownership of the feeling message.** Use words such as "I," "me," or "my" to indicate that you own the feeling.
- **Name the feeling you have.** Directly identify the emotion you feel.
- **Use positive language and a sincere tone.** State the message in the best possible tone, with the most accurate meaning. Avoid harsh language or tones. Avoid showing your feelings. Here are contrasting examples:
  - **Stating feelings:** "I was upset by those actions."
  - **Showing feelings:** "I hate when you do that."
- **Give constructive reasons to explain the basis of your feelings.** Keep your explanations brief and focus on issues and behaviours you've seen. Stick with what has happened as you've experienced it, and don't guess about the meaning behind it.

Expressing what you're feeling constructively and sincerely puts you on the road toward the solution of the conflict by opening up the dialogue. Working together to achieve a solution is the essence of what conflict resolution is all about.

SELF-CHECK

- Define positive intention, shifting and showing understanding, paraphrasing, reflective paraphrasing, describing, I-messages, stating-thoughts tool, and stating-feelings tool.
- Describe how a positive intention works in a conflict situation.
- Discuss the difference between describing and interpreting.
- Consider the role of I-messages in conflict resolution.
- Explain how the stating-thoughts and stating-feelings tools solve problems.

3.5 Bringing the Conflict to Resolution

One problem people face when they attempt to deal with conflicts on the job is that they have no problem-solving plan in mind. They talk to the other person but lack a direction to go in and, as a result, have a difficult time of reaching any kind of agreement. You have to know where you're going in such challenging meetings to reach the desired destination—a mutually beneficial solution.

One of two problem-solving models will help you bring conflicts to satisfactory resolution, whether with peers, staff members, vendors, clients, customers, even your boss: **crafting a plan** and **focusing on a solution.** This section also covers tips on how to assertively handle a few of the challenging reactions that can occur in conflict discussions.

3.5.1 Crafting a Plan

When conflict situations turn into a pattern rather than an occasional incident, you must arrange a special meeting with the other party for the situation to improve. Anxiety and tension certainly enter the picture for both parties in this kind of meeting, but it can serve as a turning point for putting the conflict on a constructive rather than destructive track.

For such meetings to be successful, you must come ready with a plan. Planning helps you stay focused and thus increases the likelihood you can keep the other person focused too. In outlining your plan for the conflict-resolution meeting, find the key points by answering the following questions:

- **Objective:** What do you want to accomplish in this meeting? What positive outcome will be mutually beneficial while still allowing you to maintain a respectful working relationship?
- **Introduction:** What will you say up front when you kick off the meeting to set a constructive tone and an organized structure? Stating positive intentions, a useful tool for setting the right tone for the meeting, is covered in Section 3.4.1.
- **Strategy:** What problem-solving model do you plan to follow to guide the flow of the meeting? (The two models are covered in depth in Sections 3.6 and 3.7.)
- **Objections:** What challenging reactions or other objections do you anticipate? How do you plan to assertively deal with them when they arise in the discussion?
- **Message:** What key points do you plan to make when you state the problem? What ideas do you have for the solution in terms of what you both can do?

The plan works best when it revolves around the problem-solving model you intend to use. Prepare yourself by filling in the blanks on what you'll say on each point that helps you work through the problem-solving model during the meeting.

3.5.2 Focusing on a Solution

People use two common mindsets (or ways of thinking) when they deal with problem situations such as conflicts. These mindsets form the attitude that you bring with you into discussions. They serve as the generator for your behaviour and attention.

With a **problem-dwelling mindset,** more of your attention is directed toward the problem. Problem-dwelling behaviours include the following:

- focusing constantly on what's wrong
- making accusations or blaming the other person for the problem
- pushing guilt or looking for the other person to admit all wrongdoing
- debating every contrary point heard.

With a **solutions-focused mindset**, more of your attention is on working out solutions. Solutions-focused behaviours include the following:

- stating a positive outcome that you're seeking for the discussion
- defining the problem in factual terms as the first step toward solving it
- listening to the other person's concerns and then working out a solution together
- brainstorming ideas and discussing solutions as a two-way conversation
- requesting what you need the other party to do to help resolve a situation and asking or offering what you'll do to help as well.

Now contrast these two sets of behaviours in terms of the dynamics or energies they create. What's in common with both sets is that they often stimulate high energy in return: With problem dwelling you get energy that adds tension and drains people, whereas with a solutions focus, you get energy that is uplifting and motivating.

Therefore, a significant part of your preparation is more than just outlining your plan for the discussion. By preparing the mindset you want to take into the discussion, reminding yourself of the behaviours that influence the solutions-focused mindset, you're more likely to work out a solution.

SELF-CHECK

- Name two methods of bringing a conflict to resolution.
- List the questions that help outline a conflict-resolution plan.
- Define problem-dwelling mindset and solutions-focused mindset.
- Discuss what the two common mindsets have in common.

3.6 Using the Resolving-Concerns Conflict-Resolution Model

The **resolving-concerns model** provides a problem-solving plan to use in situations in which the working relationship, for one reason or another, isn't working as well as needed. The resolving-concerns model happens in six steps:

Step 1: Introduce the meeting.

Step 2: Describe the concern.

Step 3: Express your feelings or explain the impact (optional).

Step 4: Let the other person respond.

Step 5: Work out the solution.

Step 6: Close.

3.6.1 Step 1: Introduce the Meeting

Your introduction sets a positive tone and organizes the structure for the meeting. By using the communication tool of stating positive intentions (covered in 3.4.1) you are saying that the actions that follow are meant to be good.

The following are the key points to express in your introduction to the meeting:

1. **State a one-sentence general purpose for the meeting.** For example, "Jack, as you know, I called this meeting to address an issue with you that has been affecting our working relationship."
2. **State a positive intention, either your own or one the other person can have, along with your own.** For example, "Jack, I want you to know my focus in this meeting is about working out ways to determine how to get the job done well when we work together. I also know that you want to have good results when you take on a job."
3. **Announce your agenda or plan for the meeting.** Keep it brief and tie it to the steps you intend to follow in the conflict-resolution model. For example, "Jack, I first want to cover the concerns that I have as I see them and the impact they've had, and then get your take on the situation. I then want to spend the majority of time exploring solutions with you about how to strengthen our working relationship, and then close by confirming an agreement to follow through on what we decide."

3.6.2 Step 2: Describe the Concern

In many respects, this is the most critical step in the whole process. You can't solve a problem unless you can clearly define it. On the other hand, if you dwell and offer too many details, you may never move forward to work on a solution. This is where the tool called describing (covered in 3.4.5) comes into play. The following guidelines can help you describe your concerns clearly and constructively:

- **State your observations, not interpretations.** Describe actions you've seen, not your characterizations or assumptions about the actions. For example:
  - ○ **Observation:** "Jack, I've noticed that usually two or three reminders are given on my part before I hear an answer from you about my requests."
  - ○ **Interpretation:** "Jack, the concern I have is that you ignore requests for information I make of you. You act like you're too busy to bother with me."
- **Be direct and sincere.** Don't use any mixed messages.
- **Be specific.** Summarize the pattern of behaviour you have seen that has caused you concern. Use a representative example or two to illustrate your points clearly, but avoid using too much detail. Be specific yet as concise as possible.

3.6.3 Step 3: Express Your Feelings or Explain the Impact (Optional)

This step is optional, and you either express your feelings or explain the impact (see 3.4.6). If you don't think you can do this step constructively and with sincerity, skip it. If you do use it, remember to hit the following basics:

- **Own the message.** Use the words "I," "me," or "my" as opposed to "you."
- **When stating feelings, identify the emotion you've felt over the situation.** For example: "Jack, because of the reminders involved in getting answers from you, I often feel annoyed that I need to keep asking."
- **When stating thoughts, explain how the situation has affected your getting the job done.** For example: "Jack, because of the reminders involved in getting answers from you, my work gets delayed as the information I need does not arrive as needed."
- **Keep the messages brief,** one to a few sentences at most.

3.6.4 Step 4: Let the Other Person Respond

For some people, this is the toughest step. Almost never do you describe the concern so well that the other person hugs you and apologizes profusely. As concretely and constructively as you've stated the problem, people still need to process what they've heard and respond to it as they desire. That starts you down the road to having two-way conversations. That's why you want to cover Steps 1, 2, and 3 quickly.

Your role in this step is to let the other person have his or her say for a bit. Listen and don't debate what you hear. Employ active listening tools (discussed in 2.4.4 and 2.4.5) to convince the person to explain the specifics of his or her thoughts or concerns. Employ the effort called shifting and showing understanding (highlighted in 3.4.3), providing verbal feedback to demonstrate your understanding of the individual's messages.

Keep in mind that you both don't have to see the problem the same way. You both want to be aware of each other's concerns so that you can take them into consideration when you collaboratively work out the solution.

3.6.5 Step 5: Work Out the Solution

This is the step with which you want to take the most time. The two of you crafting a solution is the key to success with conflicts. In this meeting, as in others, stay focused on solutions and don't dwell on problems.

Three main pieces highlight the solution stage. When applying these three pieces, you often need a transition from the problem-discussion phase to the solutions-discussion phase of the meeting. The best transition is a one- or two-sentence statement of positive intention that tells the other person where you want to go in the meeting at this time. For example: "Jack, as I mentioned at the beginning, my intent is to develop solutions that help us work productively together. Let's move ahead now and focus on doing just that." From there, follow through on the four key steps for working out the solution:

1. **Establish the desired goal.** Make this a one-sentence, positive statement that defines the picture you want to see for the working relationship when it is functioning well. Offer the goal statement as your recommendation and let the other person then respond to it. Here's an example: "Jack, how about this as the goal to shoot for in our working relationship: Establish a working relationship where we work together in a cooperative, respectful, and responsive manner. What do you think?"

2. **Develop ideas to meet the goal.** This element defines the *how*, that is, how you two are going to reach the goal. It defines the actions both parties will take to achieve the goal of the working relationship. This piece can be made to fit by one of three methods:
   ○ Recommend your ideas and ask for any others the person may have.
   ○ Solicit ideas first from the other person and then add yours into the mix.
   ○ Brainstorm in turn.

3. **Propose specific actions.** Whichever of the three methods you use to develop ideas to meet the goal, be prepared to come up with specific actions for the other person, as well as an idea of what you're willing to do. Both parties must contribute and make commitments if the conflict is to truly be resolved.

4. **Evaluate the ideas and reach consensus.** Evaluate the ideas together, trying to determine which will best meet the stated goal. Go after ideas first that are more in common so that consensus can easily be reached. With consensus,

you're asking this question: "Can you support this option or idea?" Although people don't generally agree to every idea, they're often willing to support something for the good of the cause.

Tips for Brainstorming

If you choose the brainstorming approach, set ground rules for it up front. Here are some tips for how to run an effective brainstorming session:

- Go with one idea per person per turn.
- When someone has a turn but no idea ready to offer, that person *passes* to keep the momentum going.
- Refrain from making judgements about any of the ideas until after the brainstorming is done. Thus, you have no bad ideas at this stage.
- Record the ideas as they're presented so that they are visible. Record what the other person says, not your interpretation of what is said.
- Keep going until you both run out of ideas.

3.6.6 Step 6: Close

After all of the ideas are evaluated and consensus is reached on the ones you both plan to go forward with for your solution, you're ready to bring the meeting to a close. Here are the steps to take in this final stage:

1. Confirm the plan and all the actions agreed upon by both of you.
2. Clarify which steps need to happen for implementation of the solution.
3. Close on a positive note, thanking the person for working with you.

Here are a couple of other tips to cement a strong close for this meeting:

- **Commit to typing up the agreed-upon plan and providing a copy to the other person.** Writing the agreement down as it is formed helps clarify it for both parties and gives your solutions discussion a focus. Writing down the plan also helps you both avoid having to rely on memories when honouring your commitments.
- **Set a date for the two of you to get back together in the near future, such as a month out, to review your progress with the plan.** This effort builds accountability for you and the other person and increases the likelihood that the agreement will stick.

> ### FOR EXAMPLE
>
> **An Overzealous Boss**
>
> Due to her enthusiasm for her new job, the head of a large public library quickly implemented a host of new programs and services. Her staff, however, was overwhelmed with the amount of work they were given. When an individual staffer talked to her about it, the boss assured them they "could handle it." Rather than griping behind her back, the staff's veteran librarian asked for a private meeting, where she presented her boss with a list of all their concerns. Hearing this convinced the boss that it was indeed too much to handle. The two were happy to discover that volunteers could help with many of the new tasks.

SELF-CHECK

- Define the resolving-concerns model.
- List the steps of the resolving-concerns conflict-resolution model.
- Discuss how Step 2 is often the most critical in the resolving-concerns process.
- Explain why Step 3 should be omitted in some cases.
- Discuss five tips for brainstorming ideas for conflict solutions.

3.7 Understanding the Needs-Based Conflict-Resolution Model

The second of the conflict-resolution models works well when resolving differences that are more work-issue related (as opposed to the relationship-related issues that the resolving-concerns model addresses). As you become familiar with each model, you can often mix and match what you think will result in the best problem-solving plan for handling the conflict. The five steps of the **needs-based conflict-resolution model** are:

Step 1: Introduce the meeting.

Step 2: Define the problem.

Step 3: Identify the needs of the stakeholders.

Step 4: Work out the solution.
Step 5: Close.

3.7.1 Step 1: Introduce the Meeting

This step works as follows:

1. State your general purpose for the meeting.
2. Provide a positive intention to set the tone for the discussion.
3. Briefly outline your agenda to give the meeting an organized structure.

3.7.2 Step 2: Define the Problem

In this step, you want to do two main things with the other party:

1. **Develop the problem statement.** This is a one-sentence statement that identifies the issue to be resolved. It isn't the conflict you're having but rather the issue over which the conflict stems.
2. **Clarify the source of the conflict and briefly analyze where the differences are coming from.** Differences on business issues often are around such areas as the following:
   - different ways or methods to get a job done
   - different views on how to solve a problem or what strategy to follow
   - different values or styles in how you approach work
   - different goals or expectations.

Here's a brief example that sets up how you work out Step 2: Deb and Sue are managers whose groups have to work closely together to fulfill customer orders. Currently, a fairly high number of orders, approximately 25 percent, go out incomplete or with the wrong items in them. This, of course, leads to the orders being returned for correction and a great amount of rework that slows everybody down.

Deb has proposed that work should be done to streamline the order-fulfillment process to make it simpler and more efficient. Sue has proposed implementing a formalized training program for all employees because many tend to just learn on the job. Because they disagree on which approach to take, they have a conflict.

- **Problem statement:** Customer orders aren't being fulfilled accurately on a consistent basis.
- **Source of the conflict:** Different ideas and views on how to solve this problem.

3.7.3 Step 3: Identify the Needs of the Stakeholders

This is a critical step in the problem-solving process.

- **Needs** are what drive people; they're your important interests and motivations as related to the business relationship.
- **Stakeholders** are the key parties affected by the business relationship and by what gets worked out in the conflict resolution. Usually this involves more than just the two parties having the conflict: customers, vendors, investors, other internal groups, your team, the other person's team, management above, or the company or organization as a whole.

In this step, you and the other person should identify the key stakeholders and then list the most critical needs each one has in the business relationship. You're looking at their needs, not at their positions on the issue. Looking at needs helps both of you take a broader perspective to see what's really important.

For example, in the conflict over the order-fulfillment problems in Step 2, Deb and Sue list the key stakeholders in this issue and their main needs:

- **Deb's team:**
  - has accurate customer orders delivered consistently
  - maintains high levels of customer satisfaction
  - maintains cooperative working relationships with Sue's team.
- **Sue's team:**
  - has accurate customer orders delivered consistently
  - maintains high levels of customer satisfaction
  - maintains cooperative working relationships with Deb's team.
- **The company:**
  - maintains high levels of customer satisfaction
  - ensures long-term relationships with customers
  - provides customers with value for what they buy
  - maintains an efficient operation.
- **Customers:**
  - consistently receive on-time and accurate shipments of product
  - have vendor relationships marked by reliability and high-quality service
  - pay a reasonable price and get value in return.

As this example points out, by identifying key needs, you begin moving the conflict away from two people and their own positions on an issue toward a broader view of the big picture—who is really affected by this issue and what's really important to them.

3.7.4 Step 4: Work Out the Solution

Now the problem-solving effort kicks into high gear. The following are the three main elements to work through in the solution stage:

1. **Brainstorm ideas to meet the needs.** Take turns throwing out ideas to meet the needs that were identified. Keep those needs as your visible guide and refrain from making any judgements about the ideas until after the brainstorming is done. Don't forget to record your ideas as they're stated.

2. **Evaluate the ideas against the needs.** This is the beauty of identifying the needs first. It establishes the criteria for evaluating your ideas. Therefore, the discussion no longer needs to dwell on your position versus the other person's position. You evaluate the ideas together based on how well they meet any and all of the needs you've listed.

3. **Reach consensus on what is most mutually beneficial.** Step 2 often rolls right into Step 3. You're looking to reach an agreement on the ideas that best meet needs of all of the stakeholders affected by the conflict.

3.7.5 Step 5: Close

After you reach agreement on the ideas to act upon, confirm this understanding with the other party and clarify what needs to happen to implement the solution—who's going to do what and when.

Setting a follow-up date to review progress often is a good idea. Doing so means that both of you are serious about making the agreement work. You want to give the solution time to be implemented, but at the same time, you don't want to go so far out that you forget about the agreement.

FOR EXAMPLE

Cooking Up Business

Casey's home-based muffin business had grown enough that she and an investor decided it was time for her to rent out commercial space and hire two employees. She did fine during the fall and the holiday season, but business slowed dramatically in the months following. When it became clear to the investor that Casey would have to let at least one of the employees go in order to stay afloat, Casey and the investor decided to meet. Casey was not happy about having to lose an employee, but she was equally worried about what would happen to the other stakeholders involved (she and her family, the investor, her two employees and their families, her customers, the restaurants she supplied her muffins to, her suppliers, the owner of her rental property) if she were to go out of business completely.

3.8 Dealing with the Challenging Reactions

Like anything in life, the best-laid plans don't always lead to smooth actions. Coming in with a problem-solving model that provides you with a plan to resolve the conflict, however, increases the likelihood that you'll reach a mutually beneficial solution.

Nevertheless, challenging reactions do arise sometimes, and you have to be able to deal with them constructively when they do. If you can't, you may not be able to work out a solution. Remember, you're not done until an agreement has been reached.

The following sections cover two challenging reactions that can come up in conflict-resolution discussions. You get helpful tips to work through these challenges so that you can reach the agreement you seek.

3.8.1 Handling the Defensive Reactions

When people react defensively, trying to get your point across is difficult. A loud voice, anxious body language, interruptions, and verbal counterattacks are signs of defensive reactions. In a conflict-resolution discussion, these behaviours often start right when you bring up the problem.

First, here's what to do when faced with these defensive hurdles:

- **Avoid debating.** If you counter every attack or contrary point with an argument, the great debate will rage on. Such debating tends to fuel more defensiveness.
- **Avoid abandoning ship.** Ending the conversation when the other person becomes defensive is non-assertive and counterproductive.

Therefore, here are a few tips to help you manage a challenging reaction:

- **Shift and show understanding first.** This active-listening tool (as described in Section 3.4.3), lets the other person have his or her say. After you've heard the person out, paraphrase or reflective paraphrase to check your understanding of the message.

- **Speak to clarify, not to counter.** After you've paraphrased or reflectively paraphrased to show understanding, speak only to clarify, add useful information, or address a concern that you've heard. Start out by saying such comments as "Let me clarify something for you," or "I'd like to briefly address a concern you raised."

- **Ask the other person to check understanding of your message.** In essence, you're asking the other party to paraphrase what you've said. It, too, is best done after you've shown understanding of the other person's message. Ask an open-ended question such as "Can you please describe your understanding of what I was telling you?"

- **Restate your positive intention.** By giving a reminder of the positive intention from your introduction, you refocus both of you on making something positive happen.

- **Move forward to the solution stage.** After you've heard the person out, move ahead as quickly as you can toward working on the resolution to the conflict.

3.8.2 Coping with the Reluctant Solution Maker

Sometimes the obstacle comes as you are attempting to work out the solution to the conflict. Your ideas are met with criticism and the other person offers little in return to help. You feel as though you're going nowhere and an agreement never will be reached. Here are a few tips to help you work through this challenge:

- **Uncover concerns.** When your ideas are met with responses like "That won't work," stick with the discussion. Ask questions to get an explanation for the concerns the other person has with your idea.

- **Brainstorm together.** Take the pressure to come up with all the ideas off you by setting up a brainstorming effort in which you each take turns coming up with ideas.

- **Talk benefits.** Sometimes, people need to hear about the benefits to be convinced that the solution is a good one. Benefits can be saving time, saving money, improving communication, and increasing efficiency, to name a few.

- **Explore consequences.** This is a last resort. When every other option fails to come up with a solution, explore what can happen if the conflict is left unresolved, such as getting others—usually management above you—involved. Ask an open-ended question to get the other person to think about this: "If we leave this issue unsettled, what happens for us?"

FOR EXAMPLE

Writing to Potential

Because Sean has been given more managerial duties to deal with lately, he's had to pass on more of his proposal writing to David, who has had some experience with the work. Although Sean has walked him through several proposals, he feels David is not doing as well as he should. He gives him another chance, and then decides that David might need some additional training. When the two meet to discuss the problem, David is uncharacteristically loud and belligerent. Sean listens to David, then clarifies that David's writing is not the problem; more so, the problem lies in some specific proposal-writing skills that he could learn in two or three sessions of afternoon training. Upon hearing this, David settles down, and the two work out the details of their solution.

SELF-CHECK

- Discuss ways that people react defensively in conflict resolution situations.
- Describe ways of dealing with defensive reactions.
- Explain methods of coping with people who are reluctant to work out solutions.

SUMMARY

Conflict doesn't have to be a negative part of your life. This chapter outlined how to approach and resolve such situations in a constructive way instead of turning them into major confrontations. Of the four types of approaches, the assertive approach was explained to be the most effective. Being consistently respectful is an integral part of the assertive approach. Assertive communication tools such as positive intentions, showing understanding, and describing all work to keep conflicts under control. When it comes to reaching a mutually beneficial solution, you must craft a plan. The resolving-concerns model and the needs-based model are two effective ways of reaching a resolution. Tips for handling defensive reactions and reluctant solution makers will prepare you for dealing with further challenges of conflicts.

KEY TERMS

Aggressive approach	Hard-charging method of dealing with conflict, often interpreted as hostile in manner; you come across as seeking to control or dominate; you don't back down.
Assertive approach	Expressing your rights and views in a positive and confident manner, and enabling others to do the same with the intent and effort to work out resolutions.
Conflict	A problem in which two or more people have a difference of opinions, methods, goals, styles, values, and so on.
Consistently respectful	When you have it working, you're in position to handle any conflict that confronts you, and thus keep the molehills from turning into volcanoes.
Describing	Reporting behaviours that someone displays in observable and objective terms; telling what you see, not giving your opinions about what you see.
I-messages	Statements such as "I've noticed" or "I've observed" that have you owning your message, helping you focus on actions and issues, not people.
Need	That which drives or motivates people.
Needs-based model	Works when resolving differences that are work-issue related, rather than relationship related.
Non-assertive approach	In this method of dealing with conflict, you maintain a passive manner and do not express your rights or views.
Paraphrasing	Restating the main idea of a speaker's message to verify or clarify your understanding of the facts or content of that message.
Passive-aggressive approach	Communications and actions come across as subtle, yet negative, and implied, while manipulative.
Positive intention	A statement that tells the other person in your conversation that you mean well.
Problem-dwelling mindset	When dealing with a conflict, this way of thinking directs most of your attention toward the problem.
Reflective paraphrasing	Identifying the emotion and the meaning of a message.

Resolving-concerns model	Provides a problem-solving plan to use in situations in which the working relationship isn't working as it should.
Shift and show understanding	Helps you listen actively in conflict situations by shifting your attention off of your own message and onto capturing the other person's message.
Solutions-focused mindset	When dealing with a conflict, this way of thinking directs most of your attention to working out a solution.
Stakeholders	Key parties affected by a business relationship.
Stating-feelings tool	Use it to let the other person know how a situation has made you feel; with it, you talk about emotion, rather than put it on display.
Stating-thoughts tool	Use it to indicate how the situation is impacting you; employs constructive feedback.

ASSESS YOUR UNDERSTANDING

Go to www.wiley.com/canada/brounstein to evaluate your knowledge of the basics of effective conflict resolution. Measure your learning by comparing pre-test and post-test results.

Quick Questions

1. Conflicts are more likely to be found in personal situations than business situations. True or false?

2. Which of the following is an example of what not to do in a conflict situation?
   (a) go to someone other than the source
   (b) react defensively
   (c) issue an ultimatum
   (d) all of the above

3. Being solutions focused creates an improvement, corrects an error, or makes things better than they were originally. True or false?

4. In the aggressive approach to handling conflict, which of the following behaviours are exhibited?
   (a) blaming
   (b) appeasing
   (c) rambling
   (d) all of the above

5. The passive-aggressive approach has underlying actions that may be received as hurtful. True or false?

6. In the non-assertive approach to handling conflict, which of the following behaviours are exhibited?

   (a) avoidance

   (b) withholding

   (c) going to the source

   (d) all of the above

7. A person who is consistently respectful is only able to solve issues with those people with which they share common interests. True or false?

8. Which of the following are principles of being consistently respectful?

   (a) long-term relationship building

   (b) understanding

   (c) collaboration

   (d) all of the above

9. Creative thinking is one benefit of a using a consistently respectful approach. True or false?

10. A positive intention expresses

    (a) your own statement that you mean well

    (b) your understanding of the other person's good intentions

    (c) that the discussions that follow are meant to be good

    (d) all of the above

11. To establish a structure for a meeting, an agenda should

    (a) state the issue

    (b) state the solution

    (c) describe the solution

    (d) all of the above

12. The describing tool is used to state your assumptions about another person's motives. True or false?

13. Coming into a conflict-resolution situation with a plan decreases its chances of success. True or false?

14. A problem-dwelling mindset is likely to result in a solution. True or false?

15. Work-related issues are best solved by using the resolving-concerns conflict-resolution model. True or false?

16. Which of the following belong in the introduction of a meeting?

    (a) an agenda

    (b) a positive intention

  (c) a one-sentence description of the general purpose of the meeting

  (d) all of the above

17. Express your feelings in a meeting only if you can do so with sincerity. True or false?

18. The needs-based conflict-resolution model may sometimes be combined with the resolving-concerns model. True or false?

19. The two parties in a conflict are the stakeholders. True or false?

20. Which of the following elements can help work out a solution?

  (a) brainstorm ideas to meet needs

  (b) evaluate ideas against needs

  (c) reach consensus

  (d) all of the above

21. Defensive reactions include

  (a) avoidance

  (b) anxious body language

  (c) passive-aggressiveness

  (d) all of the above

22. Which of the following can help cope with a reluctant solution-maker?

  (a) talking benefits

  (b) brainstorming

  (c) exploring consequences

  (d) all of the above

Give It Some Thought

1. Why is it important to go to the source when approaching a conflict situation?

2. Explain why avoidance is not an effective way to resolve a conflict.

3. Cite the four approaches to conflict resolution.

4. Explain why the assertive approach offers the best choice for dealing with workplace conflicts.

5. Under what circumstances is it better to wait for another time to deal with a conflict situation?

6. Being consistently respectful is a key element of the assertive approach to conflict situations. Define consistently respectful.

7. The consistently respectful approach relies on two concepts for interacting with others. Describe the two concepts.

8. Conflicts can be managed. Explain one positive benefit of conflicts.

9. A positive intention is an important conflict-resolution tool. Give an example of a positive intention.

10. What is the first step in making shifting and showing understanding work?

11. The describing tool is a way to avoid general criticism. Define describing.

12. People use two common ways of thinking to deal with conflicts. Name the mindset that is directed toward solving a problem.

13. What do the two mindsets have in common?

14. The resolving-concerns model is better suited to situations involving working relationships or work issues?

15. The fourth step of the resolving-concerns model is the toughest for some people. Explain why.

16. In the final stage, both parties work to find a solution. List the three ways that two parties can come up with ideas.

17. Which of the conflict-resolution models works well when resolving differences that are related to relationships?

18. In a situation where the security guards at an airport go on strike, who are four stakeholders affected by what gets worked out in the conflict resolution?

19. You may come across challenging situations even when you have a conflict-resolution plan. Describe two types of challenges.

20. What is the last resort when dealing with a reluctant solutions maker?

Applying This Chapter

1. You're a portrait photographer who has just received a telephone message from a client who "hates" the 18-person portrait that was shot as a gift for her great-grandmother's 90th birthday. Come up with a plan for handling the situation. Should you meet in person or speak on the phone? What communication tools will you need to resolve the issue?

2. Recall a recent conflict in which you or another party used either the aggressive, passive-aggressive, or non-assertive approach. Think about how you might have resolved the conflict using the assertive approach and write up a short dialogue to demonstrate your approach to the class.

3. In your role as a legal assistant in a criminal law office, you deal with people who've been accused of a variety of crimes. How should you apply the consistently respectful approach to your dealings with clients?

4. Think of an example in which you and another person were faced with a problem or conflict. Quickly jot down what happened in the situation, as if you were going to give it to your closest friend to read. Now, keeping in mind that describing

involves behaviours and not attitudes, rewrite the example using the describing tool. How different are the two versions?

5. One of your classmates becomes very defensive during the weekly group sessions when students are asked to critique each other's work. Often, the discussions deteriorate into a heated debate. As the leader of this week's group discussion, what strategies would you bring to the table to keep the group on track?

6. Your company midlevel managers meet once a month to give progress reports, discuss issues, and develop ideas for future projects. Each of the ten managers takes turns leading the meeting. You and several other managers have noticed that Neil, one of the newer managers, is disrespectful and speaks out of turn whenever a female manager leads a meeting. Use the resolving-concerns model to plan a conflict resolution with Neil.

7. In order for your magazine to meet its scheduled print date, many elements of the production process have to be done on time: articles written and copyedited, photos collected, designs created and laid out. As editor-in-chief, you have final say over which photos are used, and you often make last-minute changes as you see fit. Your art director typically attacks you and other staffers with statements such as: "Hey, I can't make my deadlines when things are changing so much in the final stages. The photos were fine last week; they should be fine this week. This isn't my fault!" Use the needs-based model to plan your conflict-resolution meeting

8. Your small ice-cream truck business has provided the sweet treats for a local preschool's carnival for the past six years. This year, you showed up with the usual amount of ice cream, but it won't be enough because the students' siblings were invited for the first time this year. The carnival's coordinator insists she did change the order, but you show her your records that indicate otherwise. You see that she's losing control of her emotions. How should you handle her defensive reaction?

THE NEXT STEP

The Respectful Approach

Your boss has asked you to work with another team member to plan a luncheon and tour for some board members who are coming to see your organization's new offices. Unfortunately, the last time you worked together was not a great experience; she was unpleasant to work with, you couldn't agree on anything, and she didn't do her share of the work. In spite of it all, the project was completed. Come up with a consistently respectful approach to talk with your co-worker about sharing the work more fairly in order for things to go more smoothly this time.

Planning Ahead

Rob, one of your employees, has not been very productive lately; you've noticed that he's coming in late more than twice a week, and he's been spending more time than usual on personal phone calls. You suspect that something's going on in his personal life, but it's your job to speak with him about his lack of productivity. Draft an outline for your meeting.

Food Fight

You've been elected by your co-workers to confront Tom, a long-time employee, about his lunch choices. Each day for the past six weeks, much to the dismay of the rest of the office, he heats up a pre-packaged diet meal and eats at his desk. No one enjoys the odour, but the passing comments others have made to Tom have fallen on deaf ears. Beginning with the appropriate positive intention, jot down your notes in preparation for your private conversation with Tom.

4
WRITING FOR BUSINESS AUDIENCES
Developing an Effective Message

STARTING POINT

Go to www.wiley.com/canada/brounstein to assess your knowledge of the basics of business writing. After reviewing this website, you'll be able to determine where you need to concentrate your effort.

What You'll Learn in This Chapter:

* the benefits of learning good writing skills
* how an audience factors into the writing process
* the importance of exploring ideas in the writing process
* commonly used techniques for organization
* the role of details and examples in writing.

After Studying This Chapter, You'll be Able to:

* discuss common mistakes and their relationship to effective writing
* identify the critical factors that affect the writing process
* describe ways of generating ideas
* discuss the relative merits of patterns and outlines
* explain how details and examples can strengthen writing.

INTRODUCTION

Good business writing doesn't just happen. In fact, writing is one of the more difficult challenges in the workplace. To write well—to express and deliver a clear and effective message—requires planning. Part of a plan is having a clear idea of your purpose and your audience. This chapter examines that part of the writing process as well as ways of generating and organizing ideas for communicating a message. The chapter concludes with ways of supporting a message with details and examples.

4.1 Basics of Business Writing

Good writing is a powerful tool. When you have mastered good writing, you are able to focus your ideas, present them clearly, and deliver them with impact. Good writers stand out in the business world and tend to be more successful, whether they are writing letters, reports, proposals, or memos.

Newer means of communicating, such as text messaging, blogs, and social networking sites like Facebook and MySpace™ also require business people to rely on good writing skills. A poorly written message does not improve with speed of delivery. No matter what technology you use to create and transmit your business message, you still need to win your audience's attention with your good writing skills.

4.1.1 Avoiding the Pitfalls

Good writing can be defined, as Jonathan Swift proposed two centuries ago, as "proper words in proper places." That sounds simple, but how do you know what will be proper—that is, appropriate, timely, necessary—in business messages? To better understand what good business writing is, first consider some common mistakes made in bad business writing:

Hidden meanings in your message	Solution
The reader can't figure out what the message is because the letter, report, or other communication is so poorly organized and written.	Have a plan before you start to write so each paragraph contributes to the message; this will save you time in the long run, and save your readers time because they won't have to struggle with the hidden meanings in your message.
Wrong tone	**Solution**
Even if the reader doesn't have a problem with the information in the message, the wrong tone (too formal, too casual, or too subjective) can offend the reader and render the entire message useless.	Be sure you have a firm idea of who your readers are and what they expect. You need to know demographic factors like their age, occupation, or educational background so you can focus your tone and language for their needs. For example, a letter to college students about cell phone plans would have a very different tone from a letter to seniors about pre-planning funeral arrangements.
Too much information	**Solution**
Most business readers don't have the time or patience to sort through pages, lists, tables, and sections of information.	Again, focus on your readers and their information needs and expectations. If you were writing to an engineering firm

about designs for a new bridge, your readers would expect you to provide many details in the form of tables and charts. But if you were writing to a community group about the same bridge, your letter would have an entirely different focus and a different level of detail.

The wrong information	Solution
When your message contains misleading or incorrect information, you—and your message—lose credibility with your audience.	Make absolutely sure that your information is correct before you send out a letter, email, or memo. Have a colleague proofread your document for factual errors as well as for spelling and grammar errors.

Other mistakes such as spelling and grammatical errors, long paragraphs, and poor transitions can be equally critical and will be covered in detail in Chapter 5.

4.1.2 Writing Effectively

To help you communicate the most effective message to your audience, consider three factors:

- **Tone:** No matter what the content of the message (more on that in 4.3), writers inevitably communicate their personality, intention, and image through the words they choose. When the tone (that is, the style or manner of expression) of your message is overly formal ("It has come to my attention that . . ."), your readers may feel an air of superiority. Most likely, their response to such a message will be negative or at least guarded. On the other hand, an inappropriately casual message ("Hey, boss, about that promotion . . .") can backfire if your reader resents your lack of respect or seriousness.
- **Word choice:** The words you choose also influence how willing your reader will be to grasp your message and act on it. For most business purposes, sesquipedalian vocabulary ("big words") is unnecessary for clear writing. Mark Twain once remarked, "I never write 'metropolis' when I get paid the same for writing 'city.'"
- **Length:** Even when you have chosen the right tone and words for your audience, your message can still go unread simply because it is too long. Test your own response to message length the next time you get a long-winded email. Long messages that could have been shorter add to our workday and subtract from our patience.

Notice in the cases of tone, word choice, and length that what matters are your readers. Before beginning a message, consider the best way to approach your audience. Think about your purpose in sending the message and plan how you'll achieve that purpose.

> ### FOR EXAMPLE
>
> **What's the Point?**
> Kevin was in charge of publicity for a music festival. The letter he sent out to local businesses in the hopes of getting sponsors did not do well. It turns out that Kevin spent the first eight paragraphs describing the festival and the events being planned. His key point—"We'd like you to be one of our valued festival sponsors; with your tax-free donation you'll receive an advertisement in our brochures as well as a festival booth in which you can promote your business"—was stuck in the middle of the ninth paragraph. Of the 35 businesses that received the letter, only 15 got the point.

SELF-CHECK

1. Explain the main benefits of good business writing.
2. Explain why too much information can take away from a letter's effectiveness.
3. Define tone.
4. What three factors should be considered when communicating a message?

4.2 Examining the Writing Process

The essential first step for any writing project is to focus on planning. Without planning, you may find yourself in a writer's block—those agonizing minutes or hours when words simply won't flow.

To avoid such problems, carefully plan (preferably, in writing, but at least mentally) what you'll write. In your plan, consider five questions related to five key aspects of writing:

1. **Purpose**—What are you trying to communicate?
2. **Audience**—To whom are you writing?

3. **Exploration**—What ideas should you consider?

4. **Organization**—How can you best arrange your ideas?

5. **Details and examples**—How can you support your point?

4.2.1 Knowing Your Purpose

Every communication has a purpose, and knowing that purpose before you write helps you shape your words and ideas. Think of it this way: moving targets are hard to hit with arrows or words, and non-existent targets can't be hit at all. Therefore, you should decide on your target or purpose before taking aim with your words, sentences, and paragraphs.

In general terms, your purposes will probably fall within one of the purpose circles shown in Figure 4-1. You'll notice that the circles overlap, suggesting that you can certainly have more than one purpose in a document or speech.

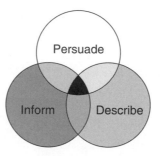

Figure 4-1 Purposes of communication

Decide at the start of any communication task what your purpose is: to inform, to persuade, or to describe. The following list of questions should help you figure out your purpose for communicating. Use some or all of the questions to help stimulate your thinking:

- What are you communicating?
- What do you want your audience to know after your communication?
- What do you want your audience to feel after the communication?
- What do you want your audience to do after your communication?

4.2.2 Knowing Your Audience

When we write friendly messages to people who like us, we usually have no trouble writing the message. On the other hand, it's much harder to figure out how to word the message when we want to complain, to give bad news, or to say almost anything to someone who doesn't want to hear our message. If we believe that the reader is hostile to us or to our message, we agonize over what and how to write the message.

For instance, you may have to say "no" to an outraged customer or draft a termination letter for an employee. At these times, words are hard to find and we often get "stalled" halfway through writing our message because we're worried about how our audience will react to our words. Instead, turn your energies toward your purpose: write and send a message as effectively as you can.

Most audiences, of course, aren't either friends or enemies. Most are neutral toward you: interested if you interest them and bored if you bore them. Imagine that your readers are your friends. When you do, you will feel yourself relax. In every way, the language that springs from you in that mood is more natural, more vivid, and more persuasive than writing that comes from hesitation, fear, and doubt.

In the following two letters, the writer is preparing a promotional letter to the community in which he is about to open a new tire store. In the first letter, the writer clearly feels distance from his audience. He sounds formal and stuffy, not friendly, because he doesn't know how the community feels about him.

1. *Our market analysis demonstrated that the northern suburbs of Halifax lacked a full-service tire store. We have decided to open such a store at 197 Atlantic Street. We are prepared to handle general tire problems, as well as specialized needs such as alignment, spin balancing, and chassis adjustment.*

2. *The northern suburbs of Halifax have deserved a full-service tire store for years. We've arrived! Visit us at 197 Atlantic Street to say "hello" and look us over. We'll take pride in providing you with the best tires at the best price. Alignment, balancing, and chassis work? Right up our alley. At Maritime Tire, we're not only new neighbours, we're also good neighbours.*

This approach of this revision may be a bit over the top for your needs, but it illustrates how your perception of your audience (hostile, neutral, or friendly) influences your ability to write with ease. And *you* control those perceptions.

4.2.3 Analyzing Your Audience

The way you think about your audience will help you communicate more effectively with them. The following list of questions may help you to analyze your audience:

- Who is your audience?
- How big is your audience? How will the size influence which method and pattern of communication you choose (see Chapter 1)?
- What does your audience know about you?
- How can you increase your credibility with your audience?
- What do you already know about your audience?
- What do you think your audience should know about your topic?
- What do you want your audience to do with the information you provide?

What you write depends in great part on your audience, so analyze that audience with care.

FOR EXAMPLE

Considering Your Audience

John, a regional representative for a paint manufacturer, needed to present some information about a new line of faux finishes and glazes being marketed. His standard approach would work fine for the meetings he had scheduled with the managers of several arts supply stores; they were familiar with manufacturers' other decorative paints. In an effort to expand his market, however, John had scheduled a meeting with someone from a local chain of hardware stores. To do so, John considered the audience; he didn't know how much experience this hardware rep had with these types of products. To cover his bases, John expanded his presentation materials to include more general information about the line of products and their growing market in home renovation and décor.

SELF-CHECK

- Discuss the five key aspects of the writing process.
- What questions can help you determine your purpose for writing?
- What questions can help you analyze your audience?
- Explain the importance of knowing your purpose and audience before writing.

4.3 Exploring Your Ideas

Once you've given some thought to your purpose and your audience, you can design your message for your audience. In other words, you need to come up with the best ideas to communicate your message to your audience.

For most writers, getting ideas down involves an expedition of sorts. Unfortunately, ideas rarely present themselves in a top-down, A, B, C order. Instead, they arrive in a jumble, awaiting some final sorting and ordering.

Take care not to reject ideas or impose a final order on them too early in your idea-design process; doing so may limit your creativity. Let a wide variety of ideas come to you—mixed up, in any order, and in any form. You'll arrange the ideas in the next step. For now, open yourself to the possibilities.

4.3.1 Idea Circle

Try using an **idea circle** to generate ideas. Here's how it works: whenever you need a variety of ideas on a topic, write the topic on a sheet of paper and draw an idea circle below it. Figure 4-2 illustrates an idea circle with eight wedges, but you can draw any number of slices you wish.

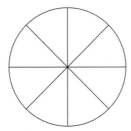

Figure 4-2 Idea circle

Now, fill in the slices of the pie as the ideas occur to you. The circular arrangement of the slices gives each idea equal weight, which can help you as you mull over which pattern of ideas works best.

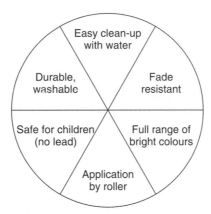

Figure 4-3 An idea circle of marketing ideas for Vinyl-Brite Paint

Figure 4-3 represents an idea circle for marketing vinylized paint; it shows how you can freely list yours ideas in any order as you search for the best marketing approach. What follows is an advertisement that grew out of this set of ideas:

Brighten up the kids' room this Saturday with the rainbow colours of Vinyl-Brite. This one-coat, lead-free, all-purpose interior paint lasts for years. Handprints wipe off with a sponge. Worried about that painting mess? No problem—Vinyl-Brite rolls on, and cleans up with water. It's on sale now for $9.99 a litre.

4.3.2 The Classic Questions

Unfortunately, there are times when the idea circle simply sits empty on the page. When that happens, try asking yourself questions in order to generate ideas (this technique is based on a system perfected by Greek orators). Mentally fill in the blank in each of the following questions with your topic. Asking the questions out loud is sometimes helpful. There is a good chance that most of the questions will produce usable ideas for your business writing.

- Why do I/others even care about _____?
- If I had to divide _____ into parts or stages, what would they be?
- What forces/circumstances led to _____?
- What kind of person is interested in _____?
- If _____ did not exist, how would things be different?
- What aspect of _____ do I (or would my readers) like best and what would they like least?
- How could _____ be explained to a 10-year-old child?

You don't need to answer every question thoroughly, and you shouldn't labour on working out perfect answers. Instead, use the questions as mental prods to get your mind moving and your ideas flowing. Then as the ideas come to you, jot them down in an idea circle.

Ideas do not usually come by simple inspiration. The idea circle and the questions can help you to generate ideas when you have time pressures. The whole process should take about five minutes, which can be a better investment in time than staring at a blank piece of paper waiting for inspiration.

FOR EXAMPLE

Questions to Develop Ideas

Jason has decided to make a move up from his customer service position with a credit card company. To be considered for a managerial position in the department, he needs to submit a short proposal of changes he would implement if hired, supporting each idea with his qualifications. Jason knows a great deal about customer satisfaction (and lack thereof); after all, he's handled thousands of calls over his five years of service. To put his experience to work, Jason uses the classic questions to help him generate his ideas. For example: "What aspects of customer service do I like best? Which aspects do I like the least?" Because he's seen a high rate of burnout in customer service representatives, Jason proposes implementing a rotating schedule that would allow reps to switch departments every four to six months.

SELF-CHECK

- Describe how an idea circle works.
- List five examples of questions that can be used in the classic-questions technique.
- How can the idea circle and classic questions be used together?
- Explain the relationship between the idea circle and business letter writing.

4.4 Organizing Your Ideas

A large part of the art of good business writing lies in finding (or inventing) the right organizational pattern in order to make sense out of the information you have. When we read a document that has either the wrong pattern or no pattern at all, we are quick to complain: "This report rambles," or "This letter just doesn't say anything."

In your work, you are often handed a collection of chaotic information that you must organize and present: financial data, test scores, consumer feedback, sales returns, and so forth. Part of your job is to choose the best way to organize it. Used with judgement, the following common patterns can help build the framework for a meaningful letter, report, or other business message.

4.4.1 Patterns of Organization

The following chart lists some examples of patterns you can use to organize your document. The constructs listed in the left-hand column can be used as part of a sentence in a short document, as a group of sentences in a longer document, or even as a set of paragraphs in a long report or proposal. The examples in the right-hand column show how you can combine the points in shorter paragraphs, but the amount of detail you need to fill in would be determined by the purposes of your document and the needs of your reader.

The Time Pattern	**Example (from an annual report)**
• In the past • At present • In the future	In the past, we supplied area retailers with prescription pharmaceutical articles. At present, we have expanded our line to include toiletries. In the future, we want to break into the over-the-counter sales.

Cause • Situation A caused event B • Event B is described • Event B can be undone/ repeated/furthered by	**Example (from a claims letter)** Poor directions in the motor scooter instruction manual caused an expensive mishap. Because you neglected to specify that oil had to be mixed with the gasoline, I had to pay $182 in repairs. Please reimburse me for that amount. You should also issue a new manual.
Emotion • Once I felt • Things changed • Now I feel	**Example (from a resignation letter)** As a new engineer at CLT, I felt that my work would earn me respect and financial rewards. However, twice in the past three years I've been passed over for raises. Therefore, I am submitting my resignation.
Perspective • One way to look at the topic • A second way to view it • Finally, a third revealing view	**Example (from a proposal)** We all agree that L&M Auto needs more exposure. The sales staff recommends a freeway sign. The advertiser favours a flyer. The approach here is new: a hot air balloon.
Doubt • Others say that A will happen • We doubt that A will happen • Here's why	**Example (from a real estate sales letter)** They're singing the old lament again; housing prices are bound to fall, so wait to buy. At Merton Realty, we just don't believe it. Land, materials, and labour costs continue to rise each year. A better buy next year? Don't bet your money on it.
Contrast • A is not like B • A has _____, but B has _____ • Only A has _____	**Example (from a relocation report)** Winnipeg differs from Vancouver in several ways. In Winnipeg, commercial office space rents for $14 per square foot; in Vancouver, a comparable property rents for $21 per square foot. As well, Vancouver offers all the rain you'll ever wish for.
Reputation • A is reputed to have _____ • In actuality, A does (does not) have _____ • A's reputation is deserved/must be adjusted	**Example (from a consumer report)** A new pain reliever, "Loado", claims to provide four potent painkillers in addition to common ibuprofen. Our lab analysis reveals only the presence of inert dyes in addition to ibuprofin. "Loado" offers more hype than common pain relievers, but not more pharmaceutical power.

Variety	Example (from a health club promotion)
• Item A comes in these sizes/ shapes/aspects • First • Next • Finally	Beauty comes in different forms: first, the irrepressible natural glow of the teen; next, the warmth of fire of young adulthood; and finally, the cultured radiance of maturity.
Opinions	**Example (from a sales report)**
• Some people say • Others claim • But most will admit	Some of my clients feel that it is a mistake to restock inventory during the next quarter. Others claim that prices will fall still lower in the coming months. However, most will admit that all retailers will have to make major purchases before the fall surge.
Likelihood	**Example (from a reply to an order)**
• A is possible • B is likely • But C is certain	While truck express may be able to deliver your parts by April 4, a somewhat later date is more likely. However, air express could deliver in time for your assembly deadline.

These brief patterns help when you need to create order out of chaos. They serve as reminders, too, that every well-written document has an easily stated chain of arguments or a "pattern" at its core. These patterns prepare you for outlining, which allows you to put your ideas into some logical sequence.

4.4.2 Using an Outline

Although patterns of organization (like those detailed in 4.4.1) provide the essential backbone for business documents, they don't have enough "meat on their bones" to guide you through the long paragraphs of writing. When you're in a rush to write something for work, you may be tempted to skip an outline. Don't yield to temptation.

Without an outline, you may waste valuable time staring at a half-finished document, wondering, "What do I say next?" Worse yet, you may get to the end of your rough draft and realize, "This doesn't make any sense." At that point, you'll be stuck trying to rearrange sentences, to cut and paste entire paragraphs, and to make some order out of what you've done.

Just as a builder follows a blueprint, a writer needs a clear outline to write efficiently. When you expand points on an outline to full or even partial sentences, much of the hard work of drafting is already done. The major phrases you've written in your outline grow into headings and topic sentences in the first draft. By filling in details, examples, definitions, and explanations, you quickly build an organized and coherent first draft.

4.4.3 Putting an Outline Together

Once you decide on a master pattern for your ideas (you can use one of the patterns listed earlier in this chapter or choose your own), you are ready to create your outline. If you're like most writers, you'll figure out your own personal system. Whether you have a system or not, the following outline structure might be helpful:

Master Pattern
Topic: Changes in How We Communicate

Past

I. Fastest forms of communication over longer distances survived slower forms

  A. The natural world

    1. Carrier pigeons vs. human runner

    2. Visual signals (smoke) vs. voice

  B. The technological world

    1. Telegraph vs. pony express

    2. Telephone vs. telegraph

Present

II. New fast modes now compete with familiar slow modes

  A. What we send and receive

    1. Word processing vs. typing

    2. Computer modem vs. traditional mail

  B. What we store and retrieve

    1. Computer memory vs. file drawers

    2. Database vs. book-like directors

Future

III. More speed lies ahead, with inevitable changes

  A. How messages are generated

    1. Artificial intelligence devices

    2. Model documents

  B. How messages are transmitted

    1. Satellite networks

    2. Speech-driven computers

This sample outline may not reflect your exact outlining habits. You may find it helpful to put down more or fewer words. The point is this: find a personal outline method and use it to guarantee orderly, logical thought development in your writing.

SELF-CHECK

- Discuss the patterns that can be used to organize information in a business document.
- Describe the importance of using an outline in writing.
- How should patterns of organization and outlines be combined to work together?

4.5 Supporting Your Ideas: Details and Examples

Ideas can be made more persuasive and memorable by supporting them with details and examples. By developing the actual details, examples, and stories, you give life and substance to your ideas.

These details and examples play three important roles in business writing:

- To provide information
- To verify, or show the truth of, an assertion
- To illustrate, or give an example of, an idea or concept

Your supporting details and examples won't do you or your audience any good if they seem forced or untrue. You have at least four ways of persuading your reader that your details and examples have credibility. Good details and examples are:

1. **Specific:** Notice how each vague detail in the following example gains strength when transformed to a specific detail.
   ○ **Vague:** Some classic automobiles have risen steeply in price in recent years.
   ○ **Specific:** Such auto classics as the gull-winged Mercedes, the MGTD, and the Porsche Speedster have risen 400 percent in real dollar value since 1965.
2. **Clearly understandable:** Your readers want to hold onto the expected and familiar as they reach for new information. Strive to keep your details and examples in touch with the common things of daily existence.
   ○ **Difficult:** Our galaxy, a protracted spheroid mass of stellar bodies and vaporous amalgams arranged along a single plane, revolves in space.
   ○ **Understandable:** The Milky Way, its countless stars drawn together into a shape not unlike an immense fried egg, revolves in space.

3. **Brief:** Although your examples should be short, they should still contain vivid details. To keep on track with your writing, omit the information that is marginally important for your reader in terms of your basic purpose.

   ○ **Too long:** To prepare for the upcoming conference, the planning committee broke into three teams of two and spent the budget of $1,000 on the following items: food ($300), beverages ($75), serving staff ($125), printed agenda ($50), folders ($50), motivational speaker ($200), and team speaker ($200).

   ○ **Brief:** To prepare for the upcoming conference, the planning teams spent $1,000 on catering services, printed materials, and speaker fees.

4. **Focused:** Studies of attention spans and reading patterns show how often readers pause, lose track, retrace, and even skip large passages of writing. Therefore, you should go out of your way to focus on your key points. Notice how the first example lacks such guidance.

   ○ **Aimless:** Few coal miners participated in the Grants-for-Education program. "I worked until six o'clock every night. Saturdays, we drove to my parents' house. Sundays, I watched football. I didn't have time, that's all."

   ○ **Focused:** Few coal miners participated in the Grants-for-Education program. Bret Jolleson, 28, explains why he turned down a $2,500 grant: "I worked until six o'clock every night. Saturdays we drove to my parents' house. Sundays, I watch football. I didn't have time, that's all."

SELF-CHECK

- Discuss the three roles that details and examples play in business writing.

- Discuss the characteristics of details and examples that make them believable.

- Explain the importance of brevity when writing examples to support your ideas.

SUMMARY

Those who master the difficult challenges of business writing are sought after and considered key players in the success of an organization. Planning, which begins with an understanding of your purpose and audience, is an integral part of the writing process. Equally important are the stages in which a writer generates and organizes ideas. In the final stage of the planning process, a writer supports those ideas with vivid and persuasive details and examples.

KEY TERMS

Idea circle   A visual tool for generating ideas before you write.

Tone   The style or manner of expression.

ASSESS YOUR UNDERSTANDING

Go to www.wiley.com/canada/brounstein to evaluate your knowledge of the basics of business writing. Measure your learning by comparing pre-test and post-test results.

Quick Questions

1. The arrival of text messaging has lowered the standards for business writing. True or false?

2. A business message will be less effective if it
   (a) contains miscellaneous information
   (b) is organized according to a pattern
   (c) includes technical information
   (d) all of the above

3. The tone of a business document should be
   (a) casual
   (b) professional
   (c) emotional
   (d) expressive

4. Writing a rough draft is the first step of any writing project. True or false?

5. A written communication can have more than one purpose. True or false?

6. Which of the following questions can help you determine the purpose of your communication?
   (a) What do you want your audience to feel after the communication?
   (b) What are you communicating?
   (c) What do you want your audience to do after the communication?
   (d) All of the above

7. Which of the following questions can help you analyze an audience?
   (a) When will the audience receive your communication?
   (b) What does the audience need to study?

   (c) What does your audience know about you?

   (d) Will the audience respond to the communication?

8. An idea circle is used to organize ideas. True or false?

9. The classic-questions technique is used to generate ideas. Which of the following questions are used in the technique?

   (a) What kind of person is interested in _____?

   (b) How could _____ be explained to a 10-year-old child?

   (c) Why do I/others even care about _____?

   (d) all of the above

10. Organizational patterns can be used to build the framework for business communications. Patterns can organize sentences into paragraphs or paragraphs into documents. True or false?

11. The perspective pattern of organization involves two views of topic. True or false?

12. An outline is

   (a) an organizational pattern

   (b) the stage in which details and examples are added

   (c) where a writer can expand on a pattern of ideas

   (d) a fixed system of organization

13. Details and supporting examples do *not* serve which of the following purposes in business writing?

   (a) verifying an assertion

   (b) providing coherent structure

   (c) illustrating a concept

   (d) giving an example of an idea

14. General examples are an effective way of supporting concepts and ideas. True or false?

Give It Some Thought

1. Which three factors most effectively address the needs of a reader?

   (a) organization, length, tone

   (b) length, word choice, tone

   (c) tone, content, length

   (d) presentation, tone, content

2. Why is it important to answer the question, "Who is my audience?" before writing a letter or memo?

3. How does knowing the purpose of a communication affect the writing process?

4. A hostile audience can make writing difficult. Create an example of a situation in which a writer needs to address a less-than-friendly audience.

5. Which of the following can help a writer cope with an unfriendly audience?
   (a) using an unfriendly tone to match that of the audience
   (b) writing as though the readers are actually friendly
   (c) ignoring any negative response
   (d) not writing for the moment

6. In the idea-exploration stage of the writing process, it is good practice to limit or edit the ideas as they come to you. True or false?

7. In which situation(s) would the idea circle and the classic-questions technique be useful for generating ideas?
   (a) developing a grant proposal for a senior citizen pet therapy program
   (b) writing a proposal to begin a company-wide internship program
   (c) writing a marketing letter for a holistic health center
   (d) all of the above

8. How can patterns be used to organize a long document?

9. How does an outline make the actual writing part of the process easier?
   (a) prevents a writer from straying off topic
   (b) outline headings translate into topic sentences
   (c) provides some partial or complete sentences
   (d) all of the above

10. What are four characteristics that make details and examples believable to readers?

Applying This Chapter

1. You need to take a day off to deal with some personal business at home. Write one version of your email to a boss who never misses a day of work, the kind of boss who expects the job to come first. Write another version of your email, this time to a much more empathetic boss, one who understands that employees sometimes have other priorities. What differences in tone and word choice can you see?

2. Imagine you're a college student, and you need some money to get you through to the end of the school term. Write three letters asking for a loan of $500 (1) to a friend, (2) to a parent, and (3) to a bank loan officer. How do your approaches to these audiences differ in tone, style, and content?

3. As the newest member of a team in charge of creating an advertising campaign for multicoloured ketchup, use the classic-questions technique to come up with five ideas.

4. Break into small groups to come up with ideas for next year's ultimate car model. Use the idea circle and then compare your results with other groups in the class.

5. Make up three specific examples to support the following assertion: "The floor plans of stores can be arranged to encourage impulse buying."

6. You've worked for the same chain of travel agencies for seven years, and although you've always said you had the best job in the world, you feel it's time to move on. You plan to leave and start your own agency, one that caters to environmentally minded clients. Write a one-page letter to your boss explaining your decision.

THE NEXT STEP

Writing Tools

In three paragraphs, describe a whitening toothpaste. In the first, simply describe its physical characteristics; in the second, inform people about it; in the third, persuade people to buy it.

Timely Ideas

As the office manager of a large law firm, you've noticed in the past two months that employees have been increasingly late for work. Come up with an incentive program to increase punctuality. Use the classic-questions technique to come up with some ideas, then draft a memo to your boss explaining the program.

Logic Talks

Use the logic pattern to argue, in writing, for higher salaries for entry-level employees. Ask your reader to consider factors like educational levels, the cost of living in a large city, or starting salaries in comparable fields. Large employment websites like monster. ca, workopolis.com, or www.jobbank.gc.ca can give you information about starting salaries in a wide range of occupations.

Aim at an Audience

Examine the following excerpt from a marketing email. Using the questions given in sections 4.2.1 and 4.2.3, determine the purpose and audience for this message:

> ### *Create Dazzling Documents in Brilliant Full Colour*
> *As a small business that's just starting to grow, you have only one chance to make a first impression to potential new clients. Get the easy-to-use* Techno Colour Laser Jet 3485 Printer *and show just how great your business is. Print full-colour, high quality brochures and price lists that are sure to get you noticed. Our printer's built-in networking capabilities will impress your clients and our industry-leading reliability will have you feeling confident in your investment. Buy now and enjoy a $110 instant rebate!*

Lines of Communication

Although he was originally hired by an engineering firm to work in-house on development planning and permit applications, much of Nate's work is taking him to work sites where he meets with contractors. To do his job effectively, he must stay in phone contact with his supervisor. The company is reluctant to provide Nate with a cell phone because other employees have abused the privilege. Imagine that you are Nate's supervisor, and, using one of the patterns outlined in this chapter, write a paragraph persuading company executives to provide Nate with a phone.

Writing Tutorial

It's clear that something must be done to upgrade the writing skills of the people you supervise in your department. Because these people are able to use the Internet, you decide to use it as a training tool. Explore writing topics on the Internet and pick three to five websites that work together to form a curriculum of sorts with which your staff can work on their writing difficulties. Write a memo to your staff in which you inform them of the training exercise; in it, list the sites and give specific directions for how you want the employees to use the websites.

5
WRITING AND REVISING BUSINESS COMMUNICATIONS
Techniques for Composing Your Message

STARTING POINT

Go to www.wiley.com/canada/brounstein to assess your knowledge of the basics of writing and revising. After reviewing this website, you'll be able to determine where you need to concentrate your effort.

What You'll Learn in This Chapter:
- the importance of word choice in writing
- guidelines for writing effective sentences
- tools for writing coherent paragraphs
- the benefits of revisions and proofreading.

After Studying This Chapter, You'll be Able to:
- discuss how word choice and voice can communicate a strong business message
- identify the critical factors that determine the effectiveness of a sentence
- discuss the relative merits of revision tools and proofreading techniques
- understand that each step of the writing process plays a critical role in the final product.

INTRODUCTION

It's not enough to know what information belongs in a letter, memo, or report. In order to do your job effectively, you need to take that information and present it in a well-written, logical, and coherent message. The foundation of a document is built on the strength of its words. Those words work together to form effective sentences. Patterns then organize these sentences into logical paragraphs. The chapter concludes with techniques for revising and proofreading, essential steps for producing a quality final product.

5.1 Writing the First Draft

The first draft is only one part of the larger writing process, but for most writers it is the most daunting part. In this stage you'll expand on your outline, fill in the content, and shape your message.

To get started, have your outline, notes, and any other resource materials you may need in front of you. If you've taken the time to develop a working outline and a good set of supporting details and examples (see Section 4.5), writing the first draft may be surprisingly easy. You know generally what you want to say and somewhere in the back of your mind, the actual words have already begun to form.

Now sit down and write—all the way through if you can. The trick to writing the first draft is letting go. Of course, you'll make mistakes. Of course, you'll use unnecessary words. Of course, you'll wander. But you should bravely let the words flow, no matter what happens.

There is a time and place to edit and polish, but that time is not while you are writing the first draft. At this stage, don't make changes, fix anything, or even check for spelling and grammar. Don't worry about these details until you're ready to revise what you wrote. Even if you get stuck on a sentence or paragraph, move on and come back to it later.

5.1.1 Choosing Your Voice

Even in business, your writing can communicate who you are as well as what you have to say. As discussed in Sections 4.1 and 4.2, your purpose, audience, and circumstances influence the voice you choose for your message. But by applying some degree of your personality and personal voice, you can catch your reader's attention and give life to your message.

As you can see, the first two voice options are not effective in business situations:

- **Encyclopedia voice:** Stiff and unemotional, but often considered a "safe" way to write. This voice sounds detached from its human speaker and is easy to tune out. For example: "It is possible to define the term *headquarters* as the central location of primary residence of a corporation. Such a definition may be said to include peripheral satellites of the central base."
- **Emotional voice:** When we revert to this voice, we sound childish and blunt; repetitive and slangy language is often used; contractions are prevalent. For example: "The company headquarters isn't just the place that we all go to work each day. It's the place where we all hang out, work hard, make friends. The powers-that-be are out there looking for a new place for us to call home and I'm telling you, it's no easy task. They've been at it for six months now."

Somewhere between the first and second examples lies your business voice, the voice that will serve you best in your career.

- **Business voice:** This voice is direct, controlled, and reasonable. It is personal but not self-centred. For example: "For six months we have sought a new headquarters without asking one basic question: do we all share the same meaning for the word *headquarters*?"

FOR EXAMPLE

Keeping Cool

Leo was one of the most ambitious employees in his accounting firm. He worked hard and earned high praise in his performance reviews. His weakness, however, was in letting his emotional voice slip into his communications, especially in high-pressure situations. After two fairly serious incidents involving this problem, Leo began working with Lila, a level-headed co-worker who had a knack for reworking Leo's writing. After less than a month of Lila's guidance, Leo's business voice was strong. Although he still maintained some of his own personality in his writing, his voice now represented that of his company, and not of his emotions.

5.1.2 Using Effective Words

Words: one at a time, these small building blocks line up to create larger structures—sentences, paragraphs, pages, and so on. The right words help ensure that your message is clear and effective. Although you shouldn't labour over every word you put on the page, certain principles can help keep your writing on track:

- **Opt for specific and concrete words.** Readers have only one motive in reading your writing. "What's here," they ask, "that can be put to use?" When you use specific and concrete words, you give your reader useful tools instead of airy approximations.

The following passage from a memo announces a client–staff meeting first in a vague way and then in a specific way. Notice the important differences.

A client wants a brief overview after lunch tomorrow. Bring along anything we can use to show off our company.

Consider the vague, abstract language:

- **"a client"**—Which client?
- **"brief"**—Twenty minutes? Two hours?

- **"overview"**—A lecture? A slide show?
- **"after lunch"**—1 p.m.? 3 p.m.?
- **"anything"**—Drapery? Pictures of the kids?
- **"company"**—The building? The logo?

Revised in a specific form, the memo passage makes its point clearly:

Ms. Allyson Royce, Operations Manager for Norton Hotels, can meet with us for 45 minutes tomorrow at 2:30 in my office. Please bring letters of appreciation, files from open accounts, photos of the buildings we now manage, and any other items that demonstrate the quality of our maintenance and rental services.

Another common way of weakening business writing is to use the vague word "very" (and its speech twin "really"). Often, a business writer uses *very* in a feeble effort to turn up the volume on another word: very nervous, very upset, very good. Business writers who know the power of specific words prefer to amplify the content of the word at hand, not its volume. Instead of "very nervous," they write "frantic"; instead of "very upset," "furious"; and instead of "very good," "outstanding." By doing so, these writers say more with fewer words.

- **Avoid vague pronouns:** Vague pronouns (this, it, that, these, those) can leave gaps of meaning in your message.

Consider the gap in meaning left by the vague use of "this":

At its last meeting, the Employee Safety Committee's discussion focused on the buddy system for particularly hazardous duty. This met with opposition from management representatives.

This what? The possibilities are many:

- This discussion met with opposition.
- This meeting met with opposition.
- This system met with opposition.
- This duty met with opposition.

To spare readers an annoying guessing game, place an identifying word or phrase immediately after "this," and revise the sentence to specify that "this safeguard met with opposition from management representatives."

The problem of the vague "it" can often be solved even more easily. Rephrase the sentence to remove the meaningless "*it*" entirely.

Johnson's perpetual questions make it impossible to concentrate.
Johnson's perpetual questions make concentration impossible.

- **Choose positive words.** Business writers recognize that happy, optimistic people are more open to new ideas and change than are discouraged, cynical people. Therefore, such writers lose no opportunity to accentuate the positive.

Notice in the following pairs how a dreary, guilt-ridden message is recast into a brighter form by positive language:

Your complaint is being dealt with by Mr. Flores.
Mr. Flores will answer your inquiry promptly.

Ten percent of the sales force failed to attend the conference.
The conference attracted 90 percent of the sales force.

Negative words such as "can't," "shouldn't," "failed," "omitted," "destroyed," and "complained" are sometimes quite accurate for the situation at hand, but they rarely have the power to change the situation for the better. Business writers wisely choose positive language whenever they can to motivate an audience.

- **Avoid sexist language.** At one time, these sentences seemed perfectly proper:

A lawyer must choose his clients carefully.
Every surgeon washes his hands before operating.

You can avoid even the appearance of sexist assumptions by using "his or her" when the gender of the person is not known.

A lawyer must choose his or her clients carefully.
Every surgeon washes his or her hands before operating.

Keep in mind that the phrase "his or her" can become awkward when repeated several times in a paragraph. In that case, consider avoiding the gender issue altogether by making your subject plural:

Lawyers must choose their clients carefully.
Surgeons wash their hands before operating.

SELF-CHECK

- Define encyclopedia voice and emotional voice, and distinguish them from the business voice.
- Identify ways of using effective words.
- Explain the benefit of choosing positive words in writing.

5.2 Developing Effective Sentences

Effective sentences are able to convey an idea with clarity and style. They have a ring to them. They have rhythm and they have focus. They give the reader a clear idea of what is most important. And they do all this with as few words as possible.

5.2.1 Begin Strongly

Effective sentences begin strongly. Readers want to know at the beginning of each sentence, "Who did what?" Writers satisfy that interest by providing the subject or a key transition word as soon as possible.

Notice what happens in the following sentence when the subject (underlined) is delayed:

Of course, without knowing the full circumstances or complete terms of agreement between the two parties, <u>my client</u> cannot . . .

As readers, we feel a growing edginess as the writer piles more and more words up before giving us the subject. Notice how it's much more satisfying to find the subject early in the sentence.

<u>My client</u>, of course, cannot act without knowing the full circumstances . . .

Transition words can also appear early in a sentence, with powerful effect.

Nevertheless, Morton kept his goal solidly before him.
On the contrary, Maxine spoke highly of her supervisor.

Keep in mind that sentences that all begin with subjects would soon make the writing sound like a story for children in grade one. For occasional variety, begin with an *-ed* phrase ("Rated first among colleges, Harvard . . .") or an *-ing* phrase ("Bracing for higher interest rates, the accountant . . .")

5.2.2 Get to the Action

Effective sentence beginnings should be followed by the central verb in the sentence as quickly as possible. When the verb is delayed, readers begin to squirm. Consider:

> *The vacation so well-deserved by Ms. Kaye but postponed by her supervisor, Ms. Virginia Ward, for petty reasons, finally took place.*

As readers we need to know "Who did what?" Once that information has been given, we can be content with long stretches of related information.

> *Virginia Ward denied Ms. Kaye her well-deserved vacation for petty reasons.*

5.2.3 Vary Sentence Length

Effective sentences should vary in length. Readers like variety in sentence rhythm, as well as in content. By mixing short, medium, and long sentences, a skilled business writer holds a reader's attention.

How long is long? In modern usage, a "long" sentence can extend to three typed lines, but rarely beyond. Short sentences, by contrast, can be as short as one or two words. Sometimes, the most powerful sentence in a paragraph contains the fewest words. The paragraph you are reading is a good example of how to vary sentence length; it contains short, medium, and long sentences.

5.2.4 Control Your Emphasis

Business writing, like speaking, has its rituals of introduction: "it is" and "there is/are." Like "uh," these sentence openers have little or no meaning. They exist merely to get things under way. Good business writers learn, though, that business prose gets underway just fine without such empty words and phrases. Notice that we lose no meaning but gain considerable sentence strength by eliminating the meaningless openers:

> *There is an oak beam supporting the roof.*
> *An oak beam supports the roof.*

> *It is possible that Williams will apply for section leader.*
> *Williams may apply for section leader.*

By removing meaningless words from the start of the sentence, the beginning of the sentence is free to contain significant words. Here, after all, is where readers look for the first clue to understanding the meaning of the entire sentence. Words placed there receive special attention and emphasis from readers. For that reason alone, waste words such as "it is" should be avoided entirely, or at least placed later in the sentence.

The process is painless. In almost all cases, meaningless phrases can simply be left out of a sentence.

There are meaningless words that should be avoided.
Meaningless words should be avoided.
Avoid meaningless words.

5.2.5 Use Active Versus Passive Verb Patterns

A verb communicates action. For example, *erasing* is the action in the sentence: "The manager erased the file." In general, English sentences work best when they pulse with action. Readers appreciate the sense of energy in the sentence. Also, sentences with active verbs are shorter and easier to read than those with passive verbs. Who did what to whom stands out loud and clear in action sentences. Compare the two sentences:

The manager delegates tasks well.
One of the manager's skills is her ability in the delegation of tasks.

Readers seldom feel much energy or motivation from sentences containing only an "is," "are," "was," or "were" at their heart. As a business writer, you should recommend, develop, suggest, argue, refute, substantiate, summarize, begin, continue, grasp, reveal, glimpse, fulfill, and all the other activities that make up business life.

One variety of the "is" construction deserves a special note: passive verb forms, such as, "The cash register is/was fixed by Henderson." These forms dilute the sense of action in business writing. That is, the victim or object appears first in the sentence. Not until the final word of the sentence does the reader discover the actor, in this case Henderson.

You don't need to completely eliminate passive and is/are constructions from your business writing. For occasional emphasis and variety, the passive form serves well. As well, the passive form is good for delivering bad news, as will be discussed in Chapter Eight.

5.2.6 Eliminate Wordiness

Wordiness has little to do with the length of a document. Even a one-paragraph memo can be guilty of excessive use of redundant and often repetitive terms—in short, wordiness.

Watch for wordiness in these two disguises:

1. **Unnecessary doubling:** Notice how the following sentence states, and then restates, its point by doubling each key word.
   - **Not:** "If and when we can establish and define our goals and objectives, each and every member will be ready and willing to give aid and assistance."
   - **Instead:** "When we define our goals, each member will be ready to help."

2. **Unnecessary modifiers:** Are the italicized modifiers really necessary in the following sentence?

   ○ **Not:** "*In this world of today, official* governmental red tape is *seriously* destroying the *motivation* for financial incentives among *relatively* small businesses."

   ○ **Instead:** "Governmental red tape is destroying financial incentives for small businesses."

Avoiding wordiness is especially important now, when most decision makers find themselves with too much to read. Each document must compete for its share of attention—and unnecessarily wordy documents lose out.

5.2.7 Avoid Jargon, Clichés, and Slang

Your business messages will be much more effective if you avoid using terms that either confuse your reader or simply don't add any useful information. **Jargon** is special terminology—usually technical in nature—that only those closely associated with a job or field of study really understand. Jargon is only appropriate if all of the readers of your document will have the technical background to understand its meaning. For example, if you are an engineer writing for an audience of engineers, then jargon will be expected. However, if you must use jargon in your writing for people who may not have a technical background, make a point of defining it first; the same rule applies to **acronyms.**

Similarly, avoid **clichés** and **slang.** Clichés are worn-out expressions that have little, if any, meaning, such as: neither here nor there, spring into action, touching base, and as luck would have it. Slang ("local street language") lowers the tone of your writing, and can offend as well as confuse readers. Remember that in today's global context, using standard English improves the chances that your writing can be understood by readers worldwide and by newcomers to Canada. For example, think for a moment about how much slang you might know from Mumbai or Glasgow, and how confused you would be if you came across it in a memo from your boss.

> ⌐ FOR EXAMPLE ⌐
>
> **Brief is Better**
> Part of Isaac's first job required him to take scientific reports and summarize them for publication in an environmental group's newsletter and annual report. His supervisor heavily edited what he wrote, with growing frustration on both sides. Isaac suffered from a case of verbosity—too many words. He worked on cutting down, but struggled. When they met to discuss the problem, his supervisor advised, "Write what you mean—nothing more. Look at each paragraph, sentence, and word with a strict eye and decide if it truly serves the meaning or is simply window dressing." Isaac began putting his supervisor's advice into action and his writing has vastly improved with practice, and he has since passed the advice on to others.

5.3 Creating Effective Paragraphs

Effective words create equally effective sentences, which, in turn, find their place in paragraphs organized around central ideas by a pattern. (Section 4.4 covers a variety of patterns that you can use to organize your sentences into logical paragraphs and your paragraphs into logical documents; you can also create patterns of your own.)

The most effective paragraphs have unity and coherence; that is, they are controlled by one idea, and each sentence within the paragraph relates to the sentences around it. The effect of a paragraph without these qualities is like that of a bad orchestra; each member is playing an instrument, but they're just not playing the same song. Simply put, your writing will not be clear.

5.3.1 Paragraph Coherence and Unity

Although the primary ingredient holding a paragraph together is the glue of logical development, paragraphs achieve coherence and unity through tools such as transitions, key words, and central ideas.

- **Use transitional words generously.** If one idea grows out of a preceding idea, tell the reader by using words like "therefore" or "furthermore." If an idea contrasts with an earlier idea, signal the difference with "however," "but," or "in contrast." In similar ways, you can signal the flow of meaning within your paragraphs with such words as "nevertheless," "of course," "in short," "consequently," and "so on."
- **Make smooth connections between sentences.** The key to tight, smooth connections between sentences lies in starting the thought of one sentence where the thought of the previous sentence left off. At no point within a paragraph should the reader be startled by a new and unexpected point of beginning.

However, the advice to start one sentence where the previous sentence left off doesn't mean you should use the same words. Avoid using the last word of one sentence as the first word of the following sentence. For example:

We received notice that the Yellowknife office was sending down a Geiger counter. The Geiger counter was supposed to help us evaluate the waste dump in the East Yard.

We received notice that the Yellowknife office was sending down a Geiger counter. The device was supposed to help us evaluate the waste dump in the East Yard.

- **Trace the relation among key words in your paragraph.** In drafting, some writers go so far as to underline every subject in a paragraph and then to ask, "How do these subjects lead from one to another?" Notice in the following paragraph how the underlined key words, including several subjects, form a meaningful progression:

   <u>Funeral homes</u> in North America have endured a decade of criticism since the early 1980s. <u>Their elaborate decoration of death</u>, some say, is grotesque and unethical. Critics point to <u>smooth-talking morticians</u> who present their sales pitch (often involving thousands of dollars) just at the time when bereaved relatives are least able to make wise financial choices.

- **Examine each paragraph to make sure it treats one central idea, not two or three.** After announcing a central point, a paragraph may go on to examine two or three aspects of that idea. However, no paragraph should include two distinct ideas. Rather, you should devote a separate paragraph to each idea.

Determining Paragraph Length

Too many business writers create paragraphs by looking at the number of lines on the page and saying, "Well, that should be long enough." A paragraph is not a measurement of length; paragraphs can be as short as two or three sentences or, under some conditions, longer than a page.

SELF-CHECK

- Name two characteristics of effective paragraphs.
- Discuss the number of ideas that should be in a paragraph.
- Explain how transition words work within paragraphs as well as between paragraphs.

5.4 Revising and Proofreading Business Messages

Although the terms are sometimes used interchangeably, revising and proofreading are not the same. Both require you to read closely and carefully, but they focus on different aspects of writing and they use different techniques.

Revision is what you do after you finish your first draft. At this stage, you'll check and tweak your content. For example, you'll reread to see if your document is well organized, that the transitions between paragraphs are smooth, and that your logic is sound. This typically requires some adding, deleting, or reorganizing so your document makes sense and is easy to follow.

In the proofreading stage, you'll read for and correct mechanical errors such as spelling, grammar, and punctuation (all those things you didn't worry about when you wrote your first draft). See Appendix B for further reference.

5.4.1 Revising Your Work: Checking Out the Big Picture

According to most professional writers, it's much more fun (though still challenging) to revise than it is to write the first draft. The rough diamond lies before you, ready to sparkle as you cut, trim, and polish.

Now is the time to take a look at your document's content and organization—the big picture, so to speak. Is your argument complete? Are all of your claims consistent? Have you supported your claims with details and evidence? Is all of the information in your paper relevant to your overall writing goal?

As tempting as it may be to make the inevitable spelling corrections during the revision stage, keep the two processes separate. If you're worrying about spelling and commas, you're not focusing on the more important development and connection of ideas that will make your writing clear and convincing.

Like your personal approach to writing the first draft, the actual steps you take to revise your work may differ in order or substance from the following steps. However, if you have no systematic method for revision, you may want to practise these steps until they become a habit.

Step 1. Check for logical connections. In the heat of argument, written or spoken, it's easy to make logical errors. Here's your chance to catch these errors before they make it into your final document. In particular, three logical errors often surface in business communication:

- **Either/or thinking:** "Either this company buys new equipment, or it faces a long and inevitable decline." (Are there really no other solutions? Should you confine your argument to a black/white, either/or presentation?)
- **Circular reasoning:** "The sales manager's poor social skills prevented him from working successfully with people." (Think about the logical circle here: the second half of the sentence repeats the meaning of the first half.)

○ **False cause:** "Johnson joined this company in 1998, and we've had nothing but problems since then." (It may be true that Johnson joined the company in 1998; and it may even be true that there have been nothing but problems since then. Does it necessarily follow that Johnson caused the problems? Of course not.)

Step 2. Check for appropriate transitions. Readers or listeners should not feel a mental lurch as you move from one sentence or paragraph to the next. When your thoughts take a significant step forward, provide a bridge by using transitional words and phrases. Notice how an appropriate transition ties these two sentences together:

Video rentals increased 80% last year. Revenues at movie theatres dropped by 15%.

Video rentals increased 80% last year. At the same time, revenues at movie theatres dropped by 15%.

Here are some transitional words that you may wish to use tie your thoughts together. (Note: Avoid using "or" or "and" to start sentences. All other words in the list may be used in almost any position where they sound alright to you.)

but, or, and still	in short	inevitably	as well
yet	because	in sum	consequently
however	although	in brief	gradually
furthermore	first, second	increasingly	thus
therefore	hence	by contrast	more and more
similarly	nevertheless	of course	for example
in addition	for instance	probably	in effect

Transitional words serve as traffic signs to your reader or listener, providing early warning of the direction in which your thought is heading. Like traffic signs on a highway, however, too many of these words can create more confusion than they resolve. Read aloud your transition words, listening to both the rhythm of your sentences and the flow of ideas. Be on the lookout for too many and too few transitions.

Step 3. Eliminate unnecessary words. As you read your rough draft, you will find words that contribute little or nothing to your message. Cut them out. Watch, in particular, for these common forms of unnecessary words:

○ **Repetitious language:** "We trusted the <u>unfounded</u> misrepresentations." (Notice that the underlined word repeats the meaning of a following word.)

○ **Meaningless language:** "<u>It was</u> the manager <u>who</u> decided which plan to accept."

Wandering language: "My uncle's company (<u>founded in 1937 by my uncle together with Al Bennett, an insurance salesman</u>) earned $.98 per share last quarter." (Note that the underlined words draw us away from the central point.)

Step 4. Test your words for power and propriety. Some words may be too weak to use. The word "nice" for example, pales in comparison to more descriptive words:

"The corporate headquarters were nice" versus *"The corporate headquarters were luxurious."*

When reviewing your choice of words, consider both the denotative meaning (dictionary meaning) and connotative meaning (emotional shading) of the language you use. Would you, for example, want to refer to the unmarried female president of your firm as a "spinster"? That word, no matter what its narrow dictionary definition, has very strong negative connotations. Exercise similar care in the words you choose.

Step 5. Make stylistic improvements. Have you used an appropriate voice? Have you varied the length of your sentences? The first part of this chapter covered these types of business style elements. When you understand each of the stylistic suggestions in that section, you may find the following checklist a useful summary:

☐ Use active verb patterns	☐ Avoid very fancy or formal style
☐ Vary sentence types	☐ Avoid unacceptable contractions
☐ Emphasize important words and abbreviations through placement	☐ Use parentheses correctly
☐ Be specific	☐ Avoid unnecessary questions
☐ Eliminate wordiness	☐ Choose words carefully
☐ Avoid awkward constructions and repetitions	☐ Choose pronouns carefully
☐ Control paragraph length	
☐ Avoid jargon and slang expressions	

By applying these five steps in your own way, you can create a polished document out of the roughest of first drafts. At times, you may have to cut out long strings of words that have no place in the final draft. At other times, you may have to be willing to give up a particularly interesting phrase or idea for the sake of general logic and clarity. Such revisions will reward you and your readers with a clear and stylish piece of writing.

5.4.2 Proofreading: The Little Things That Mean a Lot

Proofreading is the stage when you can finally focus on errors in spelling, grammar, and punctuation. You should proofread only after you have finished all of your other editing revisions.

Producing a clean, error-free final draft isn't easy. Even the most carefully edited professional publications contain occasional typos. Most readers understand this and aren't bothered by such infrequent problems. Yet when errors occur often, they undermine the writer's authority, distract the reader, and disrupt communication.

FOR EXAMPLE

Earning High Marks

Each month, the teachers at a local grade school submit short articles or classroom updates for the school's monthly newsletter. The teachers have great information for the parents to read—programs, achievements, field trips—but they have little time for the actual writing part. Even when they can find time to proofread what they've written, there's usually some activity going on around them. Inevitably, mistakes make their way into the publication. Once the principal scheduled a period each month for one teacher to proofread the entire newsletter, the mistakes began to disappear.

Most people spend only a few minutes on proofreading, hoping to catch any glaring errors that jump out from the page. But a quick reread, especially after you've been working for hours or days on a document, usually misses a lot. You're much better off working with a system that helps you to search for specific errors.

The following is a checklist of grammatical and mechanical categories.

☐ Spelling	☐ Semicolons
☐ Sentence structure	☐ Colons
☐ Fragments, run-ons	☐ Apostrophes
☐ Comma splices	☐ Quotation marks
☐ Dangling sentence parts	☐ Italics
☐ Subject–verb agreement	☐ Dashes
☐ Correct parts of verbs	☐ Parentheses
☐ Pronoun agreement	☐ Hyphens
☐ Pronoun form	☐ Capitalization
☐ Commas	

5.4.3 Proofreading Strategies

One of the best ways to catch the most errors in the least amount of time is to develop a focused and systematic proofreading process, and then stick with it. You may already use some of the proofreading strategies listed below. Experiment with different strategies and develop a system that works for you.

Remember, don't make proofreading corrections at the sentence and word level if you still need to work on the focus, organization, and development of the whole document, of sections, or of paragraphs (in other words, finish your revision stage first).

- **Set your text aside for awhile (20 minutes, or a day, or a week).** It's hard to edit or proofread a paper that you've just finished writing—it's still too familiar, and you tend to skip over a lot of errors.
- **Decide what medium lets you proofread most carefully.** Some people like to work right at the computer, while others prefer a printed copy that they can mark up as they read.
- **Find a place where you can concentrate and avoid distractions.** Don't try to proofread in front of the TV or while you're juggling other tasks.
- **Don't depend too much on spelling and grammar checkers.** Although they can be useful, they are far from foolproof. Most spelling checkers just check to see if your word is included in their dictionary, not whether you used the right word in the right place.
- **Read out loud.** Read every word and read slowly. This is especially helpful for spotting run-on sentences, but you'll also hear other problems that you may not catch when reading silently.
- **Read one sentence at a time.** This is another technique to help you to read every sentence carefully. Use a ruler or a piece of paper to isolate the line you're working on. This technique also keeps you from skipping ahead of possible mistakes.
- **Read backwards.** Start with the last word on the last page and work your way back to the beginning, reading each word separately. You'll be able to focus on the spelling of each word because content, punctuation, and grammar won't make any sense.
- **Check names and figures.** No one appreciates having their name misspelled, and incorrect figures can cause a great deal of trouble.
- **Look it up.** You'll definitely find things that don't seem quite right. A word looks like it might be misspelled, you're not sure about a comma, you can't remember if you should use "that" instead of "which." If you're not sure about something, look it up.
- **Choose the word you mean** rather than its look-alike or sound-alike double. Some examples include site/cite, lead/led, lose/loose, bear/bare, principle/principal.
- **Get another set of eyes.** Give the paper to a friend. Someone who is reading the document for the first time comes to it with completely fresh eyes.

The Look That Counts

Like it or not, the way a document looks affects the way others judge it. When you've worked hard to develop your ideas and present them for others to see, you don't want problems with the look of your document to distract your reader from your content and what you have to say. In fact, you want the visual impact of your document to entice your reader. Take some time to consider your margins, font choice, font size, and other visual elements such as bullets, headlines, and graphs as you prepare your final document. It's worth paying attention to the details that help you make a good impression.

SELF-CHECK

- List the five steps of the revision process.
- Identify three types of logical errors that are common problems in writing.
- List five proofreading strategies.
- Explain the benefit of reading one sentence at a time while proofreading.

SUMMARY

The process of writing, revising, and proofreading takes time and patience, but the resulting carefully crafted business documents are well worth the effort. Choosing the proper words and voice for a message is the first task when sitting down to write. Using guidelines for structure, length, and style, writers form these words into effective sentences. Cohesiveness is key, both in terms of sentences within a paragraph and between paragraphs. A careful examination of a document's content and organization followed by a systematic proofreading strategy ensures a well-written and effective business message.

KEY TERMS

Acronym	A word formed from the initial letters of other words (NATO—North Atlantic Treaty Organization)
Business voice	Communication that is direct, controlled, and reasonable; personal but not self-centred.

Cliché	Worn-out expressions that have little, if any, meaning.
Emotional voice	Communication with a tone that is aroused or agitated in feeling or sensibility.
Encyclopedia voice	Communication whose tone is stiff and unemotional.
Jargon	A special terminology—usually technical—that only those closely associated with the job or subject really understand.
Slang	Local street language often only familiar to a particular group; can offend as well as confuse readers.

ASSESS YOUR UNDERSTANDING

Go to www.wiley.com/canada/brounstein to evaluate your knowledge of the basics of writing and revising. Measure your learning by comparing pre-test and post-test results.

Quick Questions

1. The encyclopedia voice is considered by most to be the most professional. True or false?

2. Words such as *very* and *really* do little to strengthen a message. True or false?

3. Which of the following phrases is written in a specific way?

   (a) The meeting will begin after lunch.

   (b) Reports should be brief and to the point.

   (c) Personal items are no longer allowed in cubicles.

   (d) Submissions are due by 5 p.m. today.

4. For maximum effectiveness, all sentences should begin with the subject. True or false?

5. Which of the following was written with an active verb pattern?

   (a) The meeting was cancelled by the client.

   (b) The professor extended her office hours.

6. The best sentences are the longest. True or false?

7. "Consequently," "therefore," and "however" are examples of transitional words. True or false?

8. It is poor form to start a sentence with the same word that ended the previous sentence. True or false?

9. A paragraph should be at least two sentences but not more than 10 sentences long. True or false?

10. Revision and proofreading are best completed simultaneously. True or false?

11. The best time to worry about details such as spelling and grammar is during the revision stage. True or false?

12. Which of the following logical errors find their way into business messages?

    (a) false cause

    (b) circular reasoning

    (c) either/or thinking

    (d) all of the above

Give It Some Thought

1. How can writers avoid using sexist language?

2. Rephrasing a sentence that contains a vague pronoun is one way to clarify its meaning. But how can writers avoid vague pronouns without rephrasing?

3. What is the benefit of using positive words instead of negative words? For example, *discussion* versus *argument*.

4. How do readers respond to active verb patterns?

5. In passive construction, where does the object appear in the sentence? What is the preferred construction?

6. What are two "disguises" for wordiness?

7. List some transitional words that can be used to signal a contrasting idea.

8. How many ideas should a paragraph address?

    (a) one idea

    (b) two ideas

    (c) three ideas

    (d) as many as necessary

9. Why is it important to separate the revision process from the proofreading process?

10. What are three forms of necessary words to look for when focusing on wordiness?

Applying This Chapter

1. Take a look at the following email. Is it written in the encyclopedia or the emotional voice? Rewrite the email using the business voice.

    Hey Joe,

    You've been my boss for the past two years and things were good for the first year or so but I have to tell you, you're starting to really tick me off. The projects you've been pushing onto me show me that you don't like me. Obviously you don't think I'm any good at what I do. I want a chance to work on bigger projects. Anyways, we should talk about it. Give me a call.

2. Substitute positive words for negative ones in the following sentences:
   (a) I absolutely deny any involvement with union activists.
   (b) She refused to work overtime, claiming that she wanted to spend the weekend with her family.
   (c) Don't make the mistake of coming to work without the proper attire again, please.

3. Transform the following passive sentences into the active voice:
   (a) It was decided by the project manager that the deadline would be moved up a month.
   (b) The job was performed well by them.
   (c) The library was staffed by only two librarians this weekend.

4. The following sentences lack the appropriate transitions. Rewrite the passage, providing transitional words to tie the sentences together.

   Your company's product—Dreamboat Cupcakes—has fierce competition.
   You don't mind a fair fight for market dominance.
   You do despise the lying advertisements that appeared on television last week: "Kids everywhere are switching to Spongy Cakes because Dreamboat Cupcakes contain no real dairy products."
   You'll meet with your advertising department to issue a counterattack.
   You'll meet with stockholders to reassure them that the Spongy Cake ads are false.

5. Rewrite the following vague sentences, providing specific information:
   (a) He was tall for his age.
   (b) The company took a big loss last year.
   (c) Kumar quit because he needed more money.
   Find and correct a similar example from your own writing.

6. Proofread and correct the following paragraph, indicating reasons for corrections.

   You may have already noticed over the past decade a dramatic and amazing increase in the numbers of words your expected to process each day (by reading and writing and hearing, and etc.). Faster word-processors allow us to produce words faster and more quickly. High speed Copiers make it possible for those words to be reproduced for the entire office and beyond. Email and internet connections can be used to distribute messages across countrys and continents. Massive data storage in a very small hard-disk drive in our desk top or note book computers computers allows us to shelve words for future use.

THE NEXT STEP

Finding Your Voice

Write a paragraph about your greatest personal or professional achievement. Use a business voice and active verbs to tell your story.

The Whole Picture

Look online to find the website of a major department store, "big box" electronics store, or furniture retailer. Are there any items that you would hesitate to buy because they are not described in great enough detail? What information would you include?

Back to the Editing Room

How would a reader respond to the following short letter? Revise it and compare your results with others in the class.

Dear Sir/Madam,

For some time, as you may be aware, we have been in your neighbourhood in the cookie business in New York. And now we are seeking expansion financing, you see we need a new production oven which will cost more than we are able to raise from our own invested funds and therefore are turning to the excellent reputation of your bank for helping small businesses such as us in these matters. I will phone to arrange an appointment. Thank you.

Sincerely,

Second Impressions

Find a letter or other piece of mail that you've already read and thought was fine. Now, using the proofreading techniques covered in this chapter, reread the document, marking any corrections that you'd make if you were writing it. If you found any mistakes, did your impression of the document or its writer change?

6

MANAGING MEMOS AND EMAIL
Making the Most of Your Messages

STARTING POINT

Go to www.wiley.com/canada/brounstein to assess your knowledge of the basics of memos and email. After reviewing the website, you'll be able to determine where you need to concentrate your effort.

What You'll Learn in This Chapter:

- the importance of memos in business communications
- common types of business memos
- the advantages of using email
- situations in which email is not effective
- guidelines for writing successful emails.

After Studying This Chapter, You'll be Able to:

- discuss principles of persuasive and skillful memos
- identify four categories of memos
- identify situations in which email is a useful method of communication
- describe conditions that are not suited to email
- discuss ways of ensuring that email messages are effective.

INTRODUCTION

Despite their obvious importance in communicating countless pieces of information, memos and email messages are too often inferior and ineffective. Using the right techniques, however, business writers can deliver memos and email messages that are clear, correct, and persuasive. This chapter examines guidelines for effective memos and lists common mistakes to avoid. Four types of memos are discussed. The chapter also addresses the benefits of using email and examines the situations in which email is inappropriate. The chapter concludes with techniques for writing successful emails.

6.1 Writing Effective Memos

Second only to phone calls, memos—whether sent as hard-copy or email transmissions—are the primary means of in-house communication in business. Memos deliver questions, comments, replies, announcements, policy statements, directions, reminders, and a host of other routine but vital communications.

Unfortunately, those who would not think of sending a letter containing a typo may dash off memos marred by garbled language, half-formed sentences, and shoddy spelling and grammar.

Good business writers will keep in mind that every word matters in a memo as much as it does in letters, reports, and proposals. Every word you write helps create your business identity. If your writing is abrupt, sloppy, inaccurate, or long-winded, your associates can't help but question your professional abilities. On the other hand, your conscientious effort to write persuasive and skillful memos, letters, proposals, and reports reflects positively on your capabilities.

The following principles may guide you in writing in-house correspondence:

- **Exercise judgement.** When you need to write memos about your personal opinions or sensitive matters, use discretion and tact. One guide to help you decide whether your memo is tactful enough is the "next-week rule." Evaluate every memo, letter, report, and proposal you write against this wise criterion: will I want to see these words above my signature next week—after the feelings (of anger, excitement, etc.) have passed?

> **FOR EXAMPLE**
>
> **Using the Next-Week Rules**
> Stacy, a new programmer, stretches her lunch hour each day. Her supervisor has mentioned the problem to her, without result. Although Max's initial reaction was to write a direct, no-nonsense memo to Stacy, with a copy in her personnel file, he first took a few moments to calm down. Instead, Max decided to send a general reminder to all staff in Stacy's group regarding lunch hour regulations. On Stacy's copy, he handwrote, "Please see me if there are circumstances I should know about."

- **Use positive language to get positive results.** The meaning of your written word goes beyond the meaning you'll find in the dictionary. Words also carry feelings or connotations to your readers. Negative connotations, whether as a result of your tone or you use of language, can distort your message and cause tension between you and your reader. Notice the difference between these negative and positive statements:

Negative	Positive
You failed to notice	May I point out that
You neglected to mention	We can also consider
You overlooked the fact	One additional fact is
If you persist in	If you choose to
I see no alternative but	Our clear plan of action

- **Negative language typically points out what the reader did wrong.** Positive language shows what the reader can do right or what you and the reader can do together. Your readers are motivated and persuaded by encouragement, not by accusation and discouragement.

- **Use the proper procedures.** Individual companies develop a set of standard operating procedures for most memos. When deciding who should receive a memo, for example, use good judgement, especially when going beyond your immediate supervisor.

  ○ Take time to spell out any essential details that will help others make sense of it at a later date.

  ○ Be certain to sign your name or initials alongside your typed name on a memo. This notation shows that you have read over and approved the message. Unlike a letter, you do not sign your name at the bottom of a memo.

  ○ Decide how you'll deliver and present your memo. Consider whether memos are typically sent through company mail, hand-delivered, or sent electronically.

- **Send the whole message, but be succinct.** Memos should be brief and to the point while still delivering a complete thought. The key is to keep in mind how much detail your reader needs. When a writer focuses too narrowly on one aspect of the total message, the writer's message can go astray. Alternately, when he gives too much background information leading up to his point, the real message gets lost in the shuffle.

- **Proofread and revise your memo before you send it out.** A memo may seem like a more relaxed form of communication, but you still need to make sure you present yourself as a good business communicator. The word memo comes from *memorandum*, which is Latin for "thing to be remembered." Your memo will be put in a file and may become part of your company's official records, so make sure you present yourself as capably as you can.

The following four levels can help you think about your whole message while writing a memo:

- What has happened?
- What is happening?
- What will happen?
- How do I feel about it?

Whole communication leaves no room for misinterpretation or for the reader to postpone taking action on something because of confusion about your message.

6.1.1 Avoiding Common Mistakes

It's not unusual for business writers to ruin memos through casual, thoughtless mistakes. These errors fall into four categories; with some attention, each can be avoided:

1. **The telegram writer:** Some writers leave out major portions of sentences—sometimes even the subject itself. Their effort to save time only complicates and confuses the message, which slows the reader's ability to understand and respond to the memo.
2. **The scrawler:** Don't be so relaxed about the casual format of memos that you make mistakes in spelling, grammar, and style. Handwritten memos and glaring little mistakes indicate big mistakes in a writer's judgement.
3. **The long-winded writer:** Just as the word *memo* is short for *memorandum,* the messages in memos should be brief and to the point. Don't bore your readers before they get to *your* point.
4. **The tease:** Some memo writers consciously or unconsciously irritate their readers by hinting at information that they should just go ahead and tell. Avoid trying to build a sense of suspense at the expense of your message; a business memo shouldn't be a mystery story. First, let the message be clear. Then you can add social or personal remarks to add warmth.

SELF-CHECK

- Identify four principles for writing persuasive and skillful memos.
- Explain the benefit of using positive words when writing memos.
- Discuss four errors commonly found in memos.

6.2 Common Types of Business Memos

Business writers are likely to write memos that fall into four different categories. Notice that each of these sample memos begins with the main idea—what the writer wants the readers to know. With straightforward, direct memos, you should not waste your readers' time with introductory comments or personal pleasantries. Be a writer of efficient memos and remember the old saying that "time is money."

6.2.1 Policy Memo

This type of memo is usually sent to a wide distribution list within a company to announce or clarify company policy. The memo typically starts off with a background statement, then the policy statement, and, if necessary, a directive.

To:	*All Managers*
From:	*Sara Morgan, Vice President, Personnel*
Date:	*July 7, 2010*
Subject:	*Statements to the press*

The Globe and Mail *and other publications have recently reported takeover and/ or merger rumours with regard to our company.*

It is company policy (No. 207.I) that "no employee shall make statements to press representatives regarding company products, personnel, planning, or other proprietary concerns without written authorization."

Please review this policy with each member of your group within the next 48 hours to ensure that misstatements and misinformation do not adversely affect the company's efforts to resist hostile acquisition.

6.2.2 Notice of Change Memo

This memo describes a change in method, personnel, procedure, location, or other matter. It usually begins with a background statement, then the description of the change, and finally an interpretation, if any, for those affected by the change. The notice-of-change memo often serves to set the record straight in the face of rumours.

To:	*[distribution list]*
From:	*Dennis MacKay, Head of Engineering*
Date:	*July 7, 2010*
Subject:	*New Testing Schedule for F180 Project*

New Department of National Defence guidelines regarding the structural testing of tail components for the Air Force CF180 project require that Air Force representatives be present for field testing.

We have therefore postponed tests A24 and A25 until September 8, when Air Force Captain Vaughn Owens will visit our facility to oversee testing. All other arrangements remain unchanged.

We do not anticipate that this change in schedule will affect the ultimate delivery date of the F180 prototype on December 1.

FOR EXAMPLE

Notice of Change

Jaspreet was the office manager of a law firm about to change from one health insurance company to another. The move was being made for financial reasons; costs had risen dramatically with the original company. Jaspreet drafted a notice-of-change memo to announce the switch. Although a representative from the new company was coming in a few weeks to give a short presentation on their coverage plan and benefits, Jaspreet knew that this change would cause a great deal of anxiety for the employees. To help ease concerns, Jaspreet attached an overview of the new policy, with a comparison of both costs and benefits.

6.2.3 Update Memo

This memo tries to inform readers about developments, projects, and processes. The memo usually begins with an "at-last-report" statement, followed by the update statement, and concludes (optionally) with a forecast or future-report statement.

To:	*[distribution list]*
From:	*Peyton Janssen, Director of Advertising*
Date:	July 7, 2010
Subject:	*Update on Marketing Campaign for Vancouver Hilton*

In June, I reported to you that we had won a one-year contract to provide promotional services for the new Vancouver Hilton.

Since then, our creative teams have been hard at work on a promotional package to meet and exceed our client's goals. The package will be demonstrated in a gala dress rehearsal at the corporate theatre on July 21 at 10:30 a.m. Attendance is mandatory for Level I supervisors.

Following the presentation, the audience will be asked to complete an evaluation questionnaire on the package. I'll evaluate the results and report back to you within 10 days.

6.2.4 Inquiry Memo

The inquiry memo asks a question and may give guidelines for the reader's reply. The memo typically begins with a statement that explains why the question is being asked. The question then follows, and then a final, optional guideline statement tells how the question should be answered.

To:	*Sergey Petrovic, Supervisor, Parts Department*
From:	*Cynthia Novak, Accounting*
Date:	*July 7, 2010*
Subject:	*Inventory planning*

In the past, Sergey, I know that you have closed your department down for two days each quarter so that you could use your own personnel to do inventory counts.

Do you want me to investigate professional inventory services that can handle this chore for us each quarter? Citywide Ford has apparently had good luck with this approach for the past two years.

Please let me know today, if possible, your approximate costs in salaries and lost business for the two-day inventory period. After I've received information from external inventory companies, you and I can meet to discuss which route we'll take.

SELF-CHECK

- Discuss four types of business memos.
- Describe the typical format for an inquiry memo.

6.3 Taking Advantage of Technology: Knowing When to Use Email

Although technology has provided innovative means for person-to-person communication, it is not without pitfalls, and it has created many challenges for people as they do their jobs.

Email has quickly become a standard part of communication in today's workplace. Some people literally can spend an entire workday reading and responding to email.

Like any form of communication, you need to use skill and judgement to maximize the value of email.

The actual content of an email would be no different from the content of a hard-copy memo; the only difference would be the method of delivery. Any of the memos shown in Section 6.2 could have been formatted and sent as emails if the writers had wanted their messages to be received very quickly and if they had not been concerned about having the information filed as hard-copy records.

The popularity of email is largely due to its speed and ease of use. It is much easier to use than writing a letter and putting it in the regular mail. As a result, email can be a tool for many useful communication purposes, such as the following:

- **Sending inter-office memos:** Today, you can send memos giving news and announcements about business, personnel, and policy matters via email. Type the message and click the Send button, and you can reach as many people in the organization as you want, at one time—a much more efficient process for distributing the news than the old inter-office memo method.

- **Making requests:** Email works well for making requests. Perhaps you need assistance on a project or you want to set up a meeting. People often respond quickly to these kinds of requests.

- **Making inquiries:** Sometimes, the quickest and easiest way to find an answer to a question is to ask in an email. If the inquiry isn't overly involved and doesn't require a great deal of explanation, email is a handy communications vehicle for getting an answer.

- **Keeping in touch:** Although letters and cards make for a nice personal touch, email enables you to drop quick notes to clients, staff in other departments, and other business associates. A simple here's-what's-been-happening, how-are-you-doing communication lets business people you may not see often know that you care about how they're doing.

- **Conducting routine business transactions:** Some business relationships, such as customer–vendor ones, run under established processes. In such cases, email helps transactions run efficiently. For example, you (the customer) need some parts from your vendor. The vendor tells you the price and when he can ship them, you confirm, and you're done. When transactions and negotiations require little discussion, email helps you exchange information and get the deal done.

- **Providing status and news:** Many kinds of updates that keep fellow staff informed can usually be handled via email. For example, a manager who has salespeople in different locations can use email to find out the status of their work. If you want to keep your boss in the loop on your latest project or on what happened with that important customer issue you tackled today, email is a great option for passing on the news and highlights.

> ## FOR EXAMPLE
>
> ### Discussions and Deadlines
>
> Among other things, the managing editor of a monthly technology newsletter is in charge of seeing to it that his stable of freelance writers meets their deadlines for each issue. Calling each one to check on their progress was taking too much time away from his other work. One month, he tried a different approach and sent a quick email to each writer: "Hi. Just checking on your article for the next issue. When can I expect it? Thanks!" Although two of the twelve writers didn't respond to the email, the editor has still saved himself ten conversations.

- **Recapping agreements and discussions:** One of the best uses of email is to reinforce verbal interactions, especially when decisions or agreements are made or when action items are established. Instead of leaving what you worked out in a meeting to your memory, you can recap these important points in an email to team members. When minutes of meetings need to be recorded, email also works well.

- **Seeking ideas:** Email can be useful for generating ideas. Maybe you're working on an assignment or planning an event for which you need assistance in brainstorming ideas. Using email to solicit this input enables you to save time by skipping meetings and in-depth discussion.

- **Giving simple feedback on others' work: Simple feedback** means that the comments you write aren't long, aren't controversial, and have been requested. People often want your feedback or thoughts on their plans, proposals, or other work. If that feedback doesn't require a great deal of explanation, email can be a quick and easy way to pass along your comments.

Email can be an effective vehicle for sending and receiving various forms of news and information when live interaction isn't really needed.

SELF-CHECK

- Explain the popularity of email as a business communication tool.
- Describe nine useful purposes for using email.
- Define simple feedback.

6.4 Recognizing When Not to Use Email

Many of the problems connected with email communication result from people using email when they should be talking—and listening. Remember that email is one-way communication and isn't usually "live." You have less opportunity to be understood clearly with written messages than with live conversation because you can't use your tone of voice and body language to convey sincerity. Relying on email in situations where engaging in live conversation would be more appropriate tends to increase the tug-of-war in working relationships.

To keep working relationships on a constructive level and to enhance productivity, here are some situations in which you should not use email.

6.4.1 When You Need to Give Constructive Feedback on Performance

There are two types of constructive feedback: positive feedback for good performance and negative feedback for performance that needs improvement. Although positive feedback given in an email message may be well received, it still has less impact and seems less sincere than feedback given in person.

The recipient of negative feedback often interprets that feedback as far worse than was ever intended, and may stew about what was written. When the feedback is given via email, the giver can't help the other person understand his or her message, and the receiver doesn't have the opportunity to discuss the matter and work out solutions. The nature of giving constructive feedback—positive and negative—is verbal and informal. It works best when it's part of a two-way conversation.

6.4.2 After Your Previous Email Messages Get Little or No Response

You may encounter situations in which your inquiries made by email get no response, or your questions are met with partial answers. The reasons for this lack of response vary: disinterest in your issue, too many emails to pay attention to yours, poor follow-through skills. Just because you think that you write the message clearly doesn't guarantee that the receiver reads and acts on it.

Continuing to send follow-up email messages after a couple of tries may turn you into an irritating pest and gives those who want to ignore your messages even more reason to do so. Instead, talk to the person, either by phone or in person, to find out what has happened and determine when you can get an answer.

6.4.3 When You Address Sensitive Issues

Suppose you have a co-worker who wants to act on an idea that you know from experience will lead to problems, or you have a reservation about your boss's proposal for a business change. In these kinds of circumstances, attempting to share your feedback, thoughts, or feelings via email often exacerbates an already touchy situation.

With email, you don't have a chance to listen to what the other person is thinking. When you choose one-way communication to communicate about sensitive matters, you increase the risk of misunderstanding and tension, which is the opposite of what you're trying to achieve.

6.4.4 When You Want to Elicit Support and Understanding for Important Changes and Initiatives

Organizations are going through so much change that, in many companies, change is the only constant you can count on. Written communications can help reinforce announcements and updates about changes or new initiatives, but as the sole communications for these matters, email messages can create anxiety.

Only live and ongoing face-to-face communication about significant changes helps get people on board. The chance to explain the company's rationale, answer employees' questions, seek input and involvement, and address concerns is lost when this kind of communication is handled by email. Rumour and innuendo—key ingredients in resistance to change—often fill the voids that are created.

6.4.5 When You Need to Resolve Concerns and Conflicts

Want to aggravate a conflict? Attempt to address it in an email message. Trying to resolve conflict via email is one of the major abuses of email communications.

- **Flaming email** is a direct result of this abuse. A flaming email is an attempt by one party to voice a concern to another party through an email message that's harsh in language and tone. What often results is that the other party, hurt by the email, shoots one back through email.
- One flaming email can set off a **flame war** where the warring parties send negative email messages back and forth—sometimes copying others on them as well.

The only tried-and-true method for resolving concerns and conflicts is live, person-to-person interaction—face-to-face or by telephone when you and the other person are in different locations. Technology can't do it for you.

If you find yourself getting worked up or rewriting much of what you want to say when you're drafting an email, you shouldn't send that message. If you have an important issue or problem that involves a high degree of emotion, go directly to the source to talk and listen—that's the assertive approach introduced in Section 2.1.4.

Copying Others Not Involved with the Issue

People sometimes copy others in conflict situations, which can stir up negative energy around the office. Upper-level managers often receive too many email messages as it is, and they don't need more messages about matters in which their involvement isn't really needed. In addition, the other party in your discussion becomes aggravated by the move to notify others who aren't involved in the matter—sometimes this is also viewed as a violation of confidentiality. And when other people are copied on the news, they may get involved and make the situation worse. If you see the need to copy others on an email message that contains potentially sensitive information, make sure the other party or parties you dealt with on the issue agree that the need exists. Very simply, you should avoid other people's time and attention with unnecessary email.

FOR EXAMPLE

A Time for Face Time
Mark works from home as a technical consultant for a telephone company. Like most other off-site employees in the business world, Mark and his supervisor rely heavily on email to stay in touch with each other. For the most part, this arrangement works well. When it doesn't, it's usually because they have some issue to discuss—a problem, a difficult assignment, an error or misunderstanding. They've found that no matter how hard they try, they can never quite convey the right message in an email (in some cases, even a phone call isn't enough). In these cases, the best solution is face-to-face or telephone conversation.

SELF-CHECK

- Discuss five situations in which email is not a constructive method of communication.
- Explain the drawbacks of using email when addressing sensitive issues.
- Define flaming email and flame war.

6.5 Staying on the Right Track with Email

Use care when communicating your messages via email. Here are a few tips that will enhance rather than hinder your electronic communication:

- **Make your points directly and concisely.** Get to the point and say what you need to say as briefly as possible. Make clear use of the subject heading and your first sentence or two to communicate your central message. One popular pattern for email messages is the following:
  - Paragraph (or sentence) 1: "Here's what I want." (Main idea)
  - Paragraph (or sentence) 2: "Here's why." (Supporting information)
  - Paragraph (or sentence) 3: "Here's specifically what to do." (Close with a reminder)
- **Use your standard business voice.** In this voice (covered in Section 5.1.2), you write directly to the issue and respectively to your audience. With it, your readers are not likely to be put off by excessive emotions or formalities.
- **Go for short instead of long in your messages.** The same adage applies with emails as it does with office memos: If your email is too long, you are wasting your readers' time and your company's money. The shorter your message, the more likely people will read and comprehend it. If you find your email getting too long and you just can't edit it down, paste the information into its own document, attach the document to your email, and use your email message to briefly introduce the information in the attachment.
- **Follow accepted conventions for spelling, capitalization, grammar, and punctuation.** Early in the days of email, people tended to omit capital letters, and they allowed great latitude in spelling and punctuation. In most organizations, those days are long gone. Treat your email just as you would a printed letter.
- **Keep your language constructive.** Say—or rather, write—your messages in the best way possible. Keep the words respectful rather than harsh. Avoid anything that sounds blaming or threatening: "You didn't do what you said you would do" or "If you don't do this, I won't do that for you." Also avoid words that can trigger negative reactions, such as "always," "never," and the not-words ("don't," "won't," and "can't"). Here are a few such examples:
  - "You always forget to follow the procedure."
  - "You never help out when I request your assistance."
  - "We can't do that on such short notice."
- **Rephrase your message to be more constructive.** And in some instances, you may be better off talking to the other person rather than sending an email. The idea is to keep your language straightforward and to focus on the issue rather than the person.
- **Follow rules of capitalization.** When people use all capital letters ("caps") for some or all of an email message, others interpret it as shouting at them.

Stick to the standard practice of using caps only at the start of your sentences.

- **Write for your audience.** Just as you do when speaking or writing a traditional communication, you should understand who your audience is when sending an email. If they respond best to brief highlights, keep the message short and sweet. If they like detail, give them explanations. If they speak in technical terms, use the jargon they understand. Keeping your audience in mind helps you keep your messages clear, concise, and respectful.
- **Think cross-culturally.** The Internet has made international communication more accessible than ever. As discussed in Section 1.4.4, however, you'll need to consider the cultural differences between you and your email recipient before firing off your message.
- **Read your email message over at least twice before sending it.** Unlike traditional memos that can be fished out of the boss's mailbox, email messages are irretrievably on their way to their reader once you click the Send button. When you have a message you've written in the heat of the moment, you should let it sit for one hour, and then read it again. You may save yourself embarrassment (or worse).
- **Watch the humour.** Having a sense of humour is a great attribute, but displaying it is much harder to do in writing than it is in person-to-person interactions. If you can add an occasional lighthearted touch to your email messages, great. But the key is to focus on the content rather than the delivery.
- **Avoid off-colour jokes and ridicule.** These are offensive to readers of your email.

E-Etiquette: Attachments and Replies

No one has time for unnecessary emails or attachments that can't be opened. Increase the professionalism and efficiency of your email messages by following some common sense guidelines for attachments and replies:

- Avoid sending unnecessary attachments.
- Send attachments only when you need to include a long document or a file in another format (a spreadsheet, for example). Most people prefer to receive the information within the message of an email. Doing so eliminates the possibility that your recipient is unable to open the attachment.
- When replying to a message, include the prior email in your reply. Most email software automatically does this, a feature that allows the recipients to refer back to previous messages when necessary.
- Reserve the "Reply All" option for those cases in which you need your message to be seen by each person who received the original message.

SELF-CHECK

- Identify a popular pattern for constructing concise business emails.
- List seven ways of improving emails.
- Explain the benefit of rereading an email before sending it.

SUMMARY

Whether they are used in the wrong situations, are not taken seriously, or are simply rushed, memos and email messages often end up being inferior and ineffective. Memos, when written according to guidelines, are a primary way of communicating routine in-house messages. Avoiding common mistakes improves the success of the four common types of memos. Email is another beneficial means of communication, both internal and external. Certain situations are not suited to email. Writers can use techniques to write effective email messages.

KEY TERMS

Flaming email	An attempt by one party to voice a concern to another party through an email message that's harsh in language and tone.
Flaming war	Parties involved in a chain of flaming emails. Parties send negative email messages back and forth; messages are sometimes copied to others.
Simple feedback	Comments are brief, not controversial; comments have been requested by another party.

ASSESS YOUR UNDERSTANDING

Go to www.wiley.com/canada/brounstein to evaluate your knowledge of the basics of memos and email. Measure your learning by comparing pre-test and post-test results.

Quick Questions

1. Because memos are a somewhat informal means of in-house communication, they are not held to the same standards as other forms of business writing. True or false?

2. Which of the following principles should be used when writing memos?

    (a) Use judgement when writing memos about sensitive matters.

    (b) Follow standard operating procedures for memos.

    (c) Include the entire message.

    (d) all of the above

3. Negative language

    (a) emphasizes a message

    (b) causes tension

    (c) motivates readers

    (d) clarifies a message

4. A policy memo is typically widely distributed; it serves to announce or clarify a company policy. True or false?

5. Like a survey, an inquiry memo is used to gather information from a wide range of recipients. True or false?

6. Email messages and memos are not used together in business communications. True or false?

7. Which of the following purposes can be served by email messages?

    (a) providing simple feedback

    (b) recapping agreements and meetings

    (c) conducting routine business transactions

    (d) all of the above

8. Email messages work best when used in situations that do not require live interaction. True or false?

9. When is email not an appropriate method of communication?

    (a) when giving negative feedback

    (b) when resolving a conflict

    (c) when addressing a sensitive issue

    (d) all of the above

10. A flaming email is used to quickly distribute information to a wide audience. True or false?

11. Writing quality is as important in an email as in a formal report. True or false?

12. Email messages should be
   (a) written in a business voice
   (b) concise
   (c) written with constructive language
   (d) all of the above
13. Humour is always a good way to leave a personal mark in an email message. True or false?

Give It Some Thought

1. What is the "next-week rule," and how can you use it when writing memos?
2. Which of the following is the positive translation of "you neglected to mention"?
   (a) may I point out that
   (b) you failed to notice
   (c) we can also consider
   (d) we should seek alternatives
3. The best memos build a sense of suspense for readers. True or false?
4. Which type of memo would best serve a supervisor's need to share with employees developments of an ongoing project?
5. What is the structure of a notice-of-change memo?
   (a) background statement, description of the change, interpretation for those affected by change
   (b) description of the change, interpretation for those affected by change, background information
   (c) background statement, explanation of the policy, directive for those affected by the change
   (d) description of the change, background statement, forecast for future developments
6. How can email be used for routine business transactions?
7. When is email an effective way to provide feedback?
   (a) when it involves too many points to discuss in a face-to-face meeting
   (b) when it is not controversial in nature
   (c) when it addresses sensitive issues
   (d) when it involves a lengthy explanation
8. How should you handle a situation in which your email gets no response?
9. Define flaming war.

10. Email messages are most effective when they are a page or less in length. What is one way of handling an email that is running too long?

11. Describe a situation when it would be inappropriate to copy someone on an email.

Applying This Chapter

1. Think about an incident from your past that involved business conflict. It may be from a job, or from a retail experience. Experiment with the effects of negativity in writing: First, write an obviously angry first draft of a memo; second, revise the draft so that it still communicates your outrage but does not alienate or insult the reader. Exchange your first and second drafts with another student to review the differences.

2. You have decided to go to college to get some new skills to start a new career in an area you've always been interested in. Do some online research about the types of programs offered by your local colleges, then draft an email to a student recruitment officer requesting information about details such as application procedures or scholarship opportunities.

3. You are the customer service manager in a large car dealership. For the last few weeks, you've noticed some of the sales and support staff taking smoking breaks outside the entrance to the repair shop so customers have to squeeze past them to get in or out of the building. In a polite but firm memo to the sales and support staff, remind them of the office policies regarding smoking/coffee breaks.

4. Write an email message to your business communication instructor, updating him or her on some aspect of your school or work life. For example, you may want to update your instructor on any career developments or on a choice of academic major.

5. Your company recently expanded, so for the past few weeks you've been sharing a cubicle with a very messy and noisy individual who leaves half-empty coffee cups and used napkins all over the desk. Write an email to your immediate supervisor asking for time to speak with him about this conflict with a co-worker.

6. As the manager of the electronics department of your local All-Mart department store, you have to talk to a team member about his poor attendance and lack of participation in the weekly team meetings. You'd like to meet with him informally to work out a solution so you don't have to go to the next step of a formal reprimand. Using constructive language, draft a brief email (including the subject line) asking him to sit down with you for a chat; use the three-point pattern discussed in this chapter.

7. Get together in small groups to discuss whether the following messages should be sent as memos or emails:

   (a) instructions for using the new photocopier

   (b) a change in the company dental plan

   (c) congratulations to the sales team on an outstanding month

   (d) suggestions to the sales team on how to improve after a disappointing month

   (e) details for employees about an upcoming two-day company retreat to a provincial park.

   After you make your decisions, be prepared to discuss your reasons with the class.

8. Your only sister has decided to get married in Cuba in six weeks, and she's asked you to be in the wedding party. The only problem is that you've already used up your vacation time for this year. Write to your boss requesting special permission to make the one-week trip to be with your sister on her big day. Decide whether you should write a memo or an email, and decide what arrangements you can suggest to make up the time.

9. You're the Special Events Manager for the Montreal Tourist Bureau. Recently, the Canadian Association of Widget Promoters sent you an email inquiring about tourist attractions in the Montreal area as they are planning their upcoming biennial convention. Prepare a reply in an email with what you think are the top three attractions that will interest the widget promoters. (Do some online research first.)

10. The major project for your business writing course is due in two days. You've been working on it and making good progress, but you don't think you'll be finished in time. Prepare an email request to your teacher for an extension of two days so you can do a good job on the project. Your teacher has said that extensions can only be granted in exceptional circumstances, but you want to do the best job possible and two extra days will make a big difference.

THE NEXT STEP

Memos That Work

You are the publisher of a magazine for owners of pet reptiles like iguanas and turtles. Your magazine relies on advertising a great deal, and sales of advertising have gone down this year. You think this is due in part to the fact that you do not have a website for your magazine to bring in new readers. Write a memo to staff announcing that you're setting up a website. Brainstorm at least three advantages to a magazine having an online presence and announce these advantages in the memo. As well, you should ask your staff for suggestions. Think about the tone of the memo and how long it should be.

Group Memo

The manager of the travel agency you work for has asked you to team up with your co-workers to brainstorm ideas for new exotic vacation possibilities. The problem is that your clients can buy airline tickets online and your business is suffering. The manager feels that to survive, the agency needs to put together special adventure holidays (for example, bungee jumping in New Zealand). After a quick brainstorming session and some online research about adventure tourism, work alone or with a partner to write an email to your regular clients informing them of some of these new adventure holidays.

Constructive Communication

You are the owner of a small printing company with an unhappy customer on your hands. The menu you printed for their new restaurant has a typo in it, and you've just received their annoyed email letting you know. You've stated very clearly in your printing contracts that each customer is responsible for the quality of the text, so it would be easy enough to reply to the restaurant owner and include that portion of the agreement in your message. However, draft a constructive reply to this message instead using an alternative approach to resolving the conflict. Refer back to Chapter 3 for some useful techniques for conflict resolution.

Internet Resolution

You oversee two consultants who manage the website for your midsized import company. In the last week, at least seven customers have called to complain about technical problems with the site, particularly the ability to complete orders. You haven't experienced this problem before, but you need to resolve the situation before you begin to lose customers. Unfortunately, a face-to-face meeting is out of the question. Write an email message to the consultants.

7
WRITING POSITIVE BUSINESS LETTERS
Routine Messages That Work

STARTING POINT

Go to www.wiley.com/canada/brounstein to assess your knowledge of the basics of positive business letters. After reviewing this website, you'll be able to determine where you need to concentrate your effort.

What You'll Learn in This Chapter:

- how letters communicate information in the business world
- the parts of a standard business letter
- common letter format styles
- how positive business letters serve a customer's needs
- purpose of positive business letters
- how positive letters can resolve difficult business situations.

After Studying This Chapter, You'll be Able to:

- discuss the relationship between conversation and written words
- identify the standard and optional parts of a business-letter format
- reproduce three different letter formats
- discuss the roles of empathy and feelings in positive business letters
- understand the importance of using letters to maintain goodwill with customers.

INTRODUCTION

Your business letters are the most important written communication seen by your customers and the general public. Letters serve as important business tools and, in some cases, as legal documents. By following standards for both the elements and format of a letter, you and your communications appear professional and credible.

By showing empathy and feeling, a writer creates a critical connection with a reader. This connection carries through in those situations when a company must respond to requests, orders, and claims.

7.1 Putting Your Letters to Work

Prepare for writing a business letter by imagining yourself speaking to your reader face-to-face. Although you probably won't use all the words of an actual conversation, you can infuse the natural spirit of conversation in your written words without the "ums," "ahs," and repetitions that appear in a spoken conversation.

Although you're aiming for a conversational tone and style, your written words will be different from the actual words you use in conversation (Section 5.1 describes more on how to choose an appropriate voice and style for business writing). In general, letters are more organized than conversations and the language can be more formal depending on the subject matter.

7.1.1 Letters as Legal Documents

Business letters also differ from conversations in another way. Because business letters are written in a printed, permanent form, they can be considered legal documents. Anything you promise or even hint at promising might be considered an informal contract obliging your company to fulfill that promise.

In addition, your company can be legally obligated to make sure that it lives up to anything you state as a fact about your company's services or products. For that reason, businesses large and small now often require that letters leaving the office first be reviewed by an authorized manager.

7.1.2 Letters as a Modern Business Tool

Today, templates are available in word processing programs to help employees compose and arrange the layout of business letters. Even when a writer uses a template for a business message, however, that letter is expected to be friendlier than impersonal business letters of the past. Modern writers know the importance of motivating the reader to understand the message and to act on it. To be effective, the modern business letter must be empathetic, warm, and friendly.

Modern business letters are also expected to be more attractive and more error-free than letters used to be. Word processing, desktop publishing, high-quality printers, spell checkers, and grammar checkers have all contributed to documents that look very professional. The look of a modern letter shows the author's professionalism even before the reader sees the actual message.

FOR EXAMPLE

Legal Trouble

Helena, a real estate agent with a small realty company, was helping a couple find a vacation home in the country. The couple was planning to visit their favourite location in the next month to take another look at a possible property. The couple had asked Helena to look further into several things, in particular, the condition of the roof. Helena wrote back, "The roof is in fine shape. It was replaced in 2000 by Standard Roofing of Huntsville." Before the letter went out, Helena's boss read the letter, making one important change: "The roof is only ten years old." Her boss understood the company's potential legal problems that could result from Helena's assertion that the roof was "fine" if it then leaked disastrously.

SELF-CHECK

- Discuss ways in which a business letter is like a conversation.
- Explain the legal value of a business letter.
- Explain what information the mere appearance of a letter conveys to a reader.

7.2 Parts of a Standard Business Letter

The following are the individual parts of the standard business letter, some of which you must include and some of which are optional (you don't need them, but you might want to include them). You can find them illustrated in Figure 7-1; optional parts are marked with an asterisk.

7.2.1 Letterhead

The letterhead is the name for the text and graphics that are pre-printed at the very top of company stationery. The letterhead usually consists of the company's logo, in the company colours, with the company's address, phone and fax numbers, website address and email address. When your readers take your business letter out of the envelope, the first image to greet them is your letterhead. Take a second to flip ahead through the sample letters in this chapter to see different examples of letterheads. Ideally, a letterhead attractively displays the image your company wants to convey. Its style and information should tell your reader exactly who you are (and your necessary contact information). Knowing who you are helps your reader to decide whether to read what you have to say.

LETTERHEAD
(OR RETURN ADDRESS)

/AIA\
ACADEMY OF INDUSTRIAL ARTS
123 MAIN ST. S TORONTO, ON M9J 4C2
WWW.AIA.CA

DATE   June 23, 2010

INSIDE ADDRESS OF   Johnson & Associates Ltd.
RECIPIENT   333 Yonge St.
                              Toronto, ON M8G 6H6

ATTENTION LINE (*)   ATTN: John Loi

                              SUBJECT: 2010 Annual Industrial Arts Conference

SALUTATION   Dear Mr. Loi:

                              On behalf of the Academy of Industrial Arts, I invite you to participate as an exhibitor at our 7th
                              Annual Industrial Innovation Conference, August 6-8, 2010 at the Harbour Hotel in Halifax,
                              Nova Scotia.

BODY   The AIA's Annual Conference is the premier meeting of industrial designers, attracting nearly 300
                              participants last year, providing exhibitors an active marketplace for products and services.

                              Exhibits are located in an area to provide you with excellent access to conference participants.
                              There is time in the program each day for participants to visit the exhibits. Daily refreshment
                              breaks as well as the weekend breakfast buffets are being served in the exhibit area to encourage
                              participants to meet with you to discuss your products and services.

                              Corporate partners are an important part of the success of the Industrial Innovation Confernce.
                              Continuing the success of last year's program, we again offer the opportunity for your firm to help
                              support the conference and, most importantly, increase your exposure to the participants.
                              Partnering in a special event, sponsoring a prize draw, and presenting in the exhibit hall are all
                              great ways for your firm to get involved.   See the sponsorship information and application
                              included with this package for details.

                              As the premier meeting of industrial designers, the Annual Industrial Innovation Conference is an
                              ideal place for your company to be represented. I encourage you to return the enclosed form(s)
                              promptly so that you don't miss the opportunity to be involved in this year's meeting. I look
                              forward to hearing from you and welcoming you to the 2010 Industrial Innovation event.

COMPLIMENTARY   Sincerely,
CLOSE
SIGNATURE

                              Sriram Bhata
                              AIA President, 2010/2011

FINAL NOTATIONS(*)   *Enclosure: Sponsorship Info.doc, 2010 Application Form.doc*
                              SB/aa

Figure 7-1 Parts of a standard business letter

7.2.2 Date

Place the date that the letter is to be mailed two line spaces below the return address; and then leave two more line spaces between it and the inside address. Stick to traditional date format, without abbreviations. In Canada, the date can be written as 23 June 2010 or as June 23, 2010. Correspondence sent overseas should use day-month-year format as that is what is used in most countries around the world. Correspondence sent to the United States should use the month-day-year format that is used in that country. Because of the different systems for writing dates, you should never use only numbers; 6/8/2011 could be read as 6 August 2011 or June 8, 2011 depending where the reader lives. The international ISO standard for writing dates is all numeric, using year-month-day, so you may see June 8, 2011 written as 2011-06-08. The ISO numeric format is used by some international corporations and in some government offices in Canada.

7.2.3 Inside Address

Address your reader by his or her full professional name in the inside address, even if you plan to use a more informal name in the salutation. When you don't know the reader's name, use the job title both in the inside address and salutation. If the person to whom you are writing has no professional title, simply type the name and the company affiliation.

7.2.4 Subject Statement

A subject statement briefly describes the topic of your letter. It should have two line-spaces above it and below it, to make it stand out. It may be placed between the inside address and the salutation, or between the salutation and the first paragraph of the body of the letter. Today, business writers typically use "SUBJECT:", which is usually capitalized for emphasis. A colon follows the subject notation. Try to describe what your letter is about in as few words as possible (you don't need a complete sentence). For example:

> SUBJECT: Flood insurance

Subject announcements have the advantage of clearly stating your topic. They often have the disadvantage of sounding too urgent and impatient, however, especially in a friendly business letter where personal warmth is important.

7.2.5 Attention Line

When you address your letter directly to the company, use the attention line to name a person, position, or department. The word "ATTENTION" is often capitalized for emphasis. The use of a colon after the word is optional. Place the attention line after the inside address.

7.2.6 Salutation

The traditional greeting (such as "Dear Mr. Bevins:") appears beneath the inside address and occurs in almost all major business-letter formats. It is conventional in more formal companies or industries to address readers as "Mr." or "Mrs." unless you know them. By convention, we address business correspondents as Dear, even when our feelings are far from fond. When you don't know the name of the person you're writing to, use the job title on the inside address as the salutation. For example, "Dear Personnel Director:."

7.2.7 Body of Your Letter

The body of the letter contains the message you want your reader to receive. This is the message that motivated you to write the letter in the first place. If there were no body, there'd be no letter. The following checklist covers some key ideas for writing the body of your letter:

- **Complete:** Is the body of your letter complete? Have you included all the facts, arguments, examples, and details that you need to make your point?
- **Coherent:** Are your letter's points coherent? Do they link together in an organized, logical way? Have you helped your reader move from point to point with transitions?
- **Concise:** Are the points in the body of your letter concise? Have you used the fewest words you can? Have you cut out any padding that your reader doesn't need to get your message?
- **Concrete:** Is your letter's language concrete? Do you use easy-to-understand words that give your reader specific mental pictures about your message? Do your verbs show actions (such as direct, send, produce)?
- **Convincing:** Does your letter sound convincing? Will your letter persuade your reader to understand and trust in your message?
- **Considerate:** Is your letter and its message considerate? Do you show your readers you care about their needs? Have you looked at your letter from your reader's point of view? Have you used a warm, friendly tone?

7.2.8 Complimentary Close

This brief word (such as "Sincerely") or phrase (such as "With best wishes") is your last chance to show regard for your reader. Most business letters in Canada close with "Sincerely." After the body of the letter, insert two line spaces and then type the complimentary close that seems most appropriate.

7.2.9 Signature

Because your typed full name and professional title (optional) appear beneath your signature, you don't need to take pains to ensure that your signature shows perfect penmanship. Most business signatures have a bit of personal flair. Also, it isn't always necessary to sign your name exactly as it is typed on the letter. In a particularly friendly letter, you may wish to sign with just your first name.

7.2.10 Final Notations

A series of notations sometimes appears at the bottom of business letters, always below the signature and along the left-hand margin.

- **Copy notation:** Writers place the *cc:* notation at the bottom of letters to tell their readers to whom copies of the letter have been sent.
- **Enclosure** simply records on the business letter the list of additional items you have included with the letter. List enclosures by title whenever possible.
- **Reference initials** identify both the author of the letter and the typist. Note that the author's initials are all capitals and precede the typist's initials, which are lowercase. The initials can be separated by a colon or slash.

FOR EXAMPLE

Using Judgement

When Kate left a large financial institution to work for a local family-owned accounting firm, she found that some parts of the standard business format seemed overly formal for her client's needs. For the most part, she was dealing with people she knew personally, most of whom had long-standing relationships with the business and the family. Although she still needed to maintain the professionalism of her communications, she was able to do away with elements such as the subject line and attention line, and even overly formal salutations and closings.

SELF-CHECK

- Identify the parts of a standard business letter.
- Name the optional parts of a letter.
- List the six ideas to consider when writing the body of a letter.

7.3 Standard Formats

When seeing your letter for the first time, a reader is impressed first by overall appearance. The format—the shape, arrangement, and order of letter and envelope parts—matters not merely as a nod to business tradition but as a crucial component of your letter's success. The parts of a letter can be arranged into one of three common business format styles:

- **Block style (Figure 7-2):** In this popular business format, all parts of the letter are printed beginning at the left margin. Paragraphs are separated from one another by one or two extra line spaces. This clean, modern-looking style is the standard used in most businesses today.

Williams Electronic Supply, Inc.
1876 Bank St. Ottawa, ON K1P 5N7
613-555-9712

January 7, 2010

Mr. Frank Devlin, Manager
Devlin Industrial Wiring, Inc.
1097 Brookdale Ave.
Cornwall, ON K6J 4P5

SUBJECT: Upcoming Industrial Arts Fair, May 15-17, 2010

Dear Mr. Devlin:

Your booth at last year's Industrial Arts Fair certainly made a hit. No doubt your creative staff is already planning surprises for us at this year's fair.

Williams Electronic Supply wants to team up with Devlin Industrial Wiring for this year's fair. Together we can put on a fascinating demonstration of recent advances in domestic and industrial uses of electricity. You and I spoke briefly of this possibility at last year's fair, Mr. Devlin. We agreed then that our mutual efforts would be great for the fair and, of course, good advertising for our companies.

I'm planning to visit Cornwall on January 18, 2010. Can we meet to discuss our common interests? You can reach me weekdays at the number above. If we haven't made connection by January 15, I'll give you a call before my trip to Denver.

Until then, best wishes from all of us at Williams Electronic.

Sincerely,

Cindy Galloway

Cindy Galloway
Advertising Director

CG/woi
Enclosure: "Planning for the 2010 Industrial Arts Fair"

P.S. We have reserved the booth space next to yours in hopes that we can expand both booths into one large display area.

Figure 7-2 Block style

- **Indented style (Figure 7-3):** Three elements of the indented style are moved to the centre margin: the return address (if letterhead stationery is not being used), the date, and the signature block, including the complimentary close. Paragraphs are indented, usually five spaces. This common style is somewhat more traditional and literary in appearance than the block style.

Williams Electronic Supply, Inc.
1876 Bank St. Ottawa, ON K1P 5N7
613-555-9712

DATE MINDLINE   January 7, 2010

Mr. Frank Devlin, Manager
Devlin Industrial Wiring, Inc.
1097 Brookdale Ave.
Cornwall, ON K6J 4P5

SUBJECT: Upcoming Industrial Arts Fair, May 15-17, 2010

Dear Mr. Devlin:

    Your booth at last year's Industrial Arts Fair certainly made a hit. No doubt your creative staff is already planning surprises for us at this year's fair.

INDENTED   Williams Electronic Supply wants to team up with Devlin Industrial Wiring for this year's fair. Together we can put on a fascinating demonstration of recent advances in domestic and industrial uses of electricity. You and I spoke briefly of this possibility at last year's fair, Mr. Devlin. We agreed then that our mutual efforts would be great for the fair and, of course, good advertising for our companies.

    I'm planning to visit Cornwall on January 18, 2010. Can we meet to discuss our common interests? You can reach me weekdays at the number above. If we haven't made connection by January 15, I'll give you a call before my trip to Denver.

    Until then, best wishes from all of us at Williams Electronic.

SIGNATURE BLOCK   Sincerely,
MIDLINE

                                Cindy Galloway

                                Cindy Galloway
                                Advertising Director

CG/woi
Enclosure: "Planning for the 2010 Industrial Arts Fair"

P.S. We have reserved the booth space next to yours in hopes that we can expand both booths into one large display area.

Figure 7-3 Indented style

- **Modified block style (Figure 7-4):** Elements of both the block style and indented style appear in this format. The return address (when not using letterhead), the date, and the signature block are moved to the centre margin. All other letter parts are placed along the left margin. Paragraphs are not indented. The modified block style is less common than block style and indented style.

However attracted you may be to experimental formats that appear from time to time, consider the risk that some of your readers may expect traditional business formats as a sign of traditional business practices. Such readers may react negatively to experimental formats because business letters are still considered to be relatively more formal than other forms of communication.

Williams Electronic Supply, Inc.
1876 Bank St. Ottawa, ON K1P 5N7
613-555-9712

DATE MINDLINE

January 7, 2010

Mr. Frank Devlin, Manager
Devlin Industrial Wiring, Inc.
1097 Brookdale Ave.
Cornwall, ON   K6J 4P5

SUBJECT: Upcoming Industrial Arts Fair, May 15-17, 2010

Dear Mr. Devlin:

Your booth at last year's Industrial Arts Fair certainly made a hit. No doubt your creative staff is already planning surprises for us at this year's fair.

NO INDENTION

Williams Electronic Supply wants to team up with Devlin Industrial Wiring for this year's fair. Together we can put on a fascinating demonstration of recent advances in domestic and industrial uses of electricity. You and I spoke briefly of this possibility at last year's fair, Mr. Devlin. We agreed then that our mutual efforts would be great for the fair and, of course, good advertising for our companies.

I'm planning to visit Denver on January 18, 2010. Can we meet to discuss our common interests? You can reach me weekdays at the number above. If we haven't made connection by January 15, I'll give you a call before my trip to Denver.

Until then, best wishes from all of us at Williams Electronic.

**SIGNATURE BLOCK
MIDLINE**

Sincerely,

Cindy Galloway

Cindy Galloway
Advertising Director

CG/woi
Enclosure: "Planning for the 2010 Industrial Arts Fair"

P.S. We have reserved the booth space next to yours in hopes that we can expand both booths into one large display area.

Figure 7-4 Modified block style

Whichever business format you choose, follow these steps to check for the shape and the print quality of your letter:

1. Does the body of your letter have at-a-glance appeal? Does it look balanced, attractive, and organized on the page?
2. Have you chosen type that looks professional? Have you avoided smudges, half-printed characters, uneven spacing, and the printer-problem look?

SELF-CHECK

- Describe three common business format styles.
- Explain how the modified block style incorporates elements of two other formats.
- Review ways of checking the overall aesthetic quality of your document.

7.4 Writing Everyday Business Letters

Any business person who has contact with customers is responsible for bolstering the relationship between the company and the customer (or client, or supplier, etc.). In your business writing, the way to do that is by showing your reader that you care.

To see how quickly a reader forms an impression of a company, decide what you think about the company that allowed the letter in Figure 7-5 to be mailed to a customer.

Haeber Financial Services Inc.
5967 Maple Ave.
Winnipeg, MB   R3A 0J5   204-555-5713

Jn. 4th, 2010

Mister Bob Lee
Administater, Public Teachers Pension Fund
3908 Yonge St.
Markham, ON   L6U 9Y7

Dear. M. Thomas:

Per my call to you a couple days ago, I think we can put together a package for your membership that will earn in excess of the figures you quoted me from your experience with your previoius money management consultant.

Call me so we can move on this. I'm out of town for several days starting this coming Friday, so ring me before then, please.

Sincerly,

Burton Cay
Investment Specialist

Figure 7-5 A poorly written letter with many errors

The problem with this letter lies not only in the glaring punctuation and spelling errors. The letter reflects very poorly on the company. (How good can this company be is it hires investment specialists like this?) The letter is also self-centred and hurried. Above all, it doesn't show respect for and attention to the reader's interest. The following sections illustrate ways to connect with a reader.

7.4.1 Emphasize the Reader

As a business writer, you must show empathy for your readers, particularly in documents as personal as letters. To show empathy in your letters, focus on your reader's needs more than on your own. Think of it as the **you emphasis.** The following two examples illustrate the difference between an **I emphasis** and a you emphasis:

I emphasis: *I am sending information on optional devices suited to the computer I sold you.*

You emphasis: *You'll receive complete instructions with details and capabilities and prices of optional add-ons suited to your new computer.*

The difference in these two statements may seem slight. Yet the recurring use of *"I"* in a complete business letter causes your reader to lose interest in the letter—and lose connection with you as well. Show your genuine concern for your reader by emphasizing *"you"* and downplaying *"I"* as much as possible.

7.4.2 Include Feelings with Facts

You can show a warm, friendly tone by including some of your feelings when you're telling your reader your facts. This doesn't mean that your letters should overflow with feelings that don't belong in a business letter. The following feelings generally would be inappropriate in a business letter:

- "small talk" or comments about your personal life
- personal negative feelings about your company, your supervisor, your co-workers, your customers, or others you work with
- negative feelings toward your reader or any of your reader's associates
- intense emotions, such as love, hate, anger, or fear.

Don't make the mistake of leaving out feelings altogether, though. In modern business writing, your readers expect you to show your feelings in an appropriate way. After all, business writing takes place in a people-centred world. Business people are interested in what others do, think, and feel. For example, when reminding a client about a 3 p.m. meeting, don't hesitate to reveal your feelings:

We will meet at 3 p.m.

I look forward to talking with you at our 3 p.m. meeting.

Be as personable in business writing as you would be in a face-to-face business meeting. Your associates and customers may never know you as well as your best friends do, but you can still share many of your feelings in writing. Just as importantly, you can show that you are sensitive to the feelings of your readers.

FOR EXAMPLE

Open for Interpretation

Readers understand the force of feelings in business letters and they can accurately translate those feelings into a significant part of the message. For example, a manager's different approaches to the same subject could result in two very different reader responses. In his first approach, the manager writes: "The Sundance Peak project shows some promise." The reader interprets: "The project sounds tentative, iffy." The manager's second approach, however, conveys his feelings about the subject: "You'll probably share my excitement about the potential of the Sundance Peak project." This time, the reader interprets: "Excited? There's something worth looking into here."

SELF-CHECK

- Discuss the importance of making a connection with a reader.
- Explain the difference between an I emphasis and a you emphasis.
- List three types of personal feelings that should not appear in business letters.

7.5 Writing Positive Business Letters

Companies build goodwill, keep old customers, and win new customers not only by saying "yes" to orders, requests, and adjustment letters, but also by their skill in saying "yes, but" and even "no" when they must (Section 8.3 covers those inevitable "no" letters).

Your readers look forward to hearing you say "yes." As such, this good news should appear first in your letter. Conditions, qualifications, and other information should generally follow your clear statement of a positive response.

When clients hear "yes," they value your company's participation in their own progress. We all like the people and companies who make "yes" possible. In fact, we translate our liking into action. We tell others about the company that helped us. We return to the company for future business.

7.5.1 Format for Positive Letters

Positive letters, or yes letters, come in a wide variety of forms, but all rely on a simple four-point plan:

1. Deliver the yes message as soon as possible in the letter; always remember to put the good news up front. Reserve all the specifics and additional information for a later paragraph.

2. Keep the yes message simple. If possible, let the yes statement stand by itself without a clutter of conditions, comments, and qualifications in the same paragraph. Don't spoil this good moment for the reader.

3. Tell the reader exactly what you are saying "yes" to. Be specific. Especially in contractual matters and questions of credit, it is wise to spell out (in the next paragraph) the exact commitment you are making by your yes response.

4. Sell your company's service, product, image, or relationship. A customer who has just heard you say "yes" may be quite receptive to sales information. Here are three ways you can weave your sales message into your yes letter:
   - mention a related product or service your client might need
   - describe the future relationship you look forward to with the client
   - thank the client for past business and promise continued good service.

FOR EXAMPLE

Goodwill and Good Business

Regina Carpet Supply placed a first order for 500 boxes of carpet bonding from a supply company. Lucy, who processed the order when it arrived at the supply company, was swamped that day with orders to be filled. Although she was inclined to simply ship the order and notify the customer with a copy of the shipping order that it was on its way, she changed her mind. Instead, she shipped the order and wrote a brief letter to the manager of Regina Carpet Supply, welcoming them as new customers.

7.5.2 Responding to Customer Orders

Begin the yes letter responding to an order by stating exactly what you are saying "yes" to. You don't need to repeat the customer's entire order, of course, but

Figure 7-6 Yes letter that builds goodwill

be sure to provide all the information the customer needs to understand what order has been approved. In the next paragraph, explain any conditions, product specifications, and shipping or billing information that the customer needs to know. Conclude with a statement of appreciation and, where appropriate, a sales message.

In Figure 7-6, notice how the writer says "yes" quickly, saving details and the sales message for later paragraphs.

It may not be possible to respond to each and every order with a special letter or note. But by doing so as often as possible, you help build goodwill and pave the way to frequent reorders.

Sometimes, you will have to respond with a **partial yes** to an order that you were unable to fill completely. The letter in Figure 7-7 tells in the first paragraph what you were able to do and goes on to suggest a timely solution for filling the rest of the order.

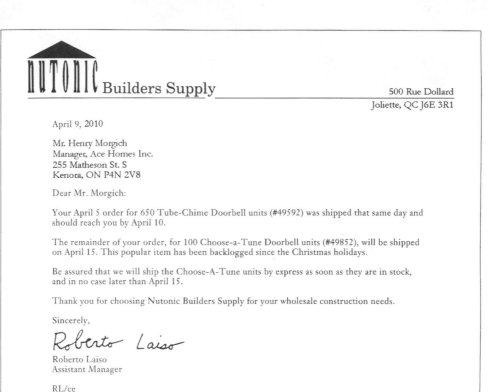

Figure 7-7 Partial yes letter

7.5.3 Responding to Information Requests

Like positive responses to orders, letters responding to information requests begin with the yes statement and then move on to other paragraphs containing additional information. If the inquiry was complicated or if a long time has passed since you received it, you can preface your yes response with a brief restatement of the inquiry. You risk repeating information the reader already knows—but that's often preferable to the larger risk of saying "yes" to a forgotten inquiry.

SELF-CHECK

- Discuss the role of positive letters in customer relations.
- List the four parts of the positive-letter format.
- Review ways of incorporating a sales message into a positive letter.
- Explain how a partial yes letter serves a customer's needs.

In Figure 7-8 the writer repeats the essence of the inquiry before answering it:

422 W. Main St.
St. John's, NL   A1B 9W5
709-555-9652

March 17, 2010

Ms. Belinda McNeil
Director, Human Resources
Tennebrach Petroleum, Inc.
495 Trent St.
Peterborough, ON   K9H 1A5

Dear Ms. McNeil:

On or before March 22, 2010, we will be pleased to ship 27 art posters from our series "Spring Morning" to your Peterborough headquarters.

The posters will arrive by United Parcel, C.O.D. Although we take extreme precautions against damage in the packaging of our framed posters, you should check all packages you receive with care. If you discover damage, please notify us immediately, including the insurance number marked on the damaged package.

We trust that you will find pleasure in seeing varieties of "Spring Morning" in your corporate offices. When making plans or decoration elsewhere in your facilities, please consider the beautiful oil paintings and watercolors now available in our fall catalog. These investment-quality art pieces would be a handsome addition to your growing collection of quality works.

Our sincere thanks and best wishes.

Cordially,

Morgan Fairmont

Morgan Fairmont
Sales Director

MF/eis

Enc.: *The Remington Fall Catalog*

Figure 7-8 Positive response to an order

7.6 Writing Yes When You're Under Stress

It's relatively easy to write yes and to share good news, and it's particularly easy to share these messages with those who like you. Sometimes, though, you're going to have to write to people who are angry with you—dissatisfied customers who are frustrated with your products or services, furious suppliers who aren't satisfied with your payment, angry co-workers who don't like their performance evaluations.

7.6.1 Responding to Criticism

It's particularly difficult to write a response to someone who has let you know that he or she is angry with you or your company. For example, a client may have tried to get

information about her account by telephone. Someone in your company (whose name you don't know) apparently told her bluntly that account information was not released by telephone. Incensed, the client writes to you:

> *After being put on hold for more than 10 minutes, I was told by a very rude man that he was not allowed to give me information about my own account. So I've had to take my extremely valuable time to write this letter.*

You realize that her complaint is probably accurate. Your company does have a policy of not releasing some account information by telephone in order to protect your customers' privacy and your accounts' confidentiality. In responding to this customer, you have a choice. On one hand, you could self-righteously tell her that your company's policy is justifiable, so her feelings are inappropriate. On the other hand, you could acknowledge her feelings and then give her some good news:

> *I apologize for any inconvenience you experienced in contacting our company. In matters involving account balances and transactions, we make every effort to protect your privacy by using only written communications, though we regret any delays this policy may have caused you. I'm happy to be able to answer each of your questions at this time.*

What's the good news here?

- You're not angry, responding blow-for-blow to her letter.
- You can do what she wants.
- Your company is doing its best to serve her interests.

In writing this kind of letter, begin by establishing the good news tone before bringing up any of the details that provoked the original bad feelings. By "starting fresh," you get the communication (and the relationship) off to a new start.

7.6.2 Responding to Claim Requests

In business, a client occasionally has bad luck with a product or service you provide. A microwave oven suddenly stops working, a television loses its picture, or a hotel reservation is unexpectedly lost. The customer writes you a letter in the heat of anger and disappointment, full of woeful descriptions of the product failure and the inconvenience and frustration you have caused. The letters often end with vague or not-so-vague threats about "further action" and "courts of law."

Prepare to write the positive adjustment letter by answering the following questions to yourself. You don't need to answer yes to each question to justify the writing

of a positive letter. You may decide to settle the issue by a positive response even if the customer is not right or cannot clearly prove fault on the part of the company. Your decision will be based on a complex set of factors, including your own judgement on a case-by-case basis and company policy.

- Is the customer right?
- Is the problem the company's fault?
- Can I admit that fault?
- Can I resolve the problem satisfactorily?

Begin your positive response by getting directly to the good news: "Yes, this company grants your claim." You don't need to repeat the details of the claim itself, except in a brief way to make clear the nature of the positive response. Especially if the details of the claim cause anger for the reader, avoid repeating what went wrong.

Let your yes statement be direct. It should satisfy the demand made against the company once and for all. Business letters cost money, and a half-yes merely invites further expensive correspondence, especially when lawyers become involved.

In the letter in Figure 7-9, the writer makes reference to the claim itself only in the subject line. Thereafter, the claim is quickly granted in the yes paragraph that begins the letter. Necessary details are provided in the second paragraph. The writer tries to restore goodwill and customer confidence in the final paragraph.

Businesses do not make a regular practice of sending blanket yes letters in response to any and all claims against them. Chapter 8 will discuss the no letter that must often be sent. Somewhere between these two answers is a middle ground: the positive adjustment letter that nevertheless takes time to educate the customer.

Let's say, for example, that Ms. Malloy's refrigerator is no longer under warranty when you receive her claim letter. Your company nonetheless decides to fix her refrigerator. In your positive adjustment letter, you take time after the initial yes paragraph to educate Ms. Malloy, in a diplomatic way, about the realities of consumer purchases:

Although your refrigerator is no longer under warranty, we will do our best to see that it is restored to good working order. At no expense to you, Garson Appliance Service will be glad to inspect your refrigerator and resolve the problem to your satisfaction.

You may want to know, Ms. Malloy, that you have purchased one of the most reliable refrigerators in the industry, according to Consumer Reports. *We're confident that the problem you are experiencing can be easily repaired. At the same time, we urge you to read warranty information carefully for each appliance you buy. In most cases repairs are the responsibility of the purchaser after expiration of the warranty period.*

1987 Central Ave.
Windsor, ON N8N 1A9
519-555-9652

April 6, 2010

Ms. Anna Malloy
495 Oak St.
Timmins, ON P4N 2R8

SUBJECT: Your letter of April 3, 2010: refrigerator malfunction

Dear Ms. Malloy:

According to our records, your refrigerator is still under warranty. At no expense to you, Garson Appliance Service in your city will be glad to inspect your refrigerator and resolve the problem to your satisfaction.

Please make arrangements for their visit by calling 427-3842.

You may want to know, Ms. Malloy, that all Reston appliances—including the revolutionary micropulse dishwashers—are on sale beginning April 15. We've enclosed a sales catalog for your review.

Thank you for giving us the opportunity to live up to our reputation for quality and service in refrigeration products.

Sincerely,

Morgan O'Neill

Morgan O'Neill
Customer Relations

MO/wo

Enclosure: Sales Catalog

Figure 7-9 Positive adjustment letter

Does such education do any good? Companies hope so. If the buying public begins to expect businesses and manufacturers to grant every claim, few companies can operate profitably. By including a brief paragraph of education, Garson Appliance Service is making an effort to retain the meaning of important business concepts such as warranty.

Finally, the positive adjustment letter provides a good opportunity to mend fences with disappointed customers. Obviously, a problem has led to the claim against the company. Your positive adjustment letter goes a long way toward repairing the feelings of disappointment and frustration. Buoyed by your yes response, in fact, the customer may be eager to learn of new products, services, sales, promotions, and so forth offered by your company. Include that information near the end of your positive adjustment letter.

> ### FOR EXAMPLE
>
> **Making Amends**
>
> A mother had searched for a particular character costume for her son's upcoming costume party. She eventually placed an order through a novelty website, calling their customer service line to make certain that the costume would arrive in time. After several days she called the company to check on the shipment of the package, and she was told it would be delivered the day before the party. When it didn't arrive as promised, she called the company again—only to discover that the item was on backorder. She related the details of the story in a scathing letter to the company, emphasizing that she would take future business elsewhere. Although the company could do nothing about the party, a customer service manager quickly responded in a letter, offering an apology for the mistake and offering a gift certificate for her next purchase.

SELF-CHECK

- Discuss the importance of writing letters to customers who are dissatisfied or frustrated.
- Explain the placement of good news in a letter responding to a claim request.
- Explain why in a positive response to a critical letter it's best not to dwell on the negative cause of the original letter.

SUMMARY

People use your business letters to form impressions about you and your organization—by the words you choose, by the way you arrange them on the page, even by the letterhead you use. Modern letters allow for a more personal approach while still maintaining a professional business approach. Standards for writing and formatting increase readability and credibility. By establishing a connection with a reader, the writer builds the customer–company relationship. This connection fosters a sense of goodwill and a willingness to handle requests and, in some cases, resolve customer-relations issues.

KEY TERMS

Block style	Business-letter format in which all parts of the letter are printed beginning at the left margin, and paragraphs are separated by one or two line spaces.
I emphasis	Writer focuses more on his or her own needs than those of the reader, limiting ability to show empathy.
Indented style	A business-letter format in which paragraphs are indented, and some elements are moved to the centre margin.
Modified block style	A business-letter format in which elements of both the block style and indented style appear.
Partial yes	A response in which the writer is unable to completely fill an order or completely satisfy a request.
Positive letters	Business letters in which the writer is able to say "yes" to a request, claim, or order.
You emphasis	Writer focuses more on the reader's needs than his or her own; this enables greater display of empathy.

ASSESS YOUR UNDERSTANDING

Go to www.wiley.com/canada/brounstein to evaluate your knowledge of the basics of positive business letters. Measure your learning by comparing pre-test and post-test results.

Quick Questions

1. Unlike a contract, a business letter cannot serve as a legal document. True or false?
2. Modern form letters are typically more personal than those of the past. True or false?
3. Every business letter should include a subject line that states the topic of your letter. True or false?
4. A company's contact information should be listed both in the letterhead and below the signature line. True or false?
5. Which of the following elements are optional in a business letter?
   (a) inside address
   (b) salutation

    (c) signature

    (d) attention line

6. The indented format is considered more traditional than the block format. True or false?

7. Both the indented format and block format are represented in the modified block format. True or false?

8. The look of a letter is not important, as long as the content is factual and well written. True or false?

9. A business letter should focus more on *you emphasis* than *I emphasis*. True or false?

10. Personal feelings should never find their way into business letters. True or false?

11. The yes message in positive letter should be reserved for the end. True or false?

12. A partial yes letter informs a customer that their item has been backordered. True or false?

13. Sales messages can be incorporated into positive letters by

    (a) describing a future business relationship with the client

    (b) thanking the client and promising continued good service

    (c) mentioning a related service or product

    (d) all of the above

14. In general, every letter from a customer deserves a response. True or false?

15. Which of the following questions can help you decide how to respond to a claim letter?

    (a) Was the claim submitted in a timely fashion?

    (b) Is there a legal precedent?

    (c) Can I resolve the problem satisfactorily?

    (d) Is there insurance coverage for this?

16. In a positive claim adjustment, the yes statement should follow an explanation of company policy. True or false?

Give It Some Thought

1. Name two ways that business letters differ from conversations.

2. List the features of an effective business letter.

    (a) empathetic, attractive, and error free

    (b) encyclopedic, modern, and error free

    (c) legally binding, friendly, and strategic

    (d) all of the above

3. What characteristics should describe the body of a letter?

   (a) long

   (b) capitalized

   (c) considerate

   (d) bulleted

4. Provide an example of a poor subject line? A good subject line?

5. How do readers react to experimental formats of business letters?

6. What is considered the most modern letter format?

   (a) block

   (b) modified block

   (c) indented

7. "I will be happy to distribute information about my services at the meeting" is an example of a sentence with you emphasis. True or false?

8. Which of the following expressions would be inappropriate in most business letters?

   (a) feelings about your personal life

   (b) sympathy for a loss

   (c) empathy about a problem

   (d) anticipation for an upcoming event

9. What four-point plan is the basis for all positive letters?

10. In an information request, why is it important to repeat the essence of an inquiry before answering it?

11. What questions should a writer ask when deciding how to respond to a claims request?

Applying This Chapter

1. Find an example of a business letter you've received and read it to find aspects such as friendliness, empathy, and warmth. Highlight instances of these aspects and describe the tone of the letter. Was it conversational, formal, overly casual?

2. Find a business letter and label each part of it according the standard described in this chapter. Is it missing any of the optional parts, and would you include them if you were writing them yourself?

3. Find a letter you've written in the past; for example a cover letter for a job. Using word processing software, reformat it using the three standard formats. Decide which letter has the best at-a-glance appeal. Compare your answer to those of three classmates. Which format is most appealing?

4. A city recreation department has just put in a large order of 300 custom-printed baseball hats with your company. Write a letter thanking them for their continued business.

5. The mayor of your town has requested that your commercial cleaning company hire unemployed teens for the summer. You've already hired your summer staff, but can take on five additional part-timers. Respond with a partial yes to the request. Include a sales message and maintain goodwill.

6. Imagine you're a customer service representative for a well-known umbrella company. A customer has written to complain that the so-called "indestructible umbrella" that she bought five years ago was torn apart during a recent storm. Write a positive adjustment letter in response to her claim letter.

THE NEXT STEP

Grading a Letter
Study a business letter you've received in the mail. In what ways does it follow and/or ignore the letter-writing principles discussed in this section? Does it serve your needs? Does it include a sense of the writer's personal feelings? Does it include the standard parts of a business letter?

Good News and Bad News
As a customer service representative for a manufacturer of high-end sport-fishing equipment, you have to deliver some good news and some bad news to a disgruntled customer. Apparently, the customer's reel broke during an expensive chartered fishing trip in the Bahamas. The reel, which is still under warranty, will be replaced and shipped for free. The customer's other request, that the cost of the chartered trip be covered, cannot be honoured. As you draft a partial adjustment letter, consider whether the good news should come first or last. Compare your results with those of your classmates.

Adjustment Reply
You work at the head office of a large furniture company. A customer emails you to say that one week after he purchased your model no. 293 dresser, the retail outlet where he bought it reduced the price by $125. He would like you to reimburse him the difference. Write a letter addressing this customer's concerns and instructing him that in order to receive an adjustment, he will have to provide you with his mailing address and a copy of his purchase receipt.

8
WRITING NEGATIVE MESSAGES
Strategies for Breaking Bad News

STARTING POINT

Go to www.wiley.com/canada/brounstein to assess your knowledge of the basics of writing negative messages. After reviewing the website, you'll be able to determine where you need to concentrate your effort.

What You'll Learn in This Chapter:

- how to use the indirect pattern when delivering negative messages
- the benefits of using a direct approach to deliver negative news
- common types of negative letters.

After Studying This Chapter, You'll be Able to:

- discuss the role of the buffer statement in the indirect pattern
- identify situations that require an indirect approach
- describe the uses of negative letters in business
- discuss the relative merits of writing techniques.

INTRODUCTION

It's not easy to write business messages that deliver bad news, whether it's denying a client's request or refuting a customer's claim. The indirect pattern is one common approach for negative letters. Certain situations call for a more straightforward delivery using the direct approach. The chapter concludes with descriptions and techniques for addressing various business situations that require a negative response.

8.1 Delivering Negative Messages with the Indirect Pattern

It's satisfying to deliver and receive good news, but in your career you'll face plenty of situations in which you must deal with bad news: saying "no," delivering distressing information, refusing customer claims, handling employment situations, or just generally delivering news that the reader doesn't want to hear. Even when the news is negative, your goal is to deliver it in a way that shows you care about your business relationship.

Section 7.5 explains how simple it is to deliver positive news: say it quickly and clearly. With negative news, you first need to think about your reader's reaction to the information. The main goals of delivering a bad news message are that the reader will understand the reasons for the decision, and that there will be no hard feelings, so future business dealings can be possible. Bad news is not news they *want* to hear, but it is news they *need* to hear. As such, you should plan your approach. Generally, the most effective way to deliver negative news is to cushion it between a positive opening statement and a friendly closing.

8.1.1 The Buffer Statement

A **buffer statement** is a positive or neutral statement—not a negative one—that serves as a starting place for your negative response or bad news. Buffers allow the reader to feel comfortable with you before experiencing the discomfort of the no message. Buffers also encourage the reader to continue reading your message; if the bad news is "up front," there is a chance the reader could be upset and not read any further. Consider the following techniques for creating effective buffers:

- **Praise the reader for personal or professional qualities.** Starting with a compliment emphasizes that you are giving bad news about a business situation, so the reader is less likely to take it personally.

  "In your interviews, Mr. Johnson, we came to know your extensive managerial skill and good business instincts."

- **Concentrate on special needs.** This focuses the bad news on a "limitation" of your business rather than on a fault of the potential customer. It preserves the possibility that you could still complete a transaction.

  "At Vector Direct Mail Sales, we have limited our new product acquisitions to cosmetics, electronic games, and jewellery."

- **Use time factors as explanations.** Discussing schedules keeps the bad news from being personal and leaves open the possibility of a future transaction.

  "Our production schedule demands that we settle upon a computer system that can be online no later than February 7."

- **Choose a positive aspect of the subject at hand.** This can be effective, but it is also a challenge because you need to make sure you don't unintentionally mislead your reader into thinking you are actually sending them a positive message.

"We were frankly surprised when our small advertisement drew over 350 responses."

By using buffers, writers try to prepare the reader to receive the negative response. Of course, you can't avoid disappointing the reader entirely. However, your effort to soften the blow of the negative response often builds a feeling of goodwill that goes beyond the momentary disappointment.

8.1.2 The Explanation and the Negative News

It's important that you explain to the reader the reasons for your decision before you give the bad news. For example, you could include a brief explanation that will help the reader understand your decision (explain a warranty policy for a product claim or a privacy policy for an information request). Providing the explanation before you provide the negative news prepares the reader for the no message and reassures him or her that this is a logical and reasonable business decision, not an arbitrary or personal decision.

Most of the time, of course, the reader will want to know why you've answered no. A good test for such occasions is to put yourself in your reader's shoes. Would you appreciate an explanation? Would being eased into a negative answer make it easier on you? If so, include an explanation in your letter. This consideration on your part builds goodwill in the long run, even for customers to whom you say "no" in the short run.

Even though you're trying to show the reader that you care with your tone and choice of words, you still have to deliver the bad news. Doing so clearly and decisively will spare your reader any confusion. If you are vague or overly apologetic, the reader can jump to the conclusion that you disagree with the decision or are open to changing your mind.

At this point, you also have the opportunity to suggest alternative ways to resolve the situation. This may involve some type of action, such as a meeting or phone call. Giving your reader a "Plan B" after you finish with the negative news shows that you are willing to find a way to continue your business relationship. It is not always possible to offer the reader an alternative; for example, you can only hire one person or award a contract to one firm, but you might want them to stay in touch for future competitions.

8.1.3 The Goodwill Closing

Do your best to end your letter on a friendly note—a statement of appreciation or goodwill. Despite the negative nature of the message, it's usually possible to find something positive to say in your closing:

- *We do appreciate you bringing this matter to our attention.*
- *Thank you for your patronage.*

- *Best wishes for a successful conference.*
- *I look forward to discussing this in person.*

FOR EXAMPLE

Letting Them Down Easy

The planner of a new senior housing community was looking for a landscape architect to work on the development's many outdoor features. A small fledgling firm sent one proposal that was quite good. In the end, the planner chose a larger, more established company, one it had worked with before. In its response to the smaller firm, however, the developer wanted to soften the blow somehow: "We were impressed by the scope of your accomplishments, given the short amount of time you've been in business. Although we chose another firm for this large-scale project, we'll keep you in mind for future smaller projects."

SELF-CHECK

- Explain the importance of using an indirect pattern to write business letters.
- Define buffer statement.
- Discuss the role of the buffer statement in considering a reader's feelings.
- List four techniques for creating effective buffers.

8.2 Delivering Negative Messages with the Direct Approach

Many business inquiries, requests, and claims ask you a simple question: Can you or can't you? Those who ask that question may not want to hear a nice buffer statement (see the preceding section) or the reasons and justifications for your answer. A firm, polite no may be all they have time to hear before setting out in new directions.

Compare the examples of negative-response letters in Figures 8-1 and 8-2. The first, although it maintains a friendly tone, does not try to explain the no answer. The letter does not spell out specifically why this applicant was denied. It would not have been helpful to tell Francine Gillings that "your grades and test scores qualified

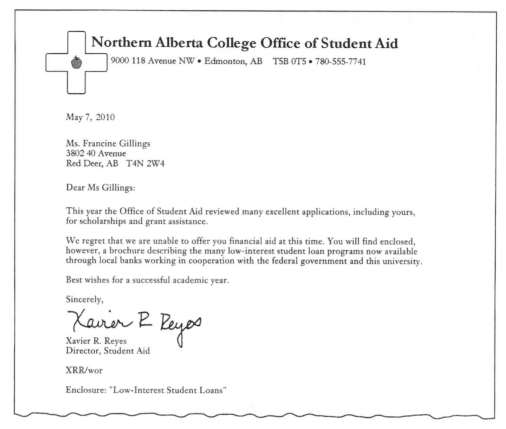

Figure 8-1 Negative response without an explanation

you for aid, but your letters of recommendation seemed hollow and restrained in their praise of you." In this case, the office chose not to tell all the reasons that led to its negative decision.

By contrast, the letter in Figure 8-2 explains the negative response. The writer wisely chooses to explain in detail why the reader's application for employment was turned down. Consider her reason for doing so: the company has a long-range interest in hiring the applicant at a later date—after his doctoral studies, perhaps, or when he has mastered UNIX. The explanation for the negative response lets the applicant know what he can do to change the no to a yes.

Consider each situation as you decide when to explain your negative response. As a general rule, include an explanation whenever it will help build goodwill or make possible future contacts. Do not explain if the reader clearly does not care for an explanation, or if your explanation will unnecessarily complicate future contacts with the reader.

Peterson Microsystems, Inc.
5000 49 Street
Yellowknife, NT   X1A 0A2
867-555-9652

January 3, 2010

Mr. Geoff Beams
37 Spencer Place
Orangeville, ON L9W 3C7

Dear Mr. Beams:

Thank you for your thorough application for the position of programmer at Peterson Microsystems and for the time you spent in interviews. We certainly enjoyed meeting you.

We regret, however, that we cannot offer you the position you seek at the present time. Our decision, made after long deliberation, is based on two factors:

- All programmers here must often work with the UNIX operating system from the first day on the job. You have not had experience with UNIX.

- Our programmers must often work overtime on high-priority projects. Your time commitments as a doctoral student, we feel, will make overtime impossible for you.

You must know, Mr. Beams, that we are interested in your abilities and thank you for contacting Peterson Microsystems. Please keep us in mind as an employer when the preceding matters no longer present obstacles to our mutual association.

Sincerely,

Berta Kiely

Berta Kiely
Personnel Director

BK/ogi

Figure 8-2 Negative response with an explanation

Getting To the Point

As the manager of a prominent import business, Adam is faced with a steady stream of inquiries and requests. He's asked about job reassignments, promotions, and raises. He's asked to donate items to the fire department's charity auction, fund a volleyball team, and sponsor a jog-a-thon. If he were to support each of his refusals with a watertight web of explanations, he would find little time for any of his other duties. Instead, Adam has learned the fine art of saying "no" simply, politely, and firmly.

8.3 Writing Letters, Memos, and Emails When You Have to Say "No"

Prepare to write a negative response by considering your reader. What language and tone will be most appropriate? What alternatives can be offered without compromising your position? How much empathy should you express, and in what form? How much can or should you explain your negative decision? The answers to these questions will guide you in organizing and wording your negative answers to orders, inquiries, requests, and other business matters. Note that although the examples are given as letters, you can use these techniques in other types of messages, for example memos or emails.

8.3.1 Responding Negatively to an Order

Businesses must often say "no" to orders. The buyer's credit may not be good, or the item ordered may be out of stock. At such times, use the following model in your letter saying "no" to the order:

1. Begin with a positive buffer (perhaps a statement of appreciation for the order or for past business).
2. Go on to a clear explanation of what you can and cannot provide.
3. Include any details or qualifications you feel will be helpful to the reader.
4. Conclude with a statement of goodwill, appreciation, or a brief sales message.

In Figure 8-3, Better Carpets regretfully must decline a huge carpet order. Notice how the writer leaves the door open for future business. He begins with a buffer of appreciation. The no message is explained in some detail. The reader understands why the small carpet company must decline the order. She may then be disposed to accept the compromise plan: a carpet order for 22 homes. The letter concludes with appreciation and an action suggestion ("meeting with you soon").

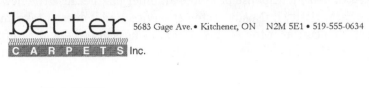

better 5683 Gage Ave.• Kitchener, ON   N2M 5E1 • 519-555-0634
C A R P E T S Inc.

March 19, 2010

Ms. Hanna Morley
Director, Interior Design
Hansen Homes Inc.
77 Kennedy Rd. S.
Brampton, ON   L6W 3C9

Dear Ms. Morley:

Thank you for choosing Better Carpets as carpeting subcontractor for the 385 homes in your Sierra Madre subdivision.

Unfortunately, we must decline your order as it now stands. Our decision, made reluctantly, is based on two considerations:

• As a relatively small carpet business, we have a limited work force. A job as large as the Sierra Madre project would require their full energies for at least two full months. We could not continue to serve the rest of our customers during this period.

• We would have to make substantial capital investment in new equipment to accomplish the Sierra Madre job in the time frame you specify. Such equipment would be idle after the job was finished.

We would like to suggest another plan for you to consider. Better Carpets will carpet the 22 model homes in the Sierra Madre tract at the discount rate you requested for the 385 homes. We would be pleased to work with you in selecting another competent carpeting contractor for the larger job.

We appreciate the confidence you have shown in Better Carpets, Ms. Morley, and I look foward to meeting with you soon to discuss our participation in the Sierra Madre project.

Sincerely,

Ronald C. Horton

Ronald C. Horton
President

RHC/iow

Figure 8-3 Negative response to an order

Other situations that require you to contact a customer or client when responding to order requests include:

• **You can't fill the order immediately.** Write a timely response, including the reason for the delay.

• **You need to make a substitution.** Write to let the customer know about any and all substitutions; include options to change an order.

• **You can't fill the complete order.** Let the customer know what is available now and when the remainder will be available; include alternatives and an apology for any inconvenience.

Don't be tempted to delay a response or ignore an order just because the news is bad. A customer's highest priority is usually customer service, and it doesn't take much of a slip on your part for a customer to take his or her business elsewhere. A carefully crafted letter shows commitment and concern, which can outweigh whether the letter bears negative or positive news.

FOR EXAMPLE

You Can't Always Get What You Want

Doris was planning a large and festive retirement party for her supervisor, who had been at the company for 30 years. She placed an order with a party supply website well in advance of the party. When the order arrived, it included the paper goods and decorations, but not the custom-printed invitations. The supplier explained in a letter that the particular style was no longer available, and gave her the option of choosing another. The supplier also offered to rush the order to meet Doris's schedule for the party.

8.3.2 Refusing Requests and Invitations

Business writers often must say "no" to inquiries, requests, and invitations. As with orders, they can do so in a polite but firm way:

1. Begin with a buffer statement that suggests, "here's a positive thought we can share." Often, the buffer helps to prevent disappointed readers from thinking, "She [or he] probably didn't understand." You do understand and must say "no."
2. Clearly say "no," and explain why, if that would be helpful. You might also suggest some alternatives.
3. Conclude with a positive message, perhaps a statement of appreciation, goodwill, or a sales message.

Notice that the writer of the letter in Figure 8-4 chooses not to provide elaborate explanations for the negative response. He does provide a buffer emphasizing a positive aspect of the inquiry (the professor's interesting research). The no message follows, supported by a brief explanation ("security regulations"). The writer is able to offer an alternative in the form of a booklet. Although it does not meet the professor's need for U.S. Army data, the booklet does provide a concrete expression of goodwill to close the letter.

When you conclude your negative responses, take care not to sound hypocritical when you can express goodwill or well-wishing for the reader and for the reader's project or request. For example, when you honestly can't wish the applicant or the project well, conclude by simply thanking the reader for contacting you.

Ft. Ebson Station
Boulder, CO 80303-0424
(303) 555-7834

April 12, 2010

Professor Andrew Higgins
Department of Biology
University of Toronto
99 Queen's Park Circle
Toronto, ON   M5S 2C5

SUBJECT: Your inquiry regarding stress testing

Dear Professor Higgins:

Thank you for your letter of April 6. We especially enjoyed hearing of your research work and wish you well on its successful outcome.

We cannot, however, provide the data you requested from U.S. Army files because of national security regulations.

However, you may find interesting a recent booklet by the Army, published for civilian researchers. I enclose it for your review.

Sincerely,

Nathan Ramirez

Nathan Ramirez
Staff Sergeant
Medical Research Unit

MR/cox

Enclosure: "Universities and the Army: Partners for Peace"

Figure 8-4 Negative response to an inquiry

Busy professionals frequently have to choose between things they can do and things they should do. As such, they often find themselves saying "no" to worthwhile projects and causes. A successful business woman is often asked to speak to groups of Girl Guides and female youth groups. Although she accepts as many as she can, she has to decline one or two each year. She uses the model listed above and concludes with the following statement to find other ways to stay involved:

As you do, I recognize the importance of this worthwhile gathering. Please let me know how else I might support the upcoming seminar.

By doing so, she can donate products or money to support an event while still maintaining her other obligations.

8.3.3 Writing No to Claims

A customer that takes the time and energy to submit a claim (or complaint) is a valuable commodity. They are giving you the opportunity to serve them and keep their business. You won't have that chance with others who simply take their business elsewhere.

When a customer makes a claim of damage, defect, or negligence against a company, someone in that company is responsible for responding positively or negatively. Of course, no business lasts long by granting every customer claim lodged against it. In learning to write negative responses to claims, use the customer's own reasonable expectations as a framework or agenda for your letter. The customer expects:

- to be heard (your positive "sharing" in the opening buffer statement tells the reader, "I heard you")
- to be answered decisively, not put off (your clear, direct no statement does this)
- to understand the grounds for your decision (your brief explanation helps the customer understand)
- to be treated with respect (your polite style of writing shows this).

Although these reasonable expectations form a blueprint for negative letters, you'll find different ways to say "no" to claim letters. Much of what you write depends on company policies that apply to the product or service you sell. Four general guidelines, however, can serve you well in your writing:

- Assess, without bias, whether the claim is justified. Make an honest effort to see the situation from the customer's point of view.
- If the claim merits it, give what you are able to give, both in words and in replacement merchandise or payment.
- Avoid language that may cause you and your company future problems. Some of the simplest phrases can cause the trickiest legal problems. In general, don't suggest company responsibility or liability for a mishap, unless you have authorization for doing so.
- Keep your answer courteous and businesslike, no matter how angry and abusive the claim letter is. Don't get caught up in your customer's anger. Your goal should be to dispense goodwill, act fairly within your limitations, and put an end to the problem.

Observe how these guidelines can be used to deal with a customer claim:

Mike Nguyen bought a pressure cooker. He took it home to cook a beef stew for friends in his newly wallpapered kitchen. About 20 minutes after the pan was put on the burner, the pan's top shot up with a roar of steam, carrying with it all the beef stew, atomized now to a fine spray. The wallpaper was ruined. Mr. Nguyen checked the pressure cooker and discovered that the entire escape valve unit had blown off the lid of the pan. In his letter to the company, he asserted his claim:

> *I demand that you replace not only my pressure cooker, but also reimburse me in the amount of $554, which is what it cost me to re-wallpaper my kitchen after your product failed in such a dangerous and destructive way.*

The company, Presley Cookware, has a strict policy on customer claims. It will grant any claim involving replacement of a returned product; it will grant no claim for cash outlay; it will accept no liability under any circumstances. The customer-relations representative operates under these guidelines. He knows, therefore, that he will say "no" to Mr. Nguyen's claim in his letter (Figure 8-5).

Notice that the writer avoids telling Mr. Nguyen that he is wrong or has not followed directions. Such direct confrontation will lead only to anger and an end to communication. The writer takes a firm stand regarding the money demanded by the customer. Subtly, the writer never mentions the exact amount, allowing it to slip from attention.

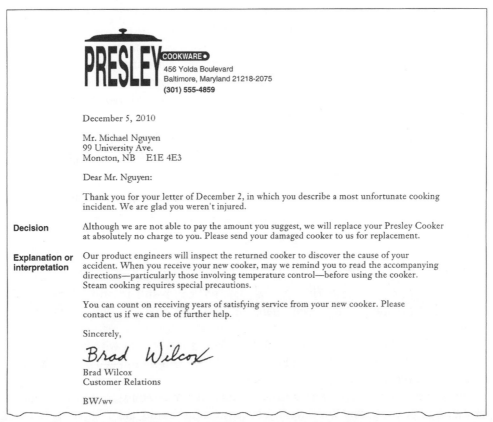

Figure 8-5 Negative adjustment letter

A form of compromise is held out in the offer of a new pot, a slight but wise concession by the company. Many angry clients seek to save face more than recover money. Mr. Nguyen may well feel that receiving a new pot, though far from his original demand, at least shows the company is willing to make amends.

Notice, too, that the writer never admits fault on the part of the company. Such an admission of liability might be used against the company in a later lawsuit. In showing professional concern for the cause of the accident, the writer invites the customer to send in the damaged pressure cooker for examination.

Instead of expressing outright sympathy, the writer tries to move the focus to positive present and future events ("you weren't injured," "a new cooker," "no charge") rather than dwelling on the event causing Mr. Nguyen's claim letter. Expressing sorrow for each detail of the incident would only stir up bad memories for the reader. Therefore, the expression of sympathy is general and brief.

At times, you may choose to explain your decision before announcing your negative response in a direct way. Consider this rearrangement of the body of the letter to Mike Nguyen:

Thank you for your letter of December 2 in which you describe a most unfortunate cooking incident. We are glad you weren't injured.

Our product engineers will inspect your cooker to discover the cause of your accident. Please return it (we will pay postage) at your earliest convenience to the address above. We will then replace your Presley Cooker at absolutely no charge to you. When you receive your new cooker, be sure to read the accompanying directions—particularly those involving temperature control—before using the cooker. Steam cooking requires special precautions.

You can count on years of reliable service from your new cooker. Please call on us if we can help you further.

You must judge whether to explain the grounds for your decision before or after the negative response. In either case, the goal is to help the reader understand and deal with your decision.

8.3.4 Writing Follow-Up Letters

Even a very polite, sympathetic letter saying "no" can result in an indignant, quite unsympathetic reply: "What do you mean, 'no'? I demand that you explain your reasons and reconsider!"

Resist the temptation to become defensive and to respond with a blunt, angry, or sarcastic letter. The test of your business maturity will be to keep your head when others are losing theirs.

First, assess your situation by taking a look at the circumstances. What did the person originally request? What were your reasons for saying "no"? What explanation did you provide at that time? What further explanation is being demanded?

Then decide what you want to accomplish in your follow-up letter. You have no obligation, of course, to agree to any demands for further explanation. In many business situations, no amount of explaining will satisfy someone who is angry and disappointed. However, ignoring a demand for explanation seldom resolves matters, and it often complicates them.

When you're faced with a demand that deserves an additional negative answer, you can choose one or more of these alternatives:

- rephrase your original explanation.
- provide the additional information requested.
- refer the matter to someone else.

The following example illustrates the options for follow-up letters and how they might be carried out.

The original response:

The repairs you request are no longer covered under warranty, which expired last year. Our factory service centre estimates a parts-and-labour cost of $485 to repair the unit. (It would then be covered under warranty again for a period of three years.)

- **Repeat your explanation in different words.** Add appropriate clarifying information. Your reader will feel insulted, and rightly so, if you simply repeat your exact words from an earlier letter:

We're happy to provide further information regarding your warranty, as you requested in your letter of June 15. The warranty on the Savage 307 unit extends from date of purchase (in your case, Dec. 2, 2010) for a period of 3 years (expiring Dec. 2, 2013). All factory repairs after the expiration of warranty are charged at industry-standard rates, with reinstatement of warranty following such factory repairs.

In this case, the writer does not try to "sell" the customer on having the factory make necessary repairs to the unit. That type of strategy might be misunderstood as manipulation ("we have you over a barrel, and here's your only way out").

- **Provide the additional information requested.** You may decide to put in some extra effort to salvage a business relationship. In the following example, the writer researched the customer's complaint and reports the results:

In response to your letter of June 15, I met with the head of our testing division for her evaluation of the breakdown you experienced with your Savage 307 unit. She reports three similar cases in the past two years. All three were associated with the customers' inadvertent use of graphite oil instead of the 30-weight oil specified in the maintenance manual. I do not know, of course, whether this circumstance is applicable to your case, but I offer the information in the hope that it will be useful to you in evaluating your difficulties with the Savage 307 unit and your plans for repair.

In this case, the writer is fairly certain that the customer has simply used the wrong oil in the unit but stops short of saying so directly. This spares the customer loss of face and avoids false accusation. The customer will probably appreciate the writer's research efforts and willingness to supply helpful information.

- **Refer the matter to someone else.** This option is helpful only when it truly helps the reader. Don't pass on a complaint to an employee who never answers the phone or responds to letters. In the following example, the writer refers a customer to a company employee specifically trained to deal with product complaints:

In your letter of June 15, you asked for additional information regarding warranty on the Savage 307 unit. I've asked Linda Conway, Customer Relations Manager, to respond to your request within the next 7 days. She and I have discussed the details of your earlier letters and I trust that the additional information she provides will prove helpful to you.

In each of these alternatives, the writer did not emphasize personal feelings of remorse or pity ("I'm so sorry that our hands are tied in repairing your unit," etc.). Such expressions may be less than sincere and may only lead the reader to feel that the request was unjustly refused. (Why else would the writer feel such emotion?)

SELF-CHECK

- Describe the four-step model of saying "no" to an order.
- Describe the three-step model of refusing a request or invitation.
- Describe the four guidelines to writing no to claims.
- Describe the three steps to writing follow-up letters.

SUMMARY

By choosing the right words and the right tone, writers can deliver negative news in the most respectful and professional way possible. With its use of the buffer statement, the indirect pattern is an effective way of considering a reader's reaction to bad news. When a more straightforward delivery is called for, the direct approach is more appropriate. Writers should follow models and use techniques to organize and write negative message that address a variety of business situations.

KEY TERMS

Buffer statement   A positive or neutral statement that serves as a starting place for a negative response or message.

ASSESS YOUR UNDERSTANDING

Go to www.wiley.com/canada/brounstein to evaluate your knowledge of the basics of writing negative messages. Measure your learning by comparing pre-test and post-test results.

Quick Questions

1. Every negative answer should be accompanied by an explanation. True or false?
2. A buffer statement is
   (a) a tool used in the indirect pattern
   (b) a neutral statement
   (c) a positive statement
   (d) all of the above
3. The buffer statement should appear between the negative news and the closing. True or false?
4. Which type of negative response is most common? Direct or indirect?
5. A direct approach to a negative response does not need to be as friendly as an indirect approach. True or false?
6. Negative adjustment letters begin with a buffer statement and then provide a rationale for the negative decision. True or false?
7. When should a negative response to an order be used?
   (a) You can't fill the complete order.
   (b) You can't fill the order on time.
   (c) You need to make a substitution.
   (d) all of the above
8. Follow-up letters can
   (a) provide additional information
   (b) refer the matter to someone else
   (c) repeat the original message in different words
   (d) all of the above

Give It Some Thought

1. How does a buffer statement build goodwill with a customer?
2. What are three types of buffers that writers can use to begin negative letters?
3. When is a buffer statement unnecessary in a negative-response letter?
   (a) when the original letter was not friendly
   (b) when the writer doesn't need one
   (c) when the explanation is too complicated
   (d) when there isn't enough time
4. What emotions are readers likely to feel when reading "no" letters that are too blunt?
5. When refusing a request or invitation, what structure should a writer use?
   (a) no message, statement of goodwill
   (b) statement of goodwill, buffer statement, no message
   (c) buffer statement, statement of appreciation, no message
   (d) buffer statement, no message, positive statement
6. What are three ways that you can follow up a letter that deserves further explanation?
7. When is it a good idea to refer a letter to someone else?
   (a) When the letter doesn't deserve another response
   (b) When the writer is extremely angry
   (c) When another person can better handle the response
   (d) When you're unable to rephrase your original response

Applying This Chapter

1. Compose a buffer statement for the following no messages:
   ○ Seaside Furnishings cannot reimburse customers for the postage cost incurred during return shipments.
   ○ You have not been selected for one of the four management-training positions at LJN Corporation.
2. Think of an occasion in which you've had to say "no" to someone. For whatever reason, you were unusually abrupt in your response. Script the situation, this time crafting an effective indirect response (you still don't want to hurt their feelings). Underline your buffer statement.
3. The trade organization you belong to has invited you to serve as chair of the annual scholarship fundraiser. Draft two versions of your letter declining the request—one with a buffer statement and one without. Which seems more appropriate?

4. Imagine you're a customer service representative for a company that makes electronic toys for children. A customer returned the broken microphone of a radio, asking for a replacement. In your original response, you wrote that you could not provide a replacement because that particular toy was no longer being produced. The customer wrote back, this time requesting a brand new radio—the new model. Choose one of the three techniques and draft a follow-up letter that will solve the problem.

THE NEXT STEP

Feeling Negative
Describe your own feelings aroused by reading a no letter at some time in the past. How could those feelings have been influenced by different words in the letter?

The Art of Saying "No"
You direct a large non-profit organization that considers grant applications from a wide variety of community, religious, and social organizations. Your employees have little trouble writing yes responses to such applications. But their no letters, by far the majority of their correspondence, are often abrupt and unsympathetic. You worry that applicants will think negatively about your organization and not make applications in the future. To help your employees help themselves in writing negative correspondence, write a memo that guides employees in how to improve their ability to say "no" with grace and professionalism.

Tending to a Request
As a claims supervisor for a small gardening supply manufacturer, you respond to a variety of customer requests and claims. How would you write a negative adjustment letter to a customer who complains that your company's plant food, Green Leaves, killed his houseplants?

9
WRITING PERSUASIVELY
Messages That Sell Your Ideas

STARTING POINT

Go to www.wiley.com/canada/brounstein to assess your knowledge of the basics of writing persuasively. After reviewing this website, you'll be able to determine where you need to concentrate your effort.

What You'll Learn in This Chapter:

- how persuasive letters address a reader's needs
- the five parts of a sales letter
- the role of persuasion in claim letters
- four common types of collection letters.

After Studying This Chapter, You'll be Able to:

- discuss the role of the reader in writing a persuasive letter
- identify three common types of persuasive letters
- describe the step-by-step plan for writing sales letters
- discuss the relative merits of writing tools and techniques
- understand how the ability to sell is a powerful business tool.

INTRODUCTION

The ability to sell an idea is a powerful tool. To persuade your audience to believe in what you're offering—a product, service, plan of action, or anything else—you must grab their attention and then prove that you can meet their needs. The first step in writing a persuasive letter, whether in print or via email, is to identify the reader's needs and interests. In a sales letter, a five-point plan captures a reader's attention and convinces him to believe in you, your product, or your service. On the other hand, customers use claim letters to convince a company to make amends. The chapter concludes with the claims letter, in which a company typically tries to motivate an individual to pay off a debt.

9.1 Selling with Persuasive Letters

To **persuade** someone is to influence a person's thoughts or actions, often by demonstrating reasons for that person to accept your influence. For example, you might persuade homeowners to buy fire insurance by showing them that if they don't have insurance, they'll lose their property in the event of a fire.

Persuasion must be based on truthful representation of the facts. When it's not, when information is distorted or misrepresented, such a persuasive appeal is unethical and manipulative. It would be wrong, for example, if homeowners were told they stood a 90% chance of losing their homes by fire, which is untrue.

If a letter is to influence a reader, it must also demonstrate that the position or action it suggests serves the reader's needs. Those needs are wide ranging, and readers often have many overlapping needs that effective persuasion may address, such as needs for:

money	health
more free time	comfort
productivity	entertainment
importance	security
power	knowledge
attractiveness	a desired skill
friends	reputation

These and other needs describe what interests a reader. If your product or service is to interest your reader, it must be linked in some way to a need he or she already feels. In other words, persuasive letters make readers understand that the product or service is not only good, but also good for them.

The majority of business letters are persuasive in the best sense. They present ideas, evidence, and beliefs in an effort to win agreement (and possibly action) on the part of the reader by considering his or her needs, point of view, and background. There are three common types of persuasive letters:

- **Sales or promotional letters,** which persuade readers to buy a product or service.
- **Claim letters,** which persuade the reader, often a company employee in charge of customer service, to make requested adjustments because of a flaw or a failure in a product or service.
- **Collection letters,** usually a series of them, which persuade the reader to pay money he or she owes.

The claim letter and the collection letter are covered in Sections 9.3 and 9.4.

SELF-CHECK

- Define persuasion.
- Describe the role of the reader's needs in a persuasive business letter.
- List three common types of persuasive letters.

9.2 Writing Sales Letters

The work of creating an effective sales letter begins in your head, not on paper. First, decide to concentrate on *you* (the reader) rather than *I* (the writer). In the following examples, notice how the focus of the sales concept changes:

The new Civic features a four-cylinder engine, revolutionary new suspension, and tinted windows.

In the you example, the writer has used the reader's needs (for economy, comfort, and security) to sell the product. "The product is not only good," the writer seems to say to the reader, "it's good for you."

The new Civic features a four-cylinder engine to save you money on gasoline, a revolutionary new suspension to take the bumps away, and tinted windows for glare-free driving.

But do readers always know what their needs are? Should you take time at the beginning of a sales letter to remind the reader of those needs?

It's an important question. On the one hand, sales letters that serve no need on the reader's part fail in their purpose. "It looks like a nice product," the reader says, "but I don't need it." On the other hand, you risk alienating your readers by assuming a set of needs in your letter that they may not feel at all.

That's where **market research** factors in. Either through professional research organizations or your own efforts, you gather, analyze, and interpret information about a market or a product or service to be offered. In doing so, you gain valuable information about the past, present, and potential customers for a particular product or service. You test your market in order to know your readers; this knowledge is a key part of being able to craft a successful sales letter.

Are your readers aware of their need for your product? If so, begin your sales letter by showing how your product meets their need. Are they unaware that your product can help them? If so, begin by reminding them in a sentence or two of a problem they have been experiencing. Then let your product come to the rescue in the letter by providing an answer to that problem.

In an example of a sales opener that assumes the reader is aware of a need related to the product or service for sale, the product or service comes first:

> *Francis Jewellery is proud to be the only wholesale jeweller in this city to offer a free X-ray with each gem it sells.*

- The opening would be ineffective for an audience that was unaware of the need for an X- ray to reveal characteristics and flaws in a gem.
- When an audience needs to be made aware of a need, begin the sales letter by describing the need that your product or service fulfills.

> *As someone who has expressed an interest in buying fine jewellery, you may already be aware of the importance of using X-ray technology to reveal characteristics and flaws in gems. Francis Jewellery is proud to be the only wholesale jeweller in this city to offer a free X-ray with each gem it sells.*

FOR EXAMPLE

No Time to Spare

When the owner of a hair salon was trying to decide if and how to expand her business, she started by doing some informal research about her clients' needs. Because most of them were business people who were only able to come in during the lunch hour, the owner knew that her expansion would have to work with that restriction. The sales letter she sent to the office managers in the building announced new services—massages, facials, and manicures—which took only 20 minutes each. To encourage new customers to try the improved and expanded service, the owner included an offer for one half-price visit.

After you have analyzed the reader's needs and determined how much or how little to assume, you can begin the S-A-L-E-S process, a step-by-step plan for each part of the sales letter:

- **S**—Spark the imagination and curiosity of the reader.
- **A**—Announce the product or service.
- **L**—List the advantages to the client.
- **E**—Express appreciation and goodwill.
- **S**—Specify exactly what the client should do—and when.

9.2.1 Spark the Imagination

The opener of a sales letter should immediately capture the reader's attention. If it doesn't, there's a good chance the reader won't read it, and it will end up in the recycling bin with the other unsolicited mail. Here are several ways to spark imagination and arouse curiosity:

- Suggest that you can do something unique for the reader. Few of us can resist reading on to find out what that "something" is.

  Rocky Mountain Tire Company offers you a new way of buying tires.

- Drop an impressive name, if appropriate, and then associate the reader with that name.

  NHL player Luke Seaborg, like you, knows the importance of regular eye examinations.

- Mention local people, places, and events, if possible.

  Winnipeg had dirt streets when my grandfather built Higgins Drug Store—and his reputation—at the corner of Portage and Main.

- Empathize—feel *with*—your reader.

  Cash emergencies occasionally catch us all off guard, especially as the holiday season nears.

  In most cases, this opener should not be more than a sentence or two long.

9.2.2 Announce the Product or Service

You've piqued your reader's curiosity with your opening sentences, and now he or she wants that curiosity satisfied. This portion should first advertise your product or service; only then can you move on to matters such as the history of your company or your product, or the expertise of your personnel. Name what you have to offer in specific terms, and do so with an honest, assertive voice. Where space permits, provide a persuasive example or two:

At Rocky Mountain Tire, just your signature, address, and driver's licence number let you drive away on a high-quality set of snow tires—with 24–36 months to pay.

Each November, we celebrate Seniors' Month at Higgins Drug Store. This November, we offer a two-for-one sale on all cosmetic items, with large reductions on all other store merchandise except pharmaceuticals. For example, school supplies have been marked down 40%.

9.2.3 List the Advantages to the Client

This section of the sales letter convinces readers that your advertised claims in the second paragraph have practical applications. Here's your chance to demonstrate the wide variety of needs your product or service can fulfill.

Because the second paragraph of a sales letter often turns out to be rather long, consider saving space by setting off major points as a list:

Floral Display, Inc. will take charge of the interior landscape of your office by:

- *placing gorgeous tropical plants throughout your workspace*
- *maintaining these plants at the peak of condition and beauty*
- *helping you make inexpensive but stunning decorating decisions using fresh, fragrant plants.*

9.2.4 Express Appreciation and Goodwill

So far, your reader has followed your train of thought through most of the sales letter. Now's the time to thank him or her for considering your ideas, or to praise the reader's company. Although compliments may seem to be unnecessary to you, they are high-interest items to readers. Everyone likes to hear nice things about themselves. You want interest to be high and dispositions to be rosy at this point in the letter because just around the corner lie the final sentences that matter most: the call to specific action. The following are typical examples of compliments and expressions of goodwill:

In its advertising and public offices, your firm is known throughout the industry for its continental flair.

We admire the standard you have set for yourself and others.

9.2.5 Specify Exactly What the Client Should Do—and When

Finally, tell the reader in a clear, specific way what you want him or her to do—and when—to bring about the advantages described in the letter. Maintain the upbeat yes attitude. Be careful not to use threats: "Your life depends on your tires. Buy Safe-T tires now before . . ."

Instead, define an easy and appealing path of action for your reader. If the action is at all complicated, break it into separate steps:

Call Marci at 555-2451 to arrange for a free decorating analysis without obligation. If you prefer, mail the enclosed card to receive our colour decorating catalogue—with no strings or plants attached.

Present the enclosed coupon on or before May 10 at your local Safe-T Tire Store, 1325 South Olive Street. You'll receive $40 off your new set of four Safe-T tires.

Specific action statements often consist of an action verb (such as "call," "present," "visit," or "email"), a specific address and telephone number, a specific time ("now" or "on or before May 10"), and perhaps one final advantage (free decorating analysis, colour decorating catalogue, $40 off) if the reader does what you suggest.

Observe each of the *S-A-L-E-S* sections working together in the complete sales letter shown in Figure 9-1:

2900 Gordon Dr. • Kelowna, BC V1Y 3H4 • 250-555-8754

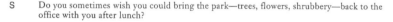

FLORAL DISPLAYS

April 10, 2010

Mr. David Jenkins
District Manager
Coleberry Financial Systems, Inc.
9465 St. George St.
Vancouver, BC   V6H 0A5

Dear Mr. Jenkins:

S   Do you sometimes wish you could bring the park—trees, flowers, shrubbery—back to the office with you after lunch?

A   Floral Displays, Inc. makes wishes come true. We rent out and maintain gorgeous tropical plants for your office and reception area. For less than $2 per day, we can surround you in lush philodendron or hide you behind an elephant plant.

L   Plants make business more pleasant and more profitable.

   • Clients appreciate your thoughtfulness and admire your taste in softening the bare edges of business life with lovely plants. Happy clients spend more, more often.

   • Employee turnover (the great hidden expense for most businesses) is drastically reduced. Employees come to think of the office as an attractive, inviting place.

E   Your reputation in Kelowna as a leading financial services company can only be further enhanced by a modest investment in a more healthful, attractive, and impressive office environment.

S   Take a moment right now to call Marci (555-9049) for a free floral decoration analysis of your office. She will come at your convenience, finish her work quickly, then dazzle you with affordable decorating ideas. If you prefer, mail in the enclosed card for our latest colour catalogue of decorating ideas.

With best wishes,

Sandra T. Lansdon

Sandra T. Lansdon
Marketing Director

STL/bck
Enclosure: "Your Catalogue Reservation" (return postcard)

Figure 9-1 Complete sales letter following the S-A-L-E-S pattern

Sales Letter Pitfalls

You've worked hard to create a sales letter that will capture your reader's attention and persuade him or her to believe in you, your product, or your service. Don't let anything stand in the way of your big sale. The following are some common sales-letter mistakes that turn away readers:

- **Being overly ambitious.** If your readers are overwhelmed with an onslaught of information, they won't be able to focus in on your main selling point.
- **Being insincere.** Don't *try* to sound sincere—simply *be* sincere and professional about what you say your product or service can do.
- **Making exaggerated claims.** Most readers know that if it sounds too good to be true, it probably is.
- **Trashing the competition.** Worry less about badmouthing your competitors and more about selling the merits of your product.

When writing any kind of persuasive letter, remember that your reader has already faced dozens of persuasive appeals that day. Television, radio, magazine, Internet, and newspaper ads have screamed or whispered, "Buy me!" Business memos, letters, emails, and conversations have been attempts to persuade ("Approve me!"). Your letter arrives in competition with these other persuasive appeals. To be effective, it must distinguish itself in a number of ways: by its readability, responsiveness to the reader's needs, persuasive logic, engaging tone, and honesty.

SELF-CHECK

- Define market research.
- Name the five parts of the sales letter.
- Discuss ways of capturing a reader's attention.
- Describe three common mistakes found in sales letters.

9.3 Writing Claim Letters

Some persuasive letters have an objective other than sales. This business letter is not selling a product or service; rather, it is persuading an organization, company, or individual to make amends.

A **claim letter** is a persuasive business letter that customers use to make and explain a demand for repayment, restitution, or replacement because of a failure in a product or service. The claim letter is one of the most powerful tools in a business writer's workshop.

Imagine, for example, that your company purchased a Model 61 photocopier for $4,021. It was delivered with several bottles of photocopy toner, which you poured into the machine according to instructions.

The toner, you discover too late, was the wrong kind. It has gummed up the machine; no copies can be made at all. The salesperson who sold you the machine says you should have noticed the error before pouring in the toner—the bottles were marked "For Model #41." He refuses to replace the machine or to pay for its repair. Meanwhile, your office work grinds to a halt for lack of a photocopier.

If you can imagine your own anger in such a situation, you know how difficult it can be to compose a steady, decisive, action-oriented letter in times of emotional stress. Without denying the validity of your feelings, use the following guidelines and questions to write a claim letter that will bring results:

- **Assess the entire situation.** Exactly what happened? Where do you place blame? Is there another side to the story? What would remedy the problem? When must action be taken? Who must take action?

- **Consider your audience.** Who is the person who has caused the problem or the person who can solve the problem? If you're not sure, call to get the name of the person who can act on your claim. Contact information and instructions from the company may help you decide whether an email or a standard letter will be the best approach for your claim.

- **Tell your story in a logical and organized way.** Present a factual, detailed description of the situation and a clear explanation for your disappointment. Include copies (keep the originals) of documentation such as invoices, cancelled cheques, or receipts if they will support your claim.

- **Be positive in your approach.** In most cases, the company will want to resolve the claim amicably (see Section 7.5). A threatening or negative approach won't help your cause. No matter how angry or upset you are, leave your emotions out of your message. If you need to, you can refer to how upset or disappointed you were, but you should do so in a logical, unemotional manner.

- **Insist on specific, timely action.** Don't leave the remedy to the imagination of your reader (as in the appeal to "Do something!"). Spell out specifically what you want done and when. If you need action by a specific date, make the deadline reasonable. If you need action to be taken very soon, for example to refund your credit card before the billing date, explain the reason to your reader.

- **Offer your co-operation.** When appropriate, offer to assist in the effort to correct the situation (send additional supporting materials, for example).

Notice how the writer in Figure 9-2 first assesses the situation by reviewing the facts and circumstances surrounding the photocopy incident. Next he considers the audience. Addressing a letter to the obstinate sales representative probably will do little good, so our writer decides to send the letter to the manager of the photocopy store:

Levi & Willard Accountants, Inc.
3459 New St.
Burlington, ON   L7R 1K3
905-555-3574

March 15, 2010

Ms. Wendy Johnson, Manager
Target Photocopy Supply
1459 Bayview Ave.
Toronto, ON   M5R 9T9

Dear Ms. Johnson:

On March 9, my firm purchased a Model # 61 photocopy machine from your salesman, Mark Trebley. As your records will show, we paid $4,021 for the machine (invoice #29843). That price included a six-month supply of toner, delivered to us with the machine.

Tell   I personally poured the toner into the machine in the way that Mark Trebley showed me. Only when the machine stopped making copies a few minutes later did we discover that the wrong toner (for Model #41) had been delivered to us with the machine.

I phoned Mr Trebley that same day. He claimed to be "swamped" with customers and promised to phone back. After my repeated efforts to reach him by phone, I called personally at your store and confronted Mr. Trebley with the error regarding the toner. He made these points:

- Someone "in the showroom" sent the wrong toner.
- In his opinion, I was largely responsible for the problem since the toner bottles were labelled "For Model #41".
- The machine would need an extensive and expensive overhaul for which neither he nor your store would be responsible.

He and I have had no further contact.

Insist   I insist that you remedy the problem caused by your personnel by replacing our photocopy machine with a free loaner during the period of overhaul. To the detriment of our accounting business, we have been without a copy machine for almost a week. Therefore, please have the loaner sent over no later than March 19.

Offer cooperation   We will not insist the loaner be a new Model #61. In fact, we are willing to make do with any serviceable model so long as it arrives by March 19.

Name specifics   Please call me (555-2943) no later than 5 p.m. tomorrow. I am confident that you are as anxious as we are to put this problem to rest. As your company has an excellent reputation for customer service, I am confident that we will be able to come to an agreement.

Sincerely,

Thomas Levi

Thomas Levi
Partner

c.c. Mr. Mark Trebley

TL/eb

Figure 9-2 Claim letter

Claims and adjustment letters, written well, can often resolve day-to-day business problems without the expensive and time-consuming involvement of lawyers and other outsiders.

Obviously, it's in a company's best interest to respond to claim letters so that they can keep customers happy whenever possible. People who work in customer service, however, admit that certain letters don't receive the same attention as others. To ensure that your claim letter gets the attention it deserves, heed the following advice when writing:

- **Stay cool.** Some people are so mad when they write that no one can figure out what went wrong, when it happened, or what they tried to do about it. Keep this in mind, particularly, when writing an email in this state of mind. (Sections 6.4 and 6.5 cover ways of writing effective emails about conflicts.)
- **Don't delay.** Send your letter as soon as the problem comes up. You weaken your case by waiting too long.
- **Be fair and polite.** Avoid depicting those who made the mistake in derogatory terms, such as "idiots" or "incompetents."
- **Be open-minded.** Don't rule out the possibility of a solution. A man who had recurring problems with his car cigarette lighter would settle, he said, for nothing less than a new replacement car. Of course, a company is left with no reasonable course of action but to refuse the request.
- **Stay on course.** Letters that wander about the topic often never quite say what the customer wants to complain about.

Learning from such experience, you can write demand letters that are controlled, realistic, and organized. That simple prescription proves easier said than done, however, when your emotions are ruling your actions.

FOR EXAMPLE

Claims and Amends

A pharmaceutical company decided to reward its employees with a catered summer barbeque at its headquarters. The weather was gorgeous and attendance was high, but the catering staff was late and the food was cold and disappointing. Nearly all the employees had left by the time the food arrived. The next morning, the company's director of human resources sent a letter to the owner of the catering company. In it, she described in detail what had happened and asked for a full refund. The caterer, knowing how influential the pharmaceutical company was, agreed and furthermore offered a 40 percent discount on the next catered event.

SELF-CHECK

- Define claim letter.
- Discuss guidelines for composing action-oriented letters.
- Review advice for writing persuasive letters that are controlled, realistic, and organized.

9.4 Writing Collection Letters

Whether it's mortgage payments, consumer loans, suppliers, or credit cards, it's a fact of life that some people and companies fail to meet their financial obligations.

If it's your job to write collection letters, then you know that your goal is to settle the account as quickly as possible. Therefore, the more effective your letter is, the better the chance that the debt will be paid. Use the following five questions to guide you as you plan your letter:

- Why has the debt not been paid?
- What tone will your letter use?
- What do you want the reader to do?
- When and where must the action occur?
- What motivational force inside the reader do you plan to address?

Collection letters range in style from friendly to final, and they are usually sent in a series, typically three to four weeks apart. The following sections will further discuss four styles of collection letters: friendly, firm, urgent, and final.

To Read or Not to Read?

Realize that the delinquent debtor will never even see your carefully written words unless he or she chooses to open the envelope. Too often, well-designed collection letters go out in less-impressive envelopes that shout "junk mail" or "collection letter," and they are promptly trashed. Put your collection letter into a good-quality, letter-sized envelope—the kind you would use for regular business communication. The address on the envelope, whether written by hand or printed, should look as though it could appear on an important letter which, of course, is exactly what your collection letter is.

9.4.1 The Friendly Reminder

In the collection letter shown in Figure 9-3, the writer assumes that the debtor simply forgot to make the payment. Business managers use this initial non-threatening approach for good reason. The first collection letter can bring more than a 50 percent response rate from delinquent debtors. These are relatively good customers who you don't want to chase away with surly collection language. The letter, therefore, is friendly. Though the action statement names a specific amount to be paid, the time is stated generally ("now," "as soon as possible," "right away"), and no specific place or person for payment is named. The letter is brief because clients will not read more. It relies on goodwill and a sense of responsibility to produce the payment of the debt:

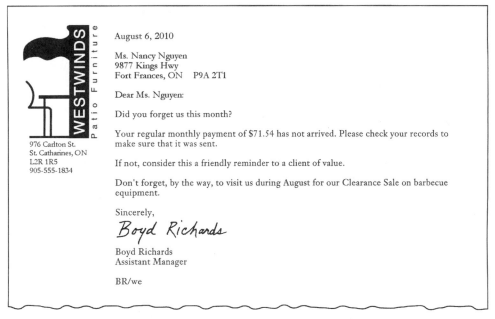

Figure 9-3 Friendly collection letter

9.4.2 The Firm Request

If the first collection letter brings no response, you can assume that a simple slip of memory is not to blame. Instead, assume that some problem (illness, layoff, travel, and so forth) has interrupted the regular flow of payments. The tone becomes firm with a hint of urgency. The specific action is spelled out, with a time and place named. You attempt to motivate the reader on the basis of a sense of fairness and business decency (see Figure 9-4):

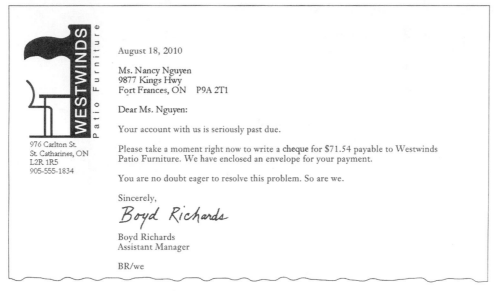

Figure 9-4 Firm collection letter

At your discretion, a pre-addressed return envelope may be included as an additional prod to put a cheque in the mail. Some businesses even include a stamped envelope, reasoning that the money spent on postage is a good investment to reclaim a bad debt.

9.4.3 The Urgent Appeal

If payment still is not received, the writer must assume that the debtor cannot or will not pay without strong motivation. The tone is now straightforward and urgent. The letter names a specific time, place, and person to whom payment must be made. The writer attempts to motivate the customer by pride, and a bit of fear.

The urgent collection letter shown in Figure 9-5 includes a name for the debtor to contact. This creates the possibility that the debtor will call and arrange payments of some kind. Note, however, that a two-month payment is now due, and it is unlikely that the debtor will write a large cheque when he could not or would not write a smaller one. The looming alternative is to turn the debt over to a collection agency.

9.4.4 The Final Demand

By now, the company has invested a considerable amount of time and expense in trying to rescue a bad debt. The last collection letter (before the collection agency begins its own series) assumes that the debtor will not pay and will make no effort to arrange partial payment.

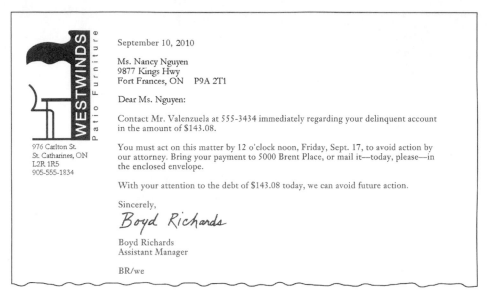

Figure 9-5 Urgent collection letter

The letter in Figure 9-6 illustrates the characteristics of the final collection effort: its emotional stance is determined, tough, but not offensive. It names a last-ditch time, place, and contact person for payment. The principal motivator now is fear of legal action. The company no longer cares to consider future patronage from the debtor. It wants its money:

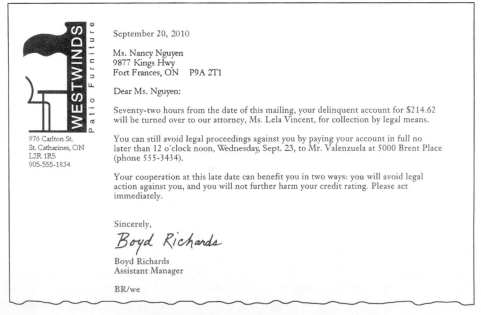

Figure 9-6 Final collection letter

> **FOR EXAMPLE**
>
> **Credit Repairs**
> Seema works in the collection department of a company that manufactures bicycle parts. Vincent, a somewhat new customer, had placed a large order for his repair shop several months ago, but had missed his second payment. Seema's first letter out informed Vincent of the payment, indicating that she expected he had simply forgotten. When the payment still did not come in, Seema's second letter was firmer. In it, she explained that his payment would ensure their continued good business relationship; she also asked that he call her to discuss the payment. Because her tone was not threatening, Vincent felt comfortable making the call, in which he explained that his business was recovering after being closed for two weeks because of an electrical problem in the building. He then promised to send in half of the owed payment immediately, and the other half in two weeks.

SELF-CHECK

- Define collection letter.
- Use guiding questions to prepare collection letters.
- Describe four styles of collection letters.
- Explain the main benefits of the four styles of collection letters.

SUMMARY

The difference between success and failure in writing persuasive letters often lies in your skill in making your points clearly and convincingly. A key element of that is identifying your reader's needs and interests. Using a five-point plan, you can capitalize on those needs and convince a reader to believe in you, your product, or your service. Customers writing claim letters use similar powers of persuasion to convince a company to make amends. Finally, collection letters motivate individuals to pay off debt.

KEY TERMS

Claim letter	A persuasive business letter that customers use to make and explain a demand for repayment, restitution, or replacement because of a failure in a product or service.

| Market research | Testing a market to gain an understanding of an audience, often done by professional research organizations. |
| Persuade | To influence a person's thoughts or actions, often by demonstrating reasons for that person to accept your influence. |

ASSESS YOUR UNDERSTANDING

Go to www.wiley.com/canada/brounstein to evaluate your knowledge of the basics of writing persuasively. Measure your learning by comparing pre-test and post-test results.

Quick Questions

1. Persuasive letters demonstrate a reason for the reader to accept the influence of the writer. True or false?

2. Examples of human needs include
   (a) reputation
   (b) entertainment
   (c) security
   (d) all of the above

3. The following three types of letters—sales, claims, and collection—are crafted to influence a reader. True or false?

4. Market research is a tool for
   (a) measuring the debt of your readers
   (b) evaluating your readers' needs
   (c) persuading a reader to believe in a product
   (d) all of the above

5. The first step in writing a sales letter is to announce the product or service. True or false?

6. A sales letter shouldn't risk putting off readers by telling them what to do. True or false?

7. Customers use claim letters to collect prepaid services or products. True or false?

8. When writing a claim letter, a customer should
   (a) consider the audience
   (b) relate the story in a logical way

(c) offer co-operation

(d) all of the above

9. A high level of emotion is an effective way of adding impact to a claim letter. True or false?

10. The goal of a collection letter is to settle a debt as quickly as possible. True or false?

11. Which of the following questions are useful for preparing a collection letter?

(a) What tone should you use?

(b) What do you want the reader to do?

(c) Why has the debt not been paid?

(d) all of the above

12. The friendly collection letter specifies when and where a debt should be paid. True or false?

13. The presentation of a collection letter is just as important as any other piece of business writing. True or false?

Give It Some Thought

1. What kind of persuasive letter addresses a reader's need for security?

2. Why should the steps of the S-A-L-E-S process be relatively short?

3. What are four ways of capturing a reader's attention?

4. To succeed in business, you need to beat the competition. What is one way of avoiding the common mistake of competition trashing in a sales letter?

(a) Bad-mouth them only once

(b) Concentrate more on your product

(c) Mention the competition in a positive way

(d) Attach a separate document

5. In what ways does anger undermine a writer's success in developing an effective claims letter?

6. Why is it important to specify the desired action of a claim letter?

7. How do a writer's assumptions change during the course of writing a series of collection letters?

8. At what point should a firm collection letter be sent?

(a) when a slip of memory is not to blame for the lack of payment

(b) after an urgent collection letter

(c) at the first sign of a late payment

(d) all of the above

9. Which type of letter comes before a collection agency becomes involved?

Applying This Chapter

1. You belong to an organization that is sponsoring a ski weekend for its members. Write a letter to members, selling them on the idea and telling them how to sign up.

2. Choose a sales letter you received recently. Find three common human needs that the letter proposes to satisfy. Note them in the margin of the letter.

3. Write a claims letter to the customer relations department of Quality Foods about the bean-sized stone you found in a can of their kidney beans. Unfortunately, you discovered the stone by biting down and cracking a $750 crown on a tooth. Decide in your claim letter what you want to ask for.

4. You've been going to the same chain of auto shops for six years to get the oil changed in your car. You've always been happy with the service until recently. The last time you went, they didn't replace the oil cap, and the time before that they cross-threaded the drain plug. Both times, you had to return to get the problems corrected. Write a claim letter to the owner of the chain in which you ask for an explanation and restitution.

5. You manage the collections department at Gold Coast Furniture. Although you have sets of form letters available, you still take the time to write some letters yourself. Write a first collection letter to the president of the city's chamber of commerce, Mrs. Doreen Frank, who purchased an expensive walnut dining set. She put 20% down two months ago, but has not made any monthly payments of $102. At last month's chamber meeting, she mentioned to you how much she was enjoying the table.

6. You own a small neighbourhood appliance store that's been in business for more than 30 years. One of your customers, Joseph Nesbitt, owes one final payment of $68 on the television set he purchased from you earlier in the year. Up until now, he's made his payments on time. Write a series of three collection letters trying to persuade him to pay off his debt.

THE NEXT STEP

Sales Pitch
Think of your company, school, or organization—what it has and what you think it needs. Choose one service that you can offer and write a letter to the person in charge selling the idea as well as your services.

Know Your Audience
You are the inventor of a new and exciting cell phone application designed to read text messages aloud. This new application will help drivers pay attention to the road while

still receiving text messages as they drive. Write a sales letter to an audience that knows about that product or service. Write a second version of the letter for an audience that might be expected to use the product or service, but that knows little about it.

Make a Claim

You have recently purchased the AmazingGro plant watering system. The product claimed that it would double the size of your house plants in 30 days or less. You have used the product as the program directed for an entire month, and none of your plants have grown any larger and one plant has actually died. Write a claim letter to the company that follows the guidelines set down in this chapter.

Prepare to Collect

Together with a group of classmates, draft a series of four all-purpose collection letters to be used by your mattress supply company as an account becomes increasingly delinquent.

10
SPOKEN COMMUNICATION
Getting Results with Words

STARTING POINT

Go to www.wiley.com/canada/brounstein to assess your knowledge of the basics of spoken communication. After reviewing this website, you'll be able to determine where you need to concentrate your effort.

What You'll Learn in This Chapter:

- the benefits of speaking assertively
- ways of delivering a positive message
- techniques for using the telephone effectively
- uses for voice mail in business
- steps for planning successful business meetings
- how to actively participate in meetings
- ways to lead effective business meetings.

After Studying This Chapter, You'll be Able to:

- discuss how honesty, directness, and constructiveness factor into speaking in the positive
- review ways of emphasizing the positive in a statement
- identify techniques for using the telephone to your advantage in business
- discuss the merits of techniques used to plan and lead business meetings
- understand the role of positive and assertive speaking skills in business communications.

INTRODUCTION

You need to choose your most effective words in order to deliver your message to others, whether in a conversation, a voice message, or a meeting. This chapter covers an approach for expressing a message the best way possible. Ways of applying assertive and positive speaking skills are described. Tools are outlined for overcoming the difficulties inherent in telephone communications, including voice mail. This chapter also covers guidelines for planning effective meetings, participating in meetings, and, finally, leading meetings.

10.1 Speaking Assertively: the Positive Approach

How you use language greatly influences how people receive and understand what you say and write. Section 2.2 focused on non-verbal tools (how the message is said) for assertively communicating your messages. This section focuses on verbal tools for assertive speaking—the substance of what you say. In business, all style and no substance often doesn't go far. You need both of them to come across positively to others.

If you're like most working people, you have colleagues, superiors, and customers who all have expectations, requests, and inquiries to which you can respond and act accordingly. They want you to provide answers to their questions. They want you to perform certain duties or functions. They want to know when you're going to get something done. Much of how you manage and then meet these expectations ties into how you communicate about them with others.

Communication starts by understanding how to use language in its most powerful and positive form. **Speaking in the positive** is about saying your messages the best way possible. When you speak in the positive, you're being honest, direct, and constructive:

- **Honest:** Communicating honestly means being straight and truthful with others, having nothing deceptive or insincere in your language. Most people are able to honestly tell what they think about an issue—as long as they feel safe in doing so.
- **Direct:** Direct means simply getting to the point and doing so with tact and respect. Sometimes people confuse directness with being blunt. Being blunt doesn't take the other person into consideration and often is hurtful in the way the speaker gets to the point. Here is an example that contrasts direct and blunt speaking:
  - **Direct:** "You have a spot on your shirt right by the pocket."
  - **Blunt:** "Look at your shirt. Ever heard of napkins?"
- **Constructive:** Being constructive is being as objective as possible in the words you say. Sometimes, people tell it like it is, but then ruin their messages by using **destructive** words. That isn't speaking in the positive. Whether the issue is a sensitive one or you have good or bad news to report, being constructive means making your point with words that make the message clear and respectful.

> ### FOR EXAMPLE
>
> **Down with Destructive**
>
> Rafael's boss recognized that although he was exceptionally talented, he didn't have much of a way with words when communicating with his staff. She even sent him to a one-day management seminar that covered, among other things, ways of using language to make a sensitive point. Now when a situation arises where Rafael would naturally use language more destructively than constructively, he can catch himself and rework what he has to say. Recently, Rafael showcased his new skill when he had to speak with a team member about her less-than-impressive marketing plan. Typically, he would have said, "That marketing plan you did just isn't going to cut it. If this is the best you can do, you've got major problems." Instead, he offered, "I had a chance to review the marketing plan that you submitted yesterday. It's going to need revision to meet our needs. Let's review what's needed and strategize on the corrections to be made."

SELF-CHECK

- Define speaking in terms of positive, constructive, and destructive patterns.
- List the three characteristics of speaking in the positive.
- Discuss how constructive language contributes to speaking in the positive.

10.2 Putting the Positive Approach to Work

When you apply the tools of assertive and positive speaking, you are better prepared to respond to and manage the countless requests and inquiries made of you by your co-workers, superiors, and clients.

10.2.1 Hold the Sugar

Sometimes, people think they are speaking in the positive (but aren't) by sugar-coating their words. **Sugar-coating** is trying to sweeten a bad message, an effort to make bad news sound better. The problem with sugar-coating is that it tends to make the message less sincere and direct.

Compare these two messages:

- **Sugar-coating:** "Jeff, I know you worked hard on this proposal. Maybe I didn't make my directions clear to you. I know you want to do good work. Next time, I'm sure you'll do even better. Just let me know how I can help you."
- **Speaking in the positive:** "Jeff, I reviewed your proposal. A few parts need some revisions. Let me show you where they are needed and then talk with you about making the corrections."

In the sugar-coated message, the speaker tries hard to be nice and not hurt Jeff's feelings. Unfortunately, Jeff doesn't get a clear picture of what was done wrong, which doesn't help him in the long run. In instances like this, the receiver often dismisses the message because no sense of importance is conveyed.

In the second case, the message is straightforward. The language is clear, indicating that parts of the report need to be fixed. The mystery is gone and no harshness is delivered. This is an assertive approach.

10.2.2 Emphasizing What You Can Do Instead of What You Can't

Sometimes when people respond to the requests of others, they hit on only one or two of the three key ingredients for speaking in the positive. Honesty is the most frequently used ingredient followed by being direct. When they leave out the constructive ingredient, they sound less than helpful.

For example, suppose someone in another department asks you to research something in your area and report back with your information tomorrow. Check out the following two responses and identify the one to which you would respond more favourably and why:

> "I can't get that information for you tomorrow. I won't be around to do any of the research."
>
> "I'm about to leave for a meeting today. What I can do is work on the research when I get back and have it to you the day after tomorrow."

The same message is evident in both responses: the request can't be handled as quickly as was requested. The first response, however, doesn't indicate when the request can be completed. The second response does, and that makes it more favourable. Not only is it honest and direct like the first response, but it's also constructive.

Emphasize what you *can* do far more than what you *can't,* especially in response to requests and inquiries. Using this language tool effectively often requires a shift in thinking. Like many people, you may be used to reacting to customer or co-worker questions with the first thought that pops into your head. Here are few common unhelpful responses that people often employ to start their replies:

- "I can't do that right now."
- "I don't know what happened to that item."
- "I won't know for at least two days."

When you lead your message with remarks like these, even if you communicate something helpful, the other person may have already dismissed you. However, when you emphasize what you can do first and foremost, you lead with a positive rather than a negative statement. Quite often, if you can steer clear of what you can't do, you come across as honest, clear, and helpful, which evokes a positive feeling in return.

Here's how the unhelpful responses like "can't do," "don't know," and "won't know" sound after changing the focus to what can be done:

- "Based on a few other matters I need to handle now, I can take care of your issue by the end of today."
- "I can give you a status on that item by the end of tomorrow. I first need to check on what happened with it."
- "I can give you an update in two days. I'll know more about where that issue stands then."

The three revised responses essentially convey the same messages as the ones emphasizing the words "can't," "don't," and "won't." The key difference is the revised responses emphasize and lead with what can be done to help—even though it won't be done right away. People can live with not having every desire or demand met immediately, as long as your message emphasizes how you can help meet them in due time.

10.2.3 Emphasizing What You Will Do

In the workplace, you're often asked to take action and make commitments, and the people doing the asking want to know when you'll be done with what they need.

For example, suppose you have told someone in another department that you can provide the information that person needs. This internal customer then asks you, "When can you get that information to me?" Which of the following two responses would you respond to more favourably and why?

I'll have that information to you by the end of this week.
I'll try to have that information to you by the end of the week.

Most people respond more favourably to the first response. The second response sounds less certain; you're just going to *try* and maybe not actually do it. The first response says that you *will* get the response done. It communicates a clear commitment—and a positive feeling.

Think about the old customer service maxim, **underpromise and overdeliver.** Sometimes you see people do just the opposite in their jobs. In essence, what they say they'll do doesn't happen. They make commitments they can't meet.

The concept of underpromise and overdeliver deals with giving yourself a large enough cushion of time to get things done as you respond to a client's *when* question, "When will you get that work done?" So when you underpromise and overdeliver, you pick a deadline that you can meet or beat. Therefore, when you say, "I can have that done and sent to you by Friday of this week," and you get the job done by Friday at the latest, then your actions have matched your words and you have managed others' expectations of you.

When you let others know what you will do to handle their requests or inquiries, you're speaking in the language of confidence and commitment. This is the language that has positive influence with others:

- "I will help you."
- "I will ensure your problems are resolved."
- "I will take care of the situation once and for all."

Telling people what you will do to handle a situation or when you will deliver on a commitment removes uncertainty for the receiver and lessens the tug-of-war feeling that interactions can have. People want to deal with others who are reliable and who meet their commitments. When you don't sound fully certain of what you'll do or when you'll do it, the level of confidence people have in you goes down.

10.2.4 Knowing When to Say "No"

On those occasions when what the other person wants you to do simply cannot be done, saying "no" is appropriate and is probably the best thing you can do. First, look to offer alternatives or options for the person to consider instead. When that isn't possible, say "no" to the request and briefly explain why it can't be done. This has you sounding firm and reasonable as opposed to unyielding and autocratic, the latter of which are aggressive characteristics as described in Section 2.1.1.

FOR EXAMPLE

Tell It Like It Is

As the volunteer coordinator for an area hospital, Rita relies heavily on volunteers for programs and patient services. Volunteers often start off strong, but get overwhelmed or lose interest. To avoid being shorthanded, Rita calls each volunteer ahead of time to confirm their schedule. Many volunteers feel guilty saying "no," even though they probably won't show. As far as Rita is concerned, she'd rather have a direct and honest answer, rather than one that falsely makes her feel better.

Conversation Comprehension

Your speaking skills become even more critical when you are communicating—whether in face-to-face conversations, in meetings, or on the telephone—with someone who primarily speaks another language. In addition to avoiding the intercultural miscommunications discussed in Section 1.6, you should consider the following three guidelines:

- **Avoid slang and idioms.** Slang and idioms involve language that is used to create an image rather than to make a literal statement. Slang and idioms tend to be too informal for many business situations, and their usage can change from city to city and from country to country. For example, the English language is rich in idioms such as "right on the money" or "run an idea up the flagpole." If someone whose first language is not English attempted to analyze those statements, they would become extremely frustrated. For the sake of clear business dealings, try to use words in their literal sense and become aware of words and phrases that might be misunderstood. Instead of "right on the money," you could say, "that's exactly what I was thinking of," and instead of "run an idea up the flagpole," you could say, "let's share the idea with some other people and get their feedback."

- **Slow down your speech.** Adjust the pace of your speaking to match the rate of understanding of your listener; however, do so without sounding patronizing. By looking directly at the person, he or she can see the words as they form on your lips and notice your hand and facial gestures, and you can monitor how well you're being understood.

- **Check your listener's understanding of what you're saying.** Learn to check often (in polite ways such as an inquiring smile or raised eyebrows) to see whether your listener is understanding. In a telephone conversation, pause to ask, "Am I being clear?" or simply "okay?" The eyes can be good barometers of understanding; a glazed, lost look means you should back up and begin again.

SELF-CHECK

- Define sugar-coating and underpromise and overdeliver.
- Explain the difference between sugar-coating and speaking in the positive.
- Discuss the importance of placing emphasis on what you can do in a situation.
- Consider the importance of knowing when to say no.

10.3 Getting the Most Out of the Telephone

Because people use them to such a great extent at work, you must be able to handle yourself on the telephone and on voice mail with customers, colleagues, and everyone else you work with.

For as much as the telephone has done in terms of efficiency and speed in business, it does have its limitations. Unlike in face-to-face interactions, you don't have visual contact in telephone conversations, so you don't experience the non-verbal cues from body language that help you use the tools of assertive speaking. The following ideas and tips can help you overcome this difference and get the most out of your telephone interactions:

10.3.1 Start with a Smile in Your Voice

You've probably met someone who's warm and friendly in person but whose voice may sound unpleasant or monotonous on the phone. Some people aren't aware of their demeanour when talking on the phone, and this comes across in the person's voice. Starting every call, whether you receive or initiate it, with a smile in your voice means that you sound upbeat and friendly.

In fact, if you consciously try to say "hello" with a smile on your face, the smile will come through in your voice. Bringing out the pleasant side of your voice at the beginning of the call helps you set a positive tone and makes others feel more relaxed with you.

10.3.2 Give a Professional Greeting

For business use, practise a smooth, friendly introduction to phone conversations. Greet the person you're calling, giving your own name as soon as possible. Jotting down the other person's name and then making a point to use it during the conversation is a good way to catch and hold someone's attention.

In some jobs, people are required to follow a four-step telephone greeting:

1. Answer with a salutation such as, "Good morning" or "Good afternoon."
2. Identify what organization or department the caller has reached.
3. Identify yourself as the receiver of the call.
4. Offer assistance, such as, "How can I help you?"

Steps 2 and 3 in this process provide information. Steps 1 and 4 make the call sound courteous and friendly. Although using all four steps may not be applicable to your job, at least use two steps, one that gives information and one that establishes a friendly tone. This starts your calls on a professional and positive note.

10.3.3 Direct People to the Right Resources

Nothing is more frustrating to a customer than giving a long explanation of his issue, only to be told that he's not talking to the right person. When answering calls from such a caller, you need to do the following:

1. Listen carefully to determine the caller's need or issue quickly.
2. Before allowing the caller to go on for too long, confirm that what you're hearing sounds like a matter that doesn't relate to your area. Briefly explain that a more suitable person can help and provide the name and number of that person.
3. If your phone system allows, transfer the call and give a heads-up to the person to whom you're sending the caller. This helps them to be ready to handle the issue, which gives the caller confidence that he or she is going to be served by the right resource.

Of course, when you transfer a caller to the right resource, you need to know how to work the transfer system. If it allows you to put the caller on hold first to see if the best resource is available, you can avoid sending the caller into a voice mail black hole. Before making the transfer, let the caller know the name and phone number of the right resource in case something goes wrong.

10.3.4 Put the Caller on Hold Smoothly

Want to aggravate callers quickly? Put them on hold abruptly and leave them holding for a long time. Even if you're receiving a high volume of calls, follow these three steps to courteously put someone on hold:

1. Briefly explain the reason for putting the caller on hold and request it. Do all this in one sentence such as, "I have another call, can you please hold?"
2. Get the acknowledgment from the caller and then place him or her on hold.
3. Return to the holding caller by saying, "Thank you for holding."

If you're putting someone on hold to check on something, don't leave that caller on hold for more than a minute. Any longer than that, even if music is playing, and callers begin to feel forgotten, and they may hang up in disgust. If you find that you need more than a minute to find information or otherwise provide the requested assistance, return to the caller within that minute and explain that your task will take longer than expected. Then, give the caller a choice of waiting longer or having you call back when you have the answer.

When you're putting people on hold because of a large volume of incoming calls and you know some calls may take you awhile to deal with, let the caller know as you make the request to put him or her on hold that you may be a few minutes. By doing so, the caller doesn't have to wonder where you went and why. Alternatively, you can offer to call the person back so they don't have to wait for you.

10.3.5 Sound Alive, Not Scripted

If the nature of your telephone interactions involves selling, avoid sounding scripted. Even if your role is to get information across to the people you call, as those in telemarketing must do, *saying* rather than *reading* your points is more likely to make you sound alive and not monotonous or robotic. More importantly, it also makes you sound as though you know what you're talking about.

10.3.6 Converse with Patience

Telephone conversations increase the tendency for you and the person on the other end of the line to talk at the same time. The visual cues that allow face-to-face conversations to flow more freely without interruptions are missing from conversations on the telephone.

For a two-way conversation to flow smoothly, you must show a little patience and slow your pace a bit, making sure that you hear the other person's entire thought before you speak. You may also want to paraphrase it first to ensure that you've captured the point being made. Then the transition for you to speak next is a natural one. Even if your waiting leaves a little silence, that's fine. Better for people to be heard than to be stepped on.

FOR EXAMPLE

Listening Ears

Mary Ellen works for a Saskatchewan social services agency pairing those in need of services with the organizations or individuals that can best help them. To do so, she spends hours on the phone each day listening to people's stories. Like many in her field, she is typically overwhelmed with people in need of help, and she feels the pressure of not having enough time for all of them. However, when she's on the phone with an individual, especially someone who is noticeably uncomfortable or nervous, she makes a special effort to give that person the extra time they may need to communicate their point. At the same time, she uses her active listening skills to confirm what she's heard and then lead the conversation on to other matters when necessary.

10.3.7 Tune in to Your Speaker's Tone

When you're listening on the telephone, you can't see (much less understand) your speaker's body language. As discussed in Section 2.2, the non-verbal part of a speaker's message (body language and tone of voice) communicates much of the emotional meaning in that message. When you can't see non-verbal messages, then you must focus on what you're hearing, not only in words but also in tone.

10.3.8 Message Control

If you make a phone call, be prepared to direct the conversation to your message. In the case of important business calls, you may even want to jot down some brief notes to refer to. Telephone conversation is much like dancing: it takes two, but one must establish the lead. In most business conversations, you may want to lead until the listener comfortably starts to respond. Occasionally ask the listener, "Do you have any questions?"

In many cases, you'll have to leave a message with someone; asking the person to repeat the message is an effective way of ensuring that they understood it properly.

10.3.9 If Your Time Is Short, Say So

Have you ever been caught in one of those phone conversations when you have only a few minutes and the person on the other end has a lot to say? You don't want to (or maybe can't) cut the person off, yet at the same time, you're struggling with trying to end the call.

In such situations, be direct and courteous instead of trying to be "nice." Announce at the beginning how much time you have and then hold to it. In cases when you thought you had the time and the call went longer than expected, give the caller a heads-up warning so that you can break away in a couple of minutes. "Jim, I have to go shortly. Let's try to wrap up this call in the next two minutes."

If more time is truly needed, you can end the call by setting up a time for the next call. Quite often, by announcing the time limit, you encourage people to get to the point and get business taken care of on the spot.

10.3.10 Close the Call Before You End It

Saying "goodbye" may end a telephone conversation, but it doesn't necessarily bring it to a close. The nature of telephone conversations, even if they are scheduled meetings, tends to be informal, so it's easy to forget to close the call.

Closing the call is remembering to check agreements made or to confirm commitments set. It sometimes involves setting up the next steps and determining who's going to call whom and when. This clear and definitive closure leaves you and the other person on the same page of understanding and feeling like your time on the call was well spent. After you're done, say your goodbyes, taking care to express your thanks and appreciation for the call. Again, using the person's name (see Section 10.3.2) is a nice touch.

SELF-CHECK

- Explain what it means to have a "smile in your voice."
- List the steps for putting a caller on hold.
- Define closing the call.

10.4 Voice Mails That Do the Job

Using **voice mail,** or the recorded verbal message you leave when someone doesn't answer the telephone, is common in today's business world, so you may find yourself talking far more often to a person's voice mail than directly to that person. Voice mail is often a much more efficient way to leave a message than to relay it to a receptionist, an assistant, or any other "live" person. You can say what you want without wondering whether the other person wrote down your message, let alone your name, correctly.

Using voice mail is like using email. It works best when its purpose is to make a request, briefly share news, or pass on basic information. It does not work for raising concerns or addressing issues of a sensitive nature. Venting on voice mail, for example, tends not to increase understanding or excite others to help you. Voice mail can be used to request a discussion, but should not be used to present details about an issue.

The intent when you leave a message is to get the other person to call you back or to give specific information. Keep your voice mail messages relatively short and include the following:

- **A brief explanation of your business or reason for calling.** Don't ramble or leave long-winded explanations. Think through your key points beforehand.
- **Your name and telephone number.** State this information slowly and clearly—it can't hurt to repeat it, either; even if you think the person knows your phone number, always leave it so that you make it convenient for him or her to return your call.
- **A request for a callback if you want one:** Don't assume that the person you're calling knows you want him or her to call you back. If you can be reached only at certain times, leave information about when you can best be reached.

Be sure to be responsive, as well. When people leave you voice mail messages asking you to call them back, do so on a timely basis. When you are responsive and follow through, you build credibility. Credibility enhances your ability to communicate effectively so that others respond to you in the ways you want.

> ## FOR EXAMPLE
>
> ### Caller Confidence
>
> When she graduated from college, Chloe began her first big job search. Her resume looked great, and she had done well in school. When it came time to make or return telephone calls, however, Chloe's shyness was overwhelming. She discovered that a bit of preparation, usually in the form of some notes, made some potentially nerve-wracking conversations go smoother. Chloe practised making and receiving those difficult calls—improving each time and building up her confidence.

SELF-CHECK

- Define the best ways to use voice mail.
- Discuss situations in which voice mail is not effective.
- List three elements that should be included in a voice mail.

10.5 Using Your Cell Phone for Business

With cell phones quickly becoming a key way that companies communicate, it is reasonable to presume that at some point you will have to use a cell phone for business purposes. A large advantage of cell phone technology is that it allows people to reach each other at any time and in anyplace. However, because it's so easy to pick up a cell phone and communicate with others, we can sometimes forget to conduct ourselves professionally on these calls. Here are a few tips to keep in mind to ensure you are projecting a professional image while using your cell phone:

- **Give your caller your full attention.** When you answer your phone, callers expect that you are free to take their call and that you will be able to communicate without interruption. If you are busy with another task or there's too much background noise, let the call go to voice mail and return the call at a more appropriate time.
- **Warn your callers that you are on a cell phone.** Avoid the surprise and possible confusion that can come from a dropped call. If the person you're speaking with knows you're on a cell phone, he or she will understand there's a possibility for the call to be dropped and that if the connection is lost, you'll call back when your signal has improved.

- **Resist the urge to get creative with your ring tone.** Nothing will take your professional credibility away faster than your co-workers or external clients hearing your phone playing the latest pop music ring tone.
- **Be aware that others may overhear your conversation.** Business calls can often involve the exchange of confidential company information. If you are talking on your phone in a public place, be aware that there is always a possibility that others may be able to hear your conversation.
- **Be courteous to those around you.** Just because you *can* answer your phone anywhere does not mean that you *should*. If you are engaged in other activities when your phone rings or you are in a place where cell phone use is discouraged, let the call to go to voice mail and return it when you are free. If you must take the call, however, politely excuse yourself and step away before answering the phone.
- **Remember your ringer.** Your phone should be on silent while you are in a meeting. If you need to be aware of incoming calls, put your phone on vibrate and keep it in a discrete place.
- **Keep business and personal calls separate.** Never take a personal call during a business meeting.

10.6 Planning Productive Meetings

Despite the reputation that meetings have for being poorly handled and for taking time away from more valuable work, business meetings are almost always unavoidable. There is no way of conducting business without occasionally planning, participating in, or leading meetings.

Meetings may be held to coordinate activities among departments or among the members of a department. Business people have meetings whenever changes arise, such as market changes, internal company changes, or external changes in suppliers. Progress meetings allow companies to monitor the work being done to meet the company's goals. Meetings are also conducted with clients or suppliers to discuss respective services.

Because you will inevitably participate in meetings during your business career, you should know how to do so effectively. Developing a plan is the best strategy when preparing for a serious or challenging meeting. When you have a plan, you'll likely achieve the positive results you're aiming for more often than when you don't have a plan.

10.6.1 Knowing When to Map Out Your Plan

In which kinds of situations is it a good idea to work out a plan? This kind of preparation is important for critical meetings in which important or sensitive issues need to be addressed, where being organized and careful in what you say are crucial for influencing positive outcomes.

Developing a plan may prove beneficial in meeting situations such as these:

- **Handling client meetings:** You need to show what you can do to win a client's business or solve a critical problem with a customer. Preparation is going to be key to achieving positive results; therefore, map out your plan first.
- **Leading group meetings:** Trying to lead a meeting without an agenda, although common, is asking for trouble. A meeting agenda is a form of mapping out your plan. It helps you establish a productive structure for the meeting and maintain the focus of the participants.
- **Addressing conflicts or concerns:** Suppose you have a problem with someone else; something is not going the way you want it to. Winging it in sensitive situations usually causes emotions to get out of control—especially your own. Thus, this is another perfect occasion for mapping out your plan before entering a sensitive situation. (Sections 3.6 and 3.7 provide you with problem-solving models for these kinds of conflict situations.)
- **Reporting important news:** When you're in a management role, you may be faced with telling others about a significant change to come—personnel changes, business changes, or cutbacks in jobs. These kinds of changes greatly affect other people in good and bad ways. A plan will help you outline your communication points in advance.
- **Persuading others to support an idea:** If you have an idea that needs the support of team members or staff from other groups to become reality, then mapping out your plan ahead of time may be helpful.
- **Delivering important presentations:** Formal presentations to fellow team members, to management, to other teams, or to customers are critical situations when you want to come off well. (Chapter 11 covers how to organize and deliver such presentations effectively.)

Your goal in planning for a meeting is to get organized for when you're speaking face-to-face with others. When you're mapping out your communication plan, you're readying yourself for the actual in-person communication, as well as preparing the written outline, supporting documents, and visual aids that you need to have with you at these meetings.

The following sections outline key tips to follow to increase the likelihood for good results in your important meetings and interactions.

10.6.2 Doing Your Homework First

Know what research you need to do, what data you need to gather, and what issues you need to understand better. Nothing is worse than communicating something important to a decision maker and leaving out vital information or not having the facts to back you up.

Sometimes you do your homework by reading reports, articles, or other records of information; sometimes you do it by talking to others and getting answers from them. At other times, you do both. When needed, homework also involves developing your visual aids and supporting documents to help make your case.

People often are impressed when you come to an important meeting and show that you've done your homework. The way you make your presentation shows preparation and thoroughness—efforts that increase the likelihood of your message being received in a positive way.

10.6.3 Considering Your Audience in Your Plans

How you develop your plan depends on who you're going to present it to. Here are some factors that you should take into account:

- Who is your target audience and what's important to them?
- What are your audience's "hot buttons" (critical points you need to address and sensitive points you want to stay away from)?
- What's their level of understanding of your issue and the best language to use to discuss the issue with them? How much detail should you use? How formal or informal should you be?
- When is the best time to discuss your issue and where is the best location to do so?
- What possible objections or negative reactions are you likely to encounter, and what's the best way to address those concerns if they come up?

Planning for these factors often is part of the homework you do prior to preparing your plan. If nothing else, homework and planning get you ready to best tailor your message to your listener.

FOR EXAMPLE

What's the Point?
Peter's boss is a key decision maker, and sometimes he needs to get her approval to make significant policy changes. Getting to know his boss better helped Peter address issues with her. First, he knows that his boss is more relaxed later in the day. Peter also knows that she has a tendency to get bogged down in details if he presents more information than what is needed to support a key point. Finally, Peter's boss wants to hear how a proposal will help the company but not be an additional burden to anyone else. Planning his meetings around these factors helps Peter achieve the results he's looking for.

10.6.4 Outlining Your Meeting Plan

With your planning complete and the audience factors considered, you're ready to map out your meeting in writing:

- **Set the opening.** Set your topic and provide context as needed.
  - ○ State your purpose; that is, say what you're trying to accomplish in this meeting. Know and state the positive outcome you're seeking. Tell your listener(s) what you want them to do so they best receive your message.
- **Organize the key points.** Determine the key points and the order in which you want to make them.
  - ○ Determine what stories and anecdotes will help illustrate your points and when to tell them. Determine, if you're using visual aids, when best to present them. Determine when you're going to provide the positive punch to your message by showing your audience the benefits from what you're proposing, the recommended solution for the problem you have defined, or the idea for change that makes the improvements desired.
- **Get the listener's response.** Determine when you want your receiver to respond, at a certain time or at anytime.
  - ○ Prepare a few questions to invite feedback, as well as responses in anticipation of possible concerns you expect to hear.
- **Bring the meeting to a close.**
  - ○ Form a recap of important points to a confirmation of an agreement or an outline of the next steps, set how you want your closure to go.

SELF-CHECK

- List six types of meetings that benefit from planning.
- Discuss what types of preparation can be done before a meeting.
- Describe how to outline a meeting.

10.7 Participating in Meetings

From ways to contribute to ways of considering the others in attendance, there are several suggestions that may help you to participate effectively in the meetings you must attend.

10.7.1 Contribute Information

It isn't enough simply to contribute or to give information. Don't say something just to be able to say that you participated in the meeting, and don't provide information that really doesn't contribute to a meeting's overall purpose. On the other hand, don't keep silent when you have an idea or some information that might be valuable to the meeting.

The information needed in meetings isn't always just facts. Sometimes your ideas or opinions may be helpful. For example, if the purpose of the meeting is to get everyone's opinion regarding how to respond to a change in your business's market, do contribute yours.

10.7.2 Show That You Can Listen

While you are speaking up and contributing to the meeting, listen carefully to what others are saying. Jot down some notes about key ideas, hints, comments, or recommendations brought up. Use these notes as a guide when you're deciding how to contribute to the meeting. Try to relate your ideas or comments to the information already given by others (see Section 2.4 for more on active listening tools).

FOR EXAMPLE

Meeting Strategy

Arda and Erica had just learned that their client was unhappy with the designs they had submitted for the client's office expansion project. It had been a difficult working relationship from the start; the client had a tendency to be abrupt and hostile in meetings. The two designers decided that for this meeting in particular, their best strategy was to do a lot of listening and simply concentrate on what specifically the client said he didn't like about the design. To do so, they took notes, letting the client have his say until it was time for their response.

10.7.3 Suggest Positive Alternatives

You may hear something in a meeting that you disagree with or that you question. If you aren't sure of something, try to word your question positively, avoiding criticism of the person you're questioning. If you disagree with something, try to suggest a positive alternative instead of focusing on how bad the original idea was. Rather than attacking the person whose idea seems questionable, focus on how to improve the idea or how to achieve the same goal in another way.

10.7.4 Notice Non-Verbal Reactions

While you are listening or speaking during a meeting, notice the faces and gestures of the other people in the meeting. Are they agreeing or disagreeing with the ideas? Are they worried about or delighted with the news of changes? Are they confused about what is going on, or do they understand what's being said? Are they enjoying the meeting or are they getting irritated that it is taking too long? Use this non-verbal information to help determine how to contribute to the meeting's goals. In addition, watch your own non-verbal reactions, to make sure that you show support when you feel it.

10.7.5 Use Your Social Skills

As with many other communication experiences in business, your social skills greatly influence how effective you will be. If you show courtesy, cooperation, and appreciation of your co-workers during meetings, you'll do very well.

SELF-CHECK

- Explain four ways of increasing the effectiveness of the meetings you attend.
- Discuss the role of active listening in meeting participation.
- Explain the importance of non-verbal reactions.

10.8 Leading Meetings

One reward for participating well in business meetings may be that you'll move up in your organization. If so, you may be asked to lead meetings. Consider the following hints and guidelines for conducting effective meetings:

- **Notify all participants about the meeting.** If possible, distribute an agenda— even a tentative one—so participants can begin to gather their thoughts and notes.
- **At the beginning of the meeting, remind the attendees to turn off their cell phones if they can.** A single phone call may be all it takes to derail a meeting's momentum.
- **If you have fewer than 20 people attending your meeting, ask all participants to introduce themselves.** These introductions not only let people meet one another by name, but also encourage free discussion. Simply by saying his or her name and company position, a participant has broken the ice. Speaking up later in the discussion may then be easier.

- **State the purpose of the meeting clearly, but not in a bossy way.** "This afternoon, we'll discuss the sales commission structure now used in the company, and any other related matters that seem important to you."

- **State an estimated time for adjournment.** Try to stick to that ending time. "We'll adjourn promptly at 4:00 so that several of you can keep other appointments."

- **Use informal rules of order.** Overly formal controls may discourage discussion in smaller meetings. Because many participants fear being out of order, they stay silent.

- **Conduct the meeting by using common sense methods: call on a variety of speakers, with fairness to each.** Don't let one member of the group dominate discussion ("Let me stop you for a moment, James. Does anyone want to respond to the point James is making?"). If the discussion turns into a free-for-all, take control of it to re-establish order. ("Just a minute, please. Katie, you had the floor, and Martina after you.")

- **Keep the meeting moving toward its goals.** Use a whiteboard, a blackboard, or a flip chart to take point-form notes to remind everyone of the major ideas discussed thus far.

- **Work toward consensus.** Because the company usually has to move ahead with one voice, the meeting should proceed with discussion until compromises and understandings that suit almost all members have been worked out. When this meeting of minds is not possible, allow some outlet for minority opinion—a minority report, for example, or a later meeting to reconsider the issues.

- **Thank all participants for attending the meeting.** As soon as possible, distribute summary notes of the meeting, organized to highlight decisions made and actions recommended.

FOR EXAMPLE

Meetings That Work

Weekly staff meetings are a time for Rohit and his employees to resolve any issues that have come up and to set down a plan for the coming week. His employees are a diverse group, ranging from outspoken and impulsive to quiet and creative—and everything in between. To keep meetings moving smoothly, Rohit sticks to a schedule: a 15-minute update, a 15-minute session for issues, a 20-minute planning session, and a final 10-minute summary and closing. Because the meetings usually involve about eight employees, Rohit makes a point of calling on each employee at least once for their news or thoughts, especially those who are content to sit and listen.

SELF-CHECK

- List techniques for leading effective meetings.
- Discuss the importance of setting a time for a meeting's end.
- Explain how to apply the rules of order in a small meeting.

SUMMARY

Through conversations, telephone calls, and meetings, your speaking skills play an enormous part in your business success, no matter what your job is. Speaking in the positive enables you to deliver your messages honestly, directly, and constructively. Emphasizing what you can and will do for those you work with inspires confidence and respect. Using the tools of assertive and positive speaking has an equally powerful effect on the success of your telephone conversations and voice mail messages. To make the most of challenging business meetings, follow guidelines for developing a strategy ahead of time. Use your communication skills to listen to others and contribute to those meetings you attend. When the time comes for you to lead meetings, more specific leadership guidelines will further increase your chances of success.

KEY TERMS

Closing the call	Checking agreements made or confirming commitments set, done near the end of a telephone call.
Constructive	Being as objective as possible in the words you say; respectful.
Destructive	Designed or tending to destroy; criticism.
Speaking in the positive	Saying your message in the best way possible; being honest, direct, and constructive.
Sugar-coating	Trying to sweeten a bad message; an effort to make bad news sound better.
Underpromise and overdeliver	Giving yourself a large enough cushion of time to get things done as you respond to a client's *when* question; when you underpromise and overdeliver, you pick a deadline that you can meet or beat.
Voice mail	The recorded verbal message you leave when someone doesn't answer the telephone.

ASSESS YOUR UNDERSTANDING

Go to www.wiley.com/canada/brounstein to evaluate your knowledge of the basics of spoken communication. Measure your learning by comparing pre-test and post-test results.

Quick Questions

1. When a person speaks in the positive, they are being
   (a) direct
   (b) constructive
   (c) honest
   (d) all of the above

2. Being direct and being blunt mean getting to the point with tact. True or false?

3. In sugar-coating a message, a speaker delivers bad news, but does so in an assertive way. True or false?

4. Which of the three elements of speaking in the positive is most often left out?
   (a) direct
   (b) constructive
   (c) honest
   (d) none of the above

5. To underpromise and overdeliver is to give yourself a cushion of time to complete a request. True or false?

6. The telephone is limited by its inability to communicate non-verbal communication cues. True or false?

7. Which of the following improves telephone communication?
   (a) professional greeting
   (b) patience
   (c) preparation
   (d) all of the above

8. Putting a "smile in your voice" means delivering only positive messages. True or false?

9. In many cases, voice mail is a more effective way of leaving a message than speaking to a live person. True or false?

10. People understand that a voice message should be returned with a phone call. True or false?

11. Meetings to discuss serious or challenging matters benefit from a pre-determined strategy. True or false?

12. A meeting plan might include which of the following?
    (a) ideas for visual aids
    (b) strategy for the face-to-face interaction
    (c) an outline
    (d) all of the above
13. A plan helps a speaker tailor a meeting's message to the audience. True or false?
14. To actively participate in a meeting, an attendee should
    (a) confront others who express contrary ideas
    (b) pay attention to how others react
    (c) listen but not share personal ideas
    (d) all of the above
15. The same principles of good behaviour can be applied to meetings as well as any other business situation. True or false?
16. Which of the following can be useful when leading a meeting?
    (a) call for introductions
    (b) set a time for the meeting's completion
    (c) include an agenda
    (d) all of the above
17. Formal rules of order encourage all attendees to participate in meeting discussions. True or false?

Give It Some Thought

1. What is speaking in the positive?
2. What is the difference between destructive language and constructive language?
3. How does sugar-coating a message differ from speaking in the positive?
4. Which way of speaking emphasizes what a speaker can or will do?
    (a) "I'll speak with the others and get back to you by the end of the day."
    (b) "It's a bit last-minute, but we'll turn the files around by next week."
    (c) "I haven't finished yet, but I will return the layouts by lunch."
    (d) all of the above
5. When is it better to say "no" to a request from a client, team member, or other co-worker?
6. What are some of the benefits of conducting business over the telephone?
7. No one likes to be put on hold, especially during a business call. What should you do when you have to put someone on hold?

8. You can't see a person's gestures, posture, or other types of body language over the phone. What non-verbal communication cues can you focus on?

9. Discuss a business situation in which leaving a voice mail message is *not* a good idea?

    (a) notification of contract termination

    (b) change of meeting date

    (c) request to resend a fax

    (d) all of the above

10. What four parts should be included in a voice mail message?

11. List three situations in which a strategy or plan is useful.

12. What questions can help a speaker develop a plan to suit a particular audience?

13. What parts should be included when outlining a meeting?

    (a) an opening that sets the topic

    (b) an order for the key points

    (c) an idea of how to handle the audience's response

    (d) all of the above

14. List some ways to ensure that others participate in and support one another during business meetings.

15. Describe how a non-verbal cue can influence others in a meeting.

16. Name three things a meeting leader can do at the beginning of a meeting.

17. What should the leader of a meeting do when, at the conclusion of the meeting, consensus has not been achieved?

Applying This Chapter

1. Revise the following statement using the speaking in the positive elements of honesty, directness, and constructiveness:

   This memo tells me nothing about what the team has accomplished with Project ABC.

2. The following statement sugar-coats the meaning of the message. Using the guidelines for speaking in the positive, revamp the statement.

   I'm sure that this type of design worked well at the other building, Jake, but we had a different vision in mind for this office. It's very confusing to go from one project to another without getting signals crossed. When this comes around again, we can discuss it further.

3. Think of a "can't do" type of statement you made in response to a request from someone. Revise it, keeping the same message, but emphasize and lead with what *can* be done to help.

4. Recall a bad experience you've had carrying out a business conversation over the phone. If you could begin that conversation all over again, how would you prepare for it to ensure that it went more successfully?

5. Think of the last three voice mail messages you've received and critique them according to the guidelines in this chapter. Did they ramble? Leave contact information? Speak clearly? Consider the recent messages you've left for others in the same way.

6. Think of a meeting you attended. Rate your level of participation on a scale of 1–10 (10 being the highest). Using the guidelines for active meeting participation, what could you have done differently to improve your performance, the meeting's success, or both?

7. Do your own survey of attitudes toward business meetings among your classmates. What specific things do they like and dislike about meetings in which they have been involved? How could someone following the principles of meeting leadership outlined in this chapter address those concerns?

8. You're meeting with two managers from your company to discuss your idea for a new type of model toy it should produce. Model kits were once all the rage, with parents buying them and assembling them with their children. You feel that today's parents are tired of the preassembled toys on the market, and that they are ripe for your great idea: a kit out of which a parent can choose from three different toys to build. Choose two classmates to meet with you and play devil's advocate in speaking against your idea. How can you control the meeting while still taking into consideration the others' feedback?

THE NEXT STEP

Attitude Adjustment
Make a point of listening for "can't do" or "won't do" responses you get from people when you make requests of them. How would you revise such responses into "can do" and "will do" types of statements? Would the revised response have made you feel any different about the answer? Why?

Put a Smile in your Voice
Work with two other classmates to practise putting a smile in your voice. One student should pretend to call a local cinema to check on show times for a very popular new movie; another student should answer the call with the "smiling" voice; the third student should observe and offer feedback after the call. Switch roles so everyone has an opportunity to practise.

Message Matters

In a mock telephone conversation with a classmate, attempt to leave a detailed business message with an obviously distracted listener. What should you do to ensure that your message reaches its intended recipient intact?

Meeting Evaluation

Take careful notes of the meeting process at the next meeting you attend—it may be a formal business meeting, a club meeting, or even a less formal meeting between yourself and a colleague or fellow student (this exercise could also be used to critique a class). Keeping in mind what it takes to lead and participate in a meeting, evaluate what went poorly or well. And why?

Planning Pays Off

Assume you've called a meeting with a close friend or family member to discuss an outstanding issue. Develop a short point-form outline of the meeting as discussed in Section 10.6.4 so you can get your points across and hear the other person's response.

Mock Meeting

A new unit supervisor has been hired to oversee seven employees who write brochures, form letters, and reports for an insurance company. On her first day, the new supervisor notices that no one begins working until after 11 a.m., and she asks why. She discovers that most of the employees feel that it takes a couple of hours to warm up, to break through their writer's block. She dismisses this concept and calls a meeting to discuss how productivity will be improved. Assign roles within a group of classmates—the supervisor, the advocate of the writer's warm-up period, a particularly lazy staffer who just hates to write, and a conscientious worker frustrated with the status quo.

11
GIVING SPEECHES AND ORAL PRESENTATIONS
Conveying Your Message to an Audience

STARTING POINT

Go to www.wiley.com/canada/brounstein to assess your knowledge of the basics of speeches and oral presentations. After reviewing this website, you'll be able to determine where you need to concentrate your effort.

What You'll Learn in This Chapter:
- ways of making and breaking a presentation
- how to present content in an organized and clear manner
- the importance of non-verbal communication tools
- ways of using visual aids to your advantage
- techniques for coping with a live audience.

After Studying This Chapter, You'll be Able to:
- discuss the relationship between preparation and effective presentations
- review the three critical parts used to organize a presentation's content
- describe the role of five non-verbal communication tools on a presenter's delivery
- prepare visual aids that add value to your presentation
- understand how to channel anxiety and stay composed in front of an audience.

INTRODUCTION

Speaking in front of a group of people is one of the most challenging—certainly the most terrifying—examples of communication at work. This chapter helps you learn from others' experiences, both their accomplishments to strive for and mistakes to avoid. The importance of organizing a presentation's content is covered. The chapter also describes ways of using non-verbal communication behaviours to deliver a presentation with impact. Techniques are outlined for supplementing your message with visual aids. The chapter concludes with ways of dealing with the anxiety and fear that may come with being in front of an audience.

11.1 Hitting the Essentials of Effective Presentations

Take a moment to think about any presentations you've attended: they could be within your organization, as well as those you've attended at seminars, lectures, conferences, and meetings. You can learn a great deal about how to give a successful presentation just by observing others, no matter what they're speaking about.

You've probably experienced a wide range of performances: the dull and distracted lecturer, the speaker who read from cue cards and never looked out at the audience, the organized and confident presenter who engaged your attention from start to finish.

As you discover in the following sections what others do, you learn not only what *to* do but also what *not* to do. In doing so, you'll increase your own likelihood for success.

11.1.1 What Breaks a Presentation

To understand what makes an effective presentation, you must be aware of what breaks or detracts from a good presentation. The following pitfalls are fairly common, but effective speakers avoid them—and so can you:

- **Looking or sounding nervous:** You can tell a presenter is nervous when he stands stiffly in one spot with his hands tucked in his pockets. Constantly pacing back and forth and fidgeting are other signs. You can also detect nervousness in the quiver in a person's voice. Even worse is when a speaker tells his audience that he's nervous; in these cases, the audience tends to focus on the high anxiety level instead of on the talk.
- **Sounding monotone:** Nothing sounds duller, regardless of the content of the speech, than a presenter's voice that has no emotion or enthusiasm to it.
- **Speaking too softly:** When speakers are barely audible past the front row, audiences tend to barely listen. Restlessness and disinterest generally take over.
- **Making little direct eye contact:** When the speaker looks down, away, or over the audience during a talk, people feel disconnected. They question the speaker's confidence level and credibility.
- **Reading slides or handouts to the audience:** Supporting materials and visual aids can do a lot for a presentation. But when speakers read nearly every item on

the slides or handouts, they insult the intelligence of their audience and render their materials non-supportive. And often, when you start reading to the audience, you sound monotone.

- **Using overloaded slides:** When presentation slides are crammed full of too much information, they lose their value. When people can't see all the tiny charts and data on the slides, they stop focusing, especially if the presentation depends heavily on slides.

- **Using too much jargon:** When the audience is less familiar with the specialized terms and language of the speaker's organization or field of expertise and the speaker uses this jargon frequently, the audience becomes disinterested.

- **Overloading with data:** This speaker is full of details—so much so that what's important in the message easily gets lost. You walk away confused or bored with no key points to remember.

- **Being vague:** This is the opposite extreme of having too much detail. When the speaker is vague, all you hear are generalizations and platitudes with no specifics and no substance.

- **Tinkering with equipment:** When speakers become preoccupied with trying to get their audio-visual equipment to work, they tend to occupy the audience's attention with everything but the speech.

- **Sounding like a know-it-all:** This happens when sounding authoritarian replaces sounding authoritative. Sometimes speakers act arrogantly in response to audience questions—responses that, in effect, say, "Didn't you know this already?" or "That's a stupid question." Obviously, if the person had known the answer, he or she wouldn't have asked the question; speakers who think a "stupid question" has been asked perhaps didn't explain their points as clearly as they should have.

- **Coming across as disorganized:** A presentation without flow or direction causes the speaker to jump back and forth between subjects, and he or she often ends up rambling. As a result, it is difficult to maintain the audience's attention for very long.

- **Trying to be funny too often:** Humour in a formal presentation can be a nice touch, but when humour is forced or excessive, the seriousness of the message gets lost, or worse, the audience can become alienated by your wisecracks. Unless we are gifted comedians, most of us should be careful when adding humour to our presentations.

- **Having no conclusion:** In some presentations, the only way you know it's over is that the speaker stops talking. The speaker offers no wrap-up and makes no other effort toward closure. When the speaker does nothing to end on a positive note, the audience walks away with less of a feel for what they heard—the presentation is incomplete.

FOR EXAMPLE

Dazed and Confused

A group of financial consultants was being trained to sell a new insurance product. The insurance representative's in-depth presentation lasted three hours, with no time for questions and answers. The consultants felt overwhelmed with the amount of material and frustrated that they were unable to ask questions. Most would have rather received a handout of the details to study later.

In many cases, speakers that behave in these ways don't even realize what they're doing. But as you prepare for a formal presentation, let this list of pitfalls serve as your checklist for what to avoid in your own performance.

11.1.2 What Makes a Presentation

People who have just heard a top-notch presentation often come away with a strong feeling about what made the speaker so effective. Here are some of the most common reasons for success:

- **Being well organized:** Presentations should flow in a logical sequence, with the points connected in an orderly fashion. The presentation should be easy to follow.
- **Getting to the point:** The speaker is direct, clear, and, most importantly, concise. You walk away understanding and remembering the key points because they are stated succinctly and in language that makes sense to you.
- **Displaying confidence:** The speaker sounds authoritative as opposed to authoritarian and knowledgeable, but not like a know-it-all. In both voice and demeanour, the speaker expresses his or her points with certainty and credibility.
- **Showing sincerity:** Often going hand-in-hand with confidence, the sincere presenter's tone and language come across with care and respect. He or she conveys a certain believability and genuineness that makes people want to listen.
- **Giving you a message:** You walk away from the presentation knowing exactly what was important. You grasp the main ideas or themes clearly and don't get lost in detail. You walk away with a message or point of view to remember.
- **Sounding positive:** The speaker's verbal and non-verbal messages match and have an upbeat feel. Points are expressed in the best way possible. Even when talking about tough issues, the speaker makes key points in a positive way.
- **Relating well to the audience:** The presenter understands your issues, speaks to them, and does so in language you can understand. You get information that's useful and relevant.

- **Having enthusiasm:** In their own style, whether low-key or full of energy, these speakers come across as animated. They sound alive and interested in what they have to say and, as a result, make their topic interesting and worth hearing.
- **Using visual aids to support the presentation:** Visual aids serve to enhance and work in tandem with the oral message. The speaker uses them as points to talk from or to help make a point.

What this and the previous checklist point out is that effective presentations involve three key ingredients, each of which will be covered further in this chapter:

- **Substance:** The content of the presentation.
- **Style:** The delivery of the presentation.
- **Supporting materials:** The visual aids that enhance the talk.

11.1.3 The Unsung Hero: Preparation

You probably do just fine in your day-to-day interactions and informal conversations at work: you respond to each situation without the need for preparation. But formal presentations are quite different. **Preparation** is the hard work you do before going "live" with your speech or presentation. Being prepared increases the likelihood that you'll deliver a winning performance, and decreases the feeling of stage fright you may get when you're put in front of an audience. When you know what you want to say and how you want to say it, you're in a much better position to be confident and in control.

You're scheduled to speak in a group setting for a longer period of time with the communication going mostly one-way: you talking to the audience. The expectation that you come across effectively—clear, organized, positive, interesting, and informative—is much higher. People want their listening time to be well spent. Coming in unprepared is usually a recipe for disaster.

Here are the key elements of preparation. Use the questions or comments listed with each step as your guide for what to do so that you're ready when speech time comes.

Step 1   Consider your audience and the amount of time you have with them.
- To whom are you presenting?
- What are the group's interests and issues? What is their technical background? How familiar are they with the subject?
- What are the group's hot buttons, those points of sensitivity to address or stay away from in the talk?
- How long do you have for your presentation?

Step 2   Determine your purpose.
- What's your goal for this talk; why are you giving this speech?
- Overall, what do you want to achieve with this audience?

Step 3 Conduct your research. Determine what homework you need to do for this talk and what answers you need to get.

Step 4 Develop your core message. Decide on the key message or themes you want to get across.

Step 5 Set your introduction. Think about how you'll grab the audience's attention.

Step 6 Organize the body of your presentation.
- What are the main points you want to cover?
- In what order will you present these points?
- What supporting data and anecdotes do you want to use?

Step 7 Set your conclusion. Decide how you want to bring the presentation to a close.

Step 8 Develop your visual aids. Consider what materials—slides, charts, handouts, and so on—will best support your main points.

Step 9 Rehearse. Practise your presentation often before the big day.
Some of these steps will need more attention than others, depending on the circumstances of your talk. But when you follow through on these steps, you'll be ready to deliver a confident and engaging presentation.

SELF-CHECK

- Describe some common pitfalls of ineffective speakers.
- Describe ways that effective speakers achieve success.
- Define preparation.
- Discuss the positive impact of preparation on a presentation.

11.2 Making the Most of Your Content

You need to do three things to deliver an organized presentation—tell the audience what you're going to tell them, tell them, and then tell them what you told them. In other words, in terms of **content,** or what you're going to say, an organized presentation contains three critical parts:

- the introduction
- the body
- the conclusion.

When you present the content in these three parts, you are better able to come across in a clear and organized fashion.

11.2.1 The Introduction

To develop an organized presentation, you'll need to start with your **introduction**—the way you open your speech. The common way in which many presenters start their talks—"My name is . . ." or "Today, I'm going to talk to you about . . ."—is not much of an introduction. The purpose of a good introduction in a formal presentation is to achieve three goals:

- grab the audience's attention
- identify the topic and the purpose or core message of the talk
- provide a brief overview or agenda of what you will cover in the talk.

Speakers often overlook the part about grabbing the audience's attention. They just start talking without creating any reason for the audience to want to listen. The key point to keep in mind here is that if you don't grab your group's attention up front, you may not have it for the rest of your speech.

Consider the following list of opening techniques to gain your audience's attention in a positive way:

- **Quote someone else. A quotation** is a line said by someone else that helps set up what you're going to talk about. When using a quote, you want to accomplish two things: cite the source of the line and tie the quote to your topic. Here's an example that a company president might use to talk about major changes happening within the organization: "'Success is a mixture of skills, competence, luck and hard work: with a bit of effort, I believe the world can be at our feet.' These were words spoken by Canadian astronaut Julie Payette and this is a message I want all of you to remember as we deal with the organizational changes that I will talk to you about today."

> ## FOR EXAMPLE
>
> **Borrowed Wisdom**
> "One hundred percent of the shots you don't take don't go in." This quote from former hockey star Wayne Gretzky has great appeal for speakers trying to motivate an audience: a company president mobilizing his employees to increase sales calls, a fitness expert inspiring overweight clients to work out, even a Scout leader cheering on his troop's fundraising efforts.

- **Share a story.** A story, sometimes called an anecdote, is another clever way to kick off a presentation. To work, the story needs to be short and make a point that you can tie to the talk that follows.

- **Make a bold statement.** This introduction technique involves a brief, thought-provoking statement that sets up your topic. Say it with a strong voice and it commands attention and gets the group ready to hear what will follow. Here's an example used in talking to groups in government organizations about customer service: "Keep this in mind: service is far more than *what* you do. It's *how* you do it."

- **Get the audience to participate.** Start your presentation by having the audience do something, from a brief exercise to responding to questions. This technique gets people's energy levels up. By using the activity as a message to relate to your topic, you really capture the group's attention. A word of caution about using this technique: be careful not to choose an activity that creates such a commotion that getting the audience's focus back on you becomes difficult.

- **Ask a rhetorical question.** A **rhetorical question** is a thought-provoking question that you ask the audience but for which you don't expect an answer out loud. When you ask the question, you want to answer it either within your introduction or a short time later in your talk. Otherwise, the question serves only to confuse people. Here's an example for a talk on customer-focus group findings: "If you were a customer doing business with your company, what would most frustrate you in this effort? As I share my findings from the customer focus groups, I'm going to tell you what these frustrations are and what you can do to address them."

- **Share noteworthy facts.** With this type of introduction, you provide the audience with some interesting statistics or facts that stimulate thinking and help set up your presentation. This technique works well when the facts you report are not common knowledge, yet are relevant. Just be sure to keep the statement brief so that you don't clutter your opening with too many easy-to-forget details.

- **Make a list of common items.** This introduction involves using a short list of at least three items that have something in common. It usually works best to say the list and then state what the items have in common with one another. For example: "Joe Davis, Sue McGee, and Jose Martinez are three people you all know well in this department. They also have used the communication techniques I'm going to tell you about today and have seen their success double in the last year."

- **Give an interesting example.** In this technique, you start with a demonstration, showing something or telling of a situation that illustrates what your core message is about. To be effective, the example must be relevant and fairly brief. A good example of this technique is the showing of before-and-after pictures from the use of a product or service; for instance, a picture of two sets of lungs—one with no history of smoking and the other with a long history of smoking.

As you prepare your introduction, carefully plan the opening technique you want to use to grab the audience's attention. Whether you start with this technique or with the component identifying your topic briefly doesn't matter. Just go with what works. Then follow these two components with a quick overview of what's to come to get your talk off to a strong start.

11.2.2 The Body

The **body** is the part of the presentation between your introduction and your conclusion (it's also the longest part). Its purpose is to get your key points across. To prepare the body of your presentation, you have two tasks—determine the key points you want to make and organize the sequence of these points. Here are some effective ways to determine the order or sequence of your body:

- **Problem to solution:** In this sequence, you first describe the problem. Then you give the recommended solution, emphasizing how it helps correct the problem.
- **Chronological:** In this sequence, you explain a series of events from past to present. It follows the element of time and moves the audience from event to event up to current times. Take care to make the dates of the events stand out clearly so that the audience is not confused as to what occurred when.
- **What once was to what needs to be in the future:** In this sequence, you describe how things once were and how they need to be in the future. You use this sequence to recommend a new direction or course of action and to highlight how the future will be different from and better than what once was—the success to aim for. Sometimes this technique is also used to highlight the dangers of staying with the status quo and describe what will happen in the future if no changes are made now.
- **General to specific:** This type of presentation flows from general information to a few key points explained in detail. Sometimes it works by starting with a main idea and then detailing how to make the main idea work.
- **Less important to most critical:** In this presentation, each piece of information or topic serves as background for the one that comes next, and the importance of each subsequent topic gets greater and greater, right up to your climactic conclusion.
- **Logical topic flow:** Sometimes the various topics in a presentation just go in a certain order that makes the most sense. Presentations that centre around processes (how to do something) work well this way, taking people through each step in the process.
- **Benefits and features: Benefits** are the gains to be made or the things that are good about your idea, product, or service. **Features** are how the idea, product, or service works. Sometimes you want to cover all the benefits first and then explain the features; sometimes you want to do the opposite. Sometimes you want to go one at a time, describing each feature and the benefits it brings. Go with the

order that works best for your subject and stick to it throughout the body of your presentation.

- **Persuasive flow:** Some presentations try to persuade others to a point of view or convince them to take action. Here are three ways to organize a presentation where persuasion is your primary purpose:
  - ○ In a sales presentation in which you want the customer to decide to buy what you have to offer, describe features and then highlight their benefits to the customer.
  - ○ When you're making recommendations to solve a critical problem, give the background of the issue first and then highlight what needs to happen and why.
  - ○ When you're convincing people to support a new process, provide the idea followed by its benefits and your recommendation for next steps.

Organizing a sequence to your presentation helps give it a smooth flow. Start by determining the key points or topics you want to cover. After you determine these key points, think of the supporting data you need for each point and any relevant stories and examples that can help.

Using Transitions and Stories

Transitions and stories are two of the finer touches that help make for a smooth flow and a more interesting presentation.

- **Transitions** move you from one topic to the next in a presentation. They create the bridges that connect points and help move a presentation forward. Transitions are one to two sentences long; the best refer to the topic just discussed and point the audience to what's coming next. For example, "Now that we've looked at the main causes of the problem, I want to outline a solution that can help."
- **Stories** are an engaging way to share life experiences, yours or others', and to highlight or illustrate a point you're making.

  To make stories work effectively in a presentation, keep these tips in mind:

- Determine the story's purpose and message.
- Plan when and where you will tell the story—when leading into a point or as an example after you have made the point.
- Have a sequence to the story. The best order to use is either chronological or building up to a climax.
- Tell the short version—not the "long-story-short" version.
- Connect the story to your key point with a sentence or two at most.

11.2.3 The Conclusion

It may feel perfectly normal to end a children's story with "The End," but it's not at all effective to use "I'm done," "The end," or "That's it" at the **conclusion** of your formal presentation. These phrases say nothing and stop your speech rather than finish it. A good conclusion brings closure to a presentation and has a lasting impact. Because the conclusion is the last part of the presentation, it is often the part the audience remembers best, so you want to leave them with something great.

Here are six techniques that can help you bring positive closure to a presentation:

- **Recap:** A recap is a summary of the main points covered in your talk. You want it brief, generally covering no more than three or four points. If you cover more than that, you're probably going to get too detailed, lose your audience, and sound like you're repeating yourself.
- **Repeat core message:** This technique ends your presentation by briefly emphasizing the theme that you have carried throughout the talk. It works really well when your introduction raised this theme and you want to wrap it up in the end.
- **Call to action:** With this closing technique, you finish by requesting that the audience take some kind of action. That action can be implementing an idea that they have gained from your talk or doing something to support a cause.
- **Quotation:** This technique works best when you can come up with a witty or interesting line that wraps up your presentation nicely. As you do in an introduction, you want to identify the source of the quote and tie it, in this case, to what you said before it.
- **Rhetorical question:** In this technique, you leave the audience with a thought-provoking question. Most often, you don't answer it for them as you would in an introduction; instead, you leave them to ponder the question for themselves. Make sure that the question is relevant to what you've said so it has them walking away thinking.
- **Story:** A story often makes for a nice close to a presentation. To make a story work in a conclusion, you want it to be relatively brief and to illustrate a point that ties to what the whole presentation was about.

FOR EXAMPLE

Skip the Tricks

Barry had worked up a new sales pitch for the line of flavoured dog toys that his company was launching, and he decided to try it out on executives from a large pet supply distributor. He had 30 minutes for his presentation, and his strategy was to build up some excitement and interest before he actually revealed the new line. His plan backfired when, after only 15 minutes, two of the three executives were suddenly called away. Although he tried to maintain his momentum, with most of the decision makers out of the picture, when he finally reached the critical point in his presentation, his big reveal fell flat.

11.3 Giving a Presentation with Impact

Once you have outlined the content of your presentation, you can focus on style, or the delivery of the content. **Delivery** is the *how* side of a presentation; delivering a presentation involves non-verbal communication. It is how you express your messages.

This section is not window dressing, however. The reality of formal presentations is simple: what you say is important, but how you say it carries more weight. The following sections explore five non-verbal behaviours of delivery and show you how to get the best out of them in your presentations. Here is where the non-verbal tools of assertive speaking, as described in Section 2.2, come into play.

11.3.1 Make Eye Contact

One thing you can usually count on when you're giving a speech is that everyone in the audience is watching you. But what are you doing with your eyes when the audience is looking at you?

In a formal presentation, eye contact is the non-verbal way of keeping the speaker and audience connected. As they watch you, you want to look at them. Here's how to do it:

- **Look at their faces.** More often than not, when you're giving a presentation you're standing above a sitting audience. Therefore, you're taller than they are. If you look straight ahead, you see no one directly, and the people in the audience wonder what you're looking at. Instead, look down a bit at the faces of the people in the audience. Your eyes give your message credibility and also serve as a magnet to draw people's attention toward you.

- **Include everyone.** As you look people in the eyes when you talk to them, scan the audience to reach everyone. Avoid locking in on a few faces and not seeing the rest of the group. Spend a few seconds on everybody and your eyes will reel their attention in to you. When you're making a point that pertains to a certain individual in particular, look at that person. Doing so makes the person feel included and important.

11.3.2 Using Gestures to Your Advantage

Gestures—what you do with your hands while you talk—are often the source of great discomfort for speakers. Clinging to the podium, clenching your hands behind your back, shoving your hands in your pockets, flailing your arms, fidgeting with your watch—these moves are all certain to detract from your message.

In a formal presentation, gestures give life to the talk and emphasize key points. Most people don't recognize what gestures can do for a presentation. Gestures help you look relaxed and animated. Here are a couple of tips to get the best from your gestures:

- **Go with the flow.** Gestures work best when they go along with the flow of what you're saying. Look for opportunities to use them. When gestures help give a visual picture of your words or help punctuate a point, they add energy to your message and greatly engage the audience's attention.
- **Vary your gestures.** If you repeat with the same gesture or two throughout your speech, they will lose their positive effect. People will walk away remembering that particular gesture like it was a nervous habit and not remember what you said. Using a variety of gestures to show you're getting into your message is the key to sparking positive attention from your audience.

11.3.3 Paying Attention to Your Posture and Body Position

You're far more likely to be standing than sitting when giving a formal presentation. But what do you do with your body? And what kind of posture should you show?

Slouching over a podium or leaning on a table as you talk makes you look too relaxed and lessens the seriousness in which your presentation is received. At the same time, standing still in one spot the whole time makes you look extremely stiff. So what do you do with yourself?

The objective with your posture and body position is to show alertness and confidence, to come across as relaxed yet with a sense of importance. Here are a couple of tips to help achieve this objective in a presentation:

- **Stand tall.** Stand at your full height. No leaning down or hunching over. Use good posture and, like your mother always told you, don't let your shoulders slump.
- **Stand steady and comfortably.** Move your body in ways that fit with the flow of your presentation. Don't stand tightly in one spot the whole time; moving around in a general area can add a feeling of positive energy to your talk. On the other

hand, don't race around or get into what looks like dance steps or rocking motions with your legs.

- **When seated, sit up.** If you are expected to sit while you present, sit up. Slouching in a chair is really easy to do. At the same time, lean forward a bit as you look at and address your audience. This motion helps you command attention and puts confidence behind your message and in your voice.

11.3.4 Taking Control of Your Voice

Your voice is one of the most powerful instruments you have to give the best of you in your presentation. It provides the volume, inflection, and tone of your message.

When using your voice in a speech, your objective is to come across with positive energy and sincerity. Your voice helps put you firmly and confidently behind your words, which has the effect of pulling the audience with you. Here are a few tips to follow to get the best out of your voice:

- **Project loudly and clearly.** In a formal presentation, you need the people at the far edges of the room to hear you easily. When you achieve that goal, everyone else will hear strength in your voice. This doesn't mean that you should shout; just turn up your volume so that no one has to strain to hear you.
- **Convey a tone of respect and importance.** The tone of your voice carries a tremendous amount of the emotion of your message and therefore greatly affects the message's overall meaning. You want your tone to say what you mean and mean what you say, and to do so with care and respect for your audience. In particular, think about the feeling you want to convey in your message—the feeling you want your audience to walk away with after hearing your presentation. Then speak with that feeling in mind, and you'll connect well with your audience.
- **Show a little enthusiasm.** In your own style, you want enthusiasm for the talk to come across in your voice. This deals with the pitch or inflection that you use. Avoid the monotone; have some life in your voice.
- **Vary at times for emphasis.** Your voice can serve as a powerful tool to emphasize key points in your talk, especially when you vary it from its normal volume and inflection. At times, get a little louder or softer on a key word or phrase, or put a little extra energy in your voice at these critical moments.

11.3.5 Pacing Yourself

Pace is your rate of speech when talking. Go too fast when you're giving a presentation and you may slur your words and confuse your audience. Go way too slowly and you may torture the group, who can't wait that long for you to make a point.

In a formal presentation, the objective of pace is to manage the flow of your delivery so that the audience hears your words clearly and leaves feeling comfortable. If the pace doesn't match what the audience is comfortable with, you lose their interest. Check out sections 2.2.7 and 2.2.8 for some tips to help you manage your pace.

- **Go at a steady rate.** You're looking for a happy medium between too fast and too slow. If you concentrate on enunciating your words clearly and easily, you'll be right where you want to be. Having said that, adding in a few slight exaggerations in your rate of speech throughout your speech can help to accentuate certain points because it helps to grab the audience's attention. Use this technique sparingly, though, or else it will lose its impact.

- **Avoid non-words and use pauses. Non-words** are words that aren't words but are said aloud—the most common being "uh," "um," "you know," and "like." They often come from thinking out loud or searching for that next word. When you feel the need to say "um" or "like," just *breathe* instead. This is a hard habit to break, but you can do it if you concentrate. Pauses are those moments of breathing and silence that occur in the midst of speaking. They work well between thoughts to help you formulate how you want to make your next point. They help you stay on top of your pace instead of racing ahead of it. Best of all, pauses help you minimize non-words, talked about in Section 2.2.8.

FOR EXAMPLE

Lame Leadership
The new president of a company gathered his employees for his first presentation. Unfortunately, nearly everyone reported that he had come across poorly—in particular, because he used more than 100 non-words in his 20-minute talk. They couldn't stop counting them. The general sentiment was that he was a nice guy but had little confidence—not exactly the leadership you'd like to see in your company president.

SELF-CHECK

- Define delivery, gestures, pace, and non-words.
- List five non-verbal delivery behaviours.
- Discuss the positive effect of using gestures in a presentation.
- Describe three ways to use posture and body position to your advantage.

11.4 Putting Your Supporting Materials to Work

Visual aids—the slides and graphics you show as you talk—are the supporting materials in a presentation. Their objective is to supplement your spoken message and add clarity and value to it.

Take care to use your visual aids to supplement your message rather than letting them be the focus of the presentation—a common mistake that some speakers make. The following sections will help you get the best out of your visual aids.

11.4.1 Avoiding the Pitfalls

The following are common mistakes presenters make when using visual aids in their talks:

- **Using visuals that are too small for the audience to read:** When the information on the slides is too small or too hard to read, the visual aids tend to distract from your talk rather than support it.
- **Handling the visuals or audio-visual equipment awkwardly:** If you're not comfortable with the equipment you're using to show your visuals, consider either not using them at all or practising their use so you don't look clumsy.
- **Focusing on the slides or graphics and not the audience:** If you look primarily at your visual aids and not much at your audience, people notice. You're usually better received when you face and talk to the live people and not to the inanimate objects.
- **Not having a clear connection to the main points of the talk:** Sometimes speakers have interesting graphics or slides but don't explain how they support the talk at hand. When the audience wonders what the point is of the visual aids you're using, using them has no purpose.
- **Reading the points instead of providing the highlights about them:** This is the cardinal sin for presenters. When you read your slides to the audience, they no longer add value. People *can* read. They come to hear what you have to say, not see how well you can read aloud.

11.4.2 Preparing Useful Visual Aids

Supporting materials can add value to your presentation. After you're aware of what not to do with visual aids, use the following tips to prepare them so that they supplement your presentation:

- **Include one idea or concept per slide.** Have each slide or graphic make its own point so that it stands on its own. This makes it easier to determine where the visual aids fit in your talk—more so than when multiple concepts are put on a slide.

- **Develop a title or heading for each visual.** Give each visual a title or heading so that it tells the audience what the points on it are all about. This organizes your presentation and helps you know why you're using a particular visual aid and where in the talk to use each one.
- **List key words or phrases.** Like talking from an outline, key words work best as points to talk from and expound on. Also, by avoiding sentences, you make it much easier for the audience to see and comprehend your visual.
- **Follow the rule of six.** This point reinforces the importance of making visuals easy to see and read—no more than six words per line, and no more than six lines per visual.
- **Use upper- and lowercase letters.** Capitalize the first letter of words, but not entire words. For example, contrast the first line, which follows this rule, with the second line:

> *Underpromise and Overdeliver.*
> *UNDERPROMISE and OVERDELIVER.*

The combination of uppercase and lowercase letters on a slide tends to be more aesthetically appealing because your eyes can follow the shapes of the letters. Again, you want the audience to see your visual aids easily.

- **Design visuals to be seen by the back row.** If the person in the back row of the audience can see your visuals clearly, so can everyone else. If necessary, check it out yourself ahead of time.
- **When in doubt, leave it out.** If you question whether you need a slide to help cover a point, or whether you should add more information to a slide, most often the answer is no.

Less is more. Remember, you can fill in the gaps or add other information when needed simply by talking. Overall, effective supporting materials are brief, clear to see, and work to highlight your verbal message.

FOR EXAMPLE

Taking It in Stride

Upon her return from a business trip to China, Andrea prepared to speak to five of her co-workers about potential business ventures for their company. When she arrived at the meeting, she found 20 staffers eagerly waiting to hear her report. She had only prepared five sets of handouts, so she was immediately shaken by the sight of the extra 15 people in the room. After a moment or two, however, she recovered enough to set those materials aside and work from a flipchart she found in the back of the room. It wasn't at all what she planned, but her brief notes and her steady smile revealed none of her anxiety to her audience.

SELF-CHECK

- Define visual aid.
- Discuss five common mistakes speakers make when using visual aids.
- Explain ways of preparing visual aids that supplement your material, not detract from it.

11.5 Going Live in Front of an Audience

Sometimes the biggest challenge in doing a presentation is not the presentation itself but contending with the audience's issues and your own fear. The following sections explore how to handle questions and stay composed while on the platform.

11.5.1 Overcoming Stage Fright

Stage fright, a feeling of anxiety or nervousness that arises when a person is expected to perform in front of others, is normal, especially when someone has to get up in front of a group to give a speech. Symptoms of stage fright can include dry mouth, sweaty hands, shaky knees, and nausea. If you have such feelings, the key is to recognize that they are normal and then take steps to deal with them.

Here are some tips that help you move from high anxiety to relative composure:

- **Come prepared.** Be in command of your material and how you want to present it before the big day. Just showing up and trying to talk off-the-cuff increases the pressure you feel. Use preparation as a primary method of preventing stage fright.

- **Recognize that nervousness can be a positive motivator.** Being nervous is a normal feeling that many entertainers and athletes experience before going on stage or into a big competition. It serves to drive them and spark energy. Think of nervousness as something that's not only okay but that's a way of stimulating positive energy.

- **Get to know the room.** Arrive early enough so you can walk around and familiarize yourself with the room in which you'll speak. Take some time to stand at the lectern and check out the microphone and any other equipment you'll be using.

- **Have note cards or an outline.** There's no need to memorize your presentation—doing so adds undue stress, especially if you lose your place. Outlines or notes serve as a reference to glance down at periodically and to then talk from to your group. If your hands are shaking, however, don't hold your notes in your hand—your audience is more likely to notice your movement.

- **Meet the audience.** If possible, greet some of the audience as they arrive and chat with them. It is easier to speak to a group of friends than to a group of strangers.

- **Relax your body.** Take a quick walk around the building to relax your muscles. Stretch your neck and back muscles, which hold a lot of tension. Take deep breaths; make yourself laugh to further release tension.

- **Don't point out that you're nervous.** Bringing attention to anything that has nothing to do with your presentation only takes your audience's attention away from your talk.

- **If you stumble, move ahead.** Musicians make mistakes all the time when they perform. In most cases, people in the audience generally don't notice because the musicians just keep on playing. The same principle applies when you're giving a presentation. If you don't say that word just right or make the point as clearly as you wanted, keep going. No one expects perfection from you; they came to hear what you had to say, so keep your focus on the next point in your presentation.

- **Use your tricks.** Take sips of water to give yourself a pause to think. Look at the friendliest faces in the audience. And, if imagining that the audience is naked works for you, then do it.

11.5.2 Responding to Audience Questions

In many business presentations, the audience wants a chance to ask questions. Allowing time for questions is to your advantage as a speaker because it gets the audience involved and gives you an opportunity to clarify key points and address concerns.

In some cases, the effectiveness of your presentation is evaluated more on how well you handle the questions that come your way than on the talk itself. Although you can anticipate some of the questions you may be asked and prepare responses to them, you won't know every question that people may ask. Yet, in order to give a successful presentation, you need to be able to handle any and all questions that come up. Here are a few tips to help you respond to an audience's questions:

- **Decide when you want to receive questions.** Some presenters like to field questions from the group as people have them. This way, they can address matters as they arrive at points in the talk. Others like to hold questions until the speech is over. They don't want their flow interrupted, nor do they want to contend with an audience that may dwell on one issue for awhile. Go with what's most comfortable for you, but communicate in your opening when you want to take questions so that your audience knows what to expect. Then, if you've asked the group to hold questions until the end, you can respectfully defer a question if someone interrupts along the way.

- **Listen closely to the questions.** Before you respond to a question, make sure that you understand what the asker is asking. If you need to, ask questions to clarify and paraphrase to check your understanding.

- **Be direct and concise in your answers.** Some people speak well when they have a prepared speech, but the minute you ask them a question where they have to talk off-the-cuff, they become verbose and vague. Your listeners want answers to their questions; they don't want to be frustrated by rambling responses.

- **Use your answers to reinforce key points or your core message.** Questions from the audience may give you the opportunity to re-emphasize key points you've made or to promote a theme from your presentation further.

- **Be positive in your responses, both verbally and non-verbally.** Just as you do in the body of your presentation, avoid coming across negatively in your language, tone of voice, and body language when you respond to questions. Also, avoid sounding annoyed with the person asking the question. Show patience and receive each question with interest. Annoyance and arrogance are major turnoffs to audiences.

- **Positively reinforce the asking of questions.** Simple remarks such as "That's a good question" or "Thanks for asking" go a long way to encourage questions and make people feel appreciated for raising them. This positive reinforcement adds to your sincerity level and helps you connect with your audience.

- **Don't make it up if you don't know the answer.** Trying to fake an answer is a bad idea. People don't want to hear misleading or inaccurate speakers. On the other hand, you may be able to give a good answer if you give yourself time to think. Sometimes paraphrasing to check that you understood the question helps to clarify the question and gives you time to think of the appropriate answer. In addition, sending the question out to the audience for their thoughts on the issue allows others to help provide an answer and gives you time to think. If you still aren't sure, tell the person that they've asked a very interesting question, and you'll check it out and get back with an answer shortly. Then follow through and do so.

FOR EXAMPLE

Q & A Derailment

A presenter who hadn't given much thought to a question-and-answer period was thrown off guard by the number of questions that popped up throughout her presentation. Instead of addressing them at the conclusion of her talk, she took them as they came. In doing so, she lost her place, her rhythm—and the audience's attention.

SELF-CHECK

- Explain the benefit of allowing audience members time to ask questions.
- Discuss the advantages and disadvantages of taking questions at the end of a presentation.
- Define stage fright.
- Explain how to cope with the feelings of anxiety associated with stage fright.

SUMMARY

As difficult as it may be, your ability to prepare and deliver a successful presentation can be a ticket to success in your career. This chapter demonstrates how preparation plays a key role in a presentation's effectiveness. The three critical pieces of a presentation's content are the introduction, body, and conclusion. Delivery is just as important as content; without impact in a presentation, your message falls flat. When used properly, visual aids can add strength to a presentation. In the end, your ability to keep your composure and work with an audience can leave a lasting—and positive—impression.

KEY TERMS

Benefits	The gains to be made or the things that are good about an idea, product, or service.
Body	The part of the presentation between an introduction and conclusion; its purpose is to get key points across.
Conclusion	The last part of a presentation; it is often the part the audience remembers best.
Content	What you say in a presentation; your message.
Delivery	How you express your messages; involves non-verbal communication.
Features	How an idea, product, or service works.
Gestures	What you do with your hands while you talk; examples include clinging to the podium and fidgeting with your watch.

Introduction	The opening of a speech or presentation.
Non-words	Words that aren't words but are said aloud—the most common being "uh," "um," "you know," and "like."
Pace	Rate of speech when talking.
Preparation	The hard work done before going "live" with a speech or presentation.
Quotation	A line said by someone else.
Recap	A summary of the main points covered in a presentation.
Rhetorical question	A thought-provoking question asked of the audience but for which you don't expect an answer out loud.
Stage fright	A feeling of anxiety or nervousness that arises when a person is expected to perform in front of others.
Stories	An engaging way to share life experiences and to highlight or illustrate a point.
Transitions	Words that move a speaker from one topic to the next in a presentation; they create the bridges that connect points and help move a presentation forward.
Visual aids	Supporting materials such as slides and graphics shown as a presenter talks.

ASSESS YOUR UNDERSTANDING

Go to www.wiley.com/canada/brounstein to evaluate your knowledge of the basics of speeches and oral presentations. Measure your learning by comparing pre-test and post-test results.

Quick Questions

1. Which of the following can spell failure for a presentation?
   (a) specialized terms and language
   (b) an enormous amount of data
   (c) rambling
   (d) all of the above
2. Regardless of whether they can handle technical equipment, a speaker should use visual aids to properly showcase his or her ideas. True or false?
3. Which of the following steps helps guide speakers in their preparation?
   (a) writing a cover letter
   (b) rehearsing

(c) mirroring

(d) monitoring

4. The content of a presentation is its method of delivery. True or false?

5. The goal of an introduction is to
   (a) identify the topic and purpose
   (b) get the audience's attention
   (c) give a short overview
   (d) all of the above

6. Which of the following patterns can be used to organize the body of a presentation?
   (a) chronological
   (b) spatial
   (c) illogical
   (d) all of the above

7. How the speaker delivers the material is more important than what she says. True or false?

8. Which of the following is an effective use of eye contact?
   (a) locking in on one or two faces for maximum impact
   (b) looking above the audience to avoid excluding some members
   (c) scanning the audience to reach everyone
   (d) all of the above

9. What should a speaker do with his or her voice in a presentation?
   (a) show enthusiasm
   (b) project clearly
   (c) vary it
   (d) all of the above

10. A visual aid should contain enough ideas to fill the entire screen. True or false?

11. Which of the following guidelines should be used when preparing visual aids?
    (a) list key words
    (b) give each visual a heading or title
    (c) follow the rule of six
    (d) all of the above

12. Why is it to a speaker's advantage to allow time for questions?
    (a) it allows a speaker to address concerns
    (b) it promotes audience involvement
    (c) it gives a speaker the chance to clarify main points
    (d) all of the above

13. In those cases in which a speaker isn't clear on an answer to a question, he or she should make an educated guess and move on. True or false?

14. Memorizing a speech is the best way to get through the material without faltering. True or false?

Give It Some Thought

1. How does an enthusiastic delivery affect an audience's perception of the presentation?

2. Stage fright is a real concern for many speakers. Explain how being prepared can decrease the feelings of stage fright.

3. What introduction techniques serve to grasp an audience's attention?
    (a) quote
    (b) story
    (c) bold statement
    (d) all of the above

4. What two tasks must be done to prepare the body of a presentation?

5. When does a quotation work best in a conclusion?

6. What are three non-verbal mistakes that speakers make when giving business presentations?

7. What can you do to reduce or eliminate the number of non-words you use in your speech?

8. Most people expect to stand while delivering a presentation. Describe the proper way to sit and present when necessary.

9. What are three mistakes speakers make with their visual aids?

10. Explain why a combination of uppercase and lowercase letters works best.

11. What are the pros and cons of taking questions from the audience only at the end of a presentation?

12. Discuss some strategies for making sure your audience is following what you are saying in a presentation.

Applying This Chapter

1. You're a representative for a uniform manufacturer who's been asked to speak to parents in a public school district that is trying to implement an unpopular uniform dress code. Come up with five questions that parents will want answered. For example: How will wearing a uniform make it easier for my child to learn?

2. You live in an oceanfront community undergoing a great deal of redevelopment. What was once a much-neglected area will now be the site of new housing, retail establishments, and a hotel. As the president of a local coalition fighting to maintain free public beach access, you've been asked to give a short presentation at a city council meeting to voice your group's concerns over proposed beach fees. Outline an effective introduction to your speech. What technique would best grab the attention of your audience?

3. You've been asked to give a presentation on how to research the job market to seniors returning to the workforce. This is a presentation designed to energize and mobilize a somewhat hesitant group of people. Jot down some ideas for ways you can use non-verbal communication behaviours to add impact to your presentation.

4. As the marketing director for a non-profit contemporary arts centre, you're trying to convince a local school district superintendent to join your organization's artistic mentoring program for area high school students. Your organization is relatively new, but the program has been successful with one other district so far. Think of three visual aids that will get the superintendent excited about the program.

5. Practise an old presentation or talk about your career goals in front of a live audience (one person will do, if necessary). Instruct your audience to ask questions as they come up during your presentation. (Use the tips outlined in Section 11.5.1 to prepare.) What happened with that approach? Would you choose the alternative, to receive all questions at the end? If so, draft a statement instructing the audience.

6. You've been asked to speak to a class at your old high school about your decision to take a business writing course. Think about what techniques you could use to begin your presentation and jot down some point-form notes about what you would say.

7. The new boss is making a presentation to your department at work and he's doing a terrible job. He's speaking too softly, he's reading from his notes, and his PowerPoint slides are not in the correct order. In a small group, discuss how the audience should react. Should you ask questions? Should you ask him to speak louder? Should you do nothing? Come up with a three-point plan for letting the boss know that you're having trouble following his presentation.

THE NEXT STEP

Peer Review

Pair up with another student and then interview each other. Choose a topic such as academic history or travel experiences and limit your questions to four. Each interviewer should take a few quick notes. Then, have the students stand and introduce their partners to the class.

Performance Evaluation

Look through different sites on the Internet until you find video of a person giving a speech. Turn down the volume and observe the person's non-verbal communication. Do they look relaxed or tense? Are they using natural hand gestures? Making eye contact? How's the posture? What could you suggest to improve your performance? If your classroom has Internet access, you could show the video to other students and share your responses with them.

Reviewing Your Notes

Go back over your notes for a section of this course and develop an outline for a two-minute impromptu talk. Don't script your entire talk, but speak informally from your notes.

Pre-Presentation Research

You've been asked to speak about a topic that interests you (for example, your favourite food or materials used to make hockey sticks). Do some research on the Internet and develop a list of six to nine points that your audience needs to know about. At least three of these points should be statistics that support what you want to say.

Stage Fright

Everyone gets stage fright: lawyers, actors, musicians, and even teachers. Talk to someone you know who speaks to groups of people about how she or he deals with nerves. Alternatively, do some online research to see how famous people calm themselves down before they step on stage.

Your Ideal Job

Prepare a two-minute presentation on your ideal job. Consider factors such as your audience, your location, and your message. You could include visual aids to illustrate your presentation.

12
WRITING BUSINESS REPORTS
Preparing Information with a Purpose

STARTING POINT

Go to www.wiley.com/canada/brounstein to assess your knowledge of the basics of writing business reports. After reviewing this website, you'll be able to determine where you need to concentrate your effort.

What You'll Learn in This Chapter:

- the importance of reports in business
- common format for short business reports
- ten steps for efficient report writing
- common format for long business reports
- widely used types of reports.

After Studying This Chapter, You'll be Able to:

- discuss how reports communicate information to an audience
- identify the key elements of a typical report
- determine the purpose of a report
- compare the ways in which a long report format differs from that of a short report
- choose the appropriate type of report for specific business situations.

INTRODUCTION

When a memo or letter isn't sufficient to communicate what you need in a business situation, or your audience needs more information with which to develop strategies or make decisions, a longer, more thorough format is required: the business report. This chapter details the differences between short and long reports in terms of purpose and audience. Common elements of the short format are outlined. Steps proven to guide other writers in efficient report writing are covered. Because of their length, long reports require extra care as far as clarity and organization. The chapter concludes with a review of common report styles.

12.1 Understanding the Purpose of Reports

Business organizations of all sizes rely on reports to help in making important decisions. They may be reports on progress, recommendations, feasibility studies, evaluations, or expenses. As the names indicate, these reports are diverse in focus and aim, and they differ in structure. However, the common goal of all reports is the same: to communicate information to an audience.

Reports help business organizations to learn what's happening (or what has happened or will happen) in two worlds:

- **The internal world:** What are employees working on? How is it going? What resources are being used, or which are required? In what ways is the company growing or shrinking? What problems need to be addressed?
- **The external world:** How is the company perceived by clients and the general public? What do clients want from the company? What are the company's SWOT factors (strengths, weaknesses, opportunities, and threats) and how can they be addressed? How can the company attract skilled workers? What social responsibilities and political challenges does the company face?

Although these issues and others can be discussed in meetings, interviews, memos, and letters, the report often addresses the issues more thoroughly, and with more formal organization than other forms of business communication.

The purpose of the report may be informative (what is known about the topic), analytical (why circumstances have developed), persuasive (how readers should respond), or portions of all three. Because reports are used for making decisions, they include enough evidence to support whatever conclusion or idea is suggested in the report.

12.1.1 The Audience for Reports

Within corporations and other organizations, reports are typically required when upper management faces a problem or a question. At this point, someone in management will delegate the task to a subordinate who, after necessary thinking and research, responds to the problem or question by means of a short report. In other words, the needs of the audience determine the purpose for a short report.

First, the report is read and approved by the person who requested it. Next, the report may be distributed within the company, or it may be stored in a company library, where others may read it. In this role, the report becomes a vehicle for getting information out to co-workers. In fact, a report writer may be asked to produce two versions of a report: (1) a complete version for the manager(s) who requested it and (2) a summary version for distribution to others in the company.

12.1.2 Short Reports Versus Long Reports

In many cases a short report—typically less than ten pages long—is adequate to communicate the information a manager or other person needs to make a decision. A short report should be able to be read in one sitting. There are cases, however, in which a short report is not sufficient.

Every major business, professional, and governmental organization regularly generates long reports; that is, reports at least 20 pages long. In an age of overflowing inboxes and hectic schedules, why do business people read or write long reports? Many such reports have to do with money. Some tell the company or government agency what it got in the past for its money. Others may look ahead to future planning for how to invest money and other resources. Still others report the present status of projects, processes, or resources on which the company is spending money.

Whether discussing the past, present, future, or a combination of the three, long reports provide key information to decision makers about how effectively they have spent their money and used their other resources. Although many short reports also provide such information, most big expenditures (including expenses for personnel and supplies) need a long report to be adequately justified.

FOR EXAMPLE

Reporting 101

In his first job as an assistant to the director of advertising for a magazine, Anthony was overwhelmed with the number of reports that he received on behalf of his boss. Because his boss would never have the time to read them all, a good portion of Anthony's time was spent on reading the reports, then summarizing them in memo form. The two met once a week to go over the reports; later, Anthony would file the information away. In the beginning, it seemed to Anthony that many of the reports were simply a waste of paper; later, as he began to use them for his own work, he realized their value.

SELF-CHECK

- Discuss three purposes for business reports.
- Describe a typical distribution flow for a report.
- Discuss a situation in which a long report would be more appropriate than a short report.

12.2 Knowing the Types of Business Reports

Among the most widely prepared reports in business are the periodic report, the progress report, the data report, and the recommendation report. These are known by various names from company to company. The periodic report may be called the "quarterly summary" or the "monthly update." The progress report may be called a "milestone report" or a "status report." No matter what they are called, these common report types have three common features. They must:

- maintain a consistent format from period to period for ease of comparison
- use direct, concise language and clear descriptions of data
- highlight particularly important developments and trends.

12.2.1 Periodic Reports

Senior management keeps its finger on the pulse of operations by requiring periodic reports from lower-level managers. These reports, usually written each month or quarter, summarize business activity during the period and comment on noteworthy developments. At the request of senior management, the report writer may offer recommendations based on factors described in the report. These recommendations may appear at the beginning or the end of the report, but they always also appear in the executive summary.

12.2.2 Progress Reports

The purpose of a progress report is to inform senior management, customers, or other interested parties about progress you've made on a project over a certain period of time. The project can be the design, construction, or repair of something, the study of a problem, or the gathering of information on a subject. Think of the structure of a progress report as having three parts: past (what's happened); present (what's happening now); and future (challenges you are anticipating). You may answer some or all of the following questions in writing a progress report:

- How much of the work is complete? (past)
- Have any problems or unexpected events arisen? (past)
- What part of the work is currently in progress? (present)
- What work remains to be done? (future)
- What challenges might be coming along in the near future? (future)

> **FOR EXAMPLE**
>
> **Making Progress**
> To keep his corporate client up to date on what's being done to remediate a toxic parcel of company property, an environmental consultant submits progress reports. In them, he outlines cleanup advancements, biological-monitoring results, how much work remains, and any delays or complications. These reports include information on unexpected expenses related to the project's budget.

12.2.3 Data Reports

Many business operations, such as cash-register sales, inventory accounting, and personnel time cards, can be monitored by computer. Management receives up-to-date results of that monitoring by means of the computer report. This document usually begins with summary statements of data and then provides specific data by date or category. Such reports can be generated periodically or as needed.

12.2.4 Recommendation Reports

For this type of report, you provide not only your recommendation, choice, or judgement, but also the data and the conclusions leading up to it. That way, readers can check your findings, your logic, and your conclusions and come up with a completely different view. But, more likely, they will be convinced by all your careful research and documentation.

For example, a company might be looking at grammar-checking software and want a recommendation on which product is the best. As the report writer on this project, you could study the market for this type of application and recommend one particular product, a couple of products (differing perhaps in their strengths and their weaknesses), or no product at all (maybe none of them are any good). The recommendation report answers the question "Which option should we choose?" (or in some cases, "Which are the best options?") by recommending Product B, or maybe both Products B and C, or none of the products.

> **FOR EXAMPLE**
>
> **Reporting to the President**
> High End Audio Outlets has expanded from one downtown location to 11 suburban stores. Along the way, it has experienced an unusually high rate of employee turnover; new hires are brought in by word-of-mouth and tend to last less than six months. The president of the company also suspects that the quick turnovers are related to the increase of internal theft. She hires a new head of personnel and assigns his first task: a report compiling data on turnover and thefts. She requests a follow-up recommendation report with a plan for solving both problems.

12.3 Following a Business-Report Format

The same tools for writing effective memos, letters, and other business communications (see Chapter 5) should be applied when writing business reports. To be successful, your report should not only communicate the required information, it must:

- capture your audience's attention
- use the appropriate tone and voice
- organize your key points in a logical way
- use correct grammar and spelling.

The format of a report may differ somewhat from corporation to corporation. One company may insist on reports in memo format (beginning with a "To:/From:/Date:/ Subject:" block), whereas another company may prefer the more traditional title page opening. Some firms bind all authorized short reports into special paper folders; others use coloured papers to signify different kinds of reports.

The format of a short report can generally be described page by page as shown in Figure 12-1 (the format for a long report will be covered later in this chapter). A sample

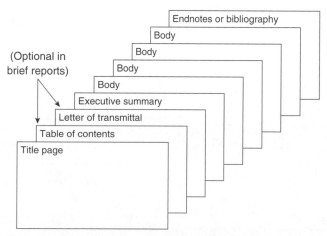

Figure 12-1 Short report format

short report can be found in Appendix A. The following sections briefly describe the common elements found in a typical short report:

- **Title page:** Centre the title of your report, your name (and the names of all other contributing writers), title, professional affiliation, and the date of the report's completion or filing. The title page must clearly show the professional quality of your report.
- **Table of contents:** This page is optional in reports of six pages or less. You can include this element if it will help your reader understand a report that is longer. Don't include it if it only makes your document longer, not better.
- **Letter of transmittal:** This optional page is a letter from the report writer to the report readers. A letter of transmittal is usually only included in very formal circumstances. It briefly provides the following:
  - reason(s) for the report
  - highlights of particularly interesting items
  - contact information for readers' questions or comments.

    Such letters usually appear in short reports that must be conveyed to their readers by mail or messenger rather than in person by the report writer. (The letter of transmittal may also be attached to but not included in the report, in which case it does not appear in the table of contents.)
- **Executive summary:** This page summarizes the purpose, organization, methods, and outcomes of the short report (sometimes called an *abstract*). The executive summary usually runs no longer than one page and may be as short as a single paragraph.
- **Body of the report:** These pages contain the actual information of the report. The development and organization of this report section is treated in depth later in this chapter.
- **Endnotes or bibliography:** Notes may be used in the text itself, placed at the foot of the page—that is, footnotes—or gathered at the end of the report as endnotes. The bibliography pages, usually the last in a short report, always follow all notes and in-text references. Many short reports don't include this documentation when the report does not cite sources or require other notes.

SELF-CHECK

- Cite four things a business report must do in order to be successful.
- Define title page, table of contents, letter of transmittal, executive summary, body of report, endnotes, and bibliography.
- Discuss why no single report format works for all business situations.

12.4 Guidelines for Report Writing

Experienced report writers in business usually develop individual approaches to their craft. Many start by reading widely in their topic area, usually while taking notes. Others like to start by making a very rough guess about the form and content of their eventual report. These writers sketch outlines for information as they shape their possibilities for research.

You too will develop personal approaches to report writing that work for you and your company. To give yourself a start on your own approach, consider ten steps that have helped many report writers get from an initial idea to a polished report in an efficient manner.

12.4.1 Step 1: Determine the Purpose of Your Report

Learn as much as possible about the purpose and intended use of your report before beginning to write. Don't be misled by the tentative title you or someone else has given to your report. Titles don't always reveal the true object of the report.

Before you start to write, find out what your report is supposed to help your key readers do. Should it help them to make a decision? If so, the report must analyze the choices, and it might need to suggest a best choice. Should it rationalize a decision that was already made? If so, it should tell why that specific choice was made and should ignore choices that seem better now, with hindsight.

Many experienced report writers jot down their object on an index card, which they keep handy while writing. The card serves as a constant reminder that every aspect of the report must help to achieve the object. Any other writing, no matter how terrific, is wasted effort.

FOR EXAMPLE

The Art of the Report
When the idea of a travelling sculpture exhibit came up at the board meeting of a contemporary arts foundation, Samantha, the assistant director, was charged with writing a short report to be presented to city leaders. She realized that artistic value alone would not convince the city to approve the exhibit. The exhibit would, however, bring positive attention and foot traffic to city landmarks and neighbourhoods. To make her case, she dedicated much of the body of the report to examples of how other cities had benefited from similar projects.

12.4.2 Step 2: Understand Your Audience's Needs

Who is your audience? What are their interests? Their needs? Their biases? The answers to these questions can help you determine what to discuss and how to shape your material to the best effect.

In actual business practice, writers too often finish a report only to be told by upper management, "You missed the point." The report writer bears primary responsibility for knowing what the reader wants. Upper management can be notoriously brief and cryptic in describing the purpose or the topic for a report.

Report writers have to learn to decode the short descriptions of upper management. Usually, this decoding process involves limiting broad, unmanageable topics. In the following passages, notice how what was said gets translated by the report writer into a limited, manageable topic:

Executive Request	Limited Topic Created by Report Writer
the minority hiring situation here	Affirmative Action Hiring at Plastron since 1992
automated tellers for the bank	Four Highly Rated Automated Tellers Suitable for Installation at Lakehead Bank

The limiting process usually happens naturally and quickly in day-to-day business conversation. When the report writer formulates a limited version of an assigned topic, he or she checks it out with upper management—usually by means of a brief memo, meeting, or phone call. These important few minutes help the writer avoid wasted days of effort on misunderstood or misdirected topics.

12.4.3 Step 3: Brainstorm About Your Topic

Consider using the classic questions technique discussed in Section 4.3.2 as a way to brainstorm your topic. The time you spend on the classic questions or other brainstorming techniques can get your mind working in productive directions, and the process can help you better understand your audience's interest in the topic.

12.4.4 Step 4: Research Your Topic

Once you have brainstormed your topic, you'll be prepared to gather the correct information from the records and files you have at your disposal as well as from other sources. A firm grasp of what you are looking for provides a powerful magnet to draw together the facts you need.

In many business situations, reports are based on primary research sources (first-hand information from surveys, interviews, measurements, samplings, and so on). You may also need to draw from secondary research materials (second-hand information from books, articles, and so on).

Inevitably, beginning report writers gather much more information than they can use in the report at hand. As your writing skills improve, you'll get better at picking the information for your report. It also helps to give careful consideration to the range of your report. How broadly should you describe and cover your topic? Do you want to summarize facts? To interpret facts? To predict future patterns of growth?

You're likely to find in your research important topics that are fascinating but don't belong in the report you're writing. Don't let your topic take you off on tangents; your report will become unmanageably long and disjointed. Instead, you must control the range of your report by deciding what belongs and what does not belong within your area of study.

The Role of Visuals

Don't overlook the value of including visual aids such as spreadsheets, graphs, and charts in a report (see Section 11.4 for more on the types of visual aids). These elements improve readability, add interest, clarify content, and help condense large amounts of information. Effective visual aids should:

- contribute to the report's text and not be redundant
- add to, but not replace, clearly written words
- be placed as close as possible to the corresponding text (text should have a reference for where to find the visual; for example, "See Figure 8A below")
- be professional-looking and easy to read.

12.4.5 Step 5: Arrange Your Major Points

A report should not just be a cover letter to a relatively disorganized collection of facts and figures. There are many patterns of thought by which you can organize your work. (Several patterns are included in Section 4.4.1.) Think not only about what you want to say, but also about placing each aspect of your argument in its appropriate location. For example, after thinking through the logical, persuasive appeal of a pattern of thought about training costs, you might write an outline resembling the one shown in the following outline:

I. **Overview**
   The purposes of the training program
   The key question: Is the company getting its money's worth?
II. **Past methods of training**
   What we used to do
   Why we did it that way
   How much it cost
III. **Present methods of training**
   What we do now

> Why we do it
>
> How much it costs
>
> **IV. Evaluation**
>
> Old methods versus new methods
>
> Old costs versus new costs
>
> **V. Conclusions**
>
> New costs are due to one-time equipment acquisition
>
> New methods are worth this expenditure
>
> Training per employee will cost less and less in the future

Some executives and managers prefer that the conclusions and recommendations portion of a report be placed at the beginning of the report. This re-arrangement is especially common when the report does not begin with an executive summary.

12.4.6 Step 6: Write Your Rough Draft

In addition to the writing tips offered in Chapter 5, a helpful way to get started writing your rough draft is to use an overview for the first section of your report. Overviews tell both the writer and the reader what to do with the report. Both look to the overview for a point of perspective, a view of the purpose of the report, and a suggestion of the approach it will take. Readers particularly like the word *overview*, with its implicit promise of orientation.

Once the overview is written, write the rest of the report, according to your outline and your research. From time to time, remind yourself that your purpose is to communicate, not to impress. If you get stuck or are faced with writer's block, study the outline again. It will show you where you are in the total report and what comes next. Your research falls naturally into place throughout the report.

At the end of your report, write down both an evaluation section (how you and the reader may think about the topic) and a conclusion (what you and the reader may decide about the topic). The evaluation unfolds the process by which you compared, contrasted, weighed, and balanced the ideas. The conclusion reveals the products of your thinking.

12.4.7 Step 7: Revise Your Rough Draft

Before you tackle the all-important task of revision, be sure you've taken a break from working on the report. Then use the following checklist to guide you through your revision. You can find more details on these and other steps of revision in Section 5.4:

- Organize the topics into a logical pattern such as chronological (past–present–future) or emphatic (most important to least important).
- Use headings to clarify and highlight the report's organization.
- Use varied sentence lengths and shorter paragraphs for better readability.

- Review your choice of words, substituting specific, vivid words for general, abstract words. Choose simple, familiar words over long or strange ones.
- Check all spelling, grammar, and language mechanics.
- Replace most status verbs (such as is, are, was, has, have, seems to be) with vivid action verbs (such as reveal, grasp, demonstrate, fall, strike, seize).
- Use the crucial first two or three words in each sentence for meaningful words and phrases (not it is, there is/are, or and).
- Define jargon or technical terms when appropriate.

12.4.8 Step 8: Review the Appearance of Your Rough Draft

Recognize that your report must please your readers' eyes if it is to please their minds. Exercise care in placing your words well on the page. First impressions are important.

Use topic headings, graphics, and tables wherever they will help the at-a-glance readability of your report. Write for the reader who will merely glance through your report as well as the reader who will read it with care.

Arrange your visuals to appeal to your reader. Use varied margins, white space, underlining, and appropriate graphics to create a document that readers will want to read. Experiment with different fonts to make your report attractive.

12.4.9 Step 9: Prepare Your Final Copy

Prepare a crisp, clean version of the report. Pay careful attention to the suggested format and other conventions of report writing specified previously. If appropriate, you may want to bind your report, either through your company or through a print or copy shop.

12.4.10 Step 10: Present Your Report

Your report is finished, but you still have to consider how to present it to your audience. Instead of sending the stack of reports to your manager by office courier, for example, you may decide to deliver the copies in person at a meeting. That way, if your manager has comments or questions, you'll be on the spot to deal with them.

SELF-CHECK

- Describe how the limiting process can define the needs of your audience.
- Discuss how primary research sources differ from secondary research sources.
- Review the steps of revision.
- Explain the importance of appearance when completing a report.

12.5 Writing Long Business Reports

In many ways, long reports are extra-long versions of short reports. However, they require special care; because they have few length restrictions, long reports can easily get sidetracked and jumbled. Clarity and organization are more important in long business reports than in almost any other business document.

Consider all of the ingredients of a long report. First, it usually includes a number of prefacing pages called front matter—a title page, letters of authorization and transmittal, tables of contents and figures (even a table of figures and/or tables), sometimes even a preface and foreword, and usually an abstract or executive summary. The body of the report is usually 15 or more pages (often many more). Concluding matter includes appendices, legal instruments (if any), endnotes, a bibliography, and perhaps a glossary and index. To view a sample of a long report, go to www.wiley.com/canada/brounstein.

Few long reports in business number less than 20 pages, and most are considerably longer. Figure 12-2 illustrates the sequence of elements in a long report:

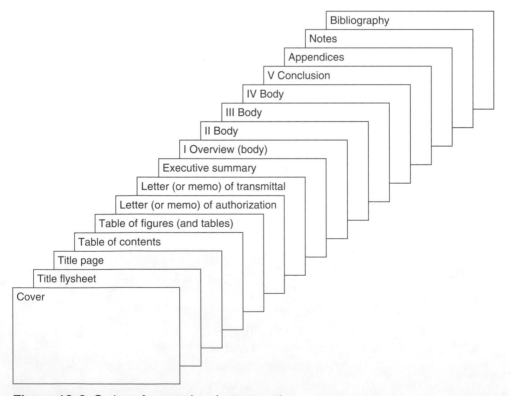

Figure 12-2 Order of pages in a long report

- **Cover:** Long reports may be bound like a softcover book. Less-expensive binding (of the sort done at photocopy shops) uses vinyl or heavy paper covers, many with windows so that the title of the report appears through the cover.

- **Title flysheet:** A single sheet of blank paper that separates the cover from the title page (unless a cover with a window is used). This sheet has no page number and bears no marks of any kind. In more formal documents, the flysheet is often parchment or translucent quality paper.

- **Title page:** The title page contains key information: what the report is about, for whom it was prepared, by whom it was written, and the date of its completion or filing.

- **Table of contents:** This familiar directory simply lists topic headings with appropriate page numbers. If your report is well organized and uses informative headings, the reader can grasp your general approach to the topic from your table of contents.

- **Table of figures and/or tables:** This table can prove useful when the reader is trying to locate charts, graphs, and statistical breakouts throughout the text of a long report. The table also helps readers gauge how much statistical information your report contains.

- **Letter (or memo) of authorization:** The letter or memo of authorization answers three key questions:
  - **Who authorizes work to be done?** Government agencies and large corporations will commonly refer not only to an authorizing individual, naming his or her position, but also to an authorizing document such as a work order, legislative measure, or Cabinet order.
  - **What work is authorized?** The letter briefly describes the scope of the work to be undertaken, referring in most cases to a more thorough description of the work contained in a request for proposal (RFP) or other documents.
  - **Who will do the work?** The letter names specific people and groups who will complete the work as described. Because the letter often serves as a binding contract, it is usually signed and dated by the authorizing official.

- **Letter (or memo) of transmittal:** Just as you would send your resumé with a cover letter, you should introduce your long report to your intended reader by means of a letter of transmittal. Three areas of focus are crucial, and a fourth is helpful:
  - **To whom are you sending the report?** Address the letter of transmittal to that person or organization. If the individual is part of your organization, you should format this message as a memo; otherwise it should be a letter.
  - **What are you sending?** Name the report by title in the letter of transmittal, then comment briefly on the highlights that might be especially interesting to your audience. You may want to mention your authorization to write the report.
  - **What do you want your readers to do after reading your report?** Spell out in specific detail any action you expect from them. (For example, "Please notify

Ms. Jill Clayton, Director of Advanced Design, when you have read this report and are prepared to meet with the engineering panel.")

- o **What are you willing to do for your readers?** Offer to help your readers or to answer any questions, if this is appropriate and you are willing to do so.

- **Executive summary:** The executive summary (also called an *abstract*) condenses or summarizes the matter of the report into one or more paragraphs (usually restricted to one page). This page typically answers five questions:

  - o What is the subject of the report?
  - o What is the purpose of the report?
  - o How is the report structured?
  - o What kind of evidence is used?
  - o What conclusions are reached and recommendations are made?

- **Body of the report:** This is the actual information of the report, as discussed earlier in this chapter. The Body section often begins with an overview, which introduces the reader to the report material and describes what the report will cover; any necessary background information about the project can be presented in the overview.

- **Conclusion:** This is where the report writer sums up all of the information presented in the report and makes the final recommendations based on his or her findings.

- **Appendices:** This section of the report contains any details or technical information that will support the report, but was not central to the report's purpose. For example, this could include detailed lists of statistics, tables of raw data, or samples of blank or completed questionnaires.

- **Notes:** This page differs from footnotes because the notes (also called *endnotes*) contained here appear at the end of the report rather than at the foot of each page. The report writer may choose to use either footnotes or endnotes. If the notes are important to the reader, grouping the notes at the end of the report makes the reader's job harder. However, if the notes aren't important for readers, endnotes are easier for both the writer and the reader.

- **Bibliography:** Aside from slightly different punctuation and ordering, the references listed in the bibliography differ in three ways from similar references contained in notes:

  - o A bibliography lists all materials the author found useful in preparing the report, not merely the works quoted or cited directly.
  - o The bibliographic list of works appears in alphabetical order, not in the order of citation in the text.
  - o Bibliographic citations do not include comments from the report writer.

You can follow several styles to prepare footnotes and bibliographies. When trying to determine which style to use, check the predominant practice within your company.

- **Pages and pagination:** Pagination for a long report is fairly straightforward if you think of your report as divided into the three sections: front matter, report body, and concluding matter. Pages in the front matter are numbered with roman numerals (i, ii, iii ...). The exception to this rule is the title flysheet and title page; these pages are included in the page count but shouldn't be numbered. Number the body of your report using Arabic numerals (1, 2, 3, ...) and begin the first page of your text as page 1. The concluding matter should be numbered with Arabic numerals continued on from the report body section. In other words, if your report's conclusion section ends on page 20, the first page of the appendix should be numbered page 21.

The following chart (Figure 12-3) maps out the pagination guidelines for each component of a long report:

Section	Components	Numbering
Front Matter (Part 1)	• Title flysheet • Title page	No page numbers required **Note:** Still include them in your front matter page count
Front Matter (Part 2)	• Table of contents • Table of figures (and tables) • Letter/memo of authorization Letter/memo of transmittal • Executive summary	Roman numerals (e.g., x, xi, xii . . .)
Main Text	• Overview • Body • Conclusion	Arabic numbers (e.g., 1, 2, 3 . . .)
End Matter	• Appendices • Notes • Bibliography	Arabic numbers (e.g., 21, 22, 23 . . .)

Figure 12-3 Pagination guidelines for a long report

SELF-CHECK

- Define cover, flysheet, title page, table of contents, table of figures, letter of authorization, letter of transmittal, executive summary, notes, bibliography, and pagination.
- List the elements of a long report's front matter.
- Discuss three critical areas of focus in a letter of transmittal.
- Explain the importance of following a standard format when writing a long report.

SUMMARY

Regardless of the information you're delivering, the business report you write must be well researched, properly formatted, and well written. Your purpose and audience will greatly determine the length and format of the report you write. By following an acceptable format, whether for a short report or a long report, you are better able to communicate the required information. By using guidelines for brainstorming, researching, organizing, writing, and revising your report, you increase its effectiveness. Having a familiarity with the types of business reports will further improve your report-writing skills.

KEY TERMS

Bibliography	Lists all materials the author found useful in preparing the report.
Body of the report	The pages that contain the actual information of the report.
Cover	Binding used to contain a report, particularly useful with long reports.
Endnote	A note that appears at the end of a report; if the notes aren't important for readers, endnotes are easier than footnotes for the writer.
Executive summary	Summarizes the purpose, organization, methods, and outcomes of the short report; sometimes called an *abstract*.
Flysheet	A single sheet of blank paper that separates the cover from the title page; in very formal documents, the flysheet is often parchment or translucent paper.
Letter of authorization	Details who authorized the work to be done, what work was authorized, and who will do the work.
Letter of transmittal	Briefly provides the reason for a report, highlights of particularly interesting items, and contact information.
Pagination	The number and arrangement of pages in a report; some pages are numbered in lowercase Roman numerals and some in Arabic.
Table of contents	A directory that lists topic headings with appropriate page numbers; especially useful with long reports.

| **Table of figures and/or tables** | Lists the location of charts, graphs, and statistical breakouts throughout the text of a long report. |
| **Title page** | Contains what the report is about, for whom it was prepared, by whom it was written, and the date of its completion or filing. |

ASSESS YOUR UNDERSTANDING

Go to www.wiley.com/canada/brounstein to evaluate your knowledge of the basics of writing business reports. Measure your learning by comparing pre-test and post-test results.

Quick Questions

1. Reports are used to distribute information about the internal workings of a business organization as well as its relationship to others. True or false?

2. Which of the following can be the purpose of a report?

   (a) persuasion

   (b) analysis

   (c) information

   (d) all of the above

3. Typical long reports are at least ten pages long. True or false?

4. Short reports should follow a single type of format, which is standard for all companies and organizations. True or false?

5. The letter of transmittal and the executive summary can serve the same purpose in a short report. True or false?

6. Which of the following should be a writer's first step in writing a report?

   (a) analyze the audience

   (b) brainstorm ideas

   (c) establish a purpose

   (d) email the person who assigned the report

7. Secondary research sources are used to support ideas near the end of a report. True or false?

8. Which of the following belongs in the front matter of a long report?

   (a) glossary

   (b) letter of authorization

   (c) bibliography

   (d) all of the above

9. Aside from differences in length, a long report follows the same format as a short report. True or false?

10. Progress reports and periodic reports share which of the following features?

   (a) use direct language

   (b) contain clear descriptions of data

   (c) maintain consistent formats for comparison

   (d) all of the above

11. Data reports are generated both periodically and on demand. True or false?

Give It Some Thought

1. Every report should have a purpose. Explain what an analytical report does.

2. When might it be necessary for a report writer to create two different versions of a report?

3. Name three standard guidelines a short report should follow.

4. When is it unnecessary to include a table of contents in a short report?

5. What are two options for where to place notes in a report?

6. In some cases, a report writer must refine a given topic before starting. Explain how this is done.

7. Which of the following revised topics is more manageable than "Social Concerns at AMN Associates"?

   (a) Employee Charitable Contributions in 2010

   (b) Holiday Event Planning Progress

   (c) Employee Morale Since Temporary Layoffs

   (d) all of the above

8. Research materials form the basis of many business reports. List four examples of research sources, both primary and secondary.

9. Because they contain a great deal of information, long reports can be difficult to navigate. What is the purpose of a table of figures and/or tables in a long report?

10. Why is the executive summary important in a long report?

11. Why is it important for a recommendation report to provide not only recommendations or choices, but also the information and data that went into that decision?

12. How does a periodic report differ from a progress report?

Applying This Chapter

1. Imagine you work in the human resources division of a company that owns a chain of amusement parks. You've been asked to write a report on the subject of employee absenteeism among the group of student workers who spend their summer breaks working at the company's various parks. Consider your audience and purpose, then determine whether you'd use a short or long format to write on the topic.

2. Write good titles for short reports on these subject areas:
   (a) medical benefits
   (b) conflict resolution among employees
   (c) employee theft

3. Create an outline for a short report on the need for energy conservation within your organization or business.

4. Write a progress report about your academic or work career. Think about the chronological structure and the reader's need for detail.

5. Your company is looking for a new multifunction laser printer that costs no more than $200 and can scan and fax as well as print. Do some online research and come up with a list of three possibilities. Think about how you would organize and present the data. Write a short recommendation report to senior management describing the three possibilities and recommending one of the three as the best candidate.

THE NEXT STEP

Writing Appeal
Find a report you've received that is visually unappealing. Give your reasons: Too much text? Too many graphics? Not enough white space? Font hard to read? Using what you've learned in this section, write a list of recommendations for how the writer could improve the report and provide the missing appeal.

Up to Speed
You're a salesperson who has been sent to a four-day conference to learn about a new line of running apparel. At the request of your manager, write a progress report to her at the conclusion of the second day.

Job Report
Together with three or four classmates, draw up a two-page informal report on why good writing is important in business. Use specific cases to make your points.

Quarterly Newsflash

The cookie business you started in your home eight years ago has grown into The Chips Corporation, which supplies delicatessens throughout the Montreal area with your cookies. Business is booming, and your investors are highly interested in your quarterly summaries—keeping track of the "dough," so to speak. Draft a short periodic report that includes news, profits, staff changes, expansion plans, and so on.

New Personal Digital Assistants

Before she went on vacation, your boss said, "We need new PDAs. Find something for us and have a report on my desk when I get back." With a partner, do some research on PDAs offered by cell phone companies in your province and draft a list of factors (like a monthly service plan) that you would consider when drafting a recommendation report for your boss.

Figuring It Out

Go online and look at the annual reports published by one of the big grocery companies in Canada, such as Loblaws or Sobeys. Have a look at how those reports use visual aids to help communicate their financial results to the public. Compare two reports from two different companies or from two different years. Which uses visual aids most effectively and why?

13
WRITING BUSINESS PROPOSALS
Techniques to Get the Job Done

STARTING POINT

Go to www.wiley.com/canada/brounstein to assess your knowledge of the basics of writing business proposals. After reviewing this website, you'll be able to determine where you need to concentrate your effort.

What You'll Learn in This Chapter:

- ways of organizing business proposals
- the five steps of the proposal-writing process
- the benefits of using visual aids in proposals.

After Studying This Chapter, You'll be Able to:

- discuss how organization can increase a proposal's persuasiveness
- determine a proposal's audience
- compare the effectiveness of visual aids in representing proposal information
- discuss the potential pitfalls associated with visual aids.

INTRODUCTION

Because proposals are the primary means by which businesses ask for work to do, and for money to earn, the proposal writer requires the sharpest writing skills. The persuasive powers of a proposal can be strengthened by the method of organization it uses to fulfill a client's or reader's needs. A writing strategy of proven steps will further guide you toward success. The chapter concludes with an overview of visual aids that you can use to make a point—and, perhaps, seal a deal.

13.1 Organizing a Persuasive Proposal

A business proposal describes ideas in such a way that they fulfill a client's needs. When a proposal does that effectively, the writer comes one step closer to earning a contract, signing a deal, or some other form of business agreement with that client.

Business proposals may be almost any length, from a single typed page to several bound volumes (as in the case of a proposal to Public Works and Government Services Canada from an energy company, for example). A proposal must be long enough to do the work it is supposed to do—no more and no less.

Although proposals differ as far as use and length, most are made up of the same parts (detailed in 13.2.3): Overview, Problem analysis, Proposal specifics, Budget, and Conclusion. Each section of a proposal should answer the following questions for the reader:

- **Overview:** Why is the proposal needed and by whom? Why should the proposal be accepted? When should the readers act on the proposal?
- **Problem analysis:** What is the problem and what caused it? What is the current scale of the problem? What will be its future scale? Who suffers from its effects? Have previous measures failed in an effort to deal with it?
- **Proposal specifics:** What is your plan to solve the problem? Are your methods proven? If so, by whom? What personnel will be involved? What is their training? What time schedule have you established for your work? What are major checkpoints in that schedule? How will you measure success?
- **Budget:** How much will it cost the reader to solve the problem? How much of the cost will be for equipment, or for research, or for salaries, or for travel?
- **Conclusion:** What's the next step? What can the reader do to get more information about your plan? What will you do to contact the reader? Are you willing to make changes to your plan?

These parts find their place according to the role they play in the overall purpose of the document. In the case of the business proposal, the central purpose is to persuade an audience to act. All parts of the proposal, then, must be arranged to serve this purpose. Consider three powerful forces to persuade your reader(s) to act on your proposal:

- logical order
- psychological order
- solid evidence.

13.1.1 Using Logical Order

Arrange the parts of your proposal in a way that appeals to your reader's sense of reason. Readers who can follow an argument point by point feel confident that the writer has thought through the material with care. Such readers are much more likely to say "yes" to the ideas proposed in the document.

Imagine the chain of logic in a proposal like a row of dominoes. Each acts on the next in an onward movement toward the conclusion of the proposal. Only a missing link—a logical flaw—can halt that movement of the reader's mind.

By carefully reviewing the logical order of the ideas within your proposal, you ensure that your reader's thoughtful consideration of the document is not interrupted or frustrated by logical errors.

Consider, for example, the sequence of logical steps at the heart of a proposal to install brighter street lights in a residential neighbourhood:

Point 1: Residents care most of all about safety and property values.

Point 2: Brighter street lights discourage crime (thereby making the neighbourhood safer).

Point 3: Brighter street lights increase property values (because safer areas have higher property values).

Point 4: Residents can be expected to support the proposal (because it gives them what they want—safety and higher property values).

Though not complex, this sequence of points serves to illustrate the domino effect of solid, logical argumentation. One point leads to the next, which in turn leads to a related point. Taken all together, the points lead to a conclusion that appeals to common sense.

Unfortunately, too many proposals (and other messages) fail because they don't have an understandable logical design. As you craft a logical argument, be on the lookout for these and other logical flaws that can stop your proposal in its tracks:

- **Circular reasoning:** What was supposed to be an explanation turns out to be a mere restatement of the problem:

  All employees are encouraged to participate in after-hours company recreation programs because such programs are especially for the use of employees after the workday has ended.

- **Hasty generalization:** The conclusion reached is based on too little evidence:

  People who don't buy organic food don't care about the environment.

- **Non sequitur:** A conclusion is reached that does not follow from the evidence presented:

  Johnson owns two homes, a boat, and a sports car, so I trust his investment advice.

- **Bias:** Personal opinions and viewpoints become the standard for evaluating objective arguments:

  Ms. Petrovic has every right to apply for the new position, but she won't get it. I just don't want to work with a woman.

- **Either/or thinking:** Two alternatives are presented as the only alternatives when others should be considered:

  Either he apologizes or I quit.

- **Straw man:** A false target is set up for the main thrust of an argument. Knocking over the target creates the illusion that the argument has succeeded when in fact nothing has changed:

  This company's problems can be blamed on poor benefits. How can anyone expect workers to concentrate on their jobs when they have doubts about their medical and dental coverage?

Such logical flaws can collapse the credibility of a proposal. Eliminate them from your own proposal writing.

13.1.2 Using Psychological Order

Skilled proposal writers want readers to want to agree with the ideas of the proposal. To do so, they try to influence feelings as well as thoughts. One technique used by such proposal writers is the careful placement and timing of good news and bad news.

Bad news can be defined as a message that threatens our welfare, stability, or reputation. A manager may hear the bad news that his or her division is being reduced in size and influence. A company may hear the bad news that it faces a major lawsuit.

Instead of shying away from bad news, proposal writers recognize bad news as the stage—the necessary precondition—for good news.

Consider, for example, a major proposal for road improvements on a mountain-pass highway. The bad news is that several accidents have occurred because of poor road conditions, particularly during bad weather. The proposal writer explains the causes of the accidents in detail, all in preparation for the proposed solution of repaving, posting better signs, and setting lower speed limits.

13.1.3 Solid Evidence

To convince readers to believe in an idea, you'll need to present them with real evidence, whether in the form of examples, illustrations, statistics, or details. Such evidence can be general or specific in nature:

- **General evidence** is made up of a great number of specific examples gathered together or "generalized." "The air in metropolitan areas is 16 percent cleaner this year because of federal pollution legislation" is general evidence.
- **Specific evidence** treats precise details in a single case. "Air quality measurements during the month of July in Toronto show a 16 percent improvement in overall air quality." Specific evidence, especially when backed by reputable sources, helps to convince the reader that the proposal writer's major ideas are sound.

To create a convincing case for your ideas, use both general and specific evidence. Too much general evidence will make the proposal sound vague and unfocused. Too much specific evidence can make the proposal sound narrow and local in its concerns. When they are balanced, however, general and specific evidence can earn your reader's acceptance of your ideas.

FOR EXAMPLE

Foreign Logic

Nick, a loyal employee for seven years, had made it clear from his first interview that he had certain goals for his career. One of the most important was that he be given the opportunity to work in his company's foreign office for at least two years. Others before him had done the same (including one of his supervisor's nephews), so it was a reasonable request. After seven years and many memos but little action on the part of the company, Nick felt it was time to make a formal proposal. In doing so, he claimed that he had not been given the opportunity because of rampant favouritism within the company. With only one instance to refer to, however, his logic—and his proposal—fell apart.

SELF-CHECK

- Define circular reasoning, hasty generalization, non sequitur, bias, either/or thinking, straw man, general evidence, and specific evidence.
- List the five parts of a business proposal.
- List three persuasive methods of organization.
- Describe the six potential flaws in logic.
- Discuss the role of bad news in using psychological order to organize a proposal.
- Explain why a mix of general evidence and specific evidence is effective.

13.2 Writing Strategies for Proposals

You will probably write proposals in your business career to attract contracts, obtain research money, change in-house procedures, fund new facilities, or argue for product or policy revisions. Use this step-by-step guide to put together proposals that are practical and successful.

13.2.1 Step 1. Determine the Requirements for Your Proposal

To get started, find out if specific guidelines already exist for developing your proposal. For example, many government agencies have strict requirements for the way topics are described, the order in which they are treated, the length of the proposal, and so forth.

13.2.2 Step 2. Determine Your Audience

Find out whether your work will be read by a general audience or by someone who specializes in your subject. Choose language that will communicate clearly to your readers.

13.2.3 Step 3. Create an Outline

Jot down ideas, examples, and details for possible use as you work your way through each section of the outline. Look at the parts of this common model used by many professional proposal writers to help you develop an outline suited to your own topic:

- **Overview:** Put together the background information your reader will need to grasp the significance of your proposed idea. Develop a clear vision of what the reader already knows and what blanks you need to fill in. If you need to provide detailed technical background information, consider adding it as an appendix at the end of the proposal to avoid bogging your reader down with details at the very beginning of the document.
- **Problem analysis:** Your readers are more likely to take action on a proposal if they believe your ideas to be necessary and timely. In this section, set the stage for this reaction by analyzing the problem with care. Use both general and specific evidence to let bad news influence your reader.
- **Proposal specifics:** Describe in detail your proposed plan of attack. Conclude this section with a summary estimation—a convincing statement of the likelihood that your plans will produce the results desired. The summary estimation is the writer's last chance to persuade the audience before introducing the key part of your proposal: the budget.
- **Budget:** Outline the costs of your proposed work, including the following items if applicable:
  - equipment acquisition
  - facility rental
  - salary and wages, with benefit allowances if applicable
  - supplies
  - travel expenses
  - research expenses
  - contingency funds.

Because funding is at the core of most proposals, your reader will be particularly interested in your section on the budget. State to the best of your ability what you will need to spend if your proposal is approved and be as specific as you can. A padded budget builds in extra costs that can later be dropped so that the project can withstand cutbacks or avoid going over budget. This technique will rarely make it past a shrewd evaluator. You also should avoid purposely underbudgeting your proposal with the false hope of presenting a real bargain. An underbudgeted proposal makes promises it cannot keep and serves no one in the long run.

- **Conclusion:** Conclude your proposal by expressing your willingness to help your readers. Offer to answer questions and to provide further information, to meet with or speak by phone to the evaluators or others, even to consider reshaping your proposal as necessary to meet the needs of the client or agency.

13.2.4 Step 4. Revise Your Proposal

Consider a few revision techniques to help create a winning proposal:

- **Use topics headings and indented material to show off your information**. Look at Figure 13-1, and judge for yourself the difference in effect.
- **Don't bury crucial information in appendices or footnotes**. If the reader needs to know a fact to make sense out of your proposal, include that fact in the text itself. If necessary, state the fact briefly in the text, elaborating elsewhere in

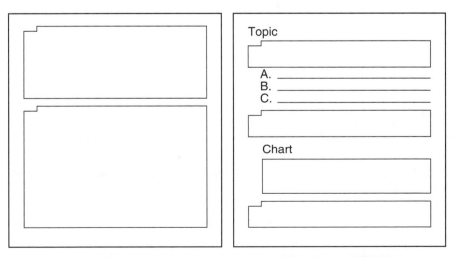

Avoid solid blocks of print   Format for readability

Figure 13-1 Using topic heading and insert material for effect

a footnote or appendix. Footnotes should be supplements and so should never contain crucial information.

- **Be direct and specific, not vague and general.** Use hard facts and statistics to support your proposal. Examine the following example from a proposal to remodel the floor plan of a factory:

  ○ **Vague, general:** *"Production has been hampered by the physical separation of related work units."*

  ○ **Direct, specific:** *"The company loses $400 per day in lost time as employees from the graphic and the word-processing units walk the 60-metre path between their two related work areas."*

13.2.5 Step 5. Polish Your Proposal

Because proposals are often judged competitively, yours will need to win attention and respect by how it looks as well as what it says. Uneven margins, complicated fonts, and amateurish graphics all say "unprofessional" and "unreliable" to an evaluator. Here are five ways to give your proposals a crisp, professional appearance:

- Use attractive, proportionately spaced fonts. In general, body text should be in traditional fonts like Times New Roman because they are easier to read.

- Use heavy-bond white paper. Beware of pastel shades, especially if you plan to photocopy the work.

- Use strict margins on all sides of the page. If you can do so without creating oddly spaced lines, justify your margins.

- Decide whether your proposal will have a more powerful effect in bound form, with a vinyl or heavy paper cover. Proposals of just a page or two, of course, are not bound.

- Double-check that photocopied versions of your proposal are comparable to your original in legibility, clarity, and crispness.

FOR EXAMPLE

Final Touches

Jackson, the owner of home renovation business, is competing against two others for a major restoration of three historical buildings for the city. His proposal explained the company's history and qualifications, detailed an acceptable schedule, and included a reasonable budget. It did not, however, present the information as professionally as the company whose proposal was chosen. If he had taken the extra steps to cover his proposal and include photographs of his previous work, the job would have been his.

SELF-CHECK

- Define overview, problem analysis, proposal specifics, budget, and conclusion.
- List the five steps of the proposal-writing process.
- Describe the parts of a typical outline for a business proposal.
- Explain the benefit of making final preparations regarding appearance (paper quality, margins, font style, etc.).

13.3 Illustrating Your Ideas with Graphics

Graphics—those interesting, attention-getting, and often entertaining forms of visual information—are what make today's business documents stand apart from those of the past. Today's communicators realize the power that graphs, charts, illustrations, photographs, and other visual aids have in making a point.

Fortunately, advances in computer graphics technology have put the artist's pen in every business communicator's hand. Many visuals are now easier to produce than ever before. Now, with the right programs and a bit of training, writers can prepare professional visual aids in a short time.

Although visual aids attract the reader's print-tired eyes, there are even more important reasons for using visual aids. Consider five key reasons for using visual aids in your business documents and presentations:

- **To clarify your point:** A visual aid can show a process, procedure, relationship, cross-section, or quantitative view of topics.
- **To emphasize your point:** Visual aids call attention to key ideas much more vividly than words do.
- **To simplify your point:** Relationships among ideas, facts, and statistics can be shown simply in graphic form.
- **To unify your points:** Several ideas can be brought together in one visual aid.
- **To make an impression on your reader:** Readers are swayed by your imaginative approach to the communication of ideas.

13.3.1 Determining Your Audience's Needs

Which graphics you use, if any, depends entirely on your audience's need for them. Begin by asking yourself what passages in your document should be enlivened and clarified for the sake of your audience. This requires reading your work as if for the first time, watching objectively for those portions that will seem difficult, vague, or complicated for your audience. Look also for emphasis opportunities—places in your communication where a visual aid would make a key point more memorable.

Once you've found possible locations for visual aids, you're ready to choose which graphics belong where. The discussion of the many visual aids depicted in this chapter can help you make an informed choice. Be cautious with graphics, though. Graphics by themselves can hurt a business communication as easily as they can help it. A chart or table that appears out of context can confuse readers, drawing their attention away from your text and undercutting your credibility.

To avoid misusing visual aids, follow five common sense dos and don'ts:

- Do point out the conclusions you want your reader to draw from a visual aid. Don't expect a reader to automatically see your point in a graphic.
- Do position your visual aids next to the text that explains them. Don't expect your reader to hunt for the text that explains a visual aid or vice versa.
- Do simplify your visual aids so that they make their primary point within a second or two of the reader's attention. Don't cram visual aids so full of information that they cannot be interpreted by the reader.
- Do provide keys, legends, captions, and titles as required by your visual aids. Don't assume that the reader will understand the intent and symbols of your visual aids.
- Do scale your graphic aids and place them on the page so that they can be seen and interpreted easily. Don't frustrate the reader with postage-stamp-sized graphs and charts.

13.3.2 Getting Acquainted with the Tools of the Trade

To be able to choose the very best graphic aid for your documents, get to know the following gallery of commonly used visual aids:

- **Photograph:** Photographs can prove invaluable in communicating product descriptions, geographical information, and personalities. Although certainly a powerful visual communicator, the photograph can be difficult and expensive to reproduce (you may also need to obtain written releases from all of the people pictured in the photo). Poorly chosen photographs can have too many details, and so can distract the reader from your point.

- **Line drawing:** Line drawings can add emphasis and attractiveness to your documents (see Figure 13-2). Because of the advanced state of line drawings (including cartoons) today, public standards for line drawings are quite high; therefore, professional quality is a must.

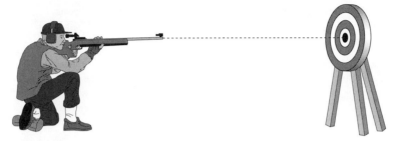

Effective marketing managers define their job as creating and delivering the proper market impact to well-defined market targets. This is a rifle approach that aims at a specific market target. This marketing manager does not waste resources and effort on the non-target area of the market.

Figure 13-2 Line drawing

- **Line graph:** This is the simplest of graphic aids; it shows trends at a glance (see Figure 13-3). Note that only the dots (the data points) represent accurate measurements. The line between the dots does not portray, point-for-point, an accurate measurement of data.

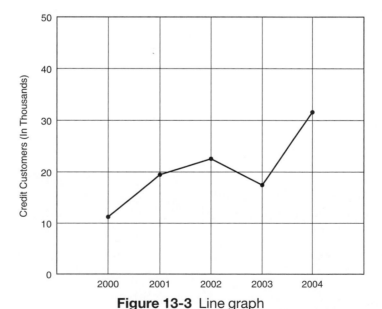

Figure 13-3 Line graph

- **Multiline graph:** By differentiating lines by colour, size, or texture, a multiline graph portrays simultaneous trends, allowing easy comparison (see Figure 13-4). Take care not to include too many different lines (three are usually the maximum) or to portray lines that intersect one another too often.

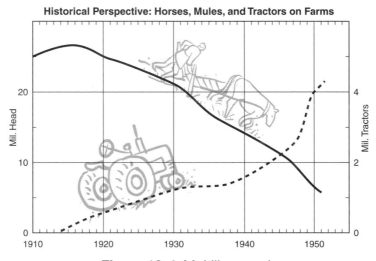

Figure 13-4 Multiline graph

- **Bar graph:** The bar graph creates strong visual statements for comparative measurement (see Figure 13-5). Trends can still be gauged but without the sloping (and often inaccurate) lines of a line graph. The simple bar chart compares two or more values and can be drawn either horizontally or vertically. Exact quantities represented by each bar are often written inside or at the top of each bar.

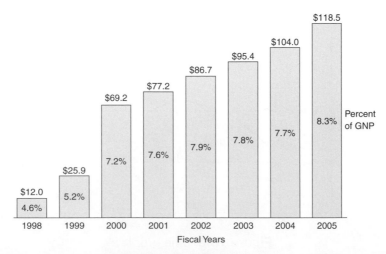

Figure 13-5 Bar graph

- **Grouped bar graph:** A grouped bar graph is, in effect, a series of simple bar charts, each measuring two or more values at specified intervals (see Figure 13-6). It allows comparison of a single element across the chart or among elements at each place on or across the chart.

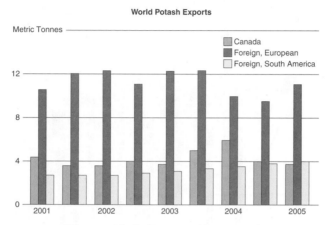

Figure 13-6 Grouped bar graph

- **Segmented bar graph:** The segmented bar graph distinguishes different parts of the whole by colour or texture (see Figure 13-7). Each bar is segmented into parts corresponding to amounts represented. This highlights the cumulative effect of the parts while still allowing for comparisons among the parts.

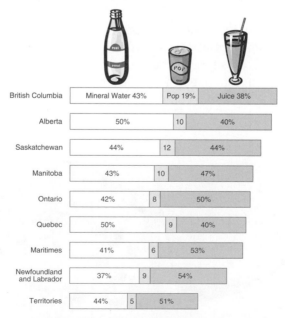

Figure 13-7 Segmented bar graph

- **Line bar graph:** The line bar graph emphasizes both individual measurements and trends (see Figure 13-8). It may offer the advantages of both bar and line graphs. However, it may also overly complicate the effects or make the graphic aid appear cluttered.

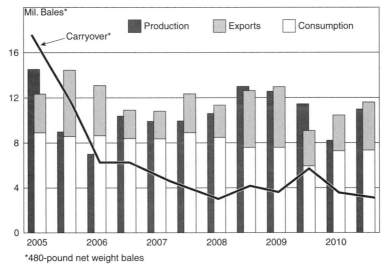

Figure 13-8 Line bar graph

- **Pie chart:** In a pie or circle chart, each portion represents part of the total amount (such as 100%) depicted in the full circle (see Figure 13-9). Portions must be proportionate in size to the value they represent. In general, a pie chart should not contain more than eight parts, to avoid clutter and confusion. Group some categories, as needed, to reduce the number of wedges. For example, "apples" and "oranges" might be put into one wedge as "fruit."

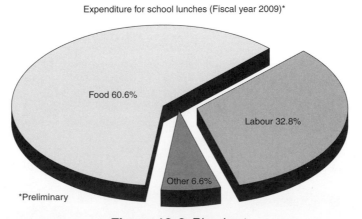

Figure 13-9 Pie chart

- **Pictogram:** Pictograms usually combine line drawings with graphics such as line, bar, and pie charts to make a point in an attractive, eye-catching way (see Figure 13-10). Pictograms are often used to try to influence emotions and attitudes. Be careful not to let your creativity become your only objective. If so, it might distort or hide the central point of the statistics you want to show.

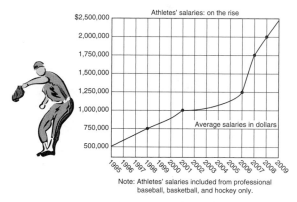

Figure 13-10 Pictogram

- **Flowchart:** Flowcharts present a process or procedure (see Figure 13-11). Examples include the steps involved in the procedure for applying to college or the stages of a chemical process. Each step should be labelled clearly and may be differentiated by shape to suggest different functions.

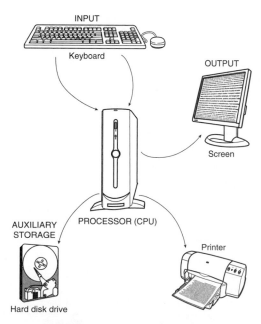

Figure 13-11 Flowchart

- **Cutaway or exploded drawing:** The cutaway or exploded drawing lets the viewer see into a structure to observe the relationships among its parts (see Figure 13-12). Such representations are often used in product descriptions and technical discussions.

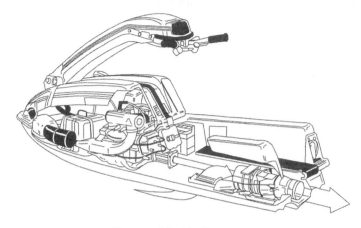

Figure 13-12 Cutaway

- **Time chart:** Time charts use bars or lines inside a work–time matrix to show when jobs, tasks, or other activities begin and end (see Figure 13-13). Used often in reports and proposals, the time chart serves as a work progress schedule. Many businesses have special project management software that generates this type of chart.

Activities	Time periods—week beginning							
	Jan. 14	Jan. 21	Jan. 28	Feb. 4	Feb. 11	Feb. 18	Feb. 25	Mar. 4
Review absentee files in personnel office	▇							
Interview supervisors and operations personnel		▇	▇					
Collect data on absentee plans from professional journals and books				▇	▇			
Organize and evaluate the data						▇	▇	
Write the report								▇
Type and proofread the report								▇
Submit final report to personnel manager								▇

Figure 13-13 Time chart

• **Organizational chart:** Organizational charts are similar to flowcharts but represent hierarchies of relationships among people rather than processes or procedures (see Figure 13-14). An organizational chart, for example, could show related functions or departments within a corporation.

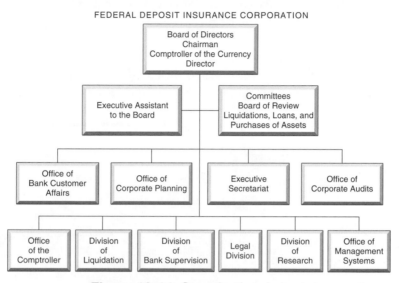

Figure 13-14 Organizational chart

• **Maps:** Maps present geographical representation of data (see Figure 13-15). Family incomes, for example, could be represented on a province-by-province or region-by-region basis. Shading, colouring, or texturing can distinguish different regions on the map.

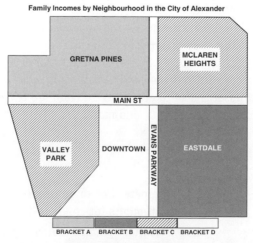

Figure 13-15 Map

> **FOR EXAMPLE**
>
> **Compelling Visuals**
>
> Anya, who worked as the coordinator for her city's community outreach division, had spent weeks gathering data on burglaries in the community. Residents had spoken up in meetings about their concerns, but the information that the city was using on crime rates was outdated. Anya's data were startling; burglaries had gone up dramatically in several quiet neighbourhoods. To make her case for more police coverage in those areas, Anya presented the information in a short proposal. Before submitting it, however, she added a detailed map, which made her case all the more compelling.

SELF-CHECK

- Define photograph, line drawing, line graph, multiline graph, bar graph, grouped bar graph, segmented bar graph, line bar graph, pie chart, pictogram, flowchart, cutaway or exploded drawing, time chart, organizational chart, and maps.
- Discuss five reasons for using visual aids.
- Discuss how technology has changed the utilization of visuals.
- Consider ways that visual aids are misused in proposals.

SUMMARY

Business writers who demonstrate the ability to write winning proposals quickly make themselves indispensable in businesses small and large. Skilled proposal writers persuade an audience to take action; they do so using organizational techniques such as logic order, psychological order, and solid evidence. Guidelines for determining an audience's needs, developing a successful outline, and revising proposal content increase your success. A winning proposal is also likely to take advantage the power of using visual aids such a photographs, charts, graphs, and maps.

KEY TERMS

Bar graph	Compares two or more values; creates strong visual statements for comparative measurement.
Bias	Personal opinions and viewpoints become the standard for evaluating objective arguments.

Budget	An outline of funding and costs.
Circular reasoning	What was intended to be an explanation turns out to be a mere restatement of the problem.
Conclusion	The end of a proposal; used to express goodwill, offer further assistance, and so on.
Cutaway or exploded drawing	The cutaway or exploded drawing lets the viewer see into a structure to observe the relationships among its parts.
Either/or thinking	Two alternatives are presented as the only alternatives when others should be considered.
Flowchart	Flowcharts present a process or procedure.
General evidence	Is made up of a great number of specific examples gathered together or "generalized."
Grouped bar graph	A series of simple bar charts, each measuring two or more values at specified intervals.
Hasty generalization	The conclusion reached is based on too little evidence.
Line bar graph	Offering the advantages of both bar and line graphs, the line bar graph emphasizes both individual measurements and trends.
Line drawing	Drawing made of solid lines; used to add emphasis and attraction to a document.
Line graph	A graph in which points of value are connected by a line; used to show trends at a glance.
Maps	Maps present geographical representation of data.
Multiline graph	By differentiating lines by colour, size, or texture, a multiline graph portrays simultaneous trends, allowing easy comparison.
Non sequitur	A conclusion is reached that does not follow from the evidence presented.
Organizational chart	Similar to flowcharts but represent hierarchies of relationships among people rather than processes or procedures.
Overview	Background information a reader needs to grasp the significance of a proposed idea.
Photograph	A picture or likeness used to communicate product descriptions, geographical information, and personalities.

Pictogram	Pictograms usually combine line drawings with graphics such as line, bar, and pie charts to make a point in an attractive, eye-catching way.
Pie chart	In a pie or circle chart, each portion represents part of the total amount (such as 100%) depicted in the full circle.
Problem analysis	An examination of a proposed idea; used to convince readers that a proposal is necessary and timely.
Proposal specifics	Detailed description of a proposal.
Segmented bar graph	The segmented bar graph distinguishes different parts of the whole by colour or texture.
Specific evidence	Treats precise details in a single case. Specific evidence, especially when backed by reputable sources, helps to convince the reader that the proposal writer's major ideas are sound.
Straw man	A false target is set up for the main thrust of an argument. Knocking over the straw man creates the illusion that the argument has succeeded, when in fact nothing has changed.
Time chart	Time charts use bars or lines inside a work–time matrix to show when jobs, tasks, or other activities begin and end.

ASSESS YOUR UNDERSTANDING

Go to www.wiley.com/canada/brounstein to evaluate your knowledge of the basics of writing business proposals. Measure your learning by comparing pre-test and post-test results.

Quick Questions

1. The main function of a business proposal is to inform an audience of a new service. True or false?
2. Which of the following can interrupt the logical flow of a proposal?
   (a) personal bias
   (b) too little evidence
   (c) non sequitur
   (d) all of the above

3. To be truly convincing in a proposal, evidence should specific in nature. True or false?

4. The first step in writing a proposal is to find out what, if any, requirements exist for your proposal regarding length, format, and so on. True or false?

5. In a proposal, the overview serves to
   (a) outline the costs
   (b) provide the reader with specifics
   (c) define the writer's approach
   (d) all of the above

6. Specialized training is required in order for a writer to include visual aids in a proposal. True or false?

7. A visual aid accomplishes which of the following in a business proposal?
   (a) unify points
   (b) make an impression
   (c) clarify a point
   (d) all of the above

8. Keys, legends, and titles only serve to complicate a proposal and confuse a reader. True or false?

Give It Some Thought

1. The placement of good news and bad news has a psychological effect in a proposal. Where should each be placed for a persuasive effect?

2. Logical flaws can destroy the credibility of a proposal. Define straw man.

3. List the five common parts of a proposal and discuss how each part meets some of the reader's needs for information.

4. For many proposals, the budget is a key item of interest. Explain why a purposely underbudgeted proposal loses out in the long run.

5. When should information be placed in an appendix?

6. What role do graphics play in the visual appeal of a business proposal?

7. Think of a situation in which words are more effective than a graphic.

Applying This Chapter

1. You own a children's clothing company and would like to expand your line to include clothing for teens. To carry out this major expansion, you need to increase your line of credit, and your bank has asked for a proposal. With a partner, brainstorm some points that you should make in your overview. (Refer back to Sections 13.1 and 13.2.3 for some reminders.)

2. Assume that you own a catering business called Sweet Treats. You know that the community organization that you belong to is thinking about hiring a new caterer for this year's thank-you luncheon for 100 volunteers because the previous year went so badly, so you are beginning to develop a proposal to get the contract for next year. Plan a menu for the luncheon and develop a budget for the event. You can look online at catering and restaurant menus to get an idea for the cost of various items.

3. You've been asked by your neighbourhood group to coordinate the hiring of a company to clear the sidewalks on your street after major snowfalls. Most companies would not submit a proposal for a small job like that, but if they did, think about what you, as a reader, would want the proposal to tell you. What are the five most important details you would need the proposal to state and in which section of the proposal would you expect each to appear?

4. Decide what kind of graphic you would use to visually depict each of the following. Explain your choice for each.
   (a) the number of European cars sold in Canada each year compared to Korean cars
   (b) the average length of employment for employees in these salary categories: to $20,000, to $30,000, to $40,000, to $50,000, to $60,000 and to $70,000
   (c) the number of departments within your company and the number of employees in each department

5. You are in your last semester of school before graduation and you are looking to make some extra money. One day after class, you notice a posting on the bulletin board from a first-year student looking for a tutor in your best subject. Think about how you would convince the student that you are the best person for the job. How would the proposal differ if you used the logical versus the psychological order?

6. Infomercials are similar to business proposals in that they identify a problem the consumer is facing and propose to fix it with their new and exciting product. Look online or flip through the channels on your television to find an infomercial. Identify in the commercial the five components of a business proposal and describe how the commercial answers the questions mentioned in Section 13.1.

THE NEXT STEP

Get Visual
Find a short document, perhaps a letter or brochure, which has no visual aids. Create a visual aid for the document—photograph and caption, map, graph, line drawing, and so on—and then place it into the document. Be sure to add into the text any words that are now required. Write a paragraph justifying your selection and handling of the visual aid you chose.

Problem and Solution

Define some problem in your municipality that you think could be handled better. Areas to be considered could include transit, garbage pick-up, hockey arenas, parking, or one-way streets. Develop a point-form outline for a short proposal to your city councillor for why and how the problem should be solved.

Career Proposal

Your goal is to get a three-month internship working with a well-known and respected individual in your chosen career. Interns do not get paid, but they get training and experience for their resumé that can lead to good permanent positions. Write an overview section for a proposal you'd send to that person to convince him or her to take you on.

Lucky Lottery

Suppose that the Lottery Corporation decided to change things up and offer its grand prize to the person who they decide deserves it most. Prepare a proposal that outlines why you should win the money and how you plan to spend it. Remember to include a detailed budget.

14
WRITING RESUMÉS AND COVER LETTERS
Promoting Yourself through Your Writing

STARTING POINT

Go to www.wiley.com/canada/brounstein to assess your knowledge of the basics of resumé writing. After reviewing this website, you'll be able to determine where you need to concentrate your effort.

What You'll Learn in This Chapter:

- ways of conducting an employment search
- the three types of resumés
- guidelines for resumé writing
- two types of cover letters
- guidelines for writing effective cover letters.

After Studying This Chapter, You'll be Able to:

- discuss the relationship between networking and potential job leads
- choose the resumé format that is best suited to your job-search needs
- explain the importance of tailoring a resumé to a job description
- identify the factors that affect your choice of cover letter.

INTRODUCTION

A company that hires you wants to know that you can present a professional and competent image through your writing; therefore, a well-written cover letter and a powerful resumé are both critical elements of your job search. This chapter outlines traditional as well as innovative ways of looking for employment. The types of resumé formats are discussed, with advantages and disadvantages for each. Ways of showcasing your writing skills in your resumé are described. The importance of a persuasive cover letter is explained. The chapter concludes with guidelines for writing cover letters that get noticed.

14.1 Conducting a Job Search

For most people, finding a job is a daunting and time-consuming chore. In difficult economic times—in the face of hiring freezes and cutbacks—the task is made even tougher. Although a winning resumé may be one key to landing a particular job, take a moment to consider what's involved in the various stages of the job-search process:

- **Think.** In this stage, you'll decide what kind of job you'd like to do (if you already know, that's great). This stage is important for those not only looking for their first job, but for those making career changes later in life.
- **Search.** Once you know what you want to do, you'll need to find a position and a company that are right for you.
- **Get hired.** Finally, you'll need to convince an employer to choose you for a position. Many elements factor into this stage, from an impressive resumé to a successful interview (Sections 15.1 and 15.2 detail the interview process).

If you're someone still deciding on a career, some research and personal contemplation can lead you down the right path. Try to find as many different kinds of jobs that might work for you. Think innovatively about your career options. What activities are you passionate about? Brainstorm with people and don't be afraid to broaden your horizons. In some cases, the very process of job hunting may help you to decide on a career.

As you get started with your job search, come up with a systematic way of keeping track of your leads and your progress. You may, at any one time, have as many as 50 resumés circulating in the professional world. To prevent yourself from accidentally applying to the same place twice or making other embarrassing mistakes, you might keep a file of index cards or use a computer record-keeping program. A system keeps your many fishing lines from becoming tangled and allows you to concentrate on pursuing job sources.

14.1.1 Having a Friend of a Friend

Personal referrals (that is, someone you know who might know someone who has a job opening) continue to be an effective way for job seekers to find out about opportunities. Let every one of your friends and relatives know that you are looking for a job. Ask them to let you know if they hear of an opening or of someone who is resigning or retiring from a job in your field.

> ### FOR EXAMPLE
>
> **Through the Grapevine**
>
> Although Sue loved her job in publishing, a recent move to the suburbs meant she was now commuting nearly three hours a day instead of 20 minutes. Because she was exhausted from spending so much time in transit, Sue didn't really have time to meet and get to know any of her neighbours except Penny, who walked her dog every day just as Sue was walking to the train. After a week or two, Sue learned that Penny's best friend, a marketing executive for a small family-run publishing house, had been in a meeting in which the company discussed a new editorial position being created. Three phone calls, a resumé, and two interviews later, Sue is happily enjoying a 20-minute commute again.

14.1.2 Networking the News

Take the friend-of-a-friend idea, translate it into the professional world, and you have yourself a network. Find out about potential job opportunities from business clients, suppliers and other contacts, co-workers, and fellow members of professional and civic organizations. Your network will continue to strengthen and grow if you maintain it (basically, keep in touch) throughout your career, not just when you're looking for a job.

14.1.3 Internet

The Internet is a repository of literally hundreds of thousands of current job openings around the world. The Internet is changing the way companies do business and the way they hire. Many companies make a practice of listing all their job openings on the company website. By going to these websites, you can access information about employment needs and policies, as well as more general information to help with your search.

In addition, Internet job sites list thousands of current job ads, typically sorted by job category, region, and company. You can spend many hours harvesting outstanding job possibilities and general job-searching advice from these sources. Typically, you can post your resumé on these sites and have the service match up your abilities and background with likely jobs.

14.1.4 Checking in with Former Employers

Review career opportunities in companies for whom you have worked in the past, even if in a part-time or other capacity. Even if your temporary or part-time job wasn't in your career field, don't overlook the career possibilities at that company. Many companies take pride in bringing someone along from the bottom of the ladder. Plus, the company knows you, and you know the company.

14.1.5 Advertisements

Don't overlook traditional advertisements, usually found in newspapers or magazines, as another source of information regarding what jobs may be available in your field or in your community. Take a look at help-wanted ads from companies as well as employment agencies. Even if an actual job doesn't come out of an ad, you may find yourself with an inspiration or useful lead.

14.1.6 Making an Appearance

Visit the human resources office of companies that interest you. Ask about job openings and pick up application packets. Human resources representatives should not mind seeing you as an uninvited visitor as long as you don't press them for what they can't provide: instant evaluations of your chances for a job, definitive lists of what positions are available in the company, or a willingness to interview you.

Of course, you could also do this by mail with less effort, but by visiting for just a moment or two in person, you show more effort than the average job seeker. Employees in the office—perhaps even the director or manager—may see your face and shake your hand and when your resumé arrives for review, they might remember you.

14.1.7 Going to School

Make use of nearby college placement services. Participate in any workshops on interviewing skills, resumé preparation, and application procedures they may offer. Companies seeking new employees in your area work closely with the campus placement office. They often send representatives to your campus to interview prospective employees. Sign up for such interviews.

SELF-CHECK

- Define network.
- Consider the benefits of networking in a job search.
- Describe some strategies for conducting a job search.
- Discuss the role of the Internet in the job market.

14.2 Formats of Persuasive Resumés

Your resumé is one of the most important ways you can demonstrate your writing skills. Not only does it communicate what you've done in the past; when written persuasively, it can convince a prospective employer that you can do the same for them.

The format you use to present your resumé is one of the first ways you influence an employer's impression of you. From the three most common formats—chronological, functional, and combination—you'll need to decide which best showcases your experience. Each has its own advantages and disadvantages, but no matter which format you choose, your goal is the same: to win an interview. Each format will be covered in more detail later in the chapter:

- **Chronological:** Organizes your experience in chronological order (starting with the most recent). By focusing on time, job continuity, and achievements, this format shows how you have made progress toward your career objective through your work history. This presentation is the popular choice for most human-resource professionals and recruiters.
- **Functional:** By focusing on your skills, credentials, and accomplishments, a functional resumé emphasizes what you did, not when or where you did it. Accomplishments, qualifications, and experience are grouped together, to emphasize your experience in specialty areas.
- **Combination:** Merges the chronological and functional styles. It begins with a functional section that lists your relevant skills and accomplishments, and is followed by a chronological section that supports the functional section with your employment history, giving specific responsibilities and accomplishments.

14.2.1 The Chronological Resumé

- **Advantages**: Information in a chronological resumé is presented in a way that clearly showcases your career progression, including the companies you've worked for, dates of employment, job titles, and your responsibilities and accomplishments. Most professionals should use this format—it's easy to read and preferred by those who review resumés.
- **Disadvantages**: This format shows gaps in employment and can highlight a lack of work experience.

The following sections describe the elements of an effective chronological resumé. Use Figure 14-1 as an example when composing your resumé:

Kikanza Brown

94 Elm Street
Winnipeg, MB R3A 0J8
Home: (204) 555-2784 Message: (204) 555-6784

Summary	To combine my two years of sales experience with my newly acquired education in advertising strategies and retail economics to provide excellent customer service as an account representative.
Education	B.A. in Marketing University of Manitoba Degree expected June, 2010

Pertinent Coursework

Professional Selling	Retail Economics
Marketing Management	Advertising Strategies
International Marketing	Management Communication

G.P.A. 3.5 on 4-point scale

Honours

Laketon Art Scholarship, 2007
University of Manitoba Marketing Award, 2008

Future Educational Plans

After completing my B.A., I plan to enroll in an M.B.A. program during non-work hours.
I am now enrolled in a B.A. program at the University of Manitoba

Experience	2006	**Field representative,** Rent-a-Treasure Art, Inc., Brandon, Manitoba (part-time)
		Responsibilities: Call on upscale corporate clients; rent, deliver, hang art in their offices; especially enjoy providing decorating advice.
	2005	**Store clerk,** Computer Village, Brandon, Manitoba
		Responsibilities: demonstrated products and closed sales on home computers.
	2004	**Designer, painter of super-graphics,** Weston Playhouse, Brandon, Manitoba (summer)
		Responsibilities: designed and painted eight wall-sized panels.
References		Available upon request

Figure 14-1 Chronological resumé

- **Summary:** Start your resumé off with one or two sentences that summarize how your strengths and contributions match the job you are applying for. Include the job title, reference to your skills or experience, and the main benefits you can offer the employer. Specifically target this section to the job and employer you are sending this resumé to. In other words, every resumé you send out should have a different career objective statement. Now that many companies scan and read resumes online, this section is growing even more important as employers often use it to see how your skills meet their needs.

- **Experience:** Use this section to outline your work experience, beginning with the name of your most recent (or current) employer. Follow the name by the city and province/territory in which it's located, and your dates of employment. State your title and follow with a short description of your responsibilities; when applicable include details such as how many stores you managed, your budget, and how many employees reported to you.

  Next, use bullets to list your accomplishments, beginning with the most relevant to the position you're applying. Include statements that begin with strong verbs (use words in the past tense such as "operated," "expanded," "directed"). Give special attention to anything innovative or different you did in your job. Use figures and percentages to illustrate and give credibility to your accomplishments ("increased sales revenues by 23%").

  You don't have to account for each and every month of your employment history. Although employers want an accurate idea of where you've done what and when, they want to get to the heart of the matter; in other words, they want to know what significant experiences you've had.

- **Professional affiliations or honours:** Include this section if it helps to persuade an employer of your qualifications; that is, list any affiliations or honours if they are relevant to the position you are seeking, or if they add to your credibility in your field.

- **Education:** Begin by listing your most recent degree, certificate, or highest level of education, then list other degrees and significant academic work. You may choose to group information pertaining to one degree beneath that degree before moving on. Mention special awards or accomplishments, but don't get bogged down in details. Highlight the items that make you perfect for *this* job in *this* company.

14.2.2 The Functional Resumé

- **Advantages:** This format de-emphasizes lack of experience in a field and minimizes possible age discrimination. It can be useful for first-time job seekers, people whose work experience or educational background is from outside Canada, those re-entering the workforce, or those changing careers.

- **Disadvantages:** Employers may expect the chronological format. This format makes it more difficult for an employer to follow your career path and can be distrusted by employers who may think an applicant is trying to conceal a liability in his or her background.

The following sections describe the elements of an effective functional resumé. Use the example in Figure 14-2 when composing your resumé:

CLIFFORD OWENS
2940 Yonge Street
Toronto, ON, M4N 2M9
(416) 555-4857

SUMMARY

Accomplished writer with proven ability to develop effective communication pieces and a demonstrated knowledge of the insurance business that will translate effectively into an editorial role within the Business Publications group.

EDUCATION

M.A. in English, Wilfrid Laurier University, 2005
B.A. in Finance, University of Waterloo, 2003

DEMONSTRATED ABILITIES

Ability to write well

Instructor, Business Writing, Wilfrid Laurier University, 2004–to present. Taught business memo, letter, proposal, and report writing.

Member, Association for Business Communication.

Ability to edit publications

Assistant editor, *Neighbours* (cottage lifestyles), 2003–2004

Editor, *News and Views* (campus newspaper), University of Waterloo, 2001

Knowledge of the insurance business

Office manager, Allstate Insurance, Cambridge, Ontario, 2000–2001. Supervised six sales people. Served as area manager for the sales region.

Insurance sales representative, Allstate Insurance, Cambridge, Ontario, 1998–1999. Sold auto, life, and fire policies; handled client claims.

References available on request.

Figure 14-2 Functional resumé

- **Summary:** As described in the chronological resumé, begin with a short introductory section.
- **Categories of success:** Instead of listing your jobs one by one in chronological order, create headings out of three or so major categories of success you have achieved (e.g., Marketing, Writing, Sales) and list the respective accomplishments under each heading.
- **Employment history:** List the names of your employers, their locations, and your dates of employment (state your job title if it will be beneficial to your application).
- **Education:** As in the chronological resumé, begin by listing your most recent degree or certificate, or highest level of education, then list other degrees and significant academic work.

14.2.3 The Combination Resumé

- **Advantages:** The combination resumé allows the ability to highlight your skills and experiences while still providing some elements of the chronological format. The combination format works best if you're someone who has a varied employment history, who is changing careers, or who'd like to include volunteer or internship experience.

- **Disadvantages:** Be aware that this format begins with elements of a functional format, and so may be dismissed by reviewers who prefer a chronological format. It may be repetitious if similar functions or skills are used in different positions and it tends to be longer than other formats.

The following sections describe the elements of an effective combination resumé. Use Figure 14-3 as a guide when you are putting together a combination resumé:

Robert C. Ortega

194 Canal St.
Ottawa, ON KIP 3R2
(613) 555-2152

SUMMARY

Detail-oriented and experienced researcher with effective leadership skills and a strong understanding of global strategy applications.

EDUCATION

Carleton University	Ottawa, ON
B.S. Marketing and International Management	May 2005

WORK EXPERIENCE

Familiar with global strategy applications
Marketing Research Assistant   Ottawa, ON
Carleton University Marketing Dept   Present
- Operate PIMS program for Global Strategy database.
- Supplement publications with research examples.
- Create file of current global strategies.

Able To Effectively Write And Review Business Proposals
Research Associate   Ottawa, ON
Carleton SBA Ethics Project   Summer 2003
- Reviewed curriculum; interviewed professors.
- Researched ethical issues in marketing, accounting, business law, and management science.
- Wrote report to dean and board of directors.

Strong and Organized Leader
Assistant Area Coordinator   Ottawa, ON
Carleton Office of Summer Housing   Summer 2003
- Supervised staff of 30.
- Created weekly and daily maintenance schedules to provide hospitality services for a 300-room dormitory.

HONOURS AND AWARDS

- Carleton SBA Invitational Leadership Retreat, 2008
- Member of Carleton Varsity Track Team

REFERENCES

References available upon request.

Figure 14-3 Combination resumé

- **Summary:** Begin with the same type of introductory section used in the chronological and functional formats.

- **Categories of success:** As in the functional format, use the major categories of success as headings and list the respective accomplishments under each heading.

- **Employment history:** In this section, include a detailed work experience section, much like that of a chronological resumé.

- **Education:** As in the chronological and functional resumés, begin by listing your most recent degree or certificate or highest level of education, then list other degrees and significant academic work.

FOR EXAMPLE

Resumé Choices

Carlos had worked for many years and for many different businesses. Although his son's chronic illness had caused him to relocate several times, he had consistently earned the respect and praise of his employers. Carlos' work history was such that a chronological format gave too much attention to the time he didn't work and not enough time to his experience. Using a combination format resumé allowed Carlos to showcase his qualifications while still providing an accurate employment history.

SELF-CHECK

- Define chronological resumé, functional resumé, and combination resumé.
- Describe the uses of each resumé format.
- Describe the major differences between the three resumé formats.
- Explain the disadvantages associated with each resumé format.

14.3 Getting Results with Your Resumé

The following guidelines will help you craft your resumé once you've established which format will be most effective:

- **Keep it short:** Most resumés are limited to one page. An employer who is going to be reading a stack of resumés would rather get what they need from you in a single-page format. Be succinct when describing your accomplishments. Use a second page only if you believe that's what it will take to get an interview; certain technical fields or upper-level positions may require more.

- **Highlight your best attributes:** Select those qualities that represent you at your highest potential—what you plan to be—instead of trying to state all the details of what you have been.

  Consider leaving out extraneous matters such as:
  ○ a brief job that has little to do with your application
  ○ personal facts that don't concern your employer
  ○ insignificant responsibilities listed under particular jobs
  ○ hobbies, affiliations, memberships, and societies that simply make the point that you are a social, likable, and active person.

- **Match your style to the job:** If you are applying for a business position, use a business style. Don't try to attract attention by being overly creative. Most interviewers prefer an attractive but traditional resumé to a flashy one. This is particularly true for traditional kinds of businesses or jobs, such as finance-related jobs and managerial positions. It may be less so for jobs in advertising or other industries in which creativity would be valued. If you aren't sure how important creativity is in getting a particular job, go with a traditional resumé.

- **Design for eye appeal:** Without resorting to trendy tactics, attract your readers' attention to your resumé at first glance. Be aware that many resumés are put through scanners to check for key words before human beings even see them, so avoid using too many graphic elements like lines and boxes that could confuse the scanner and cause your application to be rejected.

  Here are some basic techniques used to create resumés with visual appeal:
  ○ Align headings on the page.
  ○ Surround important headings with white space.
  ○ Create sections of print, not large dense blocks of type.
  ○ Use capital letters and simple font changes for special emphasis.

- **Tailor your resumé to the job:** Make sure that the details of your resumé are finely tuned to match the particular job you're trying to get. Not all companies are alike, and not all jobs are alike. When possible, match your skills and experience to the specific company to which you're applying.

  For example, suppose that you're applying for two bookkeeping positions. One of them is in a huge Fortune 500 corporation and the other is in a small non-profit agency. In the resumé for the big company, highlight how well your experience and skills fit into a large department of fellow bookkeepers. In the other resumé, highlight the ways in which you'd take initiative to single-handedly tackle all bookkeeping tasks that might come your way.

- **Eliminate mistakes:** Typos and other mistakes are certain to land your resumé in the rejection pile. Even when writing is not crucial to the job you seek, your resumé is supposed to show you at your best.

The people who see careless errors in your resumé might think, "If this person makes mistakes on the resumé, imagine how many mistakes they'll make on the job."

The Electronic Way

In this age of the Internet, many candidates look for jobs online. On the other end, companies that receive thousands of resumés and online applications for one position can scan them to narrow the field of applicants. In doing so, job-search engines and hiring professionals look for certain requirements to search for people with the right skills. To stay in the running, you'll need to write a computer-friendly resumé and, in many cases, complete an online application.

- Whenever possible, find out which resumé format is most compatible with the system used by an employer (for example, as an attachment or as part of an email message).
- Include the title of the position in the subject line of your message. Also include a signature with your full name, email address, and phone number.
- Don't use elaborate fonts, as tempted as you may be to jazz up your resumé.
- Use the right keywords to help get past the computer to a live person. Computers are instructed to look for particular words when scanning for qualified applicants. For example, if the job description says "fluent in Spanish," make sure that your resumé mentions that you speak Spanish.
- Keep formatting simple. Do not underline, put in decorative lines, use shading, or italicize. If you want to emphasize something to the person who will read your resumé, use bold font.
- Avoid graphics or unusual characters. Sometimes a computer can be baffled by a simple bullet.
- Don't assume that an employer will review your resumé; therefore, be specific about employment history in an online job application.

FOR EXAMPLE

Fatal Typo
The head of a writing and editorial service received an application for an editorial assistant position from a college graduate. Apparently she had studied English and done well in school, but she let a spelling error slip by in her resumé. Needless to say, the employer had at least ten other perfectly proofread resumés to choose from, so she was not even interviewed for the position.

SELF-CHECK

- Review guidelines for writing a winning resumé.
- Discuss the types of information that should be deleted from resumés.
- Explain how to tailor a resumé to a particular job.

14.4 Writing Persuasive Cover Letters

Any resumé you send out should be accompanied by a cover letter. This is probably going to be your first contact with an employer, so take the extra time and effort to make your letter count.

An effective cover letter can convince readers that you're worth their time. It does so by being concise and interesting. To conduct a thorough job search, you'll need to use two common types of cover letter:

- **Application letter.** This type of letter works when you're responding to a known job opening (one that a mutual friend told you about, one that was advertised, etc.).
- **Prospecting letter.** This letter is used to inquire about possible opportunities with an organization that is not currently advertising an opening. Use this letter when you've targeted a company that has a need for an employee with your qualifications.

14.4.1 The Application Letter

Application letters are written in response to advertisement or other announcement of a specific job opening. You'll use this letter to formally apply for a position and show the employer how well your qualifications match those required in the position. Use the position description and your research about the organization to compose your letter.

4857 Birch Road, Apt. 3
Red Deer, AB T4N 4R7

August 9, 2010

Ms. Gloria Hrief
Personnel Director
Benway Manufacturing, Inc.
400 Railway Center Drive
Red Deer, AB T4N 4R7

Dear Ms. Hrief:

As a June graduate in Accounting from University of Calgary, I am delighted to answer
your advertisement (*Register*, August 8) for an entry level accountant in your farm equipment division.

You may be interested not only in my accounting preparation and experience, as described in
the enclosed resumé, but also in my summer employment driving Benway tractors on my uncle's
farm.

If my application merits an interview for this position or another in your company, please
write or call (555-3948). I look forward to meeting you.

Sincerely,

Robert Collins

Robert Collins

Figure 14-4 Invited letter of application

A letter of application (see Figure 14-4) typically has three parts:

- **Why you are writing.** Identify the position you're applying for and how you found out about it (advertisement, mutual friend, company posting, etc.). Sometimes people include a brief statement about why they are interested in the organization.
- **Why they should be interested in you.** If you are responding to an ad or posting, demonstrate how your skills and background match the qualifications listed for the position. Tell the employer what sets you apart. Convince the employer that you have the qualities and motivation to perform well in the position.
- **What action needs to be taken next.** Show appreciation for the reader's time and consideration, then suggest an action; for example, state that you'll follow up by calling within ten days to set up an appointment for an interview.

Whenever possible, limit each point to one paragraph. Doing so will keep your writing on track, which will help you hold your busy reader's attention.

14.4.2 The Prospecting Letter

You don't have to wait for a company to advertise an opening. A prospecting letter is written to inquire about possible opportunities when an organization doesn't have any openings advertised.

The prospecting letter (see Figure 14-5) is similar to the application letter, but the focus is on matching your qualifications to the broader organization needs than to a specific position.

Brenda Noel
247 Levitt Street
Regina, SK S4N 0R7

June 2, 2010

Mr. Herbert Reid
Manager, Software Systems
ATC Autonetics
577 First Street
Regina, SK S4N 0R7

Dear Mr. Reid:

Your advertisements in *Byte* magazine during the past few months reveal rapid expansion in ATC software products. If your need for state-of-the-art software specialists is also expanding, my enclosed resumé may interest you.

My senior project was written in LISP—a language offering great potential for ATC's work in artificial intelligence—and I also have worked extensively in systems using FORTRAN 77, COBOL, and various forms of BASIC, which may be needed for interfacing with and updating various existing software programs.

I would like very much to meet with you to discuss how I may be of service to your organization. Perhaps we can also discuss your vision of the high-tech advances that interest both of us. I will call next Friday to see whether we may arrange to meet at a time that is convenient for you. Please feel free to call me at 555-7689, to discuss any questions or comments you may have or to arrange a meeting. I look forward to speaking with you.

Sincerely,

Brenda Noel

Brenda Noel

Figure 14-5 Uninvited letter of application

1. **Why you are writing.** Work some creativity into your reason for your letter of inquiry. You are writing, after all, to a company official who has not told you that a job is even open. How did you find out about the organization? What prompted you to send a letter? Did you receive a referral from someone who works at the organization?
2. **Why they should be interested in you.** Summarize the key strengths you bring to the employer. Include a bulleted list of achievements and qualifications that would benefit the company; do your best to show that you have researched the company and its needs. Provide examples of how you have contributed to your current or former employers.
3. **What action should be taken next.** State that you'll follow up with a phone call and inform them of when you'll call. Consider options other than securing an interview. You'd enjoy a meeting, for example, even though there may be no openings right now.

Again, the letter should not try to redo your resumé. Select one or two of your most impressive or interesting achievements and weave them into the course of your letter.

FOR EXAMPLE

Prospecting Payoffs

In the months before moving to Halifax to get married, Jack sent out dozens of prospecting letters and application letters looking for a position in advertising design. Only about one quarter of the letters earned responses, but his efforts were worth it. One prospecting letter made it into the hands of the owner of a small design firm. Jack's resumé was perfectly suited to a position about to be vacated. The owner hadn't gotten around to advertising the position and was happy to skip over that process after interviewing Jack and offering him the job.

SELF-CHECK

- Discuss the role of the cover letter in a job search.
- Define application letter and prospecting letter.
- Outline the three parts of the application cover letter.
- Explain the differences between the two types of cover letters.

14.5 Guidelines for Writing Cover Letters that Work

Each cover letter you write can mean the difference between getting an interview and getting no response. Don't put together a form letter and send it to every potential employer—your letter is certain to be ignored. The extra thought and planning you put into a well-crafted persuasive letter takes time, but the results are well worth the effort. Consider the following tips for writing cover letters:

- **Direct your letter to an individual by name and title:** Your letter and resumé are more likely to get the attention they deserve if they end up with the right person. Do some research on the Internet or make a phone call to determine the best person for the job.

> **FOR EXAMPLE**
>
> **It's the Little Things**
> As the office manager of a well-known and growing law firm, Michelle frequently runs ads in the local papers to find new support staff. In writing the ads, she deliberately leaves out her name just to see which applicants make the extra effort to call the office to find out who should receive their letters and resumes. In most cases, those that manage to send their information directly to her are more qualified than those who fall back on "To whom it may concern."

- **Match an employer's needs to your qualifications.** Use your cover letter to complement, but not duplicate, your resumé. Don't fill the page by simply listing what already appears in your resumé. Choose the skills and experience that best match those needed by the employer. In effect, write a letter that is work-centred and employer-centred, not self-centred.

- **Use research to stand out.** The more you know about a prospective employer, the better you are able to convince them that you belong in their organization. Do your homework. If, for example, you've read about a company's plans to add an in-house fitness centre, point out that you've completed two similar projects for other companies.

- **Don't mention money.** It's rarely a good idea to mention pay at this point in the process. You run the risk of devaluing yourself by naming a low salary or appearing too expensive if your price is too high. Whenever possible, indicate that you'd be happy to discuss that information during an interview.

- **Avoid mistakes and misspellings.** As with your resumé and any other business documents you write, carefully proofread your cover letter for poor grammar and typos. Such careless mistakes will likely stop your resumé from going any further with a potential employer.

- **Be yourself.** This is your chance to add the personal touch that you couldn't in your fact-based resumé. Your goal is to capture your reader's attention with your cover letter, but not detract from your resumé.

SELF-CHECK

- Discuss the relationship between a cover letter and a resumé.
- Review guidelines for writing effective cover letters.
- Explain the importance of proofreading a cover letter.

SUMMARY

The resumés and application letters you send to prospective employers are sales letters—you are selling both your job skills and your writing abilities. You're likely to draw upon a variety of sources—from the Internet to your uncle—when pursuing leads and other information about employment opportunities. A resumé is persuasive based not only on its content, but on the way in which it is organized; therefore, you must choose the most effective format. Guidelines for length, style, and strategy further increase a resumé's chance for success. When written well, the two types of cover letters persuade a reader that you and your resumé are worth his or her time.

KEY TERMS

Application letter	The type of cover letter used to respond to a known job opening.
Chronological resumé	A resumé that organizes work experience in chronological order, starting with the most recent.
Combination resumé	A resumé that merges chronological and functional styles; begins with a functional section and then lists employment history in chronological order.
Functional resumé	A resumé that groups accomplishments and qualifications together.
Network	People in your business life and personal life that can connect you with job opportunities or other job resources.
Prospecting letter	The type of cover letter used to inquire about possible job opportunities with a company that is not advertising an opening.

ASSESS YOUR UNDERSTANDING

Go to www.wiley.com/canada/brounstein to evaluate your knowledge of the basics of resumé writing. Measure your learning by comparing pre-test and post-test results.

Quick Questions

1. In a job search, a network could include
   (a) business clients
   (b) neighbours

      (c) suppliers

      (d) all of the above

2. Help-wanted ads are an ineffective means of searching for a job. True or false?

3. To make a strong impression on potential employers, visit their offices and ask about openings. True or false?

4. The functional format, chronological format, and combination format are the three most common types of resumés. True or false?

5. The functional format is the most popular choice for job seekers returning to the workforce. True or false?

6. Which of the following is a drawback of the combination format?

      (a) it may not be long enough

      (b) it shows gaps in employment

      (c) it may be repetitious

      (d) all of the above

7. As long as you're applying for jobs within the same field or industry, one version of a resumé is acceptable. True or false?

8. Intricate fonts add visual impact and appeal to a resumé. True or false?

9. The two common types of cover letters are the prospecting letter and the application letter. True or false?

10. In which of the following situations should an application cover letter be used?

      (a) in response to an ad

      (b) in response to an Internet posting

      (c) in response to a personal recommendation

      (d) all of the above

11. The goal of a prospecting letter is to convince a potential employer of your qualifications for a certain position. True or false?

12. A cover letter is a useful way to address salary issues before entering into an interview situation. True or false?

13. Which of the following can turn a typical cover letter into a letter that gets the notice it deserves?

      (a) colourful paper

      (b) references

      (c) careful presentation

      (d) all of the above

Give It Some Thought

1. What are two ways in which the Internet can be used in a job search?

2. How can a former employer be a useful resource in a job search?

3. How do the chronological and functional resumés differ?

4. What is one drawback of the chronological format?

5. When is it acceptable to have a resumé longer than one page?

6. In this age of Internet job sites, how can you increase your chances of having your resumé match the requirements of a position?

7. What are three elements of a visually appealing resumé?

8. How is a prospecting cover letter different than an application cover letter?

9. Which type of cover letter would be most appropriate in a situation in which you heard from a former colleague that a company was accepting resumés for sales positions?

10. How should you end a prospecting letter?

11. Why is "To whom it may concern" an ineffective way to direct a cover letter?

12. What kinds of research can help make a cover letter stand out?

Applying This Chapter

1. Take a few minutes to list the professional contacts you have in your network. Put a star next to those you could call today to talk about job ideas. Circle those names in your network that could be a good source but that you should work on keeping in touch with first. How could you expand your list?

2. Think about three versions of your resumé, using the chronological, functional, and combination formats. Which format works best for your background, skills, and experience? Can you think of a situation in which one of the other formats would work better? Write down your reasons.

3. Review your resumé using the guidelines from this chapter. How would you change it to increase its chances of getting results? In particular, examine your resumé in terms of its compatibility with the Internet.

4. Take a look at job postings in major job-searching websites like monster.ca or workopolis.com. Which postings seem like good leads? Choose one and write an effective application letter.

5. Find a news item from a magazine, newspaper, trade journal, or some other resource (including the Internet), and think of a way to use it in a prospecting letter.

THE NEXT STEP

Choosing a Search Approach

Start a job-search file by listing the companies or businesses you'd like to work for. Do some online research to find some potential employers. Determine the best approach for pursuing leads with your top three employer choices.

Resumé Adaptations

Choose two job ads from the newspaper or postings from the Internet. Assuming you'd like to apply for the positions, decide how, if at all, you'd need to adapt your resumé for each position.

In Pursuit of a Dream

Choose the company you'd most like to work for—your dream job. Determine who you should address your letter to, using the Internet as your first mode of research. Draft a prospecting cover letter to that person explaining the reason for your letter, your qualifications, and an appropriate closing. Share your letter with another student for feedback and ask how would he or she would react to receiving such a letter?

15
INTERVIEWING FOR EMPLOYMENT
Presenting Yourself and Your Skills

STARTING POINT

Go to www.wiley.com/canada/brounstein to assess your knowledge of the basics of job interview skills. After reviewing this website, you'll be able to determine where you need to concentrate your effort.

What You'll Learn in This Chapter:

- ways of preparing for an interview
- tips for presenting yourself successfully in an interview
- guidelines for following up after an interview.

After Studying This Chapter, You'll be Able to:

- describe the role preparation plays in the success of an interview
- identify interviewing pitfalls to avoid
- discuss assertive communication skills that lead to interviewing success
- discuss the importance of thank-you letters as follow-up.

INTRODUCTION

The interview process provides you with an opportunity to present yourself to potential employers; it's also a process that will help you decide if an opportunity is right for you. This chapter discusses how preparation increases your ability to communicate effectively in an interview. Criteria for speaking assertively and listening actively are outlined. The chapter concludes with guidelines for writing the thank-you letter that follows an interview.

15.1 Preparing for an Interview

A job interview is like a test drive with a new car: it's a limited experience from which big decisions come. The interview is a point of live contact between the seller (the job candidate) and the buyer (the hiring manager). In many respects, both are taking each other for a test drive in the interview to see whether they want to enter into a working relationship with one another.

What greatly influences whether the job interview turns out to be a positive experience is how each party communicates with the other—speaking and listening. In fact, an interview, whether you're the hiring manager or the candidate seeking a job, is one of the best forums for applying the tools of assertive speaking and active listening covered in Sections 2.1.6 and 2.4.5. How you present yourself and how you listen greatly influence how others evaluate you—and because interviews involve a relatively short time for the two parties to be together before decisions are made, you need to make your communication count in order to be successful.

Types of Interviews

Employers use a number of interview formats to find the perfect candidate for a position. Knowing what to expect from each type of interview will help prepare you for your best performance

- **Screening interview:** A representative from human resources typically conducts this type of interview, either in person or on the telephone. This person is trying to find out if you meet the minimum qualifications for the job; if so, you will move on to the next step. In many cases, a screener will focus on gaps in work history or other inconsistencies in your resumé that might disqualify you for the position.
- **Group interview:** Several candidates are interviewed at once in this format. The interviewer will use this interview to observe group interaction and participation. Coming prepared with meaningful questions will show that you are interested in the position, help you stand out from those who are not as prepared, and convince the interviewer that you are worthy of moving on in the interview process.
- **Selection interview:** At this stage, an employer knows that you have the skills that qualify you for the job, but they must still determine if you have the personality required to interact well with others in the company. Candidates may be asked to interview with different people before a decision is made.
- **Panel interview:** Several people interview a candidate at once. Because it can be an intimidating and high-pressure situation, interviewers will watch you to see how you handle stress, as well as how you will interact with different people. Be certain to make eye contact with each member of the panel as you answer questions.

Presenting yourself effectively in an interview starts with preparation. In many respects, going on a job interview is like giving a formal presentation (see Chapter 11): you need to present information—this time about yourself—coherently and positively. Like a formal presentation, preparation is key to success. In the case of a job interview, preparation means knowing about yourself as well as the employer and the industry.

15.1.1 Knowing Yourself and What You Can Do

What makes you a good candidate for the position you're seeking? Fundamentally, this question sums up everything you want to get across to the prospective employer when you interview.

To answer this essential question well (and get the job offer), you need to communicate your best skills and accomplishments. Completing the chart in Table 15-1 helps you come prepared to convey these vital points. Under the "Say It" column, list your strongest skills and accomplishments. In the "Prove It" column, give examples and stories that illuminate them.

Table 15-1: Say-it, prove-it chart

Say It	Prove It

As you outline the stories of proof, you should describe the situation, the action taken, and, as applicable, the results gained from your actions. Here's an example about one skill following this method:

- **Say it.** "Self-taught computer troubleshooter."
- **Prove it.** "Used skill to solve problem of downed computers facing many people on my team at Company X. In one day, I had every computer up and running before MIS could even come help."

As you outline the stories on the prove-it side, practise saying them concisely and giving the highlights so that they make your points with impact. As you complete Table 15-1, include as many items as possible. When you have a bag full of skills and accomplishments with appropriate stories to go with them, you are armed and ready—you can pull out the ones that help you best respond to the question at hand.

15.1.2 Researching the Position and the Field

With whatever time you have before an interview, you should do your research to learn as much as possible about a position, company, and industry. By doing so, you'll be prepared for whatever questions come your way; you'll also be able to come up with meaningful questions to bring with you to ask during the interview.

The public library and the Internet hold a wealth of information to draw from:

- company website
- websites of competitors
- investor websites, which may follow news of the company
- online research services such as LexisNexis
- books about the company or the field
- journal and newspaper articles
- business publications such as *Forbes*, *Money*, *The Wall Street Journal*, *Maclean's*.

Whenever possible, take advantage of your network to speak with someone who already works at the company or in the industry. Don't overlook the possibility of making a connection through your school's career centre or alumni office.

15.1.3 Knowing What the Interviewer Is Thinking

For hiring managers, a major emphasis of an interview is on fact-finding. To help make important hiring decisions, interviewers want to find out as much as they can about a candidate's work background and qualities. Although the person's resumé gives the interviewer a sneak preview of this background, they need live discussion to get the fullest picture of what that person can do and what that person is like.

An interviewer will begin with the job requirements for the position—a written list of the important hiring factors. The typical job description usually defines the worker's role and the job's main functions. From a job-requirements list, an interviewer can formulate the right questions to ask. The best job-requirements list outlines two sets of factors—can-do factors and will-do factors.

Can-do factors answer this question: Can the person do the job? Can-do factors define the essential qualifications for a job. Here are the more common can-do factors used by interviewers to screen resumes:

- **Education:** What level of education do you expect or need in this position? In which fields of study should the person have an education? Should the person have some specialized training for this job?
- **Technical skills and knowledge:** Every job has certain essential skills related to performing the functions of the position. Candidates may also need a certain body of technical information.

- **Computer skills:** Many positions need employees who are proficient at various computer applications, from word processing to graphic design.
- **Written communication skills/language capabilities:** Some jobs require excellent writing skills; for some, a foreign language is helpful.
- **Physical requirements:** If the job requires lifting abilities or other physical demands, an interviewer should clearly spell out the requirements for these duties.
- **Industry knowledge:** For some jobs, an interviewer may want someone who has acquired certain knowledge related to the industry or sector in which their business operates. For some positions, having someone with deep knowledge of the market in which they do business is an important can-do factor.
- **Experience:** Experience is one of the more critical can-do factors for an interviewer. They'll look at all the key areas for the role in which having previous job-related experience is important—job skills, certain work situations, management responsibilities held, and so on. An interviewer will want the level of experience as well—quantified in years as best as possible.

The other factors an interviewer will include on a job-requirements list are called *will-do factors*. Will-do factors answer this question: How will the person do the job? These are the personal attributes or qualities that make a good employee for the position. As every employer knows, many people are capable of performing a job; that is, they fit the can-do requirements. But whether those people will do the job *well* is another story.

The following are some common will-do factors important to hiring managers:

- **Team player:** Will the person work well with others in team-like situations? Does the person take a co-operative and helpful approach in such situations?
- **Track record:** Experience tells an interviewer how *long* someone has done something, not how *well*. A track record is the history of the accomplishments a person has made.
- **Interpersonal skills:** Does the employee have to interact with others to get the job done? Does the position require someone who can communicate constructively with others?
- **Organizational skills:** Many positions require attention to detail and the ability to deal with much data and keep it all organized.
- **Flexibility:** More and more jobs need people who can adapt to change—who can, as the old expression goes, roll with the punches.
- **Initiative:** Many companies need people who are self-starters. After they've acquired the essential skills, they can act without constantly being told what to do.
- **Problem-solving ability:** People who can tackle problem situations with analytical abilities and a solutions-focused mindset are critical to have in many positions.

- **Creativity:** Some roles need people who are full of ideas, who can think of new or different ways to get a job done.
- **Reliability:** This factor deals with employees who follow through, meet deadlines, are there when you need them, and can be counted on to get a job done.
- **Enthusiasm:** Some jobs require that people show a high energy level and an upbeat demeanour. Often, these jobs involve a lot of public contact.
- **Effective management style:** This factor deals with how a person leads others and what behaviours and judgement they demonstrate in a management role.

15.1.4 Thinking Ahead: Tough Questions

The earlier chart exercise helps you handle many of the common, sometimes difficult questions that interviewers ask, even if they aren't the best questions your interviewer can pose. Here are a few such questions for which you want to prepare answers, along with some recommended responses:

- **Tell me about yourself.** Respond with your 30-second commercial. This is a brief highlight of your background—three to four points at most, each said in one sentence, that summarize your **strengths** and qualifications. In particular, summarize your related experience and technical skills, your education, and something that characterizes your track record.
- **Why are you interested in this position?** "Because I need a job" is not the best answer to this common question. Emphasize how the opportunity fits with your career or job interests. Then list some of your strengths or skills and how they meet the needs of the job situation. This assertive response gives the hiring manager a strong picture of how you can be a good fit for the open position.
- **What did you like most and least about your last (or current) job?** Emphasize the most over the least. On the least side, give one or two points with brief explanations and constructive language. Go for items that sound realistic but don't have you coming across as harsh or bitter. On the "most" side, talk in terms of the accomplishments you made in that previous experience. Pull a couple of examples from your chart (see Table 15-1).
- **What are your strengths?** Pull two or three from your completed chart. Choose strengths that connect to the employer's needs for this position and tell stories that back up the strengths.
- **What are your weaknesses?** Usually asked right after the question about your strengths, the worst answer to this question is "I have no weaknesses" since that's simply not true. No one is perfect; and the interviewer isn't expecting you to be. The best approach to answering this question is to pick a couple of items to talk about and redirect to the positive strengths in your response. The interviewer expects you to only mention weaknesses that you're working to improve, so the answer can

also be interpreted as a strength. For example, don't answer the question with "I'm usually late for work in the morning" or "I can never remember people's names." Instead make statements like "I'm taking a course at night school to improve my English because it's not as strong as I want it to be" or "I like to make to-do lists to keep my projects running on time."

- **What are/were your reasons for leaving the job?** Give a brief explanation to answer this question in a way that provides the facts but not great detail. If you are sensitive about a job experience, as you would if you were fired, give the circumstances of the situation and say "laid off" or "terminated" instead of "fired," which is often a trigger word. Avoid sounding bitter, angry, or defensive.

> ## FOR EXAMPLE
>
> ### To Be Honest
> Lukas was conducting interviews for a new position in his company. Of all the candidates he interviewed, one stood out because her skills and background matched those of the position. As Lukas explored her work history, he asked for her reasons for leaving each job. For one, the candidate gave a vague and rambling answer. When Lukas called her references, he found out she had been fired from that particular job. She and her manager had clashed because she didn't want to follow his close direction. Lukas didn't hire the candidate—not because she was fired, but because she wasn't honest in dealing with it. She would have been hired had she been straightforward in handling the issue.

People make mistakes, and things go wrong in their lives. Although being terminated involuntarily isn't something most people are proud of, sounding like you've grown or learned from the experience makes you sound human and genuine. People are often willing to give you a second chance. But if you sound bitter, angry, or defensive about what happened, you tend to take away a prospective employer's comfort with giving you another shot.

Eve is applying for a position as a customer service manager. Here is how she answers four of the challenging questions following the tips outlined:

Q: Eve, tell me about yourself.

A: I bring ten years of customer service-related experience, plus five years in management roles. I have a bachelor's degree in business and bring a solid track record of training and developing staff to be service oriented in their roles.

Q: Why are you interested in this position?

A: You've mentioned you have a growing company with the need to establish a strong customer service orientation in the way you support your customers. That kind of challenge is what I'm seeking. In management roles over the past five years, I've helped organize and develop teams to provide top-notch customer service. To do this in a growing company that taps into this strength is appealing.

Q: *What did you like most and least about your last position?*

A: *I had a lot to like in my last position, which is why I was there more than five years. I had a good team to work with and enjoyed having the chance to develop them into a strongly performing team. I liked the services we provided that made customer service something I could do with real sincerity. The dislikes centred on what happened with the company. As it suffered a downturn in business, it got away from providing perks and services for both employees and customers, which is why being part of a growing company like yours is of much interest to me.*

Q: *What are your strengths?*

A: *First, my management skills. I bring a track record that shows I can develop a strong team and help people become service oriented in their roles. Second, I bring excellent written and verbal communication and interpersonal skills that have helped me not only motivate my staff but also work cross-functionally to build a strong customer-service presence in the organization. Finally, I'm a self-starter who can take initiative and develop strategies to solve problems. When I took on my management position in my last company, our customer service function was somewhat dysfunctional. I worked with both employees and management to establish procedures and a training program that turned us into an organized and service-oriented team.*

15.1.5 Weaknesses: Identification and Preparation

To one degree or another, we all have weaknesses, or flaws and shortcomings, related to our capabilities and work history. The fact that you have flaws isn't a flaw; the key is how you talk about them. If you talk about a weakness or mistake in an anxious or panicked mode, you scare off your potential employers. When you handle these issues matter-of-factly, you're a regular person who's not so bad after all.

Prepare by identifying your potential weaknesses. Here are some common examples:

- one job for a long time
- too many jobs
- experience in a different industry
- unemployed
- once got fired
- no experience in a company of this size
- unrelated or insufficient education; poor GPA
- overqualified.

After you list all the weaknesses or shortcomings that a prospective employer might see in you, practise how you'll respond to questions about them. Here is a three-step process to follow to address your potential weaknesses:

1. **Pause briefly and evaluate what qualifications or qualities the question most relates to.** Think your answer through. If you rush out with your answer and then stumble or hem and haw, your confidence and credibility will be questioned. You want to consistently answer all of the questions in the interview calmly and confidently.

2. **Respond briefly with the facts.** The emphasis here is on brief. Long explanations may sound like rationalization or defensiveness. Also, avoid remarks that go something like, "Well, but . . ." Such comments make you sound like you're making excuses or reacting defensively. Speak in a straightforward manner.

3. **Redirect to your strengths.** Focus on something positive and relevant, such as what you learned from the experience, what improvements you've made, or what you've gained and now have to offer. As much as possible, when you redirect to a positive, tie your comments to the needs for the job you're seeking.

In your preparation, define a positive strength to redirect to with every weakness you have identified for yourself. Here's an example of handling a potential weakness—having too many jobs—with this three-step process:

1. **Consider the qualities of reliability or stability that make you a good choice for the job.**

2. **Answer with something like the following:** "Layoffs and chances to grow and gain new skills have been the main reasons I've had such a variety of experiences."

3. **Redirect to strengths by stating something like the following:** "What this has done for me is help build a multitude of skills that help me in roles like the one you have available. In addition, my experience has taught me to be adaptable to change. You've talked about the need to have changes occur in your work environment, and that is one of the factors that has attracted me to this position."

15.1.6 Final Preparations

Your goal is to convince the interviewer that you are professional and competent. Taking care of a few final preparations will go a long way to ensuring your success:

• Know exactly where you are going and do whatever it takes to arrive at least ten minutes early. Drive by the location the day before if necessary. Allow plenty of time for traffic and parking.

Practice Makes Perfect

As with any skill, the more you practise interviewing, the more you'll improve. Two common ways to hone your interview skills include the mock interview and the informational interview:

- A **mock interview,** which is typically videotaped and lasts 30 minutes or less, is one of the best ways to prepare for an actual employment interview. Many career centres offer this service; you can complete similar practice sessions through online job sites. In a mock interview, the other person will take on the role of the recruiter and try to make the interview as realistic as possible by asking questions like those that might be asked during a real interview. This exercise will not only help you perfect your technique, but it'll give you a chance to get valuable feedback on your performance and boost your self-confidence.

- An **informational interview** is when you meet with someone in your chosen field to discuss career information, get advice about breaking in, and find out if you have what it takes to succeed. Although this type of interview is best suited for networking and gathering valuable career information, it is another way to build self-confidence and prepare for actual job interviews.

- The impression you make has a good deal to do with the outcome of your interview. Pick out the appropriate attire long before the interview day (a business suit is always acceptable); be certain your clothes are clean and well pressed. Minimize accessories, get a good haircut, and avoid excessive cologne and make-up.

- Bring extra copies of your resume in a folder, small briefcase, or portfolio. Bring a small notebook for notes, but plan on keeping note taking to a minimum.

- Get a good night's sleep the night before your interview. That, along with a healthy meal, will give you the stamina you'll need to stay alert and refreshed throughout your interview.

SELF-CHECK

- Describe how the Say-it, prove-it chart works in preparing for an interview.
- Describe three ways to research a potential employer.
- Discuss the importance of dealing with your weaknesses before an interview.
- List three difficult questions that come up during interviews.

15.2 Succeeding in the Interview

Your resume is your marketing piece. The interview is your sales call. During an interview, you're selling yourself, paving the way for a job offer in return. This section provides you with tips for being assertive as well as guidelines for giving a successful interview and pitfalls to avoid.

15.2.1 Going Live: Giving Your Best

Your success in an interview is ultimately based on what you do in your live performance. You know that you want to be clear, concise, positive, and confident in the way you present yourself—all important parts of assertive speaking. Here are seven communication tips that help make these results happen and help you get the best out of your interviews:

- **Make a good first impression.** Impressions form quickly in interviews, so get off to a good start. Give a warm greeting, get your interviewer's name up front and use it, speak up with energy, and engage in conversation. Like giving a formal presentation (discussed in Chapter 11), you want to use your nervousness as adrenaline to stimulate energy.

- **Truly listen to the questions.** One of the best ways to give clear and direct answers is to first truly understand the questions being asked of you. Listen patiently. Ask for clarification if a question is confusing to you. When necessary, paraphrase what you've been asked to make sure that you understand the question correctly. These active-listening efforts not only help you understand the question clearly, but also give you time to think. And when you think before you speak, you increase your chances of coming across assertively.

- **Ask for the needs early on.** Get to the heart of the matter—what are the needs for the position, the job requirements most desired in the right person? Early on in the interview, ask: "What are you looking for in the right candidate for this position?" Or "What are your needs for this position?" Gaining this information helps you know what's important for the hiring manager and, therefore, helps guide you to draw on what's more relevant from your background.

- **Tell how you can meet the needs.** After you discover the needs, such as you do when communicating effectively in a sales letter (see Section 9.2), confidently tell what you can do and have done to meet these needs at every opportunity throughout the interview. Use positive language. Keep these needs the focus of your answers.

- **Back up your key points with stories.** As you explain important points in your answers, pull real examples from your Say-it, prove-it chart (Table 15-1). Stories not only add substance to your points, but also often give them a touch of humour. They help engage others' attention and make your examples come alive.

- **Check for concerns near the end.** As the interview with the hiring manager or recruiter winds to a close, tactfully find out whether he or she has any concerns about you. After you leave the interview, you seldom have an opportunity to address any concerns the interviewer may have. To do so, ask a question like the following: "Based on our discussion today, please tell me any concerns you have regarding my background that I can address for you."

  This polite invitation often brings out a concern or two that you can address. Do so in a straightforward manner. Keep your manner patient and your tone sincere so you don't put your interviewer on the spot.

- **Ask your own questions.** The best hiring decisions are a two-way street—they are a match between the needs of the employer and the employee. Therefore, evaluate the job opportunity and the organization as much as the hiring manager evaluates you. Of course, this means arriving at the interview with your research completed (see Section 15.1.2), being prepared to ask questions, and then asking them throughout the interview with everyone you visit. Bring your notes with you—no need to memorize your questions. Keep in mind that asking questions shows interest.

  Here are some important issues to ask questions about:

- job duties
- job challenges
- needs for the position
- performance expectations
- where the position fits in the organizational structure
- reasons the position is open
- hiring manager's management style
- each interviewer's history with the business
- company history
- an overview of the company's business
- future outlook for the company
- growth opportunities
- organizational culture
- compensation and benefits package
- training and support resources available
- next steps in the hiring process.

When you present yourself clearly and confidently in both delivery and content and ask good, thought-provoking questions, you come across as a positive and motivated candidate—exactly what employers like to hire.

15.2.2 Avoiding Losing Moves

No matter how well you present yourself in an interview, there's no guarantee that you'll get the job. It's a competitive situation, and even at your best, you may not be the right match. Nonetheless, certain factors can increase or decrease your possibility for success. Be aware of the following pitfalls—in particular, the communication behaviours that have doomed some job candidates:

- **Being a distraction:** The interview is not the time to chew gum, twirl jewellery, squirm in your chair, fidget, or bite your nails. These inappropriate behaviours leave lasting impressions and cause hiring managers to hear little of what you have to say.
- **Rambling or being evasive:** When interviewers ask you questions, being verbose and not answering them directly are mistakes. Long-windedness and unclear responses are tickets for rejection.
- **Being critical of former employers or bosses:** To have a work experience that did not go well isn't unusual. But to sound bitter about it after it's over doesn't usually sit well with prospective employers. When you sound critical of past bosses, regardless of how right you may be, you sound negative.
- **Showing little interest or enthusiasm:** Looking stiff and sounding monotone give the impression that you don't care or have the energy to do a good job. Asking few or no questions also raises a concern of whether you have a real interest in the job.
- **Communicating no track record:** Experience tells how long, but not how well. If you can't articulate what you've done well in your experiences and the contributions you've made, you don't give a prospective employer a good reason to hire you.
- **Sounding distasteful:** Sounding defensive, arrogant, condescending, or insincere are big turnoffs to those who hear them. Sounding confident isn't the same as sounding cocky. Sounding smart isn't the same as sounding like a know-it-all. Being sincere and genuine in your tone still carries the day—especially in a job interview.

FOR EXAMPLE

Losing Your Nerve
David had worked hard to secure an interview with a prominent design firm. His resume was solid; so was his design portfolio, with work from design school as well as his first job. On the day of the interview, however, he couldn't get a handle on his nervousness. Instead of helping him appear enthusiastic and interested, his nerves caused him to fidget and lose track of his thought. His nervousness also caused him to lose the job opportunity.

15.2.3 Making Winning Moves

Here are some guidelines to follow to succeed in an interview. Look at them as the criteria to use to evaluate your own efforts.

- **Express yourself in a clear and concise manner.**
  - Did you answer questions directly?
  - Did you give answers in language that made sense to your interviewer instead of being full of jargon?
  - Did you answer questions with enough specifics to make them clear, yet not so overloaded on detail that you were wordy?
- **Sound positive and confident.**
  - Did you express your points in constructive language?
  - Did you give steady eye contact to your interviewer when you spoke?
  - Did your voice show expression and come across loud and clear?
  - Did you use gestures to enhance your key points?
  - Did you smile at times when sharing experiences?
- **Communicate your skills and accomplishments.**
  - Did you clearly articulate what you're good at and what you've done well in your experience?
  - Did you provide examples to back up your track record?
- **Learn about the job, the company, and the people.**
  - Did you get a picture of what the company is like?
  - Did you get a sense of what your potential boss is like, as well as your would-be team members?
  - Did you get a good understanding of what the job entails and what challenges it involves?
  - Did you ask questions to learn about these issues?

SELF-CHECK

- Discuss the role of assertive speaking in interviewing success.
- Explain the importance of active listening during an interview.
- List three positive behaviours to display in an interview.
- List three negative behaviours to avoid in an interview.
- List five questions to ask during an interview.

If you can answer yes to nearly all the questions in these four areas, you know that you did well in your interview. Regardless of whether you get a job offer, hitting the mark on these items means that you gave the interview your best. If you evaluate yourself on these factors after each interview, you'll be able to improve and be tuned in to how to present yourself assertively.

15.3 Following Up: Sending a Thank-You Letter

The days following your interview are a period of intense evaluation on the part of the company. Don't simply sit back waiting for an answer. You can still influence the process in a positive way through a thank-you letter.

After the interview, be sure to write a brief letter expressing your appreciation for the interview. Although a thank-you note doesn't guarantee that you'll get a job (or, in some cases, the chance for a second interview), employers report that a sincere thank-you letter can tip the balance in your favour. Even if the interview did not go well for you, thank the company for their interest.

As shown in Figure 15-1, begin by thanking the interviewers by name, and focus on one or two particular aspects of the interview for special comment; you may also

> 112 Smithson Street
> Niagara Falls, ON L2E 2G5
>
> December 20, 2010
>
> Mr. Richard Hall
> Personnel Director
> Tri-State Mills, Inc.
> 205 Flowertown Way
> Niagara Falls, ON L2E 2G5
>
> Dear Mr. Hall:
>
> I enjoyed meeting you, Ms. Watkins, and Mr. Valenzuela last Thursday afternoon. I was especially interested in our discussion of Japanese "just-in-time" scheduling procedures, and their possible application at Tri-State Mills.
>
> I look forward to possibly working at Tri-State, and certainly will be plased to supply any additional information you would like to support my application.
>
> Again, thank you for a stimulating afternoon. I look forward to discussing possible opportunities for me at Tri-State Mills.
>
> Sincerely,
>
> *Rose Ramirez*
> Rose Ramirez

Figure 15-1 Thank-you letter for an interview

add something you didn't get to mention in the interview. Then re-emphasize your eagerness to work for the company. Conclude in a complimentary way, mentioning the company name if possible.

Once you have written your letter, decide whether you will print it and send it by mail or whether you will send your message to the interviewer via email. If you choose the email option, you can omit the addresses and dates at the top of the page, but remember to keep the tone of your correspondence formal just like you would if you were sending a formal letter.

FOR EXAMPLE

Thank-You for Your Time

Karima was one of 400 applicants for an entry-level position in the advertising department of a national magazine. After the field was narrowed down to 15 candidates, she was asked in to interview with the director of sales. The interview went well; this was the perfect job for Karima. Somehow, in all the excitement, she forgot to send a thank-you note. When she remembered two days later, it was too late to send a proper note through the mail, so Karima emailed one. After she was hired, she found out that only 3 of the 15 candidates had followed up with a thank-you. Though it was a small gesture, the thank-you note was a critical deciding factor.

If you were interviewed by more than one person, such as in a panel interview (see Section 15.1), it's a good idea to send a note to each one. Given the circumstances, there's a good chance you won't remember every person's name, so try to ask for business cards or write down names in your notepad; you can also call the office and ask.

SUMMARY

The interview process is your chance to demonstrate your communication skills; doing so effectively is your way of earning a job offer. The key to successful interviewing lies in how you prepare for the questions that will be asked of you. By using tools of active listening and assertive speaking you can express yourself clearly, describe your accomplishments, and learn important information about the position being offered. When it comes time to follow up after an interview, you'll be prepared for the next step: writing thank-you letters.

KEY TERMS

Strengths	Something positive and relevant, such as what you learned from an experience
Weaknesses	Flaws and shortcomings; past mistakes

ASSESS YOUR UNDERSTANDING

Go to www.wiley.com/canada/brounstein to evaluate your knowledge of the basics of job interview skills. Measure your learning by comparing pre-test and post-test results.

Quick Questions

1. The Say-it, prove-it chart is
   (a) a way to determine your strengths
   (b) a way of preparing to answer difficult questions
   (c) a way of prioritizing your accomplishments
   (d) all of the above
2. Which of the following are considered potential weaknesses?
   (a) gaps in employment
   (b) unrelated education
   (c) overqualification
   (d) all of the above
3. The best approach for discussing your weaknesses is to say that you don't have any. True or false?
4. Critical statements about former employees, regardless of their merit, are not likely to be received favourably by potential employers. True or false?
5. Which of the following behaviours leave a positive impression on an interviewer?
   (a) using gestures
   (b) using jargon
   (c) being evasive
   (d) none of the above
6. Which of the following items should be explored in an interview?
   (a) organizational culture
   (b) company history

(c) growth opportunities

(d) all of the above

7. A thank-you letter can be the difference between getting a job and not getting a job. True or false?

Give It Some Thought

1. What is the best way to respond to "tell me about yourself"?

2. How can you use a weakness to your advantage in an interview?

3. What is the best response to a question about why you left a previous position?

4. Name three pitfalls to avoid in an interview.

5. What are three non-verbal communication tools you should use to make a positive impression in an interview?

6. Why is it a good idea to ask an interviewer if he or she has any concerns about you/your qualifications?

7. What's the best way to send a thank-you letter after an interview?

Applying This Chapter

1. You need to prepare for an interview, but it's been years since you last interviewed for a position. This is an excellent time to come up with your list of potential weaknesses. Have you had one job for a long time? Too many jobs? Are you over-qualified? Name three of your weaknesses, and then explain them with facts.

2. Draft a response to the common inquiry, "so tell us about yourself." Rehearse it out loud, limiting your response to 30 seconds.

3. You performed well in an interview today; you answered all of the interviewer's questions without trouble, and you asked several good questions of your own. Unfortunately, you forgot to mention a certain experience that relates to the position for which you interviewed. Draft a thank-you letter for the interview and find a way to include some mention of that experience.

THE NEXT STEP

Selling Skills

Find a job listing for a position that interests you. Come up with a list of what the employer needs for the position. Match your skills and qualifications to three of those needs. Rehearse your responses. Are you believable? Does anything sound forced or untrue? Why?

Strengths and Weaknesses

Assume you're getting ready to interview for a position in your field. Prepare an answer to the inevitable question: What are your strengths? For the same interview, prepare an answer to the question: What are your weaknesses?

Mock Interview

In a small group, have a classmate take on the role of your potential employer in a mock interview for the position you chose in the previous exercises. Ask the other group members to evaluate your perfomance. Did you stumble in your answers? Did you ramble? Were you prepared for each question? Which areas still need work?

Thank-You

Imagine that you've just interviewed for a position with a company you've always wanted to work for. The position itself was not ideal, and the interview reflected that. Even though the interview was less than stellar, you're hoping to use it as a way to secure future interviews for jobs that better suit you. Draft a thank-you note to indicate this.

Question and Answer Period

You are interviewing for a position at a popular telecommunications company. The job will require you to work independently and solve problems creatively by thinking on your feet. Practise answering the following questions from the interviewer:

- You will often have to deal with difficult customers in this position. Tell me about your ability to work under pressure.
- This job will require you to juggle several different projects at the same time. How would you decide what you will work on first?
- Much of the workday in this job is spent working alone. Do you work best independently or as part of a team?

Turning the Tables

Think of a company you would dream to work for and imagine you were being interviewed for a position there. Prepare a list of five to seven questions to ask your interviewer regarding the job and the company you would be working for.

APPENDIX A
Sample Short Report

EXECUTIVE SUMMARY

From 2003 to 2006, EEW, Inc. granted no parental leaves for workers who adopted children. As a result, more than 30 workers per year quit their jobs. Fewer than 10 percent returned after adopting. Late in 2006, the company began granting selective parental leaves, without pay, based on an employee's record of accomplishment. Because few employees applied for these unpaid leaves and even fewer received them, the number of workers who resigned following an adoption still totalled 30 to 35 workers per year between 2006 and 2007. Since that time, company policy has been liberalized to permit adopting workers to take parental leave, still without pay, but with no loss of position in seniority if they return to work within six months. While this policy has helped to stem the steady flow of this type of resignation, the company should consider a policy of parental leave with half pay as an effective way to retain trained employees and, in the long term, to save money.

I. Overview

Motivated by legislation, union demands, and its own interests, senior management has assigned the Human Resources Department the task of reporting on past, present, and future company policies regarding parental leave. This report details past practices, summarizes present policies, and evaluates the factors that will guide future policy.

The report concludes that EEW should provide up to four months of parental leave with half pay. These measures, while not yet common among our competitors, are justified in the report on the basis of employee retention and long-term savings to the company.

II. Past Policies on Parental Leave at EEW

At the time of the company's founding in 2000, it had no written policy for parental leaves among the staff. Company Human Resources files show that a few workers requested leaves of absence without pay for the preparation period before the adoption and the months after. Without exception, these requests were turned down by the company.[1] In the words of an infamous internal memo from the now-deceased former president of the company, "Absolutely no. If they adopt a child, they'll probably want more. There is no end to that kind of thing."

Under pressure from union negotiators, the company in 2006 began to grant leaves without pay to workers who had demonstrated a record of achievement and promise. While no statistics can be gathered to make the point in a concrete way, many workers seeking parental leave still were dismissed in the mid-2000s on the grounds that their records weren't "promising enough." Despite repeated efforts by the company's Human Resources director during those years, management resisted all efforts to set forth clear work standards by which "enough" could be measured. Therefore, well into 2007, employees found themselves dependent upon the whim of a supervisor for a leave of absence, of course without pay.

In 2008, a watershed event changed the company's policies overnight. Interestingly, this event came not from legislation or external pressure. During a June 2, 2008 board meeting, a talented vice-president of the company proudly announced to a somewhat shocked board that she intended to take a parental leave so that she could travel overseas to adopt a child. She went on to speak of her commitment to the company and her earnest desire to take up her duties again as soon as possible after adopting.

A discussion ensued, pitting the traditionalists in the company against those interested in finding new and more flexible policies. Traditionalists argued that profits, not parenthood, were the sole concern of the company. Employees wishing to take time away from work to spend with their families, they said, could not be retained, nor could their positions be held open for them. More liberal minds argued that companies had far-reaching obligations to their employees and could not simply turn them out for choosing to take time away from work to spend with their children.

The vice-president brought both groups up short in a brief statement still recorded in the minutes of that meeting: "Let me put it this way, members of the board. I led the successful company effort to attract over $4 million in contracts and grants last year. I have an offer to do that kind of work for your main competitor both leading up to my leave and afterward. I spoke of my commitment to this company. Now you must decide if I'm worth your commitment. In the long term, will I make you enough money to compensate for my parental leave?"[2] At that point she smiled and left the meeting.

As a result of that meeting, she was offered a leave of absence without pay for the three months leading up to the adoption and the three months after she returned home with her adopted child. (Incidentally, she left the company to accept an identical offer with pay from the competitor.) Leaves without pay were available from that time on throughout 2008 to other workers wishing to take parental leave. Relatively few workers took such leaves, however, because they could not afford to live for that period without an income. They opted instead for unemployment compensation or other work that allowed them to earn right up to the week of adoption.

III. Present Policies

Since 2008, the Human Resources Department sponsored a successful drive in the company to allow adopting workers to take parental leave. Barring company-wide layoffs, these workers could return to their jobs within six months after adopting, without loss of seniority or pay level.[3]

That policy continues to the present. No salary is paid during parental leaves of absence. Benefits may be paid, depending upon the fringe package selected by the employee. At present, the workforce of EEW totals 5,152 workers. While the Human Resources Department does not claim to know of every adoption among the workers, we estimate that each year 20 to 30 workers adopt children. Of this number, no more than 10 percent apply for a leave without pay for the period of adoption and adjustment.[4]

IV. Evaluation

Those adopting workers who do not request a leave of absence simply quit. Few return to the company in later months or years. As illustrated in Table A-1, these resignations result in a substantial loss to the company each year. Note in the table that an employee usually requires at least five months to reach the production level of our average experienced employee:

Month	Salary	Production %	Training Cost
1	$4,000	10%	$3,600
2	$4,000	30%	$2,800
3	$4,000	50%	$2,000
4	$4,000	70%	$1,200
5	$4,000	90%	$400
6	$4,000	100%	$0
			Total $10,000

Table A-1 Productivity during first five months of employment

During this period of learning, the company is paying out an average salary of $4,000 per month, only a percentage of which is earned by employee production during the learning process. Thus, the company invests on average $10,000 in the training of each employee, as demonstrated in Table A-1.

In addition to this $10,000 spent in training, the Human Resources Department spends on average $2,480 in advertising, interviewing, and processing costs for each new employee hired.[5]

Therefore, if 30 workers quit per year due to adoption, the company cost in wasted training, advertising, interviewing, and processing is $374,400 (30 × $12,480).

For prudent policy decisions on adoption, that substantial sum must be weighed against the cost of simply providing half pay for workers during the month leading up to the adoption and the first three months of parenthood. Assuming that all 30 workers accepted such an arrangement, the company would pay 30 × $2,000 (half pay) × 4 months = $240,000.

The resultant saving to the company under such a plan would be $134,400. More difficult to measure but equally important are such advantages to the company as improved employee morale, enhanced company image for job seekers, and fewer trainees in the workforce.

V. Conclusion

Over the nine years of the company's existence, policies on parental leave have been steadily liberalized in favour of the worker. Based on the training and replacement costs set forth in this report, the trend toward partial salary during parental leave is in the financial interest of the company. EEW will spend one-third less to retain adopting employees through half pay leaves than to lose them and pay for advertising, interviewing, processing, and training for replacements.

APPENDIX: FIVE CASE STUDIES

All aspects of the following five cases are factually true. Names have been changed to protect privacy.

2005—Ruth

After six years with the company as an accountant, Ruth asked her supervisor for leave without pay during the three weeks leading up to adoption and the first few months of motherhood. The request was routinely denied. Ruth resigned her position at EEW, adopted her child, then found employment with EEW's main competitor, Technoelectric Designs. Today, Ruth heads the Accounting Division at that company. Recently she was honoured by the National Accounting Association for innovative and money-saving approaches to economic forecasting at Technoelectric.

2005—Jan

Fearing that she would be fired, Jan did not tell her supervisor of her plans to adopt until she requested parental leave a month before adopting. Her supervisor recommended her dismissal at that time in spite of Jan's excellent work record at EEW. Jan's husband, a senior engineer at EEW also requested leave and was denied but was allowed to keep his job. He expressed outrage at the handling of the situation with his wife. Both found employment elsewhere.

2006—Maryam

Maryam worked in the Quality Assurance Department for three years before she requested a leave of absence without pay. Her request was turned down because her work record, in the words of the rejection memo, "did not merit such concessions by the company." Acting through her union, Maryam took the matter before the Provincial Labour Relations Board and won a judgement against the company. After receiving back pay and a settlement, Maryam voluntarily found employment at Micro-Circuitry, Inc. She now supervises a quality assurance team there.

2007—Angela

Angela applied for and received a parental leave without pay. She left EEW for six months following adoption. Faced with rising financial obligations of an international adoption, however, she found temporary work at Technoelectric Designs during the latter months of her leave. A few weeks after bringing home her child, she returned to the workforce—but not at EEW. She manages the sales support team at Technoelectric Design today.

2008—Thomas

In early 2008, Thomas came to the Human Resources Department for counselling. He and his wife planned to adopt a child, he said, but could do so only if he could be assured of returning to his job after taking two months off to bond with their child. The Human Resources officer explained that he could return to his job up to six months after adopting. Thomas kept his job at EEW, returning after his two month leave. He resigned a few months later, explaining in his exit interview that he and his wife were making plans to adopt another child. He wanted to find employment with a company that offered some kind of financial support during parental leave.

WORKS CITED

1. Annual Human Resources Summary, 2003, Vol. IV, p. 68.

2. Corporate Minutes, Oct. 2007, p. 137.

3. For a full description of this policy, see Human Resources Policies and Procedures, 2007, pp. 387–98.

4. This figure is based upon leave applications formally filed with the Human Resources Department during the 2007 fiscal year.

5. For a detailed explanation of this estimated average, see Internal Economic Report No. 7, Jan. 2008, p. 204.

APPENDIX B
Sentence Structure and Punctuation

INTRODUCTION

This concise guide focuses on writing correct English sentences, including how to use punctuation correctly and how to avoid run-on sentences, comma splices, and sentence fragments. For more information about other topics in grammar, you should refer to a grammar reference book or to the many grammar sites available online.

B.1 Smoothing Out Your Sentence Structure

In order to form a correct and complete sentence, it is important that you understand its various components. This way, you will be able to make the right choices when forming your thoughts into sentences.

B.1.1 Writing Correct and Complete Sentences

There are four different requirements for a sentence to be complete and correct. The sentence has to have:

- **A subject:** The subject is the "do-er" of the sentence:
  - ***Marco** got a promotion in the sales division.*
  - ***The manager** approved my application.*
- **A verb:** The verb expresses action or status and indicates whether the sentence refers to past, present, or future time:
  - *The customer **is running** out the door without signing the contract.*
  - *I **will submit** my report when I return from Las Vegas.*
  - *She **saw** the director to discuss her ideas.*
- **A complete thought:** The sentence must express a logical idea. Here are two examples of incomplete sentences:
  - *After your project is finished.* This is not a correct sentence because it is not a complete thought. The reader would be wondering what else is going to happen.

    ○ *Went to Toronto to close the deal.* This is also not a complete sentence. Because there is no subject, the reader would be wondering who went to Toronto.

- **Correct punctuation:** The sentence must end with a period, question mark, or exclamation mark. Note that exclamation marks are very rarely used in business writing.

B.1.2 Comparing Nouns and Pronouns

Nouns are words used to identify people, places, things, or concepts—essentially the subject of your sentence. Below are some examples of the different categories of nouns:

- **People:** Pierre Trudeau, mother, Samantha, teacher
- **Places:** Vancouver, classroom, Yukon, airport
- **Things:** tree, lamp, window, ocean
- **Concepts**: democracy, generosity, success, happiness

    Notice that nouns that refer to specific people or places, like Samantha or Yukon, are capitalized. These are called proper nouns.

    Pronouns are the short, everyday words like "she," "it," "they," "us," or "him" that are used to represent nouns to avoid excessive repetition in our writing. For example:

- **No pronouns:** *Samantha finished Samantha's report before Samantha went to the meeting.*
- **Using pronouns:** *Samantha finished her report before she went to the meeting.*

B.1.3 Using the Correct Pronoun

Pronouns in a sentence must agree with the noun to which they refer. For example, if you were referring to a single female person, you would use "she" or "her;" these are called singular pronouns. If you were referring to a group of people, you would use "they" or "them;" these are called plural pronouns.

    Here are some guidelines to follow when choosing whether to use a singular or plural pronoun:

- Use a plural pronoun to refer to two nouns joined by "and" because you are referring to more than one item:

    *Wilson **and** Chiu gave **their** resignation speeches on Wednesday.*

- Use a plural pronoun with "all" because you are referring to an entire group:

    ***All** of the salespeople submitted **their** reports on time.*

- Use a singular pronoun with "every" or "each" because you are referring to the individuals within a group:

    *Each of the salespeople submitted **his** or **her** assignment on time.*

- Use a singular pronoun to refer to any of the words that end in "–one" or "–body," such as "anyone," "anybody," "everyone," "everybody," "no one," or "nobody." Notice that "no one" is correctly written as two separate words:

    (a) ***Everybody*** *on the women's hockey team got **her** own medal.*

    (b) ***Anyone*** *could have left **his** or **her** laptop on the plane.*

    (c) ***No one*** *can approve **her** or **his** own timesheet.*

B.1.4 Verbs

Verbs are words used to describe actions or status. Here are some examples of these different types of verbs:

- **Action verbs:** run, sit, read, discuss, review, assess, speak, type
- **Status verbs:** is, feel, seem, appear, believe, consist, doubt, love, hate

Verbs are also used to define whether the sentence is referring to past, present, or future time. Notice that for most of these examples, the verb requires an auxiliary or helper verb like "is" or "have":

- **Past time:** ran, sat, was reading, have discussed
- **Present time:** run, sit, am reading, are discussing
- **Future time:** will run, will sit, will be reading, will be discussing

Notice that the words in the above list that end in "–ed" or "–ing" need helper verbs to properly express an idea.

B.1.5 Identifying and Fixing Run-On Sentences

A group of words with more than one complete thought is called a run-on sentence. The following are all examples of run-on sentences:

- *He wrote the script she designed the graphics.*
- *My boss is calling I need to pick up the phone.*

One of the easiest ways of fixing a run-on sentence is to separate the two thoughts with correct punctuation. You can use a period to create two separate sentences, or you can use a semi-colon to link the ideas together in a single sentence. Note that you cannot join two complete thoughts with a comma; this error is called a comma splice:

- *He wrote the script. She designed the graphics.* (Use a period.)
- *My boss is calling; I need to pick up the phone.* (Use a semi-colon.)

B.1.6 Identifying and Fixing Fragments

A group of words that is missing one of the four elements of a complete sentence (subject, verb, complete thought, or correct punctuation) is called a fragment. The following are all examples of fragments:

- *Called the client to set up a meeting.* (There is no subject. Who are we talking about?)
- *The employee at the front desk.* (There is no verb. What is the person doing?)
- *When you get back from lunch.* (There is an incomplete thought. What will happen then?)
- *Did you set up the meeting.* (There is incorrect punctuation. Are we being asked or told?)

A straightforward way to fix a fragment is to add what is missing:

- *The director called the client to set up a meeting.* (Now we know who you are talking about.)
- *The employee fell asleep at the front desk.* (Now we know what happened.)
- *You can write up the notes when you get back from lunch.* (Now we know what will happen then.)
- *Did you set up the meeting?* (Now we know we are being asked.)

B.2 Using Proper Punctuation

Punctuation is a very important component of sentence structure. Without it, your ideas can become unclear, which will leave your readers confused. For example, punctuation can turn a bizarre statement like "Let's eat everyone" into a friendly invitation to enjoy dinner: "Let's eat, everyone!"

There are several ways to correctly use each type of punctuation. This section outlines proper use for common types of punctuation:

B.2.1 Commas

People commonly think that they can insert a comma anywhere in their writing to create a pause, but in fact commas can only ever be used in one of the following cases:

- To separate an introductory expression from the rest of the sentence:

    When she saw the computer display, *she noticed how little space it took on the top of the desk.*
    Well, *I see your point.*
    However, *the process will need to be explained to the new employees.*

- Before a coordinating conjunction (*for, and, nor, but, or yet, so*) that links two complete thoughts:

    Landscaping for company headquarters may prove to be expensive, **but** *first impressions of the company are often important for new clients.*

- To separate "extra" information from the main idea of the sentence:

    One of our managers, who knew PASCAL, offered to help debug the program.
    The customer in Wingham, who bought three tonnes of fertilizer, will write the recommendation.
    John Singh, who is running for Parliament, spoke at the luncheon.

- To separate the name of a person being addressed from the main part of the sentence:

    We will expect your letter, Ms. Jones, no later than September 5.
    We therefore respectfully request, Prime Minister, that you consider our request.

- To separate more than two items in a series:

    We need additional funding, a new product, and some customers.
    The staples, paper clips, and pencils were stolen from my briefcase.

- To separate a quotation from the rest of a sentence:

    "We can meet our goals," proclaimed the new president.
    "We could use some new goals," responded the vice-president.

B.2.2 Semi-colons

- Use semi-colons to separate closely-related main clauses. A semi-colon creates a logical link between the two clauses. When using a semi-colon in this way, make sure that each of the clauses is a complete thought:

    Creative business managers know how to delegate authority; they give their employees a sense of importance by involving them in significant ways.

- Use a semi-colon to separate items in complex lists where commas are used within the individual list items:

    The committee was made up of Julia Sanchez, VP Finance; Francesca DiFranco, Director of Recruitment; and Paul Redman, Head of Technical Support Services.

B.2.3 Colons

- Use colons to signal the introduction of an example, an explanation, a quotation, or a list. Colons should always follow complete sentences:
    - **Error:** *The ingredients of the concrete: Portland cement, lime, sand, pea gravel, and water.*
    - **Correct:** *The concrete is made of the following ingredients: Portland cement, lime, sand, pea gravel, and water.*
- Use colons in time designations and after greetings in formal letters:

    The workday begins promptly at 8:00 a.m.
    Dear Ms. McCoy:

B.2.4 Apostrophes

- Use apostrophes to replace missing letters in contractions:

isn't	means *is not*
they've	means *they have*
she's	means *she is*

- Use apostrophes to indicate possession:

    If the word ends in any letter but *s*, add *'s* to the end of the word to indicate possession:

Simon →	*Simon's report*
company →	*company's property*
manager →	*manager's salary*
women→	*women's washroom*

    If the word ends in *s*, just add the apostrophe to the end of the word to indicate possession:

companies →	*companies' merger*
managers →	*managers' account codes*
Descartes →	*Descartes' philosophy*
Paris →	*Paris' transit system*

B.2.5 Quotation Marks

- Use quotation marks to separate others' words from your own:

    He called out, "Please step forward if you wish to bid."

- Use quotation marks to set off titles of short poems, short stories, songs, chapters, essays, or articles. In general, the title of a piece that is part of a larger work takes quotation marks:

  "How to Write a Resumé," "The Lake Isle of Innisfree"

- Use quotation marks to indicate irony or sarcasm. Be careful not to overuse quotation marks in this way:

  His "university degree" was in fact a diploma purchased for $300.

B.2.6 Parentheses

- Use parentheses to enclose explanation or details:

  The 507 Press (a fabrication press for plywood) saved the company $82,000 in one year.

- Use parentheses to enclose publisher information in a footnote:

  John Renley, Common Stock Investment Strategies (New York: Williams Press, 2003).

B.2.7 Dashes

- Use dashes to separate a series or list from the rest of the sentence:

  The essential materials of the automobile—steel, rubber, plastic, and glass—can be stockpiled in almost unlimited quantities.

- Use dashes to mark off an afterthought:

  Her resignation came only after repeated attempts to get the raise she wanted— and deserved, for that matter.

- Use dashes to separate a parenthetical comment:

  Ledger books—the kind used for professional bookkeeping—were being sold at half price.

B.2.8 Capitalization

- Use a capital letter to begin sentences, direct quotations, and most lines of poetry:

  Let your employees feel that they matter.
  He asked, "Why did you call?"

- Capitalize the names and initials of persons, places, and geographical areas:

  Henry Higgins, Hinton, Quebec, the Maritimes

- Capitalize the names of organizations and their members:

  Rotary Club, Rotarians

- Capitalize the names of ships, planes, and spacecrafts:

  Voyager II, the Queen Elizabeth II

- Capitalize the names of ethnic groups, races, nationalities, religions, languages, and historical periods:

  Jewish, Romanian, Inuit, English Renaissance

- Capitalize the names of days, months, holidays, and historical periods and events:

  Friday, October, the Roaring Twenties, Family Day

- Capitalize the first word and all other major words in titles of books, plays, poems, musical compositions, films, and works of art:

  "Some Enchanted Evening"
  The Sound and the Fury
  Star Wars

B.2.9 Italics

- Use italics (or underlining) to mark the titles of books, plays, movies, newspapers, and magazines. In general, the title of any piece that stands alone as an individual work should be appear in italics:

  The *Financial Post* reviewed the financial aspects of *Star Wars*.

- Use italics to identify foreign words and phrases:

  The visitor used the German word for work, *arbeiten*.

- Use italics to give special emphasis:

  We asked the supervisor not only *how* to do the job, but why it should be done at all.

- Use italics to set off words that you wish to call attention to as words:

  Tell the technical writers they use is *too* often.

GLOSSARY

Acronym A word formed from the initial letters of other words. For instance, NATO (North Atlantic Treaty Organization).

Active listener A person who receives a speaker's message with care and respect and then works to verify his or her understanding of that message.

Active listening Listening that captures both the facts and the feelings of a message; involves verification of the understanding of a message; sometimes referred to as responsive listening or reflective listening.

Aggressive approach Hard-charging method of dealing with conflict, often interpreted as hostile in manner; you come across as seeking to control or dominate; you don't back down.

Aggressive speaking A hard-charging speaking approach that's often hostile and comes across as controlling or dominating.

Application letter The type of cover letter used to respond to a known job opening.

Assertive approach Expressing your rights and views in a positive and confident manner, and enabling others to do the same with the intent and effort to work out resolutions.

Assertive speaking An approach to speaking that involves people expressing themselves in a positive and confident way and allowing and encouraging others to do the same.

Assumption A belief that something is true without proof or demonstration, or that a person is going to behave a certain way before they've had a chance to act.

Attentive listener Person who is engaged both non-verbally and verbally.

Bar graph Compares two or more values; creates strong visual statements for comparative measurement.

Benefits The gains to be made or the things that are good about an idea, product, or service.

Bias Personal opinions and viewpoints become the standard for evaluating objective arguments.

Bibliography   Lists all materials the author found useful in preparing the report.

Block style   Business-letter format in which all parts of the letter are printed beginning at the left margin, and paragraphs are separated by one or two line spaces.

Body   The part of the presentation between an introduction and conclusion; its purpose is to get key points across.

Body language   What a person does with their body to express their message, including facial expressions, posture, and gestures.

Body of the report   The pages that contain the actual information of the report.

Budget   An outline of funding and costs.

Buffer statement   A positive or neutral statement that serves as a starting place for a negative response or message.

Business voice   Communication that is direct, controlled, and reasonable; personal but not self-centred.

Chronological resumé   A resumé that organizes work experience in chronological order, starting with the most recent.

Circular reasoning   What was intended to be an explanation turns out to be a mere restatement of the problem.

Claim letter   A persuasive business letter that customers use to make and explain a demand for repayment, restitution, or replacement because of a failure in a product or service.

Cliché   Worn-out expressions that have little, if any, meaning.

Closing the call   Checking agreements made or confirming commitments set, done near the end of a telephone call.

Combination resumé   A resumé that merges chronological and functional styles; begins with a functional section and then lists employment history in chronological order.

Communication   A process by which information is exchanged between individuals through a common system of symbols, signs, or behaviour.

Conclusion   The final section of a proposal; used to express goodwill, offer further assistance, and so on. Or the last part of a presentation, often the part the audience remembers best.

Conflict   A problem in which two or more people have a difference of opinions, methods, goals, styles, values, and so on.

Consistently respectful   When you have it working, you're in position to handle any conflict that confronts you, and thus keep the molehills from turning into volcanoes.

Constructive   Being as objective as possible in the words you say; respectful.

Content   What you say in a presentation; your message.

Cover   Binding used to contain a report, particularly useful with long reports.

Cutaway or exploded drawing   The cutaway or exploded drawing lets the viewer see into a structure to observe the relationships among its parts.

Delivery   How you express your messages; involves non-verbal communication.

Describing   Reporting behaviours that someone displays in observable and objective terms; telling what you see, not giving your opinions about what you see.

Destructive   Designed or tending to destroy; criticism.

Either/or thinking   Two alternatives are presented as the only alternatives when others should be considered.

Emotional voice   Communication with a tone that is aroused or agitated in feeling or sensibility.

Encyclopedia voice   Communication whose tone is stiff and unemotional.

Endnote   A note that appears at the end of a report; if the notes aren't important for readers, endnotes are easier than footnotes for the writer.

Executive summary   Summarizes the purpose, organization, methods, and outcomes of the short report; sometimes called an *abstract*.

External customers   People outside the workplace with whom you need to build good working relationships for success on the job. These customers include suppliers and investors.

Features   How an idea, product, or service works.

Flaming email   An attempt by one party to voice a concern to another party through an email message that's harsh in language and tone.

Flaming war   Parties involved in a chain of flaming emails. Parties send negative email messages back and forth; messages are sometimes copied to others.

Flowchart   Flowcharts present a process or procedure.

Flysheet   A single sheet of blank paper that separates the cover from the title page; in very formal documents, the flysheet is often parchment or translucent paper.

Functional resumé   A resumé that groups accomplishments and qualifications together.

General evidence   Is made up of a great number of specific examples gathered together or "generalized."

Gestures   What you do with your hands while you talk; examples include clinging to the podium and fidgeting with your watch.

Grouped bar graph   A series of simple bar charts, each measuring two or more values at specified intervals.

Hasty generalization   The conclusion reached is based on too little evidence.

Hearing   The physical effort of taking in the speaker's message; hearing doesn't necessarily mean that the message was received, processed, or responded to.

Idea circle   A visual tool for generating ideas before you write.

I emphasis   Writer focuses more on his or her own needs than those of the reader, limiting ability to show empathy.

I-messages   Statements such as "I've noticed" or "I've observed" that have you owning your message, helping you focus on actions and issues, not people.

Indented style   A business-letter format in which paragraphs are indented, and some elements are moved to the centre margin.

Intercultural communication   Making connections between different views of the world.

Internal customers   Your fellow employees, inside and outside the department where you work, to whom you provide services or assistance.

Introduction   The opening of a speech or presentation.

Jargon: A special terminology, usually technical, that only those associated with the job or subject really understand; in-group use of language.

Letter of authorization   Details who authorized the work to be done, what work was authorized, and who will do the work.

Letter of transmittal   Briefly provides the reason for a report, highlights of particularly interesting items, and contact information.

Line bar graph   Offering the advantages of both bar and line graphs, the line bar graph emphasizes both individual measurements and trends.

Line drawing   Drawing made of solid lines; used to add emphasis and attraction to a document.

Line graph   A graph in which points of value are connected by a line; used to show trends at a glance.

Listening   The process of receiving a message from a speaker, processing that message to make sense of it, and then responding to it in ways that show understanding of what the speaker means.

Maps   Maps present geographical representation of data.

Market research   Testing a market to gain an understanding of an audience, often done by professional research organizations.

Mirroring   A person's communications match what the other person in the conversation is doing—from body language to use of words and rate of speech.

Modified block style   A business-letter format in which elements of both the block style and indented style appear.

Modulation   Having variety in pitch; a key element of assertive speaking.

Multiline graph   By differentiating lines by colour, size, or texture, a multiline graph portrays simultaneous trends, allowing easy comparison.

Need   That which drives or motivates people.

Needs-based model   Works when resolving differences that are work-issue related, rather than relationship related.

Network   People in your business life and personal life that can connect you with job opportunities or other job resources.

Non-assertive approach   In this method of dealing with conflict, you maintain a passive manner and do not express your rights or views.

Non-assertive speaking   A passive approach to speaking; a non-assertive speaker allows others to dominate the conversation.

Non sequitur   A conclusion is reached that does not follow from the evidence presented.

Non-words   Filler sounds or words that people say that do not contribute to the meaning of a message. Common forms include "Uh," "Um," "Like," "Okay," and "You know."

Organizational chart   Similar to flowcharts but represent hierarchies of relationships among people rather than processes or procedures.

Overview   Background information a reader needs to grasp the significance of a proposed idea.

Pace   The rate at which a person speaks. It determines how fast or slow the words come out and how clearly those words are heard and understood.

Pagination   The number and arrangement of pages in a report; some pages are numbered in lowercase Roman numerals (i, ii, iii) and some in Arabic (1, 2, 3).

Paraphrasing   Restating the main idea of a speaker's message to verify or clarify your understanding of the facts or content of that message.

Partial yes   A response in which the writer is unable to completely fill an order or completely satisfy a request.

Passive-aggressive approach   See Passive-aggressive speaking.

Passive-aggressive speaking   An approach in which a person comes off as subtle and indirect, but whose underlying tone may hurt or manipulate others.

Passive listening   A common way that people listen to others. In this approach, the listener is present non-verbally but verbally provides little feedback to the speaker.

Persuade   To influence a person's thoughts or actions, often by demonstrating reasons for that person to accept your influence.

Photograph   A picture or likeness used to communicate product descriptions, geographical information, and personalities.

Pictogram   Pictograms usually combine line drawings with graphics such as line, bar, and pie charts to make a point in an attractive, eye-catching way.

Pie chart   In a pie or circle chart, each portion represents part of the total amount (such as 100%) depicted in the full circle.

Positive intention   A statement that tells the other person in your conversation that you mean well.

Positive letters   Business letters in which the writer is able to say "yes" to a request, claim, or order.

Preparation   The hard work done before going live with a speech or presentation.

Problem analysis   An examination of a proposed idea; used to convince readers that a proposal is necessary and timely.

Problem-dwelling mindset   When dealing with a conflict, this way of thinking directs most of your attention toward the problem.

Proposal specifics   Detailed description of a proposal.

Prospecting letter   The type of cover letter used to inquire about possible job opportunities with a company that is not advertising an opening.

Quotation   A line said by someone else.

Recap   A summary of the main points covered in a presentation.

Receiver   A person who listens to one or more speakers.

Reflective listening   Listening that captures both the facts and the feelings of a message; involves verification of the understanding of a message; also known as active listening.

Reflective paraphrasing   Identifying the emotion and the meaning of a message.

Resolving-concerns model   Provides a problem-solving plan to use in situations in which the working relationship isn't working as it should.

Responsive listening   Listening that captures both the facts and the feelings of a message; involves verification of the understanding of a message; also known as active listening.

Rhetorical question   A thought-provoking question asked of the audience but for which you don't expect an answer out loud.

Segmented bar graph   The segmented bar graph distinguishes different parts of the whole by colour or texture.

Selective listening   An approach nearly as common as passive listening; most commonly defined as "hearing what you want to hear."

Sender   The speaker expressing his or her message to other parties.

Shift and show understanding   Helps you listen actively in conflict situations by shifting your attention off your own message and onto capturing the other person's message.

Simple feedback   Comments are brief, not controversial; comments have been requested by another party.

Slang   Informal language often only familiar to a particular group; can offend as well as confuse readers.

Solutions-focused mindset   When dealing with a conflict, this way of thinking directs most of your attention to working out a solution.

Speaking in the positive   Saying your message in the best way possible; being honest, direct, and constructive.

Specific evidence   Treats precise details in a single case. Specific evidence, especially when backed by reputable sources, helps to convince the reader that the proposal writer's major ideas are sound.

Stage fright   A feeling of anxiety or nervousness that arises when a person is expected to perform in front of others.

Stakeholders   Key parties affected by a business relationship.

Stating-feelings tool   Use it to let the other person know how a situation has made you feel; with it, you talk about emotion, rather than put it on display.

Stating-thoughts tool   Use it to indicate how the situation is impacting you; employs constructive feedback.

Stereotyping   Assuming that anyone who is from a different group than you—whether in race, ethnicity, gender, religion, sexual orientation, occupation, or other grouping— behaves and thinks in the same way as the group.

Stories   An engaging way to share life experiences and to highlight or illustrate a point.

Straw man   A false target is set up for the main thrust of an argument. Knocking over the straw man creates the illusion that the argument has succeeded when in fact nothing has changed.

Strengths   Something positive and relevant, such as what you learned from an experience

Sugar-coating   Trying to sweeten a bad message; an effort to make bad news sound better.

Table of contents   A directory that lists topic headings with appropriate page numbers; especially useful with long reports.

Table of figures and/or tables   Lists the location of charts, graphs, and statistical breakouts throughout the text of a long report.

Time chart   Time charts use bars or lines inside a work–time matrix to show when jobs, tasks, or other activities begin and end.

Title page   Contains what the report is about, for whom it was prepared, by whom it was written, and the date of its completion or filing.

Tone   The style or manner of expression.

Transaction culture   The middle ground that emerges when speakers and their own cultural background come into contact with persons of another culture.

Transitions   Words that move a speaker from one topic to the next in a presentation; they create the bridges that connect points and help move a presentation forward.

Underpromise and overdeliver   Giving yourself a large enough cushion of time to get things done as you respond to a client's *when* question; when you underpromise and overdeliver, you pick a deadline that you can meet or beat.

Visual aids   Supporting materials such as slides and graphics shown as a presenter talks.

Voice mail   The recorded verbal message you leave when someone doesn't answer the telephone.

Weaknesses   Flaws and shortcomings; past mistakes

You emphasis   Writer focuses more on the reader's needs than his or her own; this enables greater display of empathy.

INDEX